Hand and Mind

HAND AND MIND

*What Gestures
Reveal about
Thought*

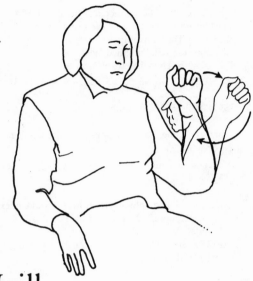

David McNeill

The University of Chicago Press
Chicago and London

David McNeill is professor of linguistics and psychology at the University of Chicago.

The University of Chicago Press, Chicago 60637
The University of Chicago Press, Ltd., London
© 1992 by The University of Chicago
All rights reserved. Published 1992
Printed in the United States of America
00 99 98 97 96 95 94 93 92   5 4 3 2 1

ISBN 0-226-56132-1 (cloth)

Library of Congress Cataloging-in-publication Data
McNeill, David.
    Hand and mind : what gestures reveal about thought / David McNeill.
        p.   cm.
    Includes bibliographical references (p.   ) and index.
        1. Gesture.   2. Thought and thinking.   3. Psycholinguistics.
    I. Title.
    P117.M36   1992
    401′.9—dc20   91-32575

For Nobuko

Contents

Acknowledgments

I began the project on which this book is based in 1980 in collaboration with Elena T. Levy. Together we collected videos of narratives in the systematic manner that has been a mainstay of the book. In the decade since, so many people have aided me that I may have left out some from this list; I hope not, but if I have I beg their forgiveness.

Several graduate students have written their doctoral dissertations on gestures. In particular Elena T. Levy, Laura L. Pedelty, Debra Stephens, Kaaren Bekken, and Justine Cassell have devoted significant parts of their graduate student careers to sharing my fascination with gestures. Their work has greatly advanced our understanding and I cite them repeatedly in the book itself.

Other students still in the midst of their graduate study or having written dissertations on other topics also have made great contributions to our research on gestures. Brecky Church, Kevin Tuite, Karl-Erik McCullough, Sotaro Kita, and Nancy L. Dray have made important contributions which I cite in the book.

The analytic study of gesture is tremendously time consuming. Just transcribing a gesture and getting the timing right can take 40 to 50 times longer than the gesture itself. Many people have cultivated the peculiarly fatiguing art of gesture observation and transcription. I am extremely grateful to everyone for their sharp eyes and open minds, not to mention their endurance; they first saw many of the phenomena that I describe in this book: Desha Baker, Kaaren Bekken, Joan Boman, Dan Bunnag, Justine Cassell, Brecky Church, Bob Czechin, Nancy L. Dray, Bill Eilfort, Anne Farley, Katie Greeno, Mitsuko Iriye, Sotaro Kita, Elena Levy, Karen Lindig, Suzanne Markel, Karl-Erik McCullough, Elizabeth McGuire, Laura Pedelty, Karen Peterson, Yukiko Shiraishi, Debra Stephens, Kevin Tuite, and Cheryl Whitmore.

My gesture research has been financially supported by the Spencer Foundation, the Linguistics Program of the National Science Foundation, and the Public Health Service (a National Institute of Mental Health Research Grant and a Biomedical Research Grant to the University of Chicago). I am grateful to these agencies for their generosity. I wish to thank in particular Paul Chapin of NSF for his insight into the relevance of gestures to linguistics as a science.

Colleagues have given me advice, ideas, hints, and have expanded my appreciation of conceptual issues. When I was a visitor at the Netherlands Institute for Advanced Study (NIAS), in Wassenaar, I had excellent discussions with Joan Bybee, then also a visitor to NIAS. Others who have been very helpful are Robin Campbell, University of Stirling; Jacques Cosnier, University of Lyon; Ino d'Arcais, University of Leiden and the Max Planck Institute for Psycholinguistics; and David Kelter, another visitor to NIAS. Here at Chicago I have enjoyed close working relations with Starkey Duncan and Susan Goldin-Meadow. Susan and I give an annual seminar entitled Communicative Uses of Nonverbal Behavior, which serves as a kind of forum for everyone with an interest in gestures.

Adam Kendon has read and commented on the entire manuscript of this book, as well as on many others things I have written, and his own contributions to the study of gesture are, I hope, evident from the many references I have made to his work.

Bob Morris, Dick Mowrey, Bill Pagliuca, Naomi Quinn, Michael Silverstein, Josef Stern, Colwyn Trevarthen, Jenny Singleton, and Dahlia Zaidel have been valuable colleagues. George Lakoff deserves special mention, since it was he who, in a conversation a decade ago, pointed out the type of gesture that I describe here as metaphoric. This is one of the most important types of gesture since it shows how abstract thought can be carried out in terms of representations of concrete objects and time and space.

The drawings of gestures add greatly to the clarity and attractiveness of the book. Most are the work of Laura Pedelty, my colleague and former student. Others are by Robert Williams, of the University of Chicago Press. I am extremely grateful to both Laura and Robert for their artistic drawings, and to Laura, not only for her skill and insights, but for her ability to find time in the midst of demanding medical work to prepare so many expressive and accurate illustrations. The index of this book was prepared by Karl-Erik McCullough.

I began writing this book during a year off from the University of Chicago which I spent at NIAS. I wish to thank NIAS for its hospitality and support during that year (1983/84). I was not able to come near finishing the book at NIAS, however, and the book was in fact not finished until 1990. By then I had two more institutions to thank. First is the Department of Anthropology at Duke University. They offered me a forum to present my ideas at an early stage of development. I am particularly grateful to Naomi Quinn for all that she did to make that visit productive and pleasant. Second is the Twelfth International Summer Institute for Semiotic and Structural Studies (ISISSS90), held at the University of Toronto in the summer of 1990. The class I taught there was the first I ever devoted entirely to gestures and the experience led me to make many structural changes in the book. I wish to express my gratitude to those who sat in on the course; their comments and questions, not to mention their facial expressions, have had a great influence: Pam Sharratt, Colwyn Trevarthen, Richard Schechner, Silja Ikäheimonen-Lindgren, William C. McCormack, Tova Meltzer, and Donna Boregham. To each of them I give my thanks.

Most of all, I wish to thank my family for all their support and guidance. My children, Cheryl and Randall, have virtually grown up with gestures as a topic of family conversation. Their reactions to things I have described have influenced my choices of examples and the ways in which I have presented them. My greatest thanks go to my wife, Nobuko, for her support and encouragement over these years, and also for her inspiration. If the book has any good qualities it owes them to her. It is to her that I dedicate this book.

December 28, 1990

David McNeill

Introduction

This is a book about gestures and language. The gestures I mean are the movements of the hands and arms that we see when people talk. Sometimes the movements are extensive, other times minimal, but movements there usually are. An example is a person narrating the story of a cartoon and raising her hand while she says, "and he climbed up the rope." The hand and its movement are symbolic; they present thought in action. The hand represents something other than itself. The hand is not a hand, but the character; the movement is not the hand moving up, but this character climbing up; the space is not the speaker's space, but a fictional space, a narrative space that exists only in the imaginary world of the discourse; and so forth. This book is about such symbols of action, movement, and space, and how they are related to spoken language.

These gestures are the spontaneous creations of individual speakers, unique and personal. They follow general principles—the subject matter of the book—but in no sense are they elements of a fixed repertoire. There is no separate "gesture language" alongside of spoken language. Indeed, the important thing about gestures is that they are *not* fixed. They are free and reveal the idiosyncratic imagery of thought. Yet, at the same time, such gestures and the images behind them coexist with speech. They are tightly intertwined with spoken language in time, meaning, and function; so closely linked are they that we should regard the gesture and the spoken utterance as different sides of a single underlying mental process. Gesture provides a new perspective on the processes of language. Language is a broader concept than we ordinarily suppose. This broadening of language is one of the major reasons for an interest in gestures. The effect is like viewing the world through two eyes rather than one. Just as binocular vision brings out a new dimension of seeing, gesture reveals a new dimension of the mind. This dimension is the imagery of language which has laid hidden. We discover that language is not just a linear progression of segments, sounds, and words, but is also instantaneous, nonlinear, holistic and imagistic. The imagistic component coexists with the linear-segmented speech stream and the coordination of the two gives us fresh insights into the processes of speech and thought.

I credit the discovery that there is a unity of speech and gesture to Adam Kendon, who presented this insight in two major papers (Kendon 1972, 1980). The present work definitely belongs to this new approach. Kendon's papers emphasized speech sounds and gesture movements in linking gestures with language. The contribution of the present book is to add other linguistic levels, specifically gestures linked with semantic and pragmatic content. My argument, in a nutshell, is that *gestures are an integral part of language as much as are words, phrases, and sentences—gesture and language are one system.*

Thus one theme of this book is that language is more than words, that a true psychology of language requires us to broaden our concept of language to include what seems, in the traditional linguistic view, the opposite of language—the imagistic, instantaneous, nonsegmented, and holistic. Images and speech are equal and simultaneously present processes in the mind.

A second theme (and seeing this took much time) is that gestures are part of the discourse in which the speaker is participating. Gestures look upward, into the discourse structure, as well as downward, into the thought structure. A gesture will occur only if one's current thought contrasts with the background discourse. If there is a contrast, how the thought is related to the discourse determines what kind of gesture it will be, how large it will be, how internally complex it will be, and so forth. Often, therefore, we can see the overarching discourse structure more clearly in the gesture than in the words and sentences.

A third theme is that the gesture itself has an impact on thought. The gesture supplies the idiosyncratic, the personal, and the context-specific aspects of thought, to be combined with the socially regulated aspects that come from the conventions of language. Such a combination implies a dialectic of gesture and language in which the gesture provides the momentary context of speaking and language carries this individuality to the social plane where it is categorized, segmented, reformatted, and dressed up for the world.

Putting these themes together, we can conceive of thought as fundamentally an inner discourse in which gestures play an intrinsic part. Each new gesture is the breaking edge of an inner discourse that we but partially express to the world. If our mode of thought is narrative, as Jerome Bruner has so eloquently argued in a recent series of books (Bruner 1986, 1990), that is, if our thought is a story that we are required to keep telling in order to think about our world at all, it is gestures that actively influence this story and carry it forward most expressively.

Gestures have attracted the attention of writers for at least two millennia.[1] However, the original interest was mainly in rhetoric. Quintilian,

---

1. I draw on a useful essay by Adam Kendon (1982) for this brief history of gesture study.

in the first century A.D., specified in detail the gestures that orators should use during their speeches. This use of gesture, as part of rhetoric, has been the theme of many later works as well, most notably, for the English speaking world, the books of John Bulwer ([1644] 1974) whose *Chirologia* and *Chironomia* were the first on gesture published in English. Both Quintilian and Bulwer took care to specify gestures that could be designed in advance as deliberate elements in a choreographed presentation. They are thus quite distinct from the *spontaneous* gestures that are the subject matter of this book. A new basis for interest in gesture developed during the Enlightenment and this interest, to some extent, continues to the present. In the eighteenth century philosophers became deeply concerned with the origin of language and the universal basis of reason. A number of thinkers supposed that the first languages were gestural. Condillac ([1756] 1971), in particular, argued that the original language emerged from "natural" signs, viz., gestures (cf. Harris and Taylor 1989). The connection of gesture to thought was the focus of interest for Wilhelm Wundt ([1921] 1973), the founder of the first modern psychological laboratory, although he confined this interest to conventionalized gestures (Neapolitan, American Indian, deaf signs), the profound differences of which from spontaneous gestures are the subject of chapter 2 of this book. Nonetheless, Wundt made gesture into a major explanatory link for how "inner form" becomes translated into "outer form"—a concept that also figures in contemporary psycholinguistics. None of these early investigators, however, considered the spontaneous gestures accompanying speech that are the chief focus of this book.

Those gestures were not described until the pioneering research of David Efron (1941), a student of Franz Boas. Several methodological issues had to be faced before ephemeral gestures could become the subject of study. Efron's dissertation was a comparison of the gestures of immigrant and "assimilated" Europeans in New York City. Along with his discussion of this question Efron, with great originality, introduced the categories of gesture that have been the foundation of all subsequent schemes of gesture classification and pioneered the method of observing gestures "from life" (see chap. 3). Efron thus opened up to scrutiny the topic of spontaneous gestures and provided the categories for describing them. Despite the pathbreaking character of this work, Efron's findings were limited by technical factors, especially the fact that his recording was done by eye, without benefit of sound film. There was no possibility of replaying gestures to extract the fine movement details that are crucial for getting their meaning and for synchronizing them with speech. (Efron made some slow-motion films, but apparently these were silent.) His book contains numerous drawings but the exact linkage of the gesture to speech cannot be examined at all.

Scientific interest in human communication took a new turn after World War II, inspired in part by information theory and cybernetics. As Kendon writes, "Once human action was conceived of as if it were a code in an information transmission system, the question of the nature of the coding system came under scrutiny" (Kendon 1982, 53). The analysis of communication fashionable in this period distinguished sharply between digital and analogical codes: a digital code was best exemplified by the linguistic system itself, while analogical codes appeared in the so-called paralinguistic signals—the very terminology asserting a dichotomy. Prosody (voice pitch and loudness), posture, facial expression, and gesture were regarded as analogical signals and thus *para*linguistic—*beside* language. However, language is digital *and* analogical, it is verbal *and* gestural. Far from being "beside" language, gesture is actively part of language. We have to stand the now traditional concept of a gesture on its head. My purpose in this book is to bring to light this new understanding and to suggest some of the far-reaching implications for psychology and linguistics.

My personal interest in gestures goes back to 1962. I can date it so precisely because that was the year I moved from Berkeley to the Center for Cognitive Studies at Harvard. Among the many remarkable things I found at the center were two individuals whose gestures differed so markedly that I could not help noticing them. They were colleagues and often talked to each other, each gesticulating in his own way. These people looked to me like sculptors working in different media. One was always pounding and pushing some heavy blocklike stuff. I imagined that his medium was clay or marble. The other was drawing out and weaving some incredibly delicate spidery stuff. His medium looked like strings or spider webs. That was my inauguration to gestures. At that early stage, I had no idea that gestures and speech should be viewed as two sides of a single system. However, by the time I took up gestures in earnest I was indeed propelled by the idea that gestures and speech must be considered jointly as components of a single process.

A first hint of this single process came in 1974; I suddenly became aware of my son's gestures. He was then four years old, and I was sure that I had earlier seen from him very few gestures of any kind. Something had taken place in his language development that suddenly triggered gestures (the emergence of abundant gestures at about this age has since been documented with larger samples of children; see chapter 11). At about this same time, I also videorecorded a technical discussion between two mathematicians expressly for the purpose of studying their gestures. Speech and gesture in this discussion were clearly linked (these gestures are described in chapter 6). So began my appreciation of the speech-gesture nexus. My first written discussions of gesture appeared as chapters in several books (Solso 1975; McNeill 1979; Rauch and Carr 1980).

I proposed writing this book in 1983, because by then I believed that I understood the phenomenon of gesture sufficiently well to expound on it at length. No doubt this self-deception served a useful purpose. I doubt now that I would have set out on a project of such vastness if I had known that it would take nearly ten years to finish. The book took this long for two reasons, both I hope respectable. First, my students and I kept finding out new things about gestures and these altered the picture, in some cases profoundly. Also, concurrently with the new discoveries and largely driven by them, my own understanding of what gestures imply for interpreting the functioning of the mind grew ever deeper. Nonetheless, I continued writing; inevitably the book passed through many revisions and with the advent of word processing the revisions have become truly innumerable. I admire and stand in awe of people who write their books in a year or two. In my case, it has taken much longer. Eventually even the name of the book changed. I mention this fact since other publications, by myself and others, have already cited the book under its old name: "Mirrors of Gesture." Although I once rather liked this title, and have even been told that it has a certain air of mystery, I gave it up when I became convinced that the metaphor of a mirror suggests a relationship of gestures to language that is altogether too static. It is at odds with the emphasis on dynamic processes that runs throughout the book. It also is at odds with the active constitutive role that I see gestures playing in our thoughts. A mirror does nothing, it is entirely passive; and passive reflection is far from the case with gestures.

I also have had a problem with nomenclature. What am I to call my subject? The word "gesture" comes from the Latin for action, for carrying out an activity, and for performing. It thus comes from a word whose reference is to serious things, and the word "gestate" has the same source. Even the *OED* does not recognize the sense of "gesture" that now seems to have become dominant. It is undeniable that the word has fallen on hard times: to many people "gesture" implies something "trivial," "ineffectual" or "empty of importance or substance." People talk about something being a "gesture," rather than being the "real thing." Commenting on a new building, one Chicago critic wrote that "they make a gesture that falls aesthetically short of the mark" (*Chicago Tribune Sunday Magazine*, 25 December 1988). Apparently "gesture" and "falling short of the mark" naturally go together. I gave considerable thought to this problem, even contemplating neologisms such as "temaniotics" (a word formed from Japanese, "temane," which means the hands picturing the world), and the word "gesticulation" that Adam Kendon prefers (Kendon 1980). But temaniotics is obscure and gesticulation conjures up, for some people, an image of windmilling arms. I have thus kept the simple word "gesture." There is also a book on Indian dance and the art of the actor, *The Mirror of Gesture* (Nandikesvara 1917), whose dedication reveals an altogether more welcoming attitude: "The movement of whose body is the world, whose speech the sum of all language, whose jewels are the moon and stars—to that pure Siva I bow!" (p. 13). And so, in this book as well, we shall bow to what, following Nandikesvara, I will simply call "gestures."

Like authors everywhere I hope that my book will be read and appreciated. However, I do not deceive myself: there is more here about gestures than many will want to know. Hence I propose a method for reading this book selectively. The text is divided into four smaller parts. I have not written these parts to be independent, and chapters from one often refer to chapters in another, but this division suggests a way to read selectively. Part 1 is Setting the Stage and consists of chapter 1, which gives an overview of the main gesture types and defends from rivals the hypothesis that gestures and language constitute a single system, and chapter 2, which compares the kinds of spontaneous gestures that accompany speech to systematic manual sign languages. Since so much has been written in recent decades on sign language, it seems appropriate and convenient to begin the exposition of spontaneous gestures by discussing the similarities and differences of gestures and signs. The next part is Varieties of Gesture, a kind of encyclopedia rich in examples that covers the different types of gesture in their great variety and gives the basic statistical data on gesture occurrence: chapter 3 is on the classification and distribution of gestures, including a complete narrative by an adult speaker; chapter 4 is on the gestures of the concrete (the iconics); chapter 5 describes an experimental proof that gestures are meaningful symbols; and chapter 6 is on the gestures of the abstract (the metaphorics, beats, spatials, and abstract deictics). The third part is Theory: chapter 7 presents the relationship of gestures to discourse; chapter 8 develops the concept of the "growth point" of utterances and presents a model of self-organization of utterances and gestures; Chapter 9 develops the concept that gestures have an impact on thought; chapter 10 describes several experiments that probe the self-organizational cycle. The final part is

Topics, which consists of applications of the theory in two important special cases: children (chapter 11) and the brain (chapter 12). The brain chapter includes descriptions of the gestures of aphasic patients and split-brain patients, and reproduces an entire narrative (including gestures) by a split-brain person. Finally, there is an appendix in which I describe in detail the methods of gesture collection, recording, description, and coding that I followed. This kind of description will be of value to researchers but would get in the way of readers who have an interest in the semiotic systems of gesture and language but no interest in carrying out a research project of this kind.

Part One

Setting the Stage

1   *Images, Inside and Out*

> If language was given to men to conceal their thoughts, then gesture's purpose was to disclose them.
>
>   —John Napier, *Hands*

This inscription provides an appropriate place to start the book that follows. Napier's book (1980) was about the evolution, mechanics, and functioning of the human hand. He ended his account with the above comment on the hands as symbolic instruments. This book starts at the same place and asks: how *are* human thoughts disclosed in gestures?

When people talk they can be seen making spontaneous movements called gestures. These are usually movements of the arms and hands and are closely synchronized with the flow of speech. The implication of gestures that interests me is the possibility of embracing in one theoretical system two forms of expression, speech and action. Gestures and speech occur in very close temporal synchrony and often have identical meanings. Yet they express these meanings in completely different ways. Comparing speech to gesture produces an effect on our understanding of language and thought something like the effect of triangulation in vision. Many details, previously hidden, spring out in a new dimension. Rather than causing us to slice a person analytically into semi-isolated modules, taking gesture into account encourages us to see something like the entire person as a theoretical entity—his thinking, speaking, willing, feeling, and acting, as a unit.

My aim is to provide a conceptual framework that includes both gesture and language. This broader framework will show how gestures and speech are linked, and how they are different. At a minimum, the framework should explain how speech, which is linear through time, is related to the type of thinking that we see exhibited in the simultaneous gesture, thinking that is instantaneous, imagistic and global—analog rather than digital.

Gestures exhibit images that cannot always be expressed in speech, as well as images the speaker thinks are concealed. Speech and gesture must cooperate to express the person's meaning. A conception of language and gesture as a single integrated system is sharply different from the notion of a "body language"—a communication process utilizing signals made up of body movements, which is regarded by its believers as separate from and beyond normal language. This concept is the product of an excessively narrow analysis, just as is the traditional linguistic notion of a

11

spoken language as exclusively comprising a system of speech sounds plus a grammar.

The topic of this book is, specifically, gestures that exhibit images. With these kinds of gesture people unwittingly display their inner thoughts and ways of understanding events of the world. These gestures are the person's memories and thoughts rendered visible. Gestures are like thoughts themselves. They belong, not to the outside world, but to the inside one of memory, thought, and mental images. Gesture images are complex, intricately interconnected, and not at all like photographs. Gestures open up a wholly new way of regarding thought processes, language, and the interactions of people.

I want now to give a sketch of the major types of gesture. I will illustrate these types and give many more details in later chapters.

Types of Gesture

Iconics

Some gestures are "iconic" and bear a close formal relationship to the semantic content of speech. For example, when describing a scene from a comic book story in which a character bends a tree back to the ground, a speaker appeared to grip something and pull it back (see fig. 1.1):

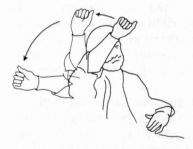

Figure 1.1. Illustration of an iconic gesture with "and he [bends it way back]." The gesture exhibits the same act referred to in speech.

(1.1) and he [bends it way back][1]

Iconic: hand appears to grip something and pull it from the upper front space back and down near to the shoulder.

1. In citing gesture examples I will use the following conventions: speech will be underscored; the extent of the meaningful part of the gesture—the stroke phase—will be shown by enclosing the concurrent segments of speech in square brackets [ ]; when the gesture is held motionlessly there will be dots (. . .); the gesture itself will be described in italics. If more than one stroke takes place, they will be numbered. Silent hesitations will be shown with slanted lines (/), and filled hesitations with a rendition of the sound. On occasion, I will also show the gesture preparation and retraction phases. In these cases, to avoid a clutter of brackets, I will show the onset of the preparation with a left bracket ([), the stroke in **boldface,** and the end of the retraction with a right bracket (]).

The speaker (not a habitual comic book reader) had been given a comic book as part of an experiment on narrative (see Marslen-Wilson, Levy, and Tyler, 1982). The gesture reveals not only the speaker's memory image but also the particular point of view that he had taken toward it. The speaker had the choice of playing the part of the agent or the tree. He was "seeing" the event from the viewpoint of the agent performing the act—otherwise his hand would not have taken the form of a grip—rather than the viewpoint of the tree undergoing the act. In the latter case, we would expect a gesture in which the arm moves back but without the grip.

The example illustrates the close connection that exists between speech and gesture. It shows how what is depicted through gesture should be incorporated into a complete picture of a person's thought processes. The gesture movement—the "stroke"—coincided with the part of the utterance that presented the same meaning. Semantically, the sentence described bending something back while the gesture concurrently exhibited the same bending back image. Moreover, the image was from the point of view of the actor, and when we look at the active form of sentence, "he bends it way back," we see that it also implies the point of view of the actor. The passive, "it got bent way back," for example, would be more appropriate for the viewpoint of the tree. Thus, both semantically and pragmatically, in terms of focus, the gesture and utterance were parallel expressions of meaning.

Along with this kind of coexpressiveness, there is also complementarity. Speech and gesture refer to the same event and are partially overlapping, but the pictures they present are different. Jointly, speech and gesture give a more complete insight into the speaker's thinking. In the following example speech conveys the ideas of pursuit and recurrence while gesture conveys the weapon used (an umbrella); both speech and gesture refer to the same event, but each presents a somewhat different aspect of it (see fig. 1.2):

Figure 1.2. Illustration of speech-gesture complementation with "she [chases him out again]." The gesture reveals the weapon while speech conveys the action (chasing) and the idea of recurrence.

(1.2) and she [chases him out again]

Iconic: hand appears to swing an object through the air.

If we were to look only at the gesture or the speech, we would have an incomplete picture of the speaker's memory and mental representation of the scene. It is only through a joint consideration of both gesture and speech that we see all the elements: the type of action, its recurrence, the weapon, and how it was used.

Metaphorics

Other gestures are "metaphoric." These are like iconic gestures in that they are pictorial, but the pictorial content presents an abstract idea rather than a concrete object or event. The gesture presents an image of the invisible—an image of an abstraction. The gesture depicts a concrete metaphor for a concept, a visual and kinesic image that we feel is, in some fashion, similar to the concept. For example, in the following, a speaker is announcing that what he has just seen and is about to recount to the listener is a cartoon (see fig. 1.3):

Figure 1.3. Illustration of a metaphoric gesture with "it [was a Sylves]ter and Tweety cartoon." The gesture is an instance of the conduit metaphor: the idea of a genre presented as a bounded container supported by the hands.

(1.3) it [was a Sylves]ter and Tweety cartoon

Metaphoric: Hands rise up and offer listener an "object."

A particular cartoon event is concrete, but the speaker here is not referring to a particular event: he is referring to the genre of the cartoon. This concept is abstract. Yet he makes it concrete in the form of an image of a bounded object supported in the hands and presented to the listener. The gesture creates and displays this object and places it into an act of offering. This is the metaphor: the concept of a genre of a certain kind (the Topic) is presented as a bounded, supportable, spatially localizable physical object (the Vehicle). Such metaphors can be documented in speech forms as well. In speech we say, for instance, "hollow words" or "a deep book"—implying that a word is a container, or a book has a vertical dimension (Reddy 1979; Lakoff and Johnson 1980). We also speak of the "presentation" of an idea or argument—implying that communication is over a path or conduit. The metaphor in which language, meaning, knowledge, genre, works of art, etc., are presented as a physical container into which substance is put and the whole is moved along a conduit has been called the *conduit* metaphor; we will see many examples of gestural conduit metaphors in this book. The conduit image of abstract ideas as physical containers is, for speakers brought up in the tradition of Western culture, a major source of metaphoric images. However, this image does not appear with speakers brought up in other, non-Western traditions (Chinese, for example).

Beats

A third type of gesture we term the "beat." Beats are so named because they look like beating musical time. Others have termed this gesture the "baton" (Efron 1941; Ekman and Friesen 1969)—naming it after the instrument rather than the function. The hand moves along with the rhythmical pulsation of speech (although the synchrony is not absolutely perfect; see McClave, 1991). Unlike iconics and metaphorics, beats tend to have the same form regardless of the content (McNeill and Levy 1982). The typical beat is a simple flick of the hand or fingers up and down, or back and forth; the movement is short and quick and the space may be the periphery of the gesture space (the lap, an armrest of the chair, etc.). The critical thing that distinguishes the beat from other types of gesture is that it has just two movement phases—in/out, up/down, etc. Iconics and metaphorics typically have three phases—preparation, stroke, and retraction. Of all gestures, beats are the most insignificant looking. But appearances are deceptive. Beats reveal the speaker's conception of the narrative discourse as a whole. The semiotic value of a beat lies in the fact that it indexes the word or phrase it accompanies as being significant, not for its own semantic content, but for its discourse-pragmatic content. Examples are marking the introduction of new characters, summarizing the action, introducing new themes, etc. Thus beats mark information that does not advance the plot line but provides the structure within which the plot line unfolds. With beats, events on the meta-level of the discourse can be inserted directly into the narrative, signaling that whatever refers in speech to the event departs from the narrated chain of events. Such departures can be brief and can be over in the confines of a single word. An example is the following, a beat that accompanied a reference to the theme of an episode. The spoken utterance does not refer to a particular incident but characterizes a class of incidents, and the beat marked the word ("whenever") that signaled this reference to the discourse as a whole rather than a specific event (see fig. 1.4):

Figure 1.4. Illustrating a beat with a summing up statement, "when[ever she]." The beat coincides with the specific linguistic segment that does the summing up.

(1.4) when[ever she] looks at him he tries to make monkey noises
Beat: hand rises short way up from lap and drops back down.

Cohesives

Another kind of discourse gesture I call "cohesive" because it serves to tie together thematically related but temporally separated parts of the discourse. This function in the case of speech is called the cohesive function (Halliday and Hasan 1976). While beats highlight discontinuities in the temporal sequence, cohesives emphasize continuities. Cohesive gestures are quite eclectic about their form. They can consist of iconic, metaphoric, or pointing gestures; they can even consist of beats. Politicians, in fact, are great demonstrators of cohesive beats. Political speeches are accompanied by an incessant beat presence. The meaning of all those beats is, I think, cohesion on the meta-level. What the politician is in effect saying is: Here is a series of points that I am making, and the crucial thing about them is that each belongs to a consistent platform (hence the cohesion of beats). Certainly every politician holds that his views on the issues are individually significant while adding up to a consistent platform. The beat is accordingly the politician's gesture par excellence.

Gestural cohesion depends on repeating the same gesture form, movement, or locus in the gesture space: the repetition is what signals the continuity. The repeated gesture shows, in the most direct way, the recurrence or continuation of a theme. An example with an iconic gesture is the following, in which a speaker describing one of the cartoon episodes first made a crisscross gesture for intersecting overhead wires, interrupted herself to make a back-and-forth movement to represent a trolley car, and then went back to the crisscross gesture. The interruption came about because the speaker realized that she had better first explain how trolleys work (no longer so obvious in some places) and broke off her narrative to do this; the back-and-forth movement was part of the explanation. Such a statement ("you know the trolley") is clearly not part of the narrative story line, so a connection back to the main theme had to be arranged after the explanation had been given, and this was accomplished by the second crisscross iconic (see fig. 1.5):

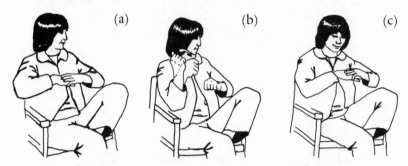

Figure 1.5. Illustrating cohesion with iconic gestures through the utilization of form. Panel (a) appeared with "[the network of wires that hooks up the cable cars]," (b) with "[you know the trolley system]," and (c) with "[right and there's a whole network of these wires]." The gesture at (c) replays the one at (a) and shows where the story resumes after the interruption at (b).

(1.5) [the network of wires that hooks up the cable cars . . . um]
Iconic: both hands, palms facing down, come together at the tips and form a crisscross.

(1.6) [you know the trolley system]
Iconic: right hand moves back and forth at side of head.

Listener: *oh across* [also gestures]

(1.7) [right and there's a whole network of these wires]
Iconic: both hands resume crisscross.

The same gesture thus occurred twice with the effect of informing the hearer where to go to get back to the story line after the interruption. The second crisscross was cohesive in that it tied together two parts of the narrative by showing, literally, where the old theme was located. Again there is speech and gesture coexpressiveness. The sentence with the second crisscross gesture also included a cohesive item, the pronoun "these." It presupposed an earlier reference to the wires in question and likewise had the effect of sending the hearer back to the interrupted theme (Halliday and Hasan 1976). Notice that the cohesive connection appeared first in the gestural channel.

Deictics

A final type of gesture important for narrative is the familiar pointing, or "deictic" gesture. Pointing has the obvious function of indicating objects and events in the concrete world, but it also plays a part even where there is nothing objectively present to point at (McNeill, Cassell, and Levy, to appear). Most pointing gestures in narratives and conversations are of this abstract kind. The following example is from a conversation between two previously unacquainted students (see fig. 1.6):

Figure 1.6. Illustration of an abstract pointing gesture with "[where did you] come from before?" The space being pointed at is not the space where the speaker and hearer currently find themselves, but an abstract space housing an introduced reference.

(1.8) [where did you] come from before?
Points to space between self and interlocutor.

The gesture is aimed not at an existing physical place where the interlocutor had been previously, but at an abstract *concept* of where he had been before. As we know from the earlier context of the conversation, the physical locus of this place was in a different city. Although the space may seem empty, it was full to the speaker. It was a palpable space in which a concept could be located as if it were a substance. Abstract pointing gestures imply a metaphorical picture of their own in which abstract ideas have a physical locus.

Gestures Don't Convey Meaning as Language

Gestures do convey meanings and their expressiveness is not necessarily inferior to that of language. If one knows how to "read" them the gesture can convey meaning no less than language, but the method used by the gesture for doing this is fundamentally different from that of language.

Language has the effect of segmenting and linearizing meaning. What might be an instantaneous thought is divided up and strung out through time. A single event, say, somebody sitting down on a chair, is analyzed into segments: the person, the chair, the movement, the direction, and so forth. These segments are organized into a hierarchically structured string of words (for example, the sentence above). The total effect is to present what had been a single instantaneous picture in the form of a string of segments. Segmentation and linearization to form a hierarchy are essential characteristics of all linguistic systems, including languages that are not spoken at all, such as American Sign Language (ASL)—the manual language of the deaf in North America (see chap. 2). Saussure ([1916] 1959) explained that the linear-segmented character of language is a property that arises because language is unidimensional while meanings are multidimensional. Language can only vary along the single dimension of time—phonemes, words, phrases, sentences, discourse: at all levels, language depends on variations along this one axis of time. This restriction forces language to break meaning complexes into segments and to reconstruct multidimensional meanings by combining the segments in time.

Gestures are different in every way. This is because they are themselves multidimensional and present meaning complexes without undergoing segmentation or linearization. Gestures are *global* and *synthetic* and *never hierarchical*. The following sections describe these properties of gestures that make them different from language.

Global-Synthetic

These terms refer to the relationship of parts to wholes in gestures. In language, parts (the words) are combined to create a whole (a sentence); the direction thus is from part to whole. In gestures, in contrast, the direction is from whole to part. The whole determines the meanings of the parts (thus it is "global"). In language, moreover, the relationship of words to meaning is analytic. Distinct meanings are attached to distinct words. In gestures, however, one gesture can combine many meanings (it is "synthetic"). An example that illustrates both the global and synthetic properties is the following typical iconic gesture (see fig. 1.7):

Figure 1.7. Illustrating the global-synthetic property of a gesture with "[and he's trying to run ahead of it]." The gesture has parts (trajectory, wiggling fingers), but the meanings of the parts depend on the meaning of the whole; the parts are not independently meaningful morphemes or words in a language.

(1.9) [and he's trying to run ahead of it]
Iconic: hand moves forward at chin level while fingers wiggle.

The gesture is a symbol in that it represents something other than itself—the hand is not a hand but a character, the movement is not a hand in motion but the character in motion, the space is not the physical space of the narrator but a narrative space, the wiggling fingers are not fingers but running feet. The gesture is thus a symbol, but the symbol is of a fundamentally different type from the symbols of speech.

This gesture-symbol is global in that the whole is not composed out of separately meaningful parts. Rather, the parts gain meaning because of the meaning of the whole. The wiggling fingers mean running only because we know that the gesture, as a whole, depicts someone running. It's not that a gesture depicting someone running was composed out of separately meaningful parts: wiggling + motion, for instance.

The gesture also is synthetic. It combines different meaning elements. The segments of the utterance, "he + running + along the wire," were combined in the gesture into a single depiction of Sylvester-running-along-the-wire.

Noncombinatoric

Gestures also are noncombinatoric: two gestures produced together don't combine to form a larger, more complex gesture. There is no hierarchical structure of gestures made out of other gestures. This noncombinatoric property contrasts with the hierarchical structure of language. In sentences, lower constituents combine into higher constituents. With gestures, each symbol is a complete expression of meaning unto itself. Most of the time gestures are one to a clause but occasionally more than one gesture occurs within a single clause. Even then the several gestures don't combine into a more complex gesture. Each gesture depicts the content from a different angle, bringing out a different aspect or temporal phase, and each is a complete expression of meaning by itself. This situation is illustrated by the next example, taken from a film narrative (see fig. 1.8):

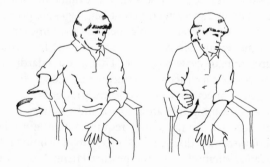

Figure 1.8. Illustrating two gestures in one clause with "[. . . and she . . .] [grabs] the knife." The gestures are two phases of an event, but do not combine into a higher level gesture.

(1.10) [. . . and she . . .][grabs] the knife
    (1)   (2)

(1) Hand gropes in a circle with the palm facing down and the fingers extended.

(2) Hand turns up and closes to a fist: gripping an "object."

The gestures are related but do not combine into a single higher gesture. The gestures, rather, present successive snapshots of the scene. The clause also describes this scene, but whereas the parts of the clause, "she," "grabs," and "the knife," combine to form the clause, groping plus grabbing do not combine to form a larger gesture. Far from combining, the two gestures maximized the contrast between them: the horizontal orientation and circling movement of (1) changed into the vertical orientation and closed fist of (2).

Other Nonlinguistic Properties

NO STANDARDS OF FORM. Linguistic systems impose standards of well-formedness to which all utterances must conform or be dismissed as "not English" or "not Japanese" or not whatever language the speaker is using. The standards are "the way we do it." Gestures have no equivalent to this implicit standard of form. Gestures by different individuals often are similar when the content of the gesture is similar, but this similarity is because of the content and not because individuals are conforming to standards for making the gesture. The gestures of different speakers can present the same meanings but do so in quite different forms. Moreover, the gestures of people speaking different languages are no more different than the gestures of different people speaking the same language. While their speech moves in different directions to meet linguistic standards, their gestures remain close together. This nonstandardized quality of gestures is important for theoretical purposes. Precisely because gestures are *not* obliged to meet standards of form, they are free to present just those aspects of meaning that are relevant and salient to the speaker and leave out aspects that language may require but are not relevant to the situation (linguists have discussed the problem of defining relevance, but have not availed themselves of the gesture channel as a source of evidence; see Sperber and Wilson 1987).

NO DUALITY OF PATTERNING. Another difference from language is that gestures lack duality of patterning. This is the property of true linguistic systems in which words enter into two patterns of contrast at once (Hockett 1958). The word "dog" differs from other words in meaning: here the contrasts are to "cat," "wolf," "monkey," etc. The word also differs from other words in sounds: now the contrasts are to "cog," "doll," "dig," etc. One pattern is a structure of meanings and the other of sounds. Duality of patterning is deeply connected to the arbitrariness of signs. Since meaning and sounds are structured separately, the two systems can be related by *arbitrary* mappings (Saussure [1916] 1959). Gestures are profoundly different from words in that they lack this duality of patterning and the associated system of arbitrary mappings. There are no separately structured systems of form and meaning in gestures. A gesture patterns in only one way, that of meaning. Kinesic form is not an independent level as sound is an independent level of language. Kinesic form in a gesture is determined by its meaning. (This is true even of beats, whose role as a universal emphasizer lacking content of its own is paralleled by its simplicity of form.) If we explain the meaning of a gesture we explain the form. Not having duality of patterning is a strength of gestures. It explains how they are able to express meanings that may be difficult to get into the verbal channel.

Yet Gestures and Language Are a Single System

Gestures and language thus differ from each other on a number of fundamental dimensions. Yet they are also closely linked. The following describes some of these linkages. Such linkages imply that gestures and speech should be viewed within a unified conceptual framework as aspects of a single underlying process (see McNeill 1985b):

1. *Gestures occur only during speech.* While emblems and pantomimes may be delivered in utter silence, the gestures that are the focus of attention for us are almost invariably accompanied by speech. In about 100 hours of recorded narratives, only one gesture was made by a listener. Gesture production and adopting the role of speaker are virtually limited to the same situations. Moreover, 90% of all gestures by speakers occur when the speaker is actually uttering something. The acts of speaking and gesturing are bound to each other in time.

2. *Gestures and speech are semantically and pragmatically coexpressive.* That is, the gestures that accompany utterances also present the same or closely related meanings semantically and perform the same functions pragmatically. Iconics accompany utterances that depict concrete objects and events and fulfill a narrative function (see chap. 5). Metaphorics accompany utterances that refer to the pragmatic structure of the discourse as a whole. They present their own image of the discourse as an object or space or other physical reality. Other gesture types have their own parallels with speech (see chap. 7).

3. *Gestures and speech are synchronous.* The specific linguistic segments

that are coexpressive with the gesture are cotemporal. The most meaningful segment of the gesture is the stroke, and it lines up in time with the
equivalent linguistic segment, as in the example given in (1.1) where the
subject said, "and he [bends it way back]," and the stroke showed bending back during the same interval of time. Such synchrony implies that
the speaker is presenting the same meaning in both channels at once.
Having a shared meaning could be the basis for integrating gesture and
speech into a single performance.

4. *Gestures and speech develop together in children.* Children's first gestures are concrete pointing and certain kinds of iconics. Much later they
add other kinds of iconics, beats, metaphorics and, last of all, abstract
pointing. In general, this progression follows the same path as the development of speech. As children's speech development moves from a
largely referential focus, through descriptive elaboration, and finally to
the ability to structure discourse, so their gestures develop from a largely
concrete deictic emphasis, through various kinds of iconic gestures, and
finally to the discourse-referring gestures—metaphors, abstract pointing, and beats. Beats do not appear at all in children much younger than 5
years and are not abundant until 11 years; yet, considered as movements,
beats are the simplest of motions—just flicks of the hand. It is the discourse structure that determines that these flicks have meaning, and the
development of this structure is late and the beat gesture itself thus
doesn't occur.

5. *Gestures and speech break down together in aphasia.* Broca's aphasia
consists of a relatively intact ability to use referring terms but a radically
impaired ability to combine terms into larger grammatical units. This
type of speech is often called "telegraphic." The gestures of Broca's aphasics are parallel in the sense that they are discrete and consist of abundant
iconics; their gesture repertoire contains almost no metaphorics or beats.
Wernicke's aphasics present the contrasting picture of fluent speech but a
more or less complete loss of the ability to make coherent semantic connections. The gestures of Wernicke type aphasics are large, mobile, but
devoid of interpretable meaning. In contrast to the Broca's aphasics they
may have few iconics but there are abundant metaphorics and beats.
Thus, the neurological damage that produces contrasting aphasic syn-
dromes affects gestures in strikingly parallel ways.

For all of these reasons gestures and speech are most appropriately regarded as two sides of a single underlying verbal-gestural process of constructing and presenting meanings. This argument will be developed in
detail over the next several chapters. Despite the fundamental character

of the differences between gestures and speech—one global and synthetic, the other linear and segmented—they are closely tied together in meaning, time, function, development, and dissolution. What we can learn about this unified process of meaning construction out of such opposite systems of symbols is the substance of this book.

Gestures and Time

The issue of how gestures and speech relate in time is crucial for understanding the system that includes gesture and speech as two parts. As shown by the phenomenon that gestures slightly anticipate speech, *gestures and speech have a constant relationship in time*. To express this relationship I will first describe the phenomenon of gesture anticipation. After that, I will describe three rules for gesture synchrony. That gestures could both anticipate and synchronize with speech is only seemingly a paradox, as I will explain.

Gesture Anticipation and Its Meaning

A prototypical gesture passes through three phases (Kendon 1980). There is first the preparation for the gesture: the hand rises from its resting place and moves to the front away from the speaker. Then there is the stroke, the main part of the gesture: the hand moves backward from the preparation phase and ends up near the shoulder. Finally there is the retraction, the return of the hand to quiescence: the hand falls back to the rest position. The preparation and retraction phases are optional but the stroke is essential. If there is a preparation phase, however, we can examine where it occurs. This phase regularly anticipates by a brief interval the coexpressive linguistic segment(s) (Kendon 1972, 1980). The "bends it way back" example cited earlier is such a case. Here is that example again now with the preparation phase indicated:

(1.11) he grabs a big [oak tree and he **bends it way back**]
      (1)   (2)

(1) Preparation phase: hand rises from armrest of chair and moves up and forward at eye level, taking on grip shape at same time.
(2) **Stroke phase:** *hand appears to pull something backwards and down, ending up near the shoulder.*

There is no explanation of the movement of the hand at (1) other than to get ready to perform the stroke at (2). The image of grasping and pulling was already taking shape when the speaker was saying "oak tree" in the previous clause. This can be taken to show that the speaker was formulating the next utterance while still producing the previous one.

The anticipation of speech by gesture is important evidence for the argument that gestures reveal utterances in their primitive form: there is a global-synthetic image taking form at the moment the preparation phase begins, but there is not yet a linguistic structure with which it can integrate. The gesture in (1.11) began in the previous clause but could integrate with speech only with the words "bends it way back." One could argue that the full sentence was planned in advance, during the preparation phase, and this is what started off the gesture preparation, but this argument is actually quite weak. I will consider it and several other counterarguments at the end of the chapter.

For the moment, I will only emphasize that gesture preparations regularly anticipate their coexpressive speech. I next will introduce what appears to be a paradox: the gesture in (1.11) also synchronized with speech.

Synchronization

I will give three "rules" governing how speech and gesture synchronize. Oddly, gestures both anticipate and synchronize with speech. This is not, however, the paradox that it may seem. Anticipation and synchronization refer to different phases of the gesture. The synchrony rules refer to the stroke phase: anticipation refers to the preparation phase. It is only the stroke of the gesture that is integrated with speech into a single smooth performance, but the preparation for the stroke slightly leads the coexpressive speech, as we have seen (also see table 4.2).

PHONOLOGICAL SYNCHRONY RULE. The synchrony rule at this level is that the stroke of the gesture precedes or ends at, but does not follow, the phonological peak syllable of speech (Kendon 1980). In other words, the stroke phase of the gesture is integrated into the phonology of the utterance. For example, the stroke phase of the "bends it way back" gesture was the hand pulling back on an imaginary tree and it ended at the word "back." This word was the phonological peak of the utterance. The speaker will temporarily cease moving his hand when phonological synchrony threatens to break down, so strong is the urge to keep the gesture and speech together. In an example cited by Kendon (1980), there was a downward stroke followed by a static post-stroke hold. The effect of the hold was to maintain the "umbrella" hand shape of the gesture until the phonologically most prominent part of the utterance could be reached (from Kendon 1980, see fig. 1):

(1.12) this patient has been a problem so far as a history is

concerned uh y'know [a] [very formal one] uh or any
(1)(2)

(1) Stroke: umbrella hand moves sharply down.
(2) Hold: umbrella hand posture held statically.

The stroke phase had taken place prematurely during the low intensity part of the utterance, but the speaker held the gesture until the phonological peak caught up.

SEMANTIC SYNCHRONY RULE. Semantic synchrony means that the two channels, speech and gesture, present the same meanings at the same time. The rule can be stated as follows: if gestures and speech co-occur they must cover the same idea unit. The term "idea unit" is meant to make provision for synchronized speech and gestures where the meanings complement one another. In the "and he bends it way back" example, the idea unit was a character seizing a tree and bending it back. The gesture, in being made with one hand, depicted the unique information that the tree was fastened at one end. It thus complemented speech by making this information specific, and speech and the gesture co-occurred. It is theoretically possible to combine gestures and speech that have different and unrelated meanings, but to do so is difficult and I have seen no spontaneous gestures that conflict with semantic synchrony. Some gestures and/or utterances are so vague that it is hard to say if they really present the same idea unit, but there are no examples of speech presenting one idea unit and gesture another. For instance, we do *not* find such pairs as "he bends it way back" with a gesture that depicts throwing something or flying or smoking a cigarette.

Three complications arise for semantic synchrony: (1) pauses, (2) multiple gestures, and (3) gestures that correspond to more than one clause. How is semantic synchrony preserved in the face of these phenomena?

1. *Pauses.* A semantically coexpressive gesture stroke will continue through the pause, thus showing that the semantic structure of the interrupted speech remains intact (Kendon 1980). Despite the interruption in

the flow of speech, semantic synchrony is preserved. Kendon gives this example:

(1.13) they wheel a big table in
[with a with a . . . (1 sec.) . . .] cake on it
Iconic: a series of circular motions with the hand pointing down and index finger extended—outlining the cake on the table.

The stroke phase continued until the word "cake," as if the gesture had to keep discharging the idea of a cake. "Cake" was still uttered with peak phonological stress, however, demonstrating that the phonological unit also was intact, and speech and gesture were integrated despite the long pause.

2. *Multiple gestures.* A small but significant proportion of clauses have two or more distinct gestures accompanying them. How do these cases of multiple gestures preserve semantic synchrony? Basically, they work the same way as single gestures when they complement speech. Each gesture covers the idea unit from a different angle. Thus, for each gesture the accompanying speech is coexpressive and there is no breakdown of semantic synchrony. The earlier example of multiple gestures in one clause (fig. 1.8) preserved semantic synchrony with each of its gestures ("[. . . and she . . .] [grabs] the knife"). The first groping gesture is coexpressive with the clause, as is the second grabbing gesture. The successive gestures depicted the temporal phases of the event, and are both synchronous on the semantic level.

3. *Multiple clauses.* Some strokes present information that is ultimately unpacked into more than one clause. Often, in this situation, the stroke is held, as in (1.12), but in some cases the hand relaxes and returns to a rest position after the first clause. The following is an instance:

(1.14) so he ig[nites himself and] flies off out the window
            (1)   (2)

(1) Stroke: hand quickly moves upward and forward, opening at the same time.
(2) Retraction: hand relaxes and falls back to armrest of chair.

The stroke illustrates both igniting (the hand opening) and flying off out the window (the hand moving up and out). Only the igniting-and-opening combination is truly synchronous. The rest of the stroke's semantic content (moving up and out) anticipates its coexpressive verbal description ("flies off out the window"). The phenomenon is the reverse of having multiple gestures in one clause: here we have one gesture and multiple clauses. Semantic synchrony would be violated if during the second clause the speaker proceeded to make a new gesture or if the second clause were not an unpacking of the stroke at (1) but some other, altogether different clause. However, neither of these breakdowns of synchrony occurred. Retraction has no significance in itself, it is semantically neutral; and the second clause was semantically a continuation of the stroke at (1). Thus examples like (1.13) do not violate semantic synchrony. In fact, such examples show an important further observation: the images exhibited in gestures might require multiple clauses to be unpacked into speech.

PRAGMATIC SYNCHRONY RULE. The rule here says that if gestures and speech co-occur they perform the same pragmatic functions. Pragmatic synchrony implies that speakers are limited to one pragmatic reference at a time. However, this does not prevent speakers from making other, semantic references in the same utterance. In the earlier example of a conduit gesture (fig. 1.3), the utterance mentioned the genre of the cartoon: "it was a Sylvester and Tweety cartoon." This semantic reference was used to identify the genre of the upcoming narrative. The gesture depicted something quite different, a bounded object. The utterance thus had one reference and the gesture a different metaphoric one, but utterance and gesture came together on the *pragmatic* level of presenting the narrative genre. The utterance did this by identifying the main characters of the story and the gesture did it by presenting the story as an object in its own right. Coexpressiveness in this case arose on the level of pragmatic meaning, not on the level of semantic meaning. Pragmatic synchrony has no exceptions so far as I am aware, even though, again, it is theoretically possible to combine gestures and sentences that perform different functions (for instance, one could combine "and drops it down the pipe" with a conduit gesture that presents the cartoon as an object, although we never find such chimerical monstrosities). Again, the effort of making the gesture have one form of pragmatic content and the utterance a different one appears to be too great for this kind of mismatch to occur during running speech.

Alternative Hypotheses

The hypothesis of this book is that gesture and speech arise from a single process of utterance formation. The utterance has both an imagistic side and a linguistic side. The image arises first and is transformed into a complex structure in which both the gesture and the linguistic structure are integral parts. The early signalling of the image in the preparation phase is one piece of evidence in support of this theory. The integration of the stroke with the utterance itself is another piece of evidence. That is, the image that is signaled in gesture preparation is tightly linked a moment later with the articulation of speech and the expression of semantic and pragmatic content. It is tightly linked despite its fundamentally different character from speech as a symbol. If the image is the primitive form of the utterance and the stroke is part of the utterance performance, we can account for the progression: a preparation phase that is separate from speech, and then the stroke phase that is integrated into speech.

Nonetheless, it is not difficult to imagine alternative hypotheses to this proposition. I have already briefly mentioned one—viz., the hypothesis that the full sentence is planned in advance during the gesture preparation phase—and I will now discuss it and several others. Such a method seems appropriate whether or not the reader also has thought of these hypotheses, since replying to them will clarify the hypothesis of a single process underlying speech and gesture.

THE SHARED PROCESS IS VERBAL. This is one version of the hypothesis of an advance sentence plan. According to it spontaneous gestures, along with speech, are generated from a common plan and this is the verbal plan of the utterance:

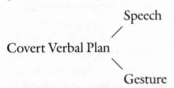

I can think of four replies to this hypothesis. First, from this theory one cannot explain the global-synthetic form of gestures. They should be linear-segmented if they are produced from a covert verbal plan.

Second, where covert linear-segmented verbal plans have been postulated (e.g., Sternberg et al. 1978) there has been an experimental procedure in which speakers were repeating verbal materials verbatim from memory; this is not planning the content of the utterance but planning only a succession of phonetic shapes. Such a verbal plan is precisely one that excludes all basis for gestures.

Third, from this theory we cannot explain the division of meaning between the gesture and speech channels as in (1.2). If there is a meaning in the gesture channel, it must have come from the covert verbal plan and should also be present in the speech channel, and to the same degree of specificity.

Finally, if gestures undergo a less complex transformation than speech after their shared computational stage, the global-synthetic image that gestures reflect can be regarded as closer to the verbal plan at an early stage of its development. This is, in fact, how I interpret gestures: gestures make manifest the utterance's primitive form, and *this* is the "verbal" plan of the utterance at an early phase of its internal development, while it is still in the form of imagery.

For all these reasons, it seems sound to conclude that speech and gesture are coexpressive manifestations of a single underlying process. The underlying process is equally speech and gesture, and there is a subsequent evolution of expressive action with outputs in both channels concurrently. The channels, moreover, have a constant relationship in time, with the gesture manifesting the primitive stage of the shared process and speech its final socially presentable stage.

THE GESTURE TRANSLATES THE SENTENCE. This is another version of the advance sentence plan hypothesis. It runs as follows. The visual-actional medium of the gesture has its own qualities, but these do not characterize the psychological structure of the sentence. There are in fact two psychological structures. The sentence medium has one characteristic set of qualities (linear and segmented), and the gesture medium has another set (global and synthetic or imagistic). The gesture is parasitic on the sentence. When a gesture occurs, this argument goes, the linear-segmented qualities of the sentence are translated into the imagistic qualities of the gesture. This does not mean that there is a shared process in which both sets of qualities exist as integral parts. On the contrary, it implies that there is computation of the sentence, then a separate computation of the gesture.

There are several replies to this hypothesis:

First, there are very few cases where speech and gesture are repaired. Rather, what typically happens is that speech is repaired and the gesture that accompanied the utterance being repaired is repeated with the repair in exactly the same form. The gesture, therefore, must not have been the output of the sentence. (This argument is due to Sotaro Kita.)

Second, there is complementarity. In the "she chases him out again" example, the gesture and speech did not manifest the same information. There was mutual complementarity in that the utterance conveyed aspects of the scene that the gesture did not convey, and vice versa. Such examples of mutual complementarity can be multiplied many fold.

Assume that gestures are copies of sentences. Then we have a situation that we can diagram as follows:

Speech → Gesture

However, there is no possibility of complementarity with this arrangement. Everything in gesture must have come from speech. Thus if a meaning appears in gesture, it must appear in speech as well. The same argument applies to the opposite diagram, with speech copying gesture (a more appropriate hypothesis in any case, in view of the anticipation of speech by gesture):

Gesture → Speech

In this case everything in speech must have come from gesture, but this also is contradicted by the phenomenon of mutual complementarity.

The DAF experiments in chapter 10 demonstrate that complexity representation spontaneously shifts from the speech to the gesture channel. The Speech → Gesture model is ruled out by this shift, since if the speech channel is blocked by DAF there is no way the gesture channel can take over its complexity if gesture is a copy of speech. Thus, complementarity of speech and gesture implies that gestures are coexpressive of meaning. Since they are so closely linked to speech, they are a manifestation of meaning that is different from but closely connected to the meaning as conveyed in spoken form.

Third, to copy speech into gesture means not only reproducing content but radically changing the form of utterance as well. Speech and gesture are representations different in form. This is most apparent in the difference between gestures and manual signs in a true linguistic system such as ASL. I will devote the entire second chapter to the contrast between spontaneous gesture and signs. For the present, I will just state that ASL signs are segmented, combinatoric, context-stable, etc., while gestures are the opposite on each dimension. It is not that gestures are uninfluenced by conventions, but that the conventions that influence them are the conventions of social life in general, not specific gesture conventions. Thus, if gestures were copies of speech, they would make the context-stable unstable, the segmented global, the combinatoric synthetic, and so on. To suppose that gesture is a copy of speech in a different medium simply overlooks the enormous complexity of such a change. Instead, I believe that gesture and speech manifest different stages of an evolution of the utterance.

Finally, the kinesic medium is pliable and has syntactic potential. This point is shown by the phenomenon of sign languages and will also be fully described in chapter 2. It is abundantly clear that the gesture medium can adopt the linguistic properties of finished utterances, which are so obviously lacking from spontaneous gestures. Linguistic properties can actually be seen emerging in gestures when a speaker is required to use gesture as his only channel of communication (Bloom 1979, described in chap. 2). If the global-synthetic properties of gestures are not inherent in the visual-kinesic medium, they must be explained in some other way. A plausible account is that they are imposed on it by a stage of processing in which the representations are imagistic. This is the primitive stage of the utterance—imagistic, analogic, global, and synthetic.

The four arguments jointly lead to the conclusion that gestures are forced to be as they are by the form of thought that exists at the moment the gesture is triggered, and this representation is imagistic. The deep time evolution of utterances carries global-synthetic imagery into a final stage of socially regulated coded symbols.

GESTURES ARE INDEPENDENT VISUAL DISPLAYS. According to this hypothesis, the gesture is just a separate display exhibited along with the utterance. It is like a photograph or drawing. And just as holding up a real photograph would have nothing to do with the process of utterance generation, so performing a gesture could have nothing to do with it either. The first point in reply is that, unlike a photograph, a gesture is something the speaker is creating while speaking. Second, the gesture is very closely connected to speech temporally, semantically, and pragmatically, all of which suggest a coordination between the gesture and the utterance that is quite different from presenting a photograph. Third, when meaning is divided between a gesture and sentence, it is a true division. It is not that the gesture is called up, as a photograph might be held up, to repair an otherwise interrupted message. We don't observe, for example,

so he . . . [*gesture to complete the idea*]

but rather,

[so he chases him out again]

Gesture shows the means.

These points reduce to one reply: gesture and speech are operations that have been connected *within*. This is the sense in which they are parts of a single process.

Moreover, there is a fundamental difference between gestures and photographs. Gestures are necessarily schematic, and are to a degree that photographs usually are not. More crucially, a gesture is structured by meaning, while a photograph is not; the meaning of a photograph is something we—the observers—bring to it whereas the meaning of a gesture is the foundation of its construction.

A further difference between a gesture and photograph, however, is that a photograph is disconnected from its original context in time. This disconnection is indeed the raison d'être of the photograph. "The most popular use of the photograph is as a memento of *the absent*" (Berger 1972, 180, emphasis added). A gesture, in contrast, exists only at a given moment and this moment must be included in the meaning of the gesture. We can video a gesture, but we also video its moment. The video itself is a photograph of sorts and is disconnected from *its* context in time, but the gesture, the subject of the video-photograph, is a real entity that exists only in context. A photograph records scene x at moment y, and this very fact is its source of significance, as Berger explains: the photograph refers to the past moment and to the recording of it. It means "I have decided that seeing this is worth recording" (Berger 1972, 179). We can then look at it with comprehension at other moments z, q, or a. The $y \neq z$, q, or a difference is what separates photos from gestures. A gesture also has its moment y, but can be comprehended only *at* y (and if we record it, we replay y too). Performing it at moments z, q, or a is play-acting, or example-citing.

THE GESTURE IS THE TIP OF THE ICEBERG. According to this hypothesis, the global-synthetic gesture is the surface manifestation of what is, underneath, a *sign*—a gesture with language-like properties.[2] If this is the case, it is a mistake to infer from the gesture a form of thought that is global and synthetic. The overt gesture is just the tip of the iceberg. The rest of the iceberg is more like language, with segmentation of complex ideas into elements, compositionality, standardization of form, distinctiveness, arbitrariness, and the rest of the properties of signs as opposed to gestures. However, this hypothesis is empirically unsound. If the observed global-synthetic gesture is just the tip of the iceberg and under the "sea of speech" is a more language-like sign, then by "raising up" the iceberg we should expose more and more language-like properties. That is, a simple gesture might be global-synthetic, but what of more complex gestures? They might be expected to be more independent of speech and display more linguistic properties of their own. However, this is not true. More complex gestures, gestures utilizing two hands

---

2. Susan Goldin-Meadow and Jenny Singleton pointed out this counterargument.

in different roles or gestures with several internal components, do not bring up latent linguistic structure and are still tied to speech. Complex gestures are global-synthetic all the way down, to keep to the iceberg metaphor. All high-complexity gestures, indeed, show global-synthetic-meaning properties. Thus, I also feel justified in rejecting the fourth hypothesis.

Conclusion

Thus, gestures are not the product of a linear-segmented verbal plan, not translations of speech into visual-kinesic form, not like photographs, and not the tip of a linguistically structured iceberg. They are closely linked to speech, yet present meaning in a form fundamentally different from that of speech. My own hypothesis is that speech and gesture are elements of a single integrated process of utterance formation in which there is a synthesis of opposite modes of thought—global-synthetic and instantaneous imagery with linear-segmented temporally extended verbalization. Utterances and thoughts realized in them are both imagery and language.

2   *Conventions, Gestures, and Signs*

Introduction

The focus of this book is on the spontaneous and idiosyncratic gestures that occur while one speaks. But it is useful to begin, not with these gestures, but with the more systematic language-like gestures that constitute sign languages. These are signs organized into true linguistic codes. We benefit in this way from the sharp contrast that we can draw between the spontaneous and the socially regulated kinds of gesture. This contrast will strengthen one of my arguments at the conclusion of the previous chapter, namely, that the visual-kinesic medium is capable of having the properties of a true language. Therefore, the *absence* of these properties from spontaneous gestures is a meaningful absence; it is a real phenomenon and can be taken to show a form of thought behind the gesture that is global, synthetic, and imagistic.

The comparison of coded signs and noncoded spontaneous gestures within the same visual-kinesic medium presents a unique view: holding constant the medium, we see what properties of signs are constant and what properties are added by the conventionally structured code. A code implies a systematic structure that is agreed on in advance and maintained by a community of users. The necessity of introducing, remembering, maintaining, and agreeing on a code has wide-ranging effects on the forms of the signs themselves. Only certain forms of signs appear in codes, presumably because of the demands placed on signs when they are parts of organized systems. This chapter analyzes these effects on signs. The properties of gestures structured under codes should also be true of spoken signs, so the findings of this chapter will have general significance for languages of all kinds.[1]

Conventional Codes

By a conventional code I mean a general prearranged agreement on the gestures (and other means) that allow individuals to coordinate communicative actions, and to achieve intersubjectivity (cf. Lewis 1968). I do not mean that people consciously apply conventions. In the case of language, speakers are generally unconscious of conventions even as they

---

1. I wish to thank Susan Goldin-Meadow and Adam Kendon for their detailed comments on this chapter. The exposition is markedly more accurate thanks to their efforts.

use them. I also do not mean that conventions are worked out face-to-face. Linguistic conventions are historical and the essential idea of having a code is precisely that it enables you to know what to do without having to discuss it.

Kendon's Continuum

To set the stage I will present an ordering of gestures that was first described by Adam Kendon in 1983, and published in 1988 (Kendon 1988a). In his honor, I will call it Kendon's continuum:

Kendon's continuum:

Gesticulation → Language-like Gestures → Pantomimes → Emblems → Sign Languages

As we move from left to right: (1) the obligatory presence of speech declines, (2) the presence of language properties increases, and (3) idiosyncratic gestures are replaced by socially regulated signs.

Kendon's continuum is important for sorting out gestures of fundamentally different kinds. Many authors refer to all forms of nonverbal behavior as "gesture," failing to distinguish among different categories, with the result that behaviors that differ fundamentally are confused or conflated. (Hecaen 1967, 1978, proposed a scheme that recognized many of the distinctions above, but did not perceive them as falling on a continuum.) I use the term "gesture" in this book specifically to refer to the leftmost, "gesticulation" end of the spectrum.

Gestures in this sense are idiosyncratic spontaneous movements of the hands and arms accompanying speech. An example is the hand rising upward while the speaker says "and he climbs up the pipe." Gestures (gesticulation) almost never occur in the absence of speech. "Language-like gestures" are similar in form and appearance to gesticulation but differ in that they are grammatically integrated into the utterance; an example is "the parents were all right, but the kids were [gesture]," where the gesture fills the grammatical slot of an adjective. In pantomime the hands depict objects or actions, but speech is not obligatory. This weakened speech presence locates pantomime in the middle of Kendon's continuum. There may be either silence or just inarticulate onomatopoetic sound effects ("whoops!" "click!" etc.). Moreover, successive pantomimes can create sequence-like demonstrations, and this is different from gesticulation where successive gestures do not combine. Emblems also occupy the middle area of Kendon's continuum. Which one—emblem or pantomime—belongs more to the right probably is arbitrary.

Emblems are the familiar "Italianate" gestures, mostly insults but some of them praise, and virtually all attempts to control other people's behavior (Kendon 1981). Emblems have standards of well-formedness, a crucial language-like property that gesticulation and pantomime lack. For example, the OK sign must be made by placing the thumb and index finger in contact; using the thumb and second finger does not produce the OK sign. Thus emblems must meet standards of well-formedness. Emblems have as their characteristic use production in the absence of speech (indeed, this is probably their raison d'être: they offer a way of getting around speech taboos). Emblems have been described by Efron (1941), Ekman and Friesen (1969), Morris et al. (1979), and Kendon (1981). Sign languages, finally, such as ASL, are full-fledged linguistic systems with segmentation, compositionality, a lexicon, a syntax, distinctiveness, arbitrariness, standards of well-formedness, and a community of users (see Klima and Bellugi 1979).

These distinctions between the different types of communicative manual actions are crucial. Not only do the different types of movements bear different logical and behavioral relations to speech, they also are affected differently following cerebral lesions. Thus highly codified sign languages such as ASL may be disrupted in ways that result in sign aphasias much like the aphasias observed in speaking patients (Poizner, Klima, and Bellugi 1987). Emblems and pantomimes might replace or supplement language to the extent that linguistic capacities remain to be exploited via another channel. Production of emblems and pantomimes, which are often tested in an attempt to quantify gestural skills (see Peterson and Kirshner 1981 for a review) do not vary systematically with the type of aphasia, but seem to be related to overall severity of the communicative deficit. Gesticulation bears a more complex relationship to speech, and varies in subtle and intricate ways in relation to the speech it accompanies (see chap. 12).

The changes that take place along Kendon's continuum have widespread consequences for the structure of the gestures themselves, considered both individually and in their collective relationships to each other. In particular, there is development of

segmentation: meaning complexes are analyzed into segments.
compositionality: meaning complexes are constructed by combining segments.
a lexicon: segments recur in the same form in different contexts.
a syntax: combinations of segments adhere to standard patterns.
paradigmatic oppositions: segments are organized into contrasting sets.

distinctiveness: details are added to the form of segments solely to distinguish segments from other segments.

arbitrariness: segments are used to refer to entities and events in contexts where their iconicity is ruled out.

utterance-like timing: segments are produced with a timing that reveals them to be the final temporal stage of the process of utterance construction, rather than the utterance's primitive form.

standards of form: signs and/or combinations of signs are held to standards of form.

a community of users: a community exists that understands the signs and sign combinations without perpetual metalinguistic explanation.

We will analyze these properties in this chapter. The accompanying chart (table 2.1) summarizes the examples and the language-like properties found in each.

An important system of gestures organized into their own code is the sign language of the deaf, known in North America as ASL, or American Sign Language (see Klima and Bellugi 1979 for a description). There have been many linguistically oriented studies of ASL, including Klima and Bellugi (1979), Stokoe (1960, 1972), Frishberg (1975), Friedman (1977), Siple (1978), Lane and Grosjean (1980), Liddell (1980), Marschark et al. (1986), and Supalla (to appear)—to give a sample.

Another gesture language is that of the women of the Warlpiri, an aborigine people living in the north central Australian desert (Kendon 1988b). (I will refer to this language as WSL.) It is the custom among the Warlpiri, as among several other aborigine groups in this region, for women to forgo speech when they are in mourning, and at certain other times as well. When they are under these speech bans, the complex sign language of WSL is used. WSL also is used as a convenient alternative means of communication even when speech is ritually permitted, and then it may be used as an accompaniment to speech during storytelling

Table 2.1 Sign Language Examples

Properties	Danny	Deaf Children	WSL	ASL	Emblems
Without speech	yes	yes	optional	yes	yes
Segments	yes	yes	yes	yes	yes
Combinations	yes	yes	yes	yes	limited
Standards	yes	yes	yes	yes	yes
Community	local	local	yes	yes	yes
Tradition	no	no	yes	yes	yes

and animated talk. When signs and speech are executed concurrently, we can investigate the timing of the two channels—invaluable for inferring the internal dynamics of conventional signs. Information on this point is not available from any other source. WSL, like the other sign languages in use among aborigine groups in this part of Australia, was developed among speakers-hearers, and thus can be directly influenced by spoken language in a way that the sign languages of the deaf, such as ASL, cannot.

A third situation is the spontaneous emergence of gesture systems in children who have not been exposed to a usable language model of any kind. These are deaf children of hearing parents who themselves do not know ASL or any other gesture system (Goldin-Meadow 1982).

A fourth example is emblems, or Italianate gestures. Emblems are but a partial code, but they still show changes of form and timing compared to spontaneous gesticulation.

Finally, I will describe an experiment in which a hearing subject (called "Danny" by the experimenter), a college student naive to any kind of sign language, invented a gesture code when he was asked to communicate a fairy story without the use of speech (Bloom 1979). All of these situations provide examples of signs at rightward locations on Kendon's continuum, and their properties can be compared to those of spontaneous gestures in speaking subjects.

The two ends of Kendon's continuum—and the different kinds of gestures that arise there—are related to speech in fundamentally different ways. Most crucially, spontaneous gestures and socially conventional signs have opposite relationships to the internal temporal dimension of utterances. While spontaneous gestures can be taken to reveal the utterance's primitive stage, conventional signs, even when they are gestural, are the *final* stage of their utterances. Comparing the properties of two ends of the continuum thus allows us to see the contrasting properties of utterances at the beginning and end of the utterance's internal evolution. The end stage is open to socio-cultural specification and control, whereas the inner symbols of the primitive stage are not. One supposes that for the deaf and others who make use of conventional sign languages the primitive stages of their sentences also include global-synthetic images, just as in the case of spoken languages, but their signs, unlike the spontaneous gestures of the hearing, do not, cannot, reflect this stage. The kinesic-visual medium is grammatical and socially regulated for the deaf, and this shifts the overt performance of deaf signers to the final stage of the internal temporal evolution of utterances.

Nonlinguistic Properties of Gesticulation

I have already mentioned in chapter 1 ways in which the gesticulation end of the continuum is unlike language. I will just summarize the properties of spontaneous speech-accompanying gestures:

GLOBAL AND SYNTHETIC. The meanings of the parts of a gesture are determined by the whole (= global), and different meaning segments are synthesized into a single gesture (= synthetic). The global-synthetic property contrasts with the combinatoric linear-segmented property of speech and sign language.

NONCOMBINATORIC. Gestures don't combine to form larger, hierarchically structured gestures. Most gestures are one to a clause, but when there are successive gestures within a clause, each corresponds to an idea unit in and of itself.

CONTEXT-SENSITIVE. Precisely because gestures are not constrained by the requirements of a code or language, they are free to incorporate only the salient and relevant aspects of the context. Each gesture is created at the moment of speaking and highlights what is relevant, and the same entity can be referred to by gestures that have changed their form. This property is shown by comparing a single speaker's gestures for an entity in different contexts, where the form of the gesture shifts to highlight different contextual aspects. For example, in one context the hand rises up and points, for the character climbing; in a later context it opens and forms a hollow space, for the character swallowing the bowling ball (see lines 28 and 33, respectively, of the narrative in chapter 3). The property of context-sensitivity contrasts with the stability of lexical forms in a linguistic system—forms recur and combine with other forms to present modifications of the core meaning in all contexts but do not give up their basic form in this process.

NO STANDARDS OF FORM. Different speakers display the same meanings in idiosyncratic ways. Here the emphasis is on different speakers in the same context. Lacking standards of form, individuals create their own gesture symbols for the same event, each incorporating a core meaning but adding details that seem salient, and these are different from speaker to speaker.

TIMING. Gestures are integrated into the speech output. They anticipate the speech in their preparation phase, and synchronize with it in the
stroke phase, which is timed to end at or before, but not after, the peak
syllable. WSL signs produced with speech, on the other hand, tend to lag
behind speech and then catch up at the start of the next idea unit. Since
WSL signs, along with speech, are socially regulated *final* products of a
speech process, they do not have the constant temporal relationship to
speech of spontaneous gestures.

These are some of the nonlinguistic properties of gestures. In all
respects—that spontaneous gestures are global-synthetic, noncombinatoric, context-sensitive, idiosyncratic in form, and timed both to anticipate and to synchronize with speech—spontaneous gestures differ
from gestures organized into a code.

Linguistic Properties of Sign Language

In this section I will illustrate the rightward end of Kendon's continuum
with examples drawn from ASL, WSL, and the gestures of deaf children
who have not been exposed to a language. This way of presenting the
material does not give a picture of the sign languages themselves since
each language is divided among different topics. Nevertheless some idea
of each sign language will emerge; more systematic descriptions of ASL
and WSL are to be found in the sources cited above (in addition to WSL,
Kendon 1988a provides valuable surveys of a number of other sign languages, including the Plains Sign Language of nineteenth-century
North America; for this language, see also Umiker-Sebeok and Sebeok
1978, and West 1960).

Each of the following properties will be illustrated with examples:
segmentation and combination (ASL, deaf children), lexicon formation
(deaf children), a syntax with paradigmatic oppositions (deaf children),
distinctiveness (WSL), arbitrariness (deaf children, ASL, WSL), standards of well formedness (deaf children, WSL), and timing (WSL). Examples could be provided from other sign languages, but the main points
will be sufficiently demonstrated with these illustrations.

Segmentation and Combination

It makes sense to consider segmentation and combination together, since
the evidence for one is simultaneously evidence for the other.

SEGMENTATION AND COMBINATION IN DEAF CHILDREN. A compell-
ing example of segmentation-combination is exhibited by a deaf child
not exposed to a usable sign language whom I will describe in a moment.

However, first a word in general about such children. Deaf children exposed to ASL from birth acquire ASL as their native language, in much the same way that hearing children acquire their spoken language (Newport and Meier 1985). Petitto and Marentette (1991) document language milestones in the learning of ASL at the appropriate ages, including the emergence of syllabic babbling before the first birthday. Similarly, hearing children of deaf parents who are exposed to ASL also learn ASL as a native language. However, deaf children of hearing parents who do not use ASL often have great difficulty acquiring any language natively. They cannot hear their parents' speech, and the parents do not have a visual sign language the children could acquire. Such children devise linguistic systems of their own based on spontaneous gestures. These gesture languages are called "home signs" by deaf people, and have been the subject of extensive research by Susan Goldin-Meadow and her colleagues (Goldin-Meadow 1982; Goldin-Meadow and Feldman 1977; Goldin-Meadow and Mylander, to appear b; Mylander and Goldin-Meadow, to appear).

Deaf children not exposed to linguistic models display a remarkable linguistic inventiveness. Although they receive no examples of language they include linguistic properties in their gestures. These properties set their performance far apart from the gestures that accompany the speech of hearing persons. It is clear that the linguistic properties arise from the children themselves. Goldin-Meadow and Mylander (1983, 1984, to appear a, to appear b) have demonstrated that the parents' gestures are radically different from the deaf children's in lacking both the children's form (morphology) and rules of combination (syntax).

The segmentation example came about in this manner. The child (a little boy known as David) was operating a toy and wanted the experimenter to put a penny down on the floor. His gesture for this was a downward motion with his hand in a ring shape (like the OK sign). In itself this could be a global-synthetic gesture presenting the shape and trajectory as an unanalyzed whole. The experimenter pretended not to understand. After several repetitions, the child (about three years old) factored the gesture into its components: first he statically held up the sign for a small round object (the OK shape) and then, quite deliberately and with his *hand no longer in the OK shape* but exhibiting a flat palm, made the trajectory for downward movement. The original gesture was thus decomposed into two elements. This example implies the presence of a system of linguistic segments in which the complex meaning of "small-round-thing-moving-downward" is broken into components and the components lawfully combined into a word. That is, the child's

gestures—unlike the spontaneous gesticulations of hearing subjects—
are complexes of simpler gesture elements.

This particular combination was one among many in David's language, for indeed the child had devised a morphemic system. Systematic
compositionality of signs within a system of contrasts is crucial evidence
of segmentation and combination. For example, he used a fist shape combined with a single arc for repositioning small long objects by hand, such
as sticks. The same handshape could be combined with a to-and-fro
movement, and this indicated a stick swinging back and forth. Thus, the
fist shape had the consistent meaning of "handling a small long object."
Similarly, movement in a single arc had the meaning of repositioning
something. These are examples of basic morphemic segments into which
the child analyzed complex meanings.

Moreover, the expressive power was doubled by giving each morpheme a different meaning depending on the perspective of the gesture.
For example, arcing to-and-fro would mean swinging a long thin object
by hand when it was a Hand morpheme (the viewpoint of a "character,"
cf. chap. 4) but would mean repositioning a bulky object in a circle when
it was an Object morpheme (the viewpoint of an "observer," cf. chap. 4).
The Hand morpheme involves the hand playing the part of a hand, in

Table 2.2 Handshape Morphemes in Child's Gesture Code (from Goldin-Meadow
and Mylander, to appear b)

Hand-shape	Hand Morphemes ("character" VPT)[a]	Object Morphemes ("observer" VPT)
	Meaning of Morpheme	Meaning of Morpheme
Fist	Handle small, long object (e.g., spoon, drumstick, balloon string, handlebar)	Bulky object (hammer, head, block)
O	Handle small object (e.g., crank, shoe lace)	Round compact object (e.g., round hat, tree ball, bubble)
C	Handle large object (e.g., cup, horn, guitar)	Curved object (e.g., cowboy's legs around horse, turtle)
Palm flat	Handle flat surface (e.g., sides of toy bag, chair back)	Flat wide object (e.g., fish, flag, bird wings)
Point	Handle small surface (e.g., trigger)	Thin straight object (e.g., straw, bubble, wand, pinwheel)

[a]Key: VPT means viewpoint; "Fist" means the fingers and thumb curled into the palm;
"O" means the index finger or 4 fingers bent toward the thumb with 1/2 inch or less space
between them; "C" means index finger or 4 fingers curled toward the thumb with 3 inches
between them; "Palm" means 4 fingers extended; "Point" means the index finger extended
(Mylander and Goldin-Meadow, to appear b; table 2).

Table 2.3 Motion Morphemes in Child's Gesture Code (from Goldin-Meadow and Mylander, to appear b)

Type of Motion	Form	Meaning of Morpheme
Change of Location	Linear	Change of location by moving along path
	Long Arc	Change of location by moving along path typically to or from a particular endpoint
Change of Position	Arc To and Fro	Reposition by moving back and forth
	Circular	Reposition by moving in a circle or rotating around an axis
	Short Arc	Reposition or reorient in place
Change of Shape	Open/Close	Open or close, expand or contract, or flicker on and off
	Bend	Bend at joint
	Wiggle	Wiggle back and forth
No Change	No Motion	Hold in place, or exist

which case the hand appears to be grasping a long thin object, while in the Object morpheme the hand is playing the part of the object itself, and the hand configuration appears to depict a bulky object. Tables 2.2 and 2.3 show David's morphemes of shape (with two viewpoints) and movements (based on Mylander and Goldin-Meadow's tables 2 and 4).

The motion and handshape morphemes, finally, were combined to form complex meanings. For instance, the Arcing To and Fro morpheme combined 28 times with the Fist morpheme (in the Hand morpheme category), compared to combining with Flat palm only 8 times, a difference that very likely corresponds to the number of opportunities a small child has for repositioning small long objects compared to repositioning large flat surfaces. In any case it reflects his use of the morpheme structure to analyze event structure.

The above are combinations of morphemes. Compositionality also appeared at the sentence level. For example, pointing at a jar (= reference to the jar) followed by a twisting gesture (= twisting the lid) was used to request that the jar lid be taken off. This compositionality also implies segments and hierarchical structuring—pointing was one segment, which indicated the topic of the child's statement, and twisting the other; together they formed a unified structure. I will describe these word-level segmentations in the section dealing with the lexicon, below.

SEGMENTATION AND COMBINATION IN ASL. In ASL, too, there is segmentation and combination. A particularly striking example was presented by Klima and Bellugi (1979). The sign for "slow" is made by moving one hand across the back of the other hand. The movement is performed slowly, and thus iconically demonstrates slowness. However, when the sign is modified to be "very slow" it is made *more rapidly* (Klima and Bellugi 1979). In ASL, that is, modifying the meaning of a sign can reduce its iconicity. In contrast, the addition of semantic information to a spontaneous gesture always increases its iconicity—if something is thought of as very slow, the gesture for it is also very slow. In ASL there is a systematic way of showing intensification in general, which is by making the adjective sign more rapidly:

Intensification = Adjective + Rapid Execution

This rule is the language's way of analyzing an intensification of a quality into two components: an adjective and sign of intensity. The composition method is the reverse of the nonanalytic expression of meaning via a global-synthetic gesture.

Creating a neologism is another example of composition. Consider the ASL word for a streaker (the name of one who runs unclothed through a public place—a fad in the late 1970s). In ASL this comes out something like "nude-zooms off" (Klima and Bellugi 1979). Here two signs combine into one. The sign for "zoom off" is made by moving the hand forward and simultaneously changing the shape from open to closed. To get "streaker" the hand moves forward, as in a normal "zoom off," but the motion starts out with the handshape of "nude." So the new word is formed out of a combination of "nude" and "zoom off."

A third example is the interconversion of nouns to verbs and vice versa (Supalla and Newport 1978). To make a noun out of a verb in ASL, the sign is performed in a restrained manner and repeated, but otherwise the sign is unchanged. The rule is

Noun = Verb + Restraint and Repetition

For example, "to fly" is made by moving the hand once forward with the thumb, forefinger and pinkie extended, the other fingers curled in; "airplane" is this same shape and movement but the movement is repeated and made in a smaller space. Again, there is analysis and rule-governed combination: an object-word is derived from an action-word by combining the action-word with a generalized sign of objecthood—restraint and repetition. The relationship between an airplane and flying is thus built into the language. The same kind of derivation exists for many other verbs and nouns in ASL: in every case the noun is the verb but repeated and made in a restricted space; thus,

Verb (unrestrained, not repeated)	Noun (restrained, repeated)
fly	airplane
sweep	broom
iron (V)	iron (N)
sit	chair
hammer (V)	hammer (N)

Spoken English also has such pairs as "hammer" (verb, noun) and "iron" (verb, noun) and many others, but these have identical forms and do not manifest the kind of systematic shift we see in ASL. A closer English parallel would be the regular pattern of stress shift that accompanies the conversion of verbs to nouns—"recórd" to "récord" for example.

The unique qualities of ASL arise from the ability of the language to use movements, shapes, and space that are iconic in some contexts and exploit them for wider grammatical purposes. The word for a streaker was ordered as "nude" and "zoom off." The very structure of the word shows what to do—disrobe and zoom off, in that order—but the result is a word of ASL, not a pantomime. The adjective intensification rule takes the intensification of motion that is iconic in some contexts and uses it in all contexts, without regard to iconicity. The derivation of nouns from verbs also grammaticizes iconicity, in that the kinesic features added to a verb to make the noun (restraint and repetition) convey objecthood (something static and repeatable). The ASL linguistic system thus offers numerous illustrations of how iconic gestures are restructured when they become parts of a linguistic code.

A Lexicon

The signs that are used to carve up complex meanings and then reconstitute the meanings through combinations must also be stable and recallable, and this implies a lexicon. Both deaf children and ASL clearly have lexicons. The children are the more interesting, since their system is closer to spontaneous gesticulation, and this highlights the changes that come about when gestures are stabilized in a lexicon. Moreover, their lexicon is their own invention, and thus manifests what Susan Goldin-Meadow calls the "resilient" properties of language, the properties of language that are capable of development under conditions of deprived input (Goldin-Meadow 1982).

The children's lexicon is organized into two classes, referring signs and characterizing signs. Referring signs are various kinds of pointing gestures and characterizing signs are iconics and stylized pantomimes. The above shape and motion morpheme categories exist within the class of characterizing signs. Pointing gestures are used to refer to people, places, or things. The things deaf children point at encompass the same range of entities that hearing children refer to with nouns (Feldman, Goldin-Meadow, and Gleitman 1978). Pointing thus seems to be the deaf child's noun category. Further evidence that pointing is part of the system of signs for deaf children is that it undergoes systematic development (Butcher 1989; Butcher et al., to appear). Pointing for the child at a young age is literal, concrete deixis—pointing at real objects in the immediate environment. These points may or may not yet be lexical words. An example is pointing at the battery compartment of a toy, and then pointing at the batteries (asking for the batteries to be put in). Later the child points to objects similar to the intended object when the intended object is not in view. This distancing from the here-and-now is more clearly like a noun. For example, David pointed to a box of Christmas tree balls, and then pointed at an empty corner of the room (where the Christmas tree is usually placed, but not at the moment). Another form of abstract pointing is to point at a perceptually similar object. For example, David touched a picture of a toy train track, then pointed through the floor to the basement, to refer to a toy train in the basement of his grandparents' house. A third stage carries the abstraction further. The child becomes able to designate a space and point at it to stand for an object. This is like the use of abstract space by adult narrators. An example is making a movement in space for hanging something, then making an O-shape in the same space, and finally pointing to a spot on this O. The reference is to an absent Christmas tree ornament. In all of this development, a stable gesture form recurs in wider and ever more abstract contexts, showing some of the essential properties of a lexical word.

The characterizing signs, the stylized pantomimes, correspondingly, are the child's verb and adjective categories (with no apparent distinction between verbs and adjectives). An example (verb) is the gesture for "eating," which is pantomimic and made by holding a fist near the mouth and making chewing movements. An example of an adjective is "round," an O-hand (the gesture used, for example, to describe the Christmas tree ornament).

A Syntax

In a code, combinations of signs permit the speaker to reconstitute meanings when they have been broken down into segments. A syntax is apparent in the deaf children not exposed to language models in their predicate structures, deletions of elements as a function of semantic complexity, and their ability to form complex structures. The patterning of the children's sign sentences, moreover, suggests an ergative structure, a grammatical pattern that is often seen in gesture derived languages but is fundamentally different from the English of the children's parents.

PREDICATE STRUCTURE. Predicate structures were revealed in the following ways: (1) Gesture sequences expressed the semantic relations typically found in early hearing child utterances, with characterizing gestures fulfilling the role of the predicate; for example "Mickey" (point) "walk" (walking movements with hands). (2) The mean length of utterance (MLU) increased systematically with age, as in hearing children, implying that expanding the length of sentences is not just adding words but is an extension of structural possibilities and thus part of a developmental process. (3) The order of this development was the same as with hearing children: first a one-word stage when they produced just one gesture at a time; then two-gesture sequences; finally complex sentences, in which the relationships between gestures were similar to those in speech (coordination, temporal sequence, and subordination).

DELETION REGULARITIES. At the two-gesture stage, characterizing gestures (verbs) whose meanings implied one, two, or three logical arguments (agent, object, recipient) had different probabilities of including the different arguments. Specifically, the larger the number of implicit arguments, the lower the probability of including a gesture for the agent. A systematic regularity in selecting arguments also implies a syntax. It implies a structure within which the arguments are differentiated and rank-ordered in terms of importance. With a one-argument verb such as "sleep" or "dance," an agent was usually included; this produces a sequence that stays within the general two-sign limit of length. With a two-argument verb, such as "eat" or "go," the probability of the agent was lower, the two slots being given to the action and direct object ("cheese eat"). With a three-argument verb like "give," the probability of an explicit agent was very low, the two positions in the sentence being turned over to the action and the recipient ("give me") or the direct object and recipient ("cheese me"). Although limited to two gestures, the children do not select the two randomly, but follow a systematic principle to select the most informative arguments.

Ordering regularities also appear in the deaf children's two-sign sequences in that only half of the logical possibilities appear: object-action (cheese + eat), object-recipient (hat + head), and action-recipient (move-to + table), but not action-object, recipient-object, or recipient-action. Again, this suggests an underlying system that allows some combinations and outlaws others.

ERGATIVE STRUCTURES. Being unconstrained by adult models (models that for these children would have been of the accusative type), the children devised ergative patterns that would not be found in the development of hearing children in the same environment.[2] They had many sentences like the following:

"boy run" (intransitive agent, i.e., "the boy runs")
"boy hit" (transitive object, i.e., "hits the boy"),

but few sentences like:

"hit girl" or "girl hit" (transitive agent, i.e., "the girl hits").

This is ergative-like in that the case treated as unique is the transitive agent. It is an ergative-like *deletion* pattern, and it appeared with all the deaf children in Goldin-Meadow's study. With one child (the remarkable David) there also was an ergative *inclusion* pattern. David provided a sufficient number of transitive agent sentences for this analysis to be carried out, and in these sentences he tended to put gestures for the transitive agent after the verb. This arrangement contrasted with gestures for the transitive object and the intransitive agent, which he placed before the verb. Thus David came close to an explicit ergative system:

"boy run" (intransitive agent, "the boy runs")
"boy hit" (transitive object, "hits the boy")
"hit boy" (transitive *agent,* "the boy hits").

2. In an ergative language the ergative case is the unique case and is given to the transitive agent; the intransitive agent and transitive object are treated in the same uniform way, different from the ergative, and are called the absolutive case. This contrasts with an accusative language, such as English, where the unique case is the transitive object, called the accusative, and the two agents, transitive and intransitive, are treated in the same uniform way, called the nominative case. Examples of ergative languages are Georgian or Warlpiri. To see the accusative pattern in English, it is necessary to look at the one place where case marking exists: "*he* sleeps," "*he* cuts the cheese"—intransitive and transitive agents, respectively, both marked with the nominative case; and "the girl hits *him*"—direct object in the accusative case.

Ergative-like arrangements are patterns that appear repeatedly in gestures, including gestures invoked experimentally in adult hearing subjects (Bloom 1979, described later in this chapter). The most convincing explanation of such gestural ergativity is that by Tuite (n.d.). In gesture, he observed, the configuration of the hand can convey the properties of the arguments of the verb. Since an intrinsic part of the gesture, its hand configuration, is used to convey these arguments, the gesture naturally favors including semantic roles that are most closely linked to the verb, namely, the intransitive agents and transitive objects. This produces the ergative-like pattern. In ergative languages, such as Georgian, the cases divide along lines of being more closely linked to the verb (the absolutive) and less closely linked (the ergative). In accusative systems, in contrast, the cases cut across this semantic grouping. The nominative includes one closely linked role, the intransitive agent, together with the less closely linked role, the transitive agent, while the accusative includes the other closely linked role, the transitive object. For this reason, gestures are unlikely to take on accusative structures, but, following intrinsic semantic groupings, can and do emerge with ergative-like structures.

COMPLEX SENTENCES. Finally, deaf children are able to form complex sentences out of simple sentences. The combinations are based on specific semantic relationships (coordination, temporal sequences, and relative clause subordination). As in hearing children exposed to language models, complex sentences do not emerge immediately but only after an extended period of development.

Coordination is the semantic relationship in this example:

Points at Mickey Mouse + swinging pantomime + walking pantomime, i.e., "Mickey swings and walks" (action of a toy).

Temporal sequence is the semantic relationship in this example:

Points at tower + hitting pantomime + falling over pantomime, i.e., "I hit the tower and it falls over" (action of self on a toy).

Finally, *a complex NP through subordination of a relative clause* is the semantic relationship in the following:

"Roundness" + points at penny + points at self, i.e., "give me the penny that is round."

To gloss this as a relative clause assumes that the child employs here his usual lexical distinction between characterizing signs (for predicates) and pointing signs (for nominals). If this is the correct analysis, the sentence was predicating two propositions (i.e., penny, give; penny, round), one of them subordinate to the other.

The deaf children thus found ways to relate sentences to each other, through coordination, temporal sequences, and (possibly) subordination, and thus to create complex sentences.

SUMMARY OF SYNTAX. The emergence of a syntax is spontaneous in these deaf children. They show a capacity to create predicate structures, select the most informative elements from larger underlying structures, organize sentence constituents into grammatical patterns (which is the ergative pattern), and construct complex sentences out of simple sentences. There was no instruction or even clue given by the parents that gestures could be structured in these ways and such combinations do not occur in the parents' own gestures.

Distinctiveness

Signs in a linguistic system may have details added to them solely to distinguish them from other signs. The additions have no semantic motivation and exist just to make the sign distinguishable from other signs with which it might be confused. Distinctiveness is convincing evidence of incorporating gestures into a linguistic system.

Kendon (1988b) gives many examples of distinctiveness in WSL. The sign for "turaki" (a truck) is made by rotating the forearm into an upward (supine) position. This is performed twice in rapid succession while the hand is held in a kind of O-shape (the first three fingers curled in toward the thumb). The added feature is that the pinkie sticks out in a little crook. This has no function other than to keep the sign distinct from another sign, "kurdu" (child), which is made the same way but with the little finger curled in.

Distinctiveness appears in WSL in other ways. As women learn the sign language, they usually start out with pantomimes and gradually shift to more standard signs. Distinctiveness is apparent at several points in this process. The sign for "playing cards," for example, is performed by older women in the following way: they hold out a single fist-hand and twice rotate it downward with the thumb sticking out. Novices, in contrast, pantomime dealing cards: they use two hands, rather than one, and repeatedly move the thumb of one hand along the upright palm of the other hand. The mature sign thus retains some features of the pantomime. In the pantomime the dealing hand moves repeatedly and in the mature sign the hand rotates outward two times (the other hand is not involved). However, the mature sign is also altered to fit into the system of other WSL signs. By extending the thumb, the mature sign is distinguished from two other signs, "water" and "not ready," which are made in the same or almost the same way. By rotating the hand downward the sign is differentiated from "washing," which otherwise is identical to it, and so forth.

Arbitrariness

Arbitrariness means disregarding the potential iconicity of the gesture (this narrow definition is sufficient for present purposes). An example is the ASL sign for "very slow," which was "slow" made more rapidly; the speeding-up feature is arbitrary. An example from David, the deaf child, is patting his stomach; the movement iconically depicts patting or deictically refers to the stomach itself, but here the movement means Santa Claus. In WSL the hooked pinkie in "turaki" is an arbitrary feature.

Gestures, while potentially iconic, are thus capable of arbitrariness. However, there must be some reason for disregarding iconicity. If the gesture is part of a code, the code can supply this reason. Spontaneous gesticulation lacks a code and everything in the gesture—form, space, movement, etc.—is potentially iconic.

Standards of Well-Formedness

There is one recorded instance where David corrected his hearing sister's performance of a gesture, and this implies a standard of well-formedness. The segmentation example cited above also shows that the child was able to exaggerate his sign, and this implies a standard. Just looking at the videos of the child's gesture performance, one is struck by the differences from the gestures of hearing children and adults: the child's movements are clearly articulated, disciplined, reproducible, and schematic; in all these respects they are unlike the contextually varying gestures of hearing persons, and this also suggests standards.

Standards of well-formedness in other gesture codes are rigorously applied. To take a familiar example, emblems must adhere to standards that specify the limits within which the gesture is to be made if it is to be recognized. The OK sign *must* be made by contacting the index finger and thumb while the other fingers are extended. If the contact is between the second finger and thumb or if the other fingers are not extended, the gesture is not the OK sign. Another example is the sign in WSL for dealing out cards in contrast to the novice sign. Thus, the properties retained or altered in the mature sign are often explainable in terms of standards of form and the requirement of meeting them.

Timing

Although WSL is meant for silent communication, expert signers also use the sign language when speaking is not prohibited; then they might sign and speak concurrently. This situation provides a natural experiment on the timing of one code, gestures, in relation to that of another, speech. One of Kendon's (1988b) informants, Winnie Nangala, an expert Warlpiri signer, spontaneously adopted this dual method of communication during the recounting of a story, and her narrative was videotaped. The temporal relationships of signing and speaking are summarized in five points (based on Kendon 1988b, 305–308):

1. Each new speech phrase begins simultaneously with the *stroke* of the first sign.
2. The preparation phase of the first sign begins before speech.
3. Speech may be delayed if it gets ahead of the stroke.
4. Late in a speech phase, speech is allowed to get ahead of the stroke, and a sign might take place after the speech phrase has been completed.
5. The onset of the next speech phrase is delayed until the last sign from the preceding phrase is completed.

The first three points are familiar from spontaneous gesticulation, since here, too, the stroke synchronizes with speech and the preparation anticipates speech, and if synchrony threatens to break down speech may be delayed. As Kendon writes, these points provide "clear evidence that the planning processes for speech and sign are carried out in a completely integrated fashion. That is to say, spoken forms and signed equivalents are co-selected and their production is coordinated" (307). This suggests that Winnie's speech and signs had the same primitive stage. The last two points, however, are quite different from spontaneous gesticulation. They show that, once speech is underway, signs and spontaneous gestures proceed independently. Unlike spontaneous gestures, gestures and speech are not integrated into one performance where coexpressive signs and spoken words are presented at the same time. This is a direct consequence of the gestures' belonging to their own linguistic code. The gesture words are seen, not as the accompaniments of the verbal message, but as symbols presenting meanings within their own system. Moreover, since the planning phases of speech and signs are shared, the separation

of the signs and spoken words would occur during the actual performance phase when speaking and gesturing are taking place.

The following example is from Winnie Nangala's narrative (based on
Kendon 1988b, 306). The format is that used by Kendon: the first line, in
capitals, is the Warlpiri sign language, each written word corresponding
to a different sign; the second line is the gesture time-line showing the
preparations and strokes; the third line is the Warlpiri speech; and the
fourth line is Kendon's translation into English.

(1)RDARRI   (2)MARDARNI
[prep **stroke**   ][prep **stroke**   ]

rdarri m a r d a ka   wajalunyanu . . .

'grab   hold of her yourself

(3)NGANGKIRI (4)NYANU
[prep **stroke**   ] [prep   **stroke**]

. . . ngang   kiri nyanurlulunyanu

husband   of my niece'

At (1) and (3), Winnie began new speech phrases. The stroke of the
accompanying sign exactly coincided with the spoken word and the
preparation phase slightly anticipated it. At (2) and (4), in contrast,
the signs were at late positions and speech was allowed to get ahead of the
sign. The spoken word at (2), "marda" even began before the preparation
phase of the signed word MARDARNI, and the spoken word at (4),
"nyanu," preceded the stroke of the signed NYANU. Speech flow was
interrupted briefly after (2), the end of a speech phrase, and this enabled
the spoken word "ngangkiri," at (3), to start simultaneously with the
stroke of the signed word NGANGKIRI, which was the beginning
of the next phrase. Thus, the spoken words and signed words
"rdarri"/RDARRI (grab hold) and "ngangkiri"/NGANGKIRI (husband) seemed to have been part of the planning phases of the utterances
and were planned together, but the spoken words and signed words
"marda"/MARDARNI and "nyanu"/NYANU unrolled independently
each within its own utterance program.

At least one reason why the timing of signs is different from that of
spontaneous gestures is because signs are structured by their own code.
They have their own plan of execution and once planned are not integrated with speech into a single performance. This ensures that speech
and signs will be temporally related in different ways from speech and
spontaneous gestures.

Emblems

A widely known type of gesture that shows cultural specificity is the emblem, or Italianate gesture.[3] Emblems are part of a social code but are not fully structured as a language. They have names or standard paraphrases, are learned as specific symbols, and can be used as if they were spoken words; in fact they are unspoken words (and phrases); but there is no grammar, and emblems are rarely if ever combined. An example of the cultural specificity of emblems is the so-called Hand Purse, in which the fingers and thumb are pressed together at the tips and held upright. This is not in use at all by North Americans and, in Europe, it has six or seven different meanings, depending on the region. In Spain, for example, it has the meaning of "lots of people," in Italy "a query," in Belgium and France "fear," etc. (Morris et al. 1979). Thus there is extensive cultural determination of this gesture: it doesn't appear at all in some areas, and when it appears it has different uses. In contrast to spontaneous iconics and metaphorics, there is no way to understand the Hand Purse without the appropriate cultural knowledge.

Emblems are signs but the code that structures them is incomplete. Emblems have but limited contrasts and these exist only for certain individual sets of gestures. Emblems show restricted compositionality, and no real syntax at all; and the functions of emblems fall within a narrow range of speech acts. Emblems nonetheless still have certain language-like properties. They have segmentation, standards of well-formedness, an historical tradition, and a community of users that understands them without metalinguistic explanations. All these things considered, emblems belong in the middle section of Kendon's continuum.

Probably every society has culturally prescribed emblems, some more than others. Precisely because emblems are culturally specific, they differ from culture to culture, with some societies having quite elaborate emblem systems. Sparhawk (1976), for example, analyzed more than 200 Persian emblems in use in modern Iran. I will first describe a survey of 20 European emblems conducted by Morris et al. (1979) and summarize their results. I will add material from Kendon's (1981) review of their book, and then present Kendon's analysis of the restricted range of speech acts that emblems characteristically perform. I will conclude this discussion of emblems with a description of the code-like aspects of emblems, including Italianate and Persian.

3. The term "emblem" was used by Ekman and Friesen (1969) following Efron (1941), who used the term "emblematic gesture" for the same type of culturally specified gesture form. "Italianate" recognizes the richness of this type of gesture in parts of Italy.

The Survey by Morris et al.

Morris and his associates (1979) traveled across Europe testing local residents for their interpretation of 20 preselected emblems and photographing people performing them. This very procedure—studying gestures that are specified in advance by form—is possible only at the rightward end of Kendon's continuum. Morris's group present their results gesture by gesture, giving the geographical distribution of each one, its major interpretations and where it appears, comments on the history of the gesture, and speculations on the motivation of the form of the gesture in terms of ancestral iconic forms. Kendon (1981) added to this a number of historical details and an important set of observations on speech act functions.

THE 20 EMBLEMS. A description of the first 11 of the emblems, their interrelations, locations, possible iconic origins, and historical notes are given in the following list; this is a combination of information from Morris et al. (1979) and Kendon (1981). The names of the gestures are from the Morris publication.

1. *The Fingertip Kiss:* fingers and thumb contact the pursed lips and move away, possibly with a puff of air from the mouth at the same time. This means "praise" in Holland, Belgium, Yugoslavia, and Turkey. It is a salutation in Portugal, Sardinia, Malta, and Corfu. The movement is supposed to evoke the idea of a mouth kiss (which itself is considered to derive from feeding movements). The Fingertip Kiss is a gesture of great antiquity, existing for more than 2,000 years. It was common in Greece and Rome, and in Biblical times in the Near East. Greeks and Romans threw kisses when they entered and left a temple, and threw them at sacred objects of various kinds. The gesture gradually shifted from religious adoration to general praise or salutation.

2. *The Fingers Cross:* the middle finger crosses over the index finger. This invokes protection in England, Scandinavia, parts of Sicily, and Yugoslavia. In Corfu and Turkey, in contrast, it means breaking a friendship. Its connection with the "protection" meaning is as a disguised version of the sign of the cross, presumably used as a secret sign, and thus its origin is not as ancient as the preceding.

3. *The Nose Thumb:* the thumb contacts the tip of the nose, the fingers extended and wiggling. This means "mockery" everywhere; in fact, it is the most widely known emblem of the 20 Morris and his group tested. The earliest reference to it is in the fifteenth century. Morris and his group believe the origin of the Nose Thumb may have been an ancient

practice of making mocking effigies out of wax, which featured long noses.

4. *The Hand Purse:* the thumb and fingers are in contact at the tip, the hand facing upward. This means (as noted earlier) "query" in Italy, Sardinia, and Sicily; "good" in Portugal, Greece, and Turkey; "fear" in Belgium and France; and "emphasis" in Holland and Germany. There is clearly regional grouping of these different meanings, suggesting separate historical traditions for the same hand shape. Morris and his group think that the "query," "good," and "emphasis" meanings could have arisen originally from the precision grip (the hand posture for precise manipulative movements). The "emphasis" meaning suggests a beat. The Hand Purse is described in a book on Neapolitan gestures by Di Jorio in 1832.

5. *The Cheek Screw:* the extended index finger touches the cheek and the whole hand rotates back and forth. In Italy, Sicily, and Sardinia this means something that is deemed good to eat. In Germany it means "crazy," which Morris and his group take to be a disguised version of a "crazy" gesture made on the side of the head (a movement that is, they say, illegal as a public gesture in Germany). In its "good to eat" meaning, the movement could have arisen from the expression in Italian *al dente* 'on the tooth', or just right for eating, and in any case is appropriate for pointing to the mouth.

6. *The Eyelid Pull:* the index finger pulls down the skin under one eye. In Italy this means "watch out, be alert" and everywhere else it means "I am alert." The one whose alertness is invoked is thus the variable element. In either case the gesture exaggerates opening the eye. It too is mentioned by Di Jorio in 1832.

7. *The Forearm Jerk:* the forearm is pulled up abruptly while the opposite hand chops down on the inside crook of the arm. North Americans refer to this as the "Italian Salute." Morris and associates describe it as an enhanced version (a "supernormal stimulus") of the ancient Roman *digitus impudicus*. The Forearm Jerk may be no more than a century old, but the *digitus impudicus* is 2,000 years or more old. Caligula is said to have used it scandalously when he offered his hand to be kissed. The phallic imagery of the gesture requires no explanation.

8. *The Flat-Hand Flick:* the fingers of one hand are rapidly drawn to the front across the back of the other hand. This means "beat it!" in Belgium, France, Italy, and Greece. The gesture is quite iconic, but nonetheless has a standard form in the regions of its use, and is not recognized as a departure signal elsewhere at all.

9. *The Ring:* the thumb and first finger in contact at the tips, the other

fingers extended. This means OK everywhere except Tunisia, where it is a threat and in Brazil where it is an insult (a more unfortunate form of polysemy would be hard to imagine). It also means an orifice in Germany, northern Italy, northern Sardinia, and Malta; and it means "zero" in Belgium, France, and Tunisia. The crucial feature for the OK meaning, Morris and associates believe, is the precision contact of the first finger and thumb. The traditional explanation is that the gesture is an attempt to form an O and a K. However, the earliest reference to the gesture with an OK meaning is in the first century A.D., in a Roman text. The orifice meaning is also ancient, at least 2,000 years old (Greece).

10. *The Vertical Horn:* the first finger and pinkie are extended, the other fingers curled in with the thumb on top of them; in this version, the palm faces outward. The gesture accuses someone of being a cuckold in Spain, Portugal, and Italy. It is very ancient, and while the iconic element in the gesture of depicting horns is clear, the connection of horns themselves to cuckoldry remains obscure. The gesture is now restricted to Catholic countries, but it was once widespread throughout Europe.

11. *The Horizontal Horn:* the same as the Vertical Horn, except that the palm faces down. The gesture also is now an accusation of cuckoldry in the same regions, but had an original meaning of "protection" (warding off the evil eye). In Malta and Italy this use of the gesture is still quite active. The gesture in this meaning is extremely ancient, Morris and associates dating it back 2,500 years or more. The orientation of the gesture makes iconic sense for protection, since it is aimed at the source of evil.

These are the first 11 of the 20 emblems that Morris and his group tested. The others, without discussing them, are (12) *The Fig* (sexual comment or insult), (13) *The Head Toss* (negation or beckoning), (14) *The Chin Flick* (disinterest or negation), (15) *The Cheek Stroke* (thin and ill), (16) *Thumb Up* (OK), (17) *The Teeth-Flick* (nothing or anger), (18) *The Ear Touch* (effeminate or watch out), (19) *The Nose Tap* (secrecy), and (20) *The Palm-Back V-Sign* (victory but, in Britain, a sexual insult; the Churchillean V-for-victory sign carefully has the palm to the front).

COMMENTS ON THE 20 EMBLEMS. In emblems we can see a microcosm of the changes wrought in gestures when they become elements in a socially regulated code.

1. *Distribution.* In contrast to the near universality of spontaneous iconic and metaphoric gestures, there is much regional variation with emblems. This variability appears in both the number of emblems that are recognized and the meanings that they have. Such is just the distribution that would result from separate historical traditions. The importance of

cultural specification for emblems is evident in another way. The meanings of emblems vary from place to place, even though the gesture form is the same. Each cultural region determines a meaning on its own. The Hand Purse is a clear case of such variation. There is no sensible connection among the "query," "good," or "fear" meanings, and to these can be added "slowly" (Tunisia), "large quantity" (Spain), and "emphasis" (Holland, Germany). This kind of wide variation among regions combined with stability of meaning in each region is possible only by conventions that are culturally reinforced.

2. *Iconicity*. Nonetheless, the different cultural varieties of emblems could still stem from a common core. Kendon (1981) argued that emblems do not arise from other emblems, but in many cases could have begun as iconic gestures which then were ritualized and stabilized as part of a gesture code. Consistent with this idea is the preservation of an element of iconicity in many of the emblems described by Morris and associates. This iconicity seems to have little essential role in the gesture's current function, this function being carried by the recognition of the gesture as part of a code. But the iconic element remains—a vestige of the emblem's past. The Finger Tip Kiss, for example, iconically depicts emanations from the lips toward the object of praise: it would misfire if one were to make the movement off to the side toward some other object. The Fingers Cross iconically depicts the Christian Cross; the Nose Thumb depicts an elongated nose; the Hand Purse depicts a precision grip on something small, and this metaphorically presents the ideas of "query" and "excellence" (however, the "fear" meaning is not explained this way). The Cheek Screw actually points to the locus of something that has excellent taste. The Eyelid Pull, Forearm Jerk, Flat-Hand Flick, and the two Horn-Signs all contain iconic elements. The Ring depicts a precision grip and this could metaphorically present the abstract meaning of sufficiency and adequacy (OK). The Teeth Flick for anger enacts biting (one's own thumbnail). Some of the others, however, seem to lack iconicity, at least any now discernible. The Chin Flick for "disinterest" or "negation" seems wholly arbitrary as far as one can tell.

3. *Historical longevity*. One of the most impressive findings from the investigation of emblems is their extraordinary longevity. While no spoken languages have lasted unchanged since Roman times, a number of emblem gestures are Roman and some are older than that. We apparently would have no difficulty making ourselves understood to a legionnaire if all we wanted was to say OK or offer a sexual insult. Kendon (1981) attributes this great stability over historical time to the absence of compositionality: emblems can change only as wholes and this encourages

conservatism since there is no way for historical processes to chip away bits of emblems, the way they can erode bits of spoken symbols, without having the entire gesture change or lose its meaning. A striking illustration of the historical stability of emblems is the Head Toss with the meaning of negation. This gesture appears in Italy south of the Volturno River near Naples, whereas north of this river negation is conveyed with the familiar Head Wag (Morris et al. 1979). The same Head Toss gesture meaning negation also appears in Greece and nowhere else. It thus appears to have been a gesture of Greek origin. What is remarkable is that the southern region of Italy was colonized by the Greeks in the seventh or eighth century B.C., and the Head Toss for negation apparently dates from then. Once settled in, tucked behind a natural barrier, it neither spread out nor changed for all these centuries.

Code-like Properties

Emblems comprise a partial code, as I mentioned earlier. They are segments, are lexicalized, have standard forms, belong to historical traditions, have arbitrary or ritualized uses, and are understood by a community of users. The code is partial, however, because emblems lack the crucial linguistic property of compositionality. There are however two cases of limited compositionality with emblems, and these exceptions I will describe below. Sparhawk (1976) described sentence-like combinations of Persian emblems, and the familiar European emblems of beckoning and waving appear to be gestural words composed out of quasi-morphological elements.

Sentence-like compositionality with Persian emblems. Sparhawk (1976) found rare occurrences of topic-comment and comment-comment sequences of emblem gestures. The topic-comment sequences followed the SOV order that is common in Persian clause roots but also is identical to the preferred sequence of constituents in the signing of deaf children not exposed to linguistic models. Some examples of these topic-comment "sentences":

"talks too much": moves lips + sign for "a lot"
"what time is it?": points at watch + sign for "don't know"
"give me a cigarette": taps extended fingers on lips + sign for "give"

Despite these examples, Sparhawk regards emblems as fundamentally lacking compositionality: her informants also stressed that emblems were used singly rather than in sequence. The regulation of gesture sequences does not appear to be part of the standard repertoire. She says, "emblems do not function as a system separate from and parallel to language, or at least, . . . they function separately only in a very rudimentary manner" (87). Even so, the sequence of topic and comment forms a higher unit of meaning, and this possibility of combining elements into a hierarchical structure sets the emblem apart from spontaneous gesture.

MORPHEME-LIKE COMPOSITIONALITY WITH WAVING. In northern Europe and North America, to beckon someone you point your hand up and turn its palm toward yourself: this is UP and HIDE (meaning the hand is pointing up and the palm is hidden from whoever is being summoned; Morris et al. 1979). In these same regions, to wave goodbye you again point your hand up but now turn the palm toward the person you are seeing off: UP and SHOW. Morris and associates present these facts, and we can see that there is a certain iconicity in the orientation of the palm in these gestures. If the palm surface is thought of as facing the locus of the addressee, then you beckon by turning this locus towards you, and you wave goodbye by turning it away from you. Thus the gesture rotates the space iconically to depict the acts of arriving and departing.

In the Mediterranean parts of Europe the gestures are different in a way that suggests a deictic system rather than an iconic one. Beckoning is done by turning the hand downward: the gesture is DOWN and HIDE. As in the northern beckoning emblem, we can see again that there may be something iconic in the hidden palm for beckoning, but there also is something deictic in the downward orientation of the hand. This could be understood as pointing at the ground where the new locus of the addressee should be. In Italy, waving goodbye is yet different: the hand points up but the palm is hidden, so the gesture of waving goodbye is UP and HIDE. Since the beckon is DOWN and the goodbye is UP, the interpretation of the UP-DOWN dimension as deictic seems most appropriate (a common spontaneous deictic gesture for a remote locus in fact is to point up).

Table 2.4 gives the beckoning and waving gestures for the three regions mentioned—northern Europe (and North America), non-Italian Mediterranean Europe, and Italy—defined in terms of the featural components of UP/DOWN and HIDE/SHOW. The table makes clear an important principle: the contrast of meaning between beckoning and waving is everywhere registered with a contrast of gesture form. In this sense, the beckoning-waving gesture system is motivated by a semantic distinction. However, the contrasts are organized in terms of different principles. The underscored terms in table 2.4 mark the feature(s) that appears to be

Table 2.4 Compositionality of Two Emblems

Region	Beckoning	Waving
Northern Europe	UP + <u>HIDE</u>	UP + <u>SHOW</u>
Mediterranean Europe (non-Italy)	<u>DOWN</u> + HIDE	UP + <u>SHOW</u>
Italy	<u>DOWN</u> + HIDE	<u>UP</u> + HIDE

distinctive, which set the emblems apart. Given the remarks above, we can say that in northern Europe the principle of distinguishing beckoning and waving is the iconic use of the hand to depict a trajectory. In Italy the principle is the deictic use of the hand to indicate a locus near or far from the speaker. In the rest of the Mediterranean region, both iconicity and deixis seem to be involved and the gestures convey beckoning and waving redundantly.

NOVEL FORMS OF WAVING. If this compositionality of emblems is true, it should be possible to find novel forms of beckoning and waving in which gestures depart from canonical waves or beckons but preserve standards of form by honoring the semantic features of the system. I have observed a case of waving goodbye in which the SHOW dimension (the northern European system) was realized in a novel form. The person doing the waving was driving a car past the addressee; the addressee was standing to the left (the driver's side). Thus there were two lines in conflict: the forward trajectory of the car and driver, and the line between the driver and the addressee, to the left. Since the driver could not turn to face the addressee, he came up with a different form of waving in this context. The gesture was formed by awkwardly turning the left hand so that the palm faced the addressee on the left (i.e., SHOW) and moving the hand up and down from the waver's own perspective. From his own point of view this was a kind of chopping motion, but from the addressee's point of view it was a side-to-side waving motion. The direction of the wave was thus dissociated from the direction in which the waver was facing and moving. The gesture makes sense in terms of the SHOW parameter. The palm was turned in the direction of the addressee, and it is this addressee whose locus the palm represents in the northern system as being away. Once facing the right direction, the side-to-side direction of the waving action was determined as appropriate even though it was, from the perspective of the waver himself, the wrong direction. The gesture was a departure from a canonical wave but remained within the system of the SHOW parameter and realized it in a novel way. The example

demonstrates compositionality of waving in that the gesture was not activated as a whole but was constructed out of features that proved open to
independent manipulation.

Nonetheless, in having compositional structure beckoning and waving are unique. The system of features out of which they are composed is
an apparently isolated pocket within a code characterized more appropriately by the earlier list—segmentation, lexicalization, etc., but not compositionality.

Restricted Speech-Act Functions

Emblems are complete speech acts in themselves, but the speech acts they
perform are restricted to a certain range of functions (Kendon 1981).
They regulate and comment on the behavior of others, reveal one's own
emotional states, make promises, swear oaths, etc. They are used to salute, command, request, reply to some challenge, insult, threaten, seek
protection, express contempt or fear. In contrast to spontaneous gestures, however, they do not represent objects or events. Even when the
iconicity of emblems is taken into account, the function is not referential
or propositional. The precision grip involved in forming the Ring (the
OK sign) is not a comment on the roundness or smallness, delicacy, or
manner of manipulation of some object or situation: it is an expression of
approbation, viz., that something is adequate by some standard.
Sparhawk (1976) made the same observation for Persian emblems: her
examples fell into the categories of questions, impositions, offers, and
comments, not statements of fact or of ideas. Combinations could be
construed as propositional in character, but even they were used to express one's own state, not to describe objects or events (e.g., "cold +
sleepy"). Kendon (1981) reviewed a number of published lists of emblems and categorized the speech acts they apparently performed. Over
80% were used for interpersonal control, announcement of one's own
current state, or evaluation of another person. In contrast, gestures that
were labels for objects or actions were the least frequent of all types,
down to 5% in some lists.

Kendon raises the question of why the social code of emblems is so
restricted. Why are so few referential and propositional? He suggests a
number of factors, among them the suitability of emblems for collusive
and secret messages being exchanged at the same time as speech interactions are taking place. Related to this, gestures can have communicative
effects outside of awareness, a point also demonstrated in the "mismatch"
experiments described in chapter 5. However, these reasons do not
uniquely explain why emblems are restricted to the speech acts of

social commentary/regulation and self-expression. Propositional content could be quite important for collusive speech, and such content is conveyed out of awareness in the mismatch experiments. I believe there is another important factor, the belief in word magic. Spoken words are special and carry with them the responsibility for being articulated. However, conveying the same meaning in gesture form avoids the articulatory act and, thanks to word magic, this lessened responsibility for speaking transfers to the speech act itself. Thus, the responsibility for commentary, regulation, or self-expression is reduced if you don't actually speak it. The pressure to invoke gestures and specify them by conventions would therefore be most strongly felt for those speech acts where the cultural sanctions are most severe, and these are the acts of commentary, control, and self-expression. This theory holds that from knowing the areas where a culture places sanctions we can predict the emblems that will be developed and maintained.

Inducing Signs Experimentally

One of the most remarkable demonstrations of the changes made in gestures organized under a code comes from an experiment carried out by Ralph Bloom (1979) as his undergraduate thesis at the University of Chicago. The importance of this study is in how it shows linguistic properties taking their place in a gesture system. They make their appearance almost immediately. Within a remarkably short period of time the subject's gestures become well organized into what must be regarded as a *linguistic* system. There is, therefore, no resistance from the gesture medium to taking on language-like properties. From this rapid linguistic buildup with gestures that do not accompany speech, we can be confident that when gestures do accompany speech and lack linguistic properties, the lack is an interpretable phenomenon that reveals the existence of a nonlinguistic imagistic mode of thought.

Bloom had normal, hearing adult subjects recount fairy stories to listeners without any use of speech. The subjects and the listeners were university students with no prior knowledge of a sign language. The following description is based on the performance of one subject whom Bloom identified as "Danny," who decided that he would tell the story of Snow White (other subjects chose Hansel and Gretel or Little Red Ridinghood). The listener, another university student, did not know in advance which story Danny would attempt to narrate. The listener was also banned from using speech, and in fact began to make some use of the gestural linguistic system. After the narrative was over, Bloom then had

the listener retell the story (in speech) and had Danny review his performance and explain his signs (all of this was also recorded on videotape).

What occurs in these circumstances is a very rapid introduction of linguistic properties into the gesture channel. Within 15 or 20 minutes a
system has emerged that includes segmentation, compositionality, a lexicon, a syntax with paradigmatic oppositions, arbitrariness, distinctiveness, standards of well-formedness, and a high degree of fluency. The
subject quickly moved to the right-hand end of Kendon's continuum.
Since nothing in Danny's past experience included acquaintance with a
sign language, we can visualize him traversing all the way across it.[4] I will
first summarize the system that Danny devised, and then comment on its
linguistic properties.

Summary of Danny's Performance

LEXICON.   Danny developed a lexicon of stable gestures that had recognizable referents in the story and that recurred in the same forms. Each
main character had its own sign, and so did attributes of the characters
and other entities, as well as the principal actions (in the examples below
words in double quotes are specific signs in Danny's lexicon). For example, there was a sign for "King" made in two parts.

> "King": first the two hands outlined a *crown* on the head (each hand
> points to the head on opposite sides, and then moves up and down
> while the hands rotate around the head); then *has-muscles* (the hands
> moved quickly down to the sides and, while sitting very straight,
> clenched and moved rapidly across the chest).

There was also a sign for "Queen," again made in two parts:

> "Queen": first the same *crown;* then *has-breasts* (two hands form
> cups facing upward at the chest).

The sign for "shooting" simulated holding a rifle (although in the
story actual shooting was done with a bow and arrow).

The sign for "goodlike" was made by drawing a smiling mouth over
Danny's mouth, an opposed sign for "evillike" was made by drawing a

---

4. Kendon (personal communication) has pointed out that the continuum might be
multidimensional. One dimension, clearly, is the extent to which speech is obligatory; another is the extent to which the code is socially shared; others are usages of different linguistic properties, which may appear at different places on the continuum. These different
dimensions, since they are less than perfectly correlated, would be expected to emerge at
different places. The continuum also might be better presented as a circle, since gesticulations can accompany the production of signs.

frowning mouth. "Womanlike" or "female-shaped" was a two-handed outline of an hourglass figure.

VIEWPOINT. The viewpoints of iconics is discussed in chapter 4. Basically, two viewpoints appear in the gestures people perform during narratives: the gesture may seem to reenact the character, and this is character viewpoint (C-VPT), or the gesture may appear to display an event from the viewpoint of an observer, and this is observer viewpoint (O-VPT). In Danny's narration both viewpoints appeared, with C-VPT outnumbering O-VPT 62% to 38%. Exploiting a tendency also present in spontaneous gestures, the viewpoints were used systematically to distinguish transitive and intransitive actions:

Character viewpoint was strongly connected with transitive situations (accounting for 80% of C-VPT gestures) in which an actor acted on an object. An example is "sweeps," where Danny's body represented Snow White's body and mimed actions of sweeping the floor.

Observer viewpoint was even more strongly associated with intransitive situations (accounting for 88% of O-VPT gestures) where an actor changes location or performs an act that lacks an object. An example here is "walks from," where Danny's hand represented the hunter's body walking away from Snow White and Danny himself was an onlooker.

PRONOUNS. Pronouns were defined by Bloom as gestures that substituted for entity names; thus there had to be an entity name in order for the pronoun substitute to be defined. Danny devised three kinds of pronouns, each with a distinct and more or less fixed kinesic form:

Hand pronouns consisted of the hand held out in front of the body, usually in the shape of a V, with the palm facing down. The sole function of this gesture was to refer to a person; for example:

points to right + the V-shape (= the hunter) + "perplexed" for "the hunter was perplexed."

Body pronouns consisted of Danny's body or the listener's body with the sole function of referring to a person. An example:

"walks" gesture + points to left in V-shape (= the hunter) + "shoots" + points to listener (= Snow White) for "the hunter shoots her."

Space pronoun consisted of a hold-up gesture indicating a fixed location in the gesture space for each main character. This was worked out over the course of the narrative. The right space was for the Queen, the left space for the King, and the space in front at stomach level for Snow White. Here is an example:

hold-up in King's space + "joins" + right hand moves + "produce" + hold-up in Snow White's space + "cradles" for "the King joins the

Queen and produces a baby, Snow White" (the right hand, for the Queen, was brought into the gesture space at the moment the "joins" sign was made).

CASE INCORPORATION IN VERBS. These cases provide information that depicts an aspect of an action—the actor, the object, location, etc. The case is built directly into the action gesture, and there need not be a separate gesture for the case. Some examples (which have no parallel in Danny's English-language speech):

"opens" (hand appears to pull on door) made with hunched shoulders to indicate the actor (one of the dwarves).

"shoots" (hands appear to hold a rifle) to indicate the animacy of the actor.

"looks-at" (two O-shaped hands move toward target) to show the shape of the eyes.

"drips" (precision-grip hand moves down repeatedly, turning into a spread 5-hand at the bottom) first to outline the agent (the blood) and then the manner and location (splattered on the floor).

ERGATIVITY. Just as deaf children not exposed to linguistic models create an ergative-like organization, Danny also emerged with an ergative-like structure. Ergativity appeared in his patterns of case incorporation with verb gestures. Verbs incorporated an intransitive actor 45 times and a transitive object 55 times, but a transitive actor only 15 times—the rest of the time this actor was conveyed in a separate gesture. Thus, in terms of the incorporation of the entity into the action, the most prominent cases were the transitive object and intransitive actor; in terms of separate specification, the most prominent case was the transitive actor: either way, the system is ergative-like.

An example with transitive objects is the way Danny signed "the Queen threads the needle." The gesture movement incorporated the object in the hand shape (the hand appearing to hold a needle and thread). Similarly, a gesture incorporated the shape of the intransitive subject in "the sun sets" (a round hand shape went down). In contrast, the subject of a transitive verb was signed separately in "Snow White eats food." Danny first moved his body to a place where he had previously made a "Snow White" gesture, and then made the gesture for eating. These examples again illustrate Tuite's (n.d.) suggestion that gestures show ergative patterns because they directly incorporate the semantic arguments most closely connected to the action. Thus, to convey food Danny performed a gesture for the act of eating, and this incorporated food within it, but to convey the agent, Danny had to make a separate gesture for Snow White.

WORD ORDER. This tended to be SV and SVO, following English word order, but there were many one-word "sentences."

Linguistic Properties

Some properties in this system were derived from English (such as word order) but many others were unique and exotic from the point of view of English (lexical incorporation, three kinds of pronoun, association of viewpoint with transitivity, ergativity). Since this entire code emerged in about 20 minutes, we have a telescoped view of the birth and development of a fairly complex system that includes several linguistic properties.

SEGMENTATION AND LEXICON. There were recurrent gestures for the King and the Queen, Snow White, the Dwarves, and the Hunter—the latter both in an iconic sign (holding a rifle) and in a classifier-like gesture (inverted V) that was incorporated into verb gestures. Moreover, all the gestures fell into recognizable classes of noun-like entity-terms, adjective-like attribute-terms, and verb-like action-terms.

PARADIGMATIC OPPOSITION. The "King" and "Queen" signs were both made with two elements one of which was shared (crown) and the other of which contrasted (has-muscles vs. has-breasts). Thus the two referring terms were organized into a paradigmatic set that shared one feature and contrasted on the other. Exemplifying a different method, the good Queen and the evil Queen were made with the same sign, and the opposition between them was made predicatively: e.g., "Queen evillike" or "Queen #2" both distinguished from "Queen goodlike."

ARBITRARINESS. An iconic gesture for Snow White (female-shaped) was initially used to describe Snow White; in this use it was an attribute-sign based on iconicity referring to Snow White's being configured in a certain way. This is apparent in the sign's early uses, such as:

<u>she (= Snow White) + grows-up + female-shaped</u> ("she, Snow White, grows up and becomes female-shaped").

In later uses, however, the same sign was used purely denotatively, as a proper name, where being female-shaped was not being attributed. For example,

<u>female-shaped + draws-water + tired + sweeps</u> ("Snow White draws water, sweeps, and is tired").

In this later use, the potential iconicity of the female-shaped sign was disregarded in favor of pure denotation of Snow White.

DISTINCTIVENESS. The sign for King acquired an extra kinesic feature (flat-chested) in a context where Danny felt the distinction between the King and Queen was crucial and believed the listener was likely to mix the two up (as he explained in the postexperimental interview). This was an added feature—a downward chop of both hands in front of the chest—purely for the purpose of distinguishing one sign from another. It proves conclusively that the signs were organized into contrastive sets for Danny. Another illustration of distinctiveness was that as the Queen sign became more and more schematic with repetition, it never lost distinctiveness with respect to the King sign. At first "Queen" was the elaborate two-step sign described previously with (a) the crown gesture (itself involving several up-and-down movements and a slow rotation around the head) and (b) the has-breasts gesture. With repetition, the crown gesture was reduced to simply a twirl of one hand near the head and the has-breasts gesture to a backwards flip of one hand (by now facing down) near the chest. The backwards flip, however minimal, distinguished the Queen sign from the King sign and was never omitted.

COMPOSITIONALITY. This existed on two levels, morphological and syntactic. Morphologically, "King" and "Queen" were formed out of a combination of the crown and has-muscles or has-breasts features. Syntactically, "King," "Queen" and other gestures combined linearly or incorporated case features to construct propositions.

STANDARDS OF WELL-FORMEDNESS. Standards seem to have been consciously applied, as indicated by the following: (a) there was a high degree of streamlining of gestures but distinctiveness was preserved; (b) the listener adopted some of the same gestures, e.g., the female-shaped sign for Snow White; (c) Danny's remarks during the postexperimental interview which implied that he had conscious standards. For example, he could answer questions about the form of the crown gesture and when he would make it with one or two hands.

FLUENCY. This is difficult to demonstrate quantitatively or illustrate in examples, but is very clear upon inspection of the video of the narrative. The speed of the gestures picked up enormously, the signs became streamlined by cutting them down to their essential features, and the listener began to learn the system well enough to formulate questions in it.

Summary of the Experiment

It is undeniable that Danny's gestures developed many linguistic properties. This itself is proof that gesture is capable of showing the qualities of a language and that, when it does, it changes from global-synthetic: it becomes standardized, lexicalized, decomposable, combinable, used in arbitrary extensions, streamlined for efficient performance, and so forth. Language properties emerged simply by forcing the subject to pay attention to the gesture channel. This is perhaps the most surprising aspect of Bloom's results: how quickly and with what little guidance language properties come into play.

Sources of Change

What is the source of the language-like properties that appear in the gesture channel? The channel itself cannot explain them. While the medium is the same, language-like and non-language-like gestures are widely different in numerous respects. Transfers from speech also do not explain them, at least not all of them. The deaf children of hearing parents have no spoken language source. While transfers from spoken Warlpiri to the WSL system definitely can be shown to have taken place, and ASL may have been influenced historically by the English-language speech of the wider community, the gesture performance of Danny showed many language-like features that have no counterparts in English, the only possible source in his case. Thus, the gesture medium is capable of incorporating language-like features, but these emerge, somehow, seemingly on their own. These spontaneous language-like features are of the greatest interest. They seem to have been produced out of the necessity of using gestures in a communicative system. Their changes from spontaneous gestures may reflect the constraints on symbols when the symbols are the focus of communicative intentions.

This kind of shift in the form of representation when the representation becomes self-contained has been studied by Karmiloff-Smith (1979b) who wrote as follows regarding the spontaneous notation systems of children; her remarks seem equally relevant to the emergence of linguistic properties in gestures:

The stepping up to a metaprocedural level seems to occur each time the child has a handle on his currently functioning, goal-oriented system. This enables the child to treat the system, or procedures which are part thereof, as units of functioning in their own right. Thus there appears to be a deep-rooted psychological tendency for a representational tool which functions well procedurally to become subsequently a problem space per se. (P. 91)

This shift of attitude alters the relationship between the speaker and gesture. Innovations appear that make sense if gestures are no longer unwitting expressions of meaning but are units of functioning of their own, which are compared to one another and organized into a system designed for ready access and good memory. Linguistic properties imply a meta-level awareness of gestures as signs. A lexicon requires recognizing that form-meaning pairings repeat themselves. Arbitrariness depends on extending a form into contexts where the referent is preserved but the original form-meaning pairing is lost. Compositionality is a product of segmentation and arises when the speaker realizes that meaning complexes that have been broken into segments must be reconstituted. Bloom's subject did this spontaneously once he invented his gesture words for the King and Queen. Standards of form summarize and codify as intuitive restrictions the speaker's solutions in the problem space mentioned by Karmiloff-Smith, and are the linguistic property that most clearly reflects a meta-level awareness. Paradigmatic oppositions reveal an attitude of differentiation toward the gestures as units in which sets of minimally contrasting units are set up. Distinctiveness implies a system in which the speaker realizes that gestures are similar to one another in absentia, and adds form details solely to keep gestures apart within this system.

The idea is thus that a meta-level of awareness of gestures in their own right releases the "resilient properties" of linguistic systems, properties that appear even when input is lacking or is degenerate (Goldin-Meadow 1982). Long ago Condillac ([1756] 1971; see Harris and Taylor 1989) regarded gestures as human language precursors that were supplanted by words and sentences to aid making one's own thoughts intelligible to others (what Harris and Taylor refer to as "telementation"). The linear and segmented character of language was necessary, in Condillac's view, for the full development of human consciousness and must have arisen from the preceding experience of people without a language. In the release of resilient properties by meta-level attention to gesture we may see—over a very short period of time—a partial replay of what Condillac regarded as linguistic evolution.

Such then is the state of gestures at the rightward end of Kendon's continuum, where gestures are focused upon as the sole means of communication. The rest of this book is concerned with the contrasting "gesticulation" end of the continuum, where gestures are the unwitting accompaniments of speech. Here, utilizing a channel of which the speaker is largely unaware, we can use gestures to see into his thoughts.

Part Two

Varieties of Gesture

3   *Guide to Gesture Classification, Transcription, and Distribution*

Introduction

With this chapter I begin my description of the varieties of gestures. In the course of Part 2, I will discuss the different kinds of gestures and the coding scheme that we have used to transcribe and analyze them. I will present information on the contexts in which they appear and on how they relate to semantic meaning and pragmatic function. I will also present statistics of their distribution.

This particular chapter describes the coding scheme, our methods for collecting and coding gestures, and the basic statistics of gesture occurrence. It also reproduces the transcript of a full narrative by an adult speaker, including all of the gestures. Chapter 4 is devoted to the variety of gestures of the concrete (iconics of different degrees of elaboration). Chapter 5 presents an experiment on gestures and how they effect listeners to narratives. Chapter 6 explains the gestures of the abstract (metaphorics, beats, abstract pointing). The four chapters together form a kind of encyclopedia of the gestures and their effects at the gesticulation end of Kendon's continuum.

Types of Gesture

Classification Schemes

A number of gesture classification schemes have been proposed over the years. I will mention three in addition to our own. All four are summarized in table 3.1. The justification for our own scheme is that it does not require overly fine distinctions and that it is gauged to identify the types of gesture that appear in narratives. All of the schemes are basically the same, a fact explained by their common descent from Efron's (1941) classification. Efron (1941) and Ekman and Friesen (1969) subdivide gestures more finely than we have; Freedman and Hoffman (1967) have built in a somewhat different orientation—toward the gestures that take place during psychotherapy sessions rather than during storytelling. While each scheme has its own special usefulness, they are interconvertible in the sense that they regard the same movements as gestures and differ only in their grouping and subdividing strategies. An investigator

Table 3.1 Four Gesture Classification Schemes

Present Categories	Efron	Freedman and Hoffman	Ekman and Friesen
iconics	physiographics kinetographics	literal-reproductive	kinetographs
			pictographs
metaphorics	ideographics	concretization minor and major qualifying	ideographs underliners
			spatials
deictics	deictics		diectics
beats	batons	punctuating	batons rhythmics
Butterworths		speech failures	

could, if he wished, employ all three schemes or start with one and switch to another and cover the same gestural movements.

In our approach we classify gesture movements into four major categories: iconic, metaphoric, deictic (pointing), and beat gestures; definitions are provided later in the chapter. The gesture classifications we have used have validity inasmuch as the four types are *not* uniformly divided among discourse functions, but some are strongly associated with metanarrative functions, other with narrative, and so forth. All of this is shown in table 3.7 and explained in detail in chapter 7. Also, the four categories have different histories of development in children (chap. 11) and different breakdown patterns in aphasia (chap. 12).

The scheme was have used has the goal of identifying the referential values of gestures. The orientation of the scheme is toward the entities, actions, spaces, concepts, relationships, etc., that the gestures refer to. The classification scheme thus requires asking what meanings and functions a gesture possesses. It provides a guided, systematic, and disciplined method for inferring these meanings and functions. (It thus differs from schemes that make physical form differences into the primary basis of categorization.) The gesture categories, iconic, metaphoric, deictic, and beat, distinguish references to concrete events, to abstract concepts and relations, to orientations and reorientations, and to discontinuities: these are the goals of the scheme. The classification also makes essential linkage to the accompanying speech. A gesture category is formulated only in coordination with the speech content. An iconic gesture, for example, is one that, in its execution and manner of performance, refers to a concrete event, object, or action that is also referred to in speech at the same time. The iconic category expresses directly a category of meaning that must be compared to speech, and the other gesture categories are meant to have their own linkages to speech functions as well.

Our purpose is thus to bring out semiotic values, and this has led us to build semiotic distinctions directly into the gesture classification; that is, to classify the gesture by means of asking (a) is the movement a symbol? and (b) what type of symbol is it? The categories of iconic, metaphoric, deictic, or beat correspond to the fundamental types of semiotic sign (Peirce 1931–58).

One category requires a bit of explanation. This is the "Butterworth," corresponding to the "speech failure" category in Freedman and Hoffman's scheme (neither Efron nor Ekman and Friesen included such a category). I have named this category after Brian Butterworth, a scholar in Britain who has argued that many gestures arise in response to speech failures (see, e.g., Butterworth and Beattie 1978; Butterworth and Hadar 1989). I do not agree with this view that speech failures are a necessary or even an important condition for gesture occurrence in a general sense, but I would not deny that there are gestures that occur specifically as part of an effort to recall a word and/or find an appropriate sentence structure. However, they are a small fraction of all gestures, at least in narratives. A prototypical instance of a Butterworth is a hand grasping or plucking in the air while the speaker is trying to recall a word. Typically, there is no speech and this not-speaking places the Butterworth away from the leftward, gesticulation, end of Kendon's continuum (see chap. 2).

Experimental Paradigm

Basic Situation

Most of our gesture examples have been recorded during narrative discourse. Some other examples are taken from video recorded conversations, anthropological films, TV broadcasts, and naturally observed academic discourse. The narrative situation is quasi-experimental in that a speaker is shown a "stimulus"—a film, animated cartoon, or comic book—and then after this exposure the speaker immediately recounts the story of the stimulus from memory to a listener, and we videotape the performance. The listener is a genuine listener who does not have prior knowledge of the stimulus and does not see it. The speaker is told to present the story in as clear and complete a fashion as possible, for the listener will have to retell it later to a third person. Neither the speaker nor the listener knows that gestures are of interest and the instructions do not even mention the word. The speakers have been adults and children, and a number have been speakers of non-English languages (German, French, Italian, Georgian, Swahili, Chinese, and Japanese—the last four non-Indo-European). In addition, we have tested both Broca-type and Wernicke-type aphasics and two commissurotomy patients (so-called split-brains; see chap. 12). A major methodological advantage of this procedure is that, since we know the source of the narration independently of the narration itself, comparisons among speakers narrating the same episodes are possible. A detailed description of the methods used in this research will be found in the Appendix.

Coding

The following is a sketch of the methods that we have developed for coding iconic, beat, metaphoric, and deictic gestures. The Appendix gives the details.

DEFINITIONS. All visible movements by the speaker are first differentiated into gestures and non-gestures; the latter comprise self-touching (e.g., stroking the hair) and object-manipulations. The rest are considered gestures and are classified as to type. Gestures are distinguished basically as imagistic and non-imagistic types, depending on whether they depict imagery. In addition, the imagistic types are often triphasic (preparation-stroke-retraction), while the non-imagistic type, the beat, is biphasic.

A gesture is *iconic* if it bears a close formal relationship to the semantic content of speech. As noted previously, an iconic gesture displays, in its form and manner of execution, aspects of the same scene that speech also presents (McNeill and Levy 1982). An example is a gesture that accompanied the utterance, "he tries going up inside the pipe this time," in which the hand rises upward: this depicts, in its manner of execution, a feature also referred to in speech, namely, upward motion. The gesture omits other features (interiority, the identity of the character, etc.) but is classified as iconic because of the upward trajectory. Another iconic gesture is the "bends it way back" example (ex. 1.1). As the speaker described this scene he appeared to grip something in his own hand and pull it back toward his shoulder. The grip shape of the hand and the backward trajectory displayed aspects of the scene that speech also was presenting ("and he bent it way back"). Thus the gesture is classified as iconic:

(3.1) and he [bends it way back]
Iconic: right hand appears to grip something and pull it back from front to own shoulder.

Note that to judge this or any other gesture iconic, we compare it to our knowledge of the scene, not just to the speech. Speech is necessary inasmuch as we rely on the spoken text to know which scene the speaker is describing, but the iconicity of the gesture is determined by whether it exhibits aspects of the same scene described in speech, not the speech itself. It is our independent knowledge that a character seized hold of and bent back a tree that enables us to recognize the iconicity in the gesture above. This may seem like an overly precious distinction, but it is logically important. It underlies the concept of gestures and speech presenting overlapping but different aspects of the same scene. Since we refer the gesture to the independently known scene, we can logically define cases of complementarity of speech and iconic gesture.

The "bends it way back" gesture in fact complemented speech, in that it presented explicitly an aspect of the scene that is only implicit in the utterance. We note that the gesture was performed with a single hand; from this we can infer that the object being bent back was fastened down at one end (in fact, it was a tree). A two-handed gesture would have been used to depict an object like a stick or ruler that had to be held in place to be bent back. Speech does not convey this detail explicitly (it may be implicit in the verb and particle "bends way back"), but it is from his gesture that we see most clearly that it was part of the speaker's representation of the scene.

It is examples such as this that imply that gesture and speech jointly comprise a single integrated expression of meaning (chapter 1 presented arguments in support of this view). Gesture and speech convey information about the same scenes, but each can include something that the other leaves out. The bending way back example is in no way unique. Many other iconic gestures display this relationship to speech, coexpression combined with complementation.

While the semiotic definition of iconic gestures refers to the content of the gesture, it is possible to identify iconic gestures without any reference to the accompanying speech. Gestures have been coded as beat or iconic based solely on formal movement characteristics. This method has been crucial for coding the gestures of aphasic speakers for whom we cannot assume that speech presents meaning in a normal manner (Pedelty 1987). Because we have repeatedly used the same narrative stimuli we have been able to examine the gestures of many normal speakers narrating these stories, and to derive "canonical" gesture forms used to depict certain scenes. Gestures of special populations of subjects (such as aphasics) can then be classified with high reliability by comparing their movement features with the movement features of the canonical gestures.

Metaphoric gestures are similar to iconics in that they present imagery, but present an image of an abstract concept, such as knowledge, language itself, the genre of the narrative, etc. Metaphorics are, therefore, intrinsically more complex than iconics. Whereas an iconic gesture depicts some concrete event or object by creating a homology to aspects of the event/object, a metaphoric must depict two things. There is the Base (this term is from Mandel 1977), which is the concrete entity or action that is actually presented in the gesture. An example is a gesture presenting the concept of a question as a cupped hand: the Base is this cup, iconically depicted in the gesture. There is also the Referent (Mandel 1977), which is the concept that the metaphoric gesture Base is presenting: the concept of a question or of the answer (in either case, an abstract concept). Thus, a cupped hand accompanying the question, "I wanted to ask you something," presents a Base (the cup) and the Referent (the concept). The coding of metaphorics takes this dual structure into account.

Deictic gestures are pointing movements, which are prototypically performed with the pointing finger, although any extensible object or body part can be used, including the head, nose, or chin, as well as manipulated artifacts. The deictic gestures that appear during narratives rarely if ever point to concrete entities. They select a part of the gesture space and the meaning of the gesture depends on the referential value attached to this region.

Beats are defined as movements that do not present a discernible meaning, and they can be recognized positively in terms of their prototypical movement characteristics. They are typically biphasic (two movement components), small, low energy, rapid flicks of the fingers or hand; they lack a special gesture space, and are performed indeed wherever the hands happen to find themselves, including rest positions (the lap, next to the cheek, etc.). Some of the positive movement properties of beats have been organized into a "beat filter," which I describe below.

CODING METHODS. The coding of gestures is hierarchical in the sense that some coding categories are introduced only for gestures of the imagistic type (iconics, metaphorics). The Appendix presents the coding scheme in detail, along with example transcriptions. Coding proceeds by answering a series of questions. For those gestures considered to be iconic or metaphoric, each is coded in terms of

1. hands, which includes handedness, shape of hand, palm and finger orientation, and gesture space;
2. motion, which includes shape of trajectory, space where motion is articulated, and direction;
3. meaning, which is coded for hands, motion, and body separately:
   a. For the hand, what does it represent, and what viewpoint does it entail?
   b. For the motion, what does it represent and what viewpoint does it entail? In addition, are there any marked features, such as manner, direction, kind of path, or locus?
   c. For the body, is it representing a different entity from the hand or motion?

For metaphoric gestures, we specify both the vehicle of the metaphor (the image—the Base—that the gesture is depicting) and the tenor (what the abstract meaning is—the Referent—that is being presented in the metaphoric image). If the gesture is a beat, we code timing with respect to speech but not the form of the gesture, unless this varies from the typical (i.e., if the shape is other than an open palm and the movement other than short and up-and-down or side-to-side strokes. If the gesture is deictic, we code only the handedness, shape, and the locus where the hand (finger) is directed.

To time gestures in relation to speech, a movement is located using slow motion, the tape stopped, and then the tape released and the speech recorded: this provides the alignment within a syllable (it is crucial to have a VCR modified so that it reproduces sound in slow motion). To aid the temporal alignment, we add to each video field a sequential number and oscilloscope trace of the speech wave form. With such data, based entirely on visual information, speech and gesture can be lined up to an accuracy of $1/30$th sec. (one video field). The auditory and visual methods can be used jointly. The duration of pauses, both filled and silent, and pauses for breath can be measured from sound spectrographs.

BEAT FILTER. This is a formal method of differentiating imagistic (iconic and metaphoric) from non-imagistic (beat) gestures. It is called a beat filter because it filters out the imagistic gestures: what passes through are the beats. The filter is a series of questions, and a score of 1 is added for each yes answer: (1) Does the gesture have other than two movement phases (i.e., either one phase or three phases, or more)? (2) How many times does wrist or finger movement or tensed stasis appear in any movement phase not ending in a rest position? (add this number to the score).

(3) If the first movement is in a non-center part of space, is any other movement performed in center space? (4) If there are exactly two movement phases, is the space of the first phase different from the space of the second?

A score of 0 means no imagery on formal grounds, and the gesture probably is a beat. A score of 5 or 6 means high imagery on formal grounds, and the gesture is probably iconic or metaphoric (which it is depends on the relationship to meaning).

In addition, meaning judgments can be rated on a confidence scale with 1=marginally convinced and 5=totally certain.

Kinesic Structure

Gesture Form

Kendon (1972, 1980) wrote of the hierarchy of gesture movements that it "may be seen to provide at least a partial diagram of the relations between the units of the speaker's discourse" (207); we have found ample reason to agree with this statement. The following diagram summarizes the hierarchy (from McNeill, Levy, and Pedelty 1990).

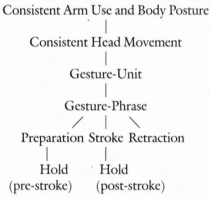

Consistent Arm Use and Body Posture
|
Consistent Head Movement
|
Gesture-Unit
|
Gesture-Phrase
/ | \
Preparation Stroke Retraction
| |
Hold   Hold
(pre-stroke)   (post-stroke)

ARM USE AND BODY POSTURE. Within units on this level, the speaker adopts different body postures and arm usage patterns. Kendon observed stretches in which all gestures were made with the right arm or left arm, or both. Shifting between arm options and body postures defines a kinesic unit on this level. The discourse stretches marked by consistent arm usage and body postures correspond roughly to a "paragraph" (Kendon 1972).

HEAD MOVEMENTS. Within stretches of a consistent arm and body use shorter sketches occur in which the same head movements take place; for example, first the head moves from the center of the gesture space to the right, and this occurs several times.

GESTURE-UNIT (G-UNIT). The G-unit is defined as the period of time between successive rests of the limbs; a G-unit begins the moment the limb begins to move and ends when it has reached a rest position again.

GESTURE-PHRASE (G-PHRASE). The G-phrase occurs within a G-unit (several G-phrases may cluster together within one G-unit).

A G-phrase in turn consists of one or more movement *phases* (preparation, various holds, stroke, retraction):

1. *Preparation* (optional), in which the limb moves away from its rest position to a position in gesture space where the stroke begins. The preparation phase typically anticipates the linguistic segments that are coexpressive with the gesture's meaning.

1h. *Pre-stroke hold* (optional) is the position and hand posture reached at the end of the preparation itself; this may be held more or less briefly until the stroke begins (cf. chap. 10; the terms "pre-stroke" and "post-stroke hold" are from Kita 1990). Pre-stroke holds occur when, for some reason, the stroke onset is delayed (chap. 10).

A *hold* in general is any temporary cessation of movement without leaving the gesture hierarchy (in contrast to a rest, which means exiting the hierarchy).

2. *Stroke* (obligatory) is the peak of effort in the gesture. It is in this phase that the meaning of the gesture is expressed. The stroke is synchronized with the linguistic segments that are coexpressive with it. It typically is performed in the central gesture space bounded roughly by the waist, shoulders, and arms; the head also becomes involved occasionally.

2h. *Post-stroke hold* (optional) is the final position and posture of the hand reached at the end of the stroke; this may be held more or less briefly until the retraction begins. Post-stroke holds occur when, for some reason, the coexpressive spoken utterance is delayed (chap. 10).

3. *Retraction* (optional) is the return of the hand to a rest position (not necessarily the one occupied before the G-phrase).

While a G-phrase cannot exist without a stroke, by definition, the other phases are optional. However, the option to omit the preparation phase is rarely taken in our narratives. Virtually all gestures contain a preparation component, and one may be added, apparently superfluously. Retraction phases are often omitted when one gesture passes directly into a succeeding gesture. The preparation and the two stroke-hold phases can compensate for mismatches of speech-gesture synchrony.

To illustrate these phases I will use the following examples from Kendon (1980):

1. The hand rises up and takes an umbrella form, and then moves down sharply.
   Preparation: hand rising up and taking umbrella form.
   Stroke: hand moving down sharply.
   Post-stroke hold: hand held in position reached at end of stroke.
   Retraction: fingers relax into loose bunch.
2. The arm rises up and sweeps side-to-side two times.
   Preparation: arm rises upward.
   Stroke: arm swings in and out twice. Note that this is considered to be one stroke even though the arm moves in and out two times.
   Retraction: arm returns to the rest position it was in before the gesture.

In this book most of our observations refer to the lowest level of the kinesic hierarchy, and within this level, to the stroke phase. (The strokes in the examples appear within square brackets except when the example also shows the preparation and retraction phases; in this case the brackets mark the beginning and end of the entire gesture and the stroke is in boldface.) The stroke is the phase that carries the gesture content. The preparation phase is crucial for the question of gesture timing. I discussed this earlier, in chapter 1; experiments on timing are described in chapter 10.

GESTURES AND SPEECH PHONOLOGY. In an analysis of the relationship of gesture movements to speech sounds, Kendon (1972) compared the kinesic hierarchy above to the tone units comprising a natural conversation. He could define a phonological hierarchy (Kingdon 1958) and observed that the two hierarchies—sound and gesture—were remarkably parallel to one another. On the lowest phonological level is the *most prominent syllable*, the phonological peak within a single clause. Just above this is the *tone unit*, a grouping of syllables over which there is a complete intonation tune (e.g., rise-fall, etc.). Tone units in turn form *locutions*, mapping typically onto complete sentences. A locution is separated from its neighbors by distinct pauses and begins with increased loudness. A series of locutions forms a *locution group*. At this level there may be phonological variation but some common phonological feature will be preserved throughout, such as the same, e.g., low-rise, tune. The highest level is the *locution cluster*, which is marked by pauses, repeated or repaired phrases, altered pitch and/or voice quality, and a thematic shift of content.

Table 3.2 Kinesic and Phonological Hierarchies Combined

Kinesic Hierarchy	Phonological Hierarchy
Consistent Arm Use and Body Posture	Locution Cluster
Consistent Head Movement	Locution Group
One G-Unit	Locution
One G-Phrase	Tone Group
One Stroke	Most Prominent Syllable

The phonological and kinesic hierarchies line up such that boundaries between the highest, middle, and lowest levels of each hierarchy co-occur in time (table 3.2, based on Kendon 1972, 1980). It appears from table 3.2 that each speech unit has its equivalent unit of body motion, and the larger the speech unit, the greater the change in the kinesic sphere, perhaps as a form of working memory control (Kendon 1972).

LENGTH OF G-UNITS. Given that G-units can encompass more than one G-phrase, or gesture, how long in fact do G-units tend to be? Table 3.3 answers this question for six cartoon narratives, and shows the percentage of G-units that contain one, two, three, etc., G-phrases. About half of all G-units consist of a single gesture, a few of two successive gestures, and the rest of a range of longer sequences.

Table 3.4 gives the converse distribution, the empty spans between G-units. These were stretches of speech where there were no gestures; the length of a span is indexed in terms of clauses. Most G-units had no clauses between them. This means that 70% of the time the hands returned to rest between successive clauses and then immediately returned to action to make a new gesture. Of the remaining spans, two-thirds contained just one clause. Thus, while gesture activity is fairly continuous, there are almost as many rests as there are gestures.

From tables 3.3 and 3.4 we learn that most gestures occur one gesture at a time. Gestures tend to occur as singletons and between gestures the hands return to a rest position. (Along with the obligatory presence of speech, this predominance of singletons also differentiates gestures from pantomime.)

Table 3.3 Percentage of G-Units of Different Lengths

	Number of G-Phrases in G-Unit							Number of G-units
	1	2	3	4	5	6	>6	
Percentage of G-units	56	14	8	8	4	2	8	254

Table 3.4 Percentage of Non-Gesture Intervals of Different Lengths

	Number of Clauses between G-Units								Number of Intervals
	0	1	2	3	4	5	6	>6	
Percentage of Intervals	70	19	5	3	1	2	—	1	275

GESTURE HAND SHAPES. Table 3.5 summarizes the hand shapes that have appeared as iconic gestures in the six cartoon narratives. The ASL shapes in the table are only approximated by spontaneous gestures; we describe the gesture with the ASL shape that the gesture most closely resembles, but nearly all gestures are deficient from an ASL point of view (too loose, not clearly enough marked). Narratives in other genres (such as films) would undoubtedly produce a different distribution of shapes, but the most common hand shapes are likely to occur in all narratives. Indeed, the most frequent of all is the 5-hand, which is the ASL approximation to a relaxed, semantically unmarked hand in the loose way it is made. The bent 5-hand, in contrast, is semantically motivated: it can be used to depict removing a hat from a character's head, for example. Over the six narratives twenty different shapes were used. Different speakers had individual favorites: for example, speaker 1 preferred the G-hand; speaker 3 the O-hand; speaker 4 the C-hand; speaker 6 the S-hand; and so forth. Most shapes, whether the favorite of one speaker or of all, correspond to semantic distinctions, and these are described in chapter 4.

Gesture Space

The gesture space can be visualized as a shallow disk in front of the speaker, the bottom half flattened when the speaker is seated (see fig. 3.1). Adults usually perform gestures within this limited space (with children the space is larger; see chap. 11). Figure 3.2 shows the density of gesture occurrence in this space (all six speakers combined). The fore-aft dimension is shorted and almost never extends behind the body; gestures behind the frontal plane of the body are rare and have marked status. Speakers from different cultures appear to organize their gesture spaces somewhat differently. Turkana speakers, for example, make more use of the space around the head than speakers of European languages (see chap. 6). The latter, in turn, do not noticeably differ from one another (this includes observations of speakers of English, French, German, Italian, and Georgian).

For transcription purposes, the gesture space can be divided into sectors using a system of concentric squares; the sector directly in front of the chest is Center-Center; surrounding this is the Center, then the Pe-

Table 3.5 Hand Shapes Used for Iconics in Six Cartoon Narratives (ASL hand shapes from Friedman 1977)

		1	2	3	4	5	6	All
	Speaker							
Number of Iconics		56	63	83	77	70	67	416
ASL Hand Shape		Percentage of Iconics						
A		4	11	11	8	23	13	12
S		5		4	3		33	7
O		4	6	14	1	1		5
tapered O		9			1			1
baby O		5	6	4	1	3	9	5
B		4	3		1	3	9	3
B spread		7	6	6	1	3		4
C		7	10	16	24	6	9	12
5		21	42	31	34	49	10	31
4				1				<1
bent 5		5	3	7	10	4	12	7
F			2	1				<1

continued

Table 3.5 Continued

		Speaker					
	1	2	3	4	5	6	All
Number of Iconics	56	63	83	77	70	67	416
ASL Hand Shape				Percentage of Iconics			
G	12			3	4		3
X1	5			2	3		2
L				2	5		1
bent L	4			8	1		2
H	4	2					1
bent 3			10				1
7						4	1
D	4						<1

riphery (divided into upper, lower, right, left), and finally, at the outer limit, the Extreme Periphery (also divided).

The panels in fig. 3.2 are filled in different regions depending on the type of gesture. Iconics fill the Center-Center space. Metaphorics congregate below in the lower Center space. Deictics extend to the Periphery. Beats form bunches at several places and each bunch is due to a different speaker. That the four types of gesture utilize space in such different ways is, in itself, a strong justification for subdividing gestures according to the iconic, metaphoric, deictic, and beat scheme.

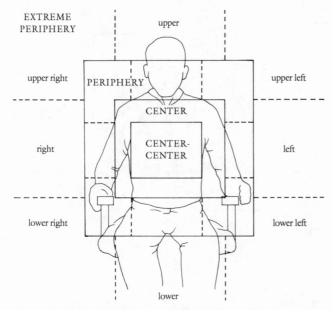

Figure 3.1. Drawing of the typical gesture space of an adult speaker.

Statistics

The following statistics of gesture occurrence are based on the six cartoon narratives mentioned earlier by young adult English-language
speakers (university students). Such statistics provide a general orientation to the incidence of gestures and their distribution in relation to
speech during narrative discourse.

CO-OCCURRENCE OF GESTURE WITH SPEECH. In many hours of recorded narratives, we have observed only one instance of a gesture by a
listener. The passive comprehender role does not evoke gestures to anything like the same degree as the active producer role. The cause of this
huge difference is unclear. The listener is experiencing the same content
and linguistic forms and presumably is constructing imagistic representations of the narrative in parallel with the speaker; yet there are no gestures. It is possible that gestural production is suppressed along with
speech as part of the turn-taking conventions regulating face-to-face interactions, where a sharp distinction obtains between the speaker and the
listener (Duncan and Fiske 1977). It is also possible that gesture production requires motor activity in the speech channel. Whatever the explana-

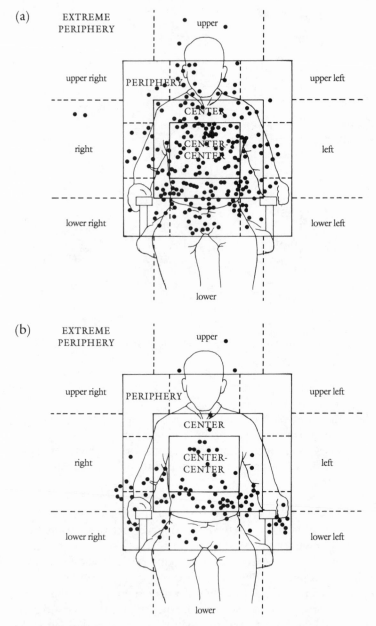

Figure 3.2. Density of space usage in six cartoon narratives. Panel (a) shows iconics, most of which are in the C region; (b) shows metaphorics, mostly in lower C region; (c) shows deictics and they tend to be in more peripheral regions; (d) shows beats and they are bunched up into tight clusters (each cluster is from a different speaker, who has her own favorite part of space for this gesture).

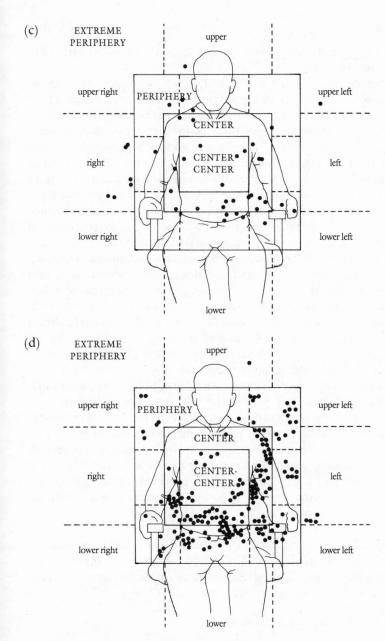

Figure 3.2. continued

tion, the production of gestures and speaking are virtually restricted to the same situations.

Focusing, then, on the speaker we find that the majority of his or her gestures occur during actual speech articulation. Gestures during hesitant periods (pauses, silent or filled) are in a distinct minority. Table 3.6 shows the distribution of gestures in five categories: co-articulated speech, filled pauses ("um," "uh," and extended phonation of the vowel portions of words), unfilled pauses, breath pauses (i.e., audible breathiness during an unfilled pause), and false starts (the speaker interrupts his or her utterance and immediately begins a repair). The decisive component of the gesture in table 3.6 is the stroke phase. If the stroke coincided with speech, the gesture was counted as coinciding with speech even if there was silence during the preparation or retraction phase; conversely, if the stroke coincided with silence, the gesture was counted as coinciding with silence even if there was speech during the preparation or retraction phases. With beats (which have only two phases), the entire gesture had to coincide with speech to be counted as occurring during speech. Table 3.6 shows that 90% of all strokes occurred during the actual articulation of speech. Slightly less than 4% took place during false starts and slightly more than 3% during breath pauses; only between 1% and 2% occurred during filled and unfilled pauses respectively.

This result superficially contrasts with that of Butterworth and Beattie (1978), who found nearly identical *rates* of gestures per 1000 seconds of speech and 1000 seconds of hesitation. However, their way of presenting data is not directly comparable to that in table 3.6, which shows the percentage of gestures made during speech and hesitation, not rates per unit of time. To normalize during hesitations and speech to get equal baselines of time might be useful for some purposes but it gives a grossly distorted picture of the actual distribution of gestures during narrations since speech is, by far, more copious than hesitation.

FREQUENCY OF GESTURE TYPES. Table 3.7 is an expanded version of a table in McNeill and Levy (1982). It shows the relative frequency of iconics, beats, metaphorics, and deictics, as well as the frequency of clauses with no gestures accompanying them at all.

Table 3.6 Speech and Gesture Co-Occurrence

	Percentage of Gestures in Category				
Co-articulated Speech	Filled Pauses	Unfilled Pauses	Breath Pauses	False Starts	Total
90	1	2	3	4	100

The type of clause in table 3.7 will be explained briefly; more details are given in chapter 7; also McNeill and Levy (1982). A narrative level clause presents a step in the plot-line development of the story; it is therefore subject to sequential constraints (Labov and Waletsky 1967; Hopper 1979; Hopper and Thompson 1980). An extranarrative clause is any other clause in the storytelling act that is not on the plot line (e.g., describing the setting, summing up the action, introducing characters, forecasting what is to come, mentioning the video, etc.) and is not subject to sequential constraints. Extranarrative clauses will eventually be differentiated into subvarieties (metanarrative and paranarrative), but this distinction is not crucial in this chapter and will be overlooked (see chap. 7). More than half of the clauses in narratives were accompanied by gestures, and narrative and extranarrative clauses did not differ in the frequency of gestures that occurred with them.

One generalization that fits table 3.7 is this: although there are similar numbers of iconics and beats, iconics occur overwhelmingly in narrative clauses, while beats can occur in both narrative and extranarrative clauses. Thus, iconic gestures are limited by the sequentiality constraint, but beats can appear anywhere. The difference in distribution reflects the different functions of the two kinds of gesture. The events that iconics illustrate inherently progress in temporal and causal sequences in the real or fictive world, while beats occur at points of significant discontinuity in discourse and function to highlight atemporal relationships (Silverstein 1984). Another generalization we can make is the following: abstract pointing occurs chiefly with narrative clauses, whereas metaphorics appear chiefly with extranarrative clauses.

Thus, while each type of gesture has its own way of correlating with narrative and extranarrative contexts, the gestures fall into two larger groups:

1. *Sequence related* iconics and deictics appear in narrative contexts.
2. *Structure related* beats and metaphorics appear in extranarrative contexts. Of these structure related gestures, beats appear in all contexts, while metaphorics appear primarily in extranarrative contexts.

Table 3.7 Frequency of Gesture Types in Different Contexts

Type of Clause	Type of Gesture					
	Iconic	Beat	Metaphoric	Deictic	None	Total
Narrative	226	134	12	25	146	543
Extranarrative	35	134	31	3	44	247
Total	261	268	43	28	190	790

GESTURE TO CLAUSE CORRESPONDENCE. As a general rule there is one gesture, one clause. Narrators, nonetheless, depart from this rule and depart in both directions. Some clauses have more than one gesture and some gestures cover more than one clause. Table 3.8 (based on a similar table for aphasic speakers in Pedelty 1987, which appears later as table 12.2) tallies the correspondence of gestures and clauses in the six cartoon narrations.

As can be seen, most departures from a one-to-one ratio are in the multiple gesture to one clause direction. If we equate gestures with "idea units" (Kendon 1980), we can say that the speaker is attempting to cover more than one idea unit with a single clause. Not surprisingly, given the overloading of the linguistic program this implies, multiple gesture to single clause utterances are often accompanied by dysfluencies. For example, one speaker performed two distinct gestures during the following: "[and she . . .][grabbed a knife]." A lengthy pause interrupted the speech flow before the gesture boundary, as if the speaker were waiting for the next gesture. The multiple clause for one gesture combinations are, by comparison, rare, but they occur frequently in the gestures of Wernicke's aphasics (chap. 12).

Example of a Narration by an Adult Speaker

To provide an extended example of adult narrative performance, I reproduce in full one speaker's narration of the cartoon story. The narration will illustrate the full range of gestural phenomena, including the inevitable residue of gestures that are difficult to classify. Such difficulties are pointed out in the comments. The narrative is typical of an adult performance in most respects. It lasted slightly more than four and a half minutes. The speaker has a high proportion of iconics relative to other gesture types, and in this respect goes farther than other adults. Her beats almost never appear in isolation but are superimposed on other gestures, and her deictics are usually combined with iconics; in these respects she also differs somewhat from other adults, but the differences are of proportion, not of kind. In common with other narrators she pro-

Table 3.8 Correspondence of Gestures to Clauses[a] (as a percentage of total gestures)

	Gesture to Clause Ratio						
	1:4	1:3	1:2	1:1	2:1	3:1	N (g)
Normal Speakers	<1	1	4	67	19	8	433

[a] Based on a method devised by Pedelty, (1987).

duces no emblems. She also has no Butterworths, although her speech has many hesitant phases, and the hesitations are characterized by an *absence* of gesture of every kind (cf. Butterworth and Beattie 1978, who seemingly observed the opposite). Also, as is common in narratives, the listener is not entirely passive, but asks questions and reacts to the speaker's narrative, to which the speaker in turn responds. Worth noting in particular is the variety of semantic relationships and shifts of viewpoint conveyed in the iconic and metaphoric gestures, and the variety of pragmatic references conveyed in the metaphoric beats, and deictics. I have indicated the gesture strokes with brackets but not the other gesture phases (thus the boldface convention for indicating the stroke is not used). All hesitations and false starts are shown, as well as their durations in tenths of a second. The transcript is the work of many individuals. It was prepared in this very full version by Karl-Erik McCullough with the assistance of Desha Baker. The conventions are as follows:

[ ]	stroke phase of gesture
♯	audible breath pause with duration in seconds
/	silent pause with duration in seconds
*	self-interruption
=	other interruption
< >	filled pause with duration in seconds
C-VPT	character viewpoint of an iconic gesture
O-VPT	observer viewpoint of an iconic gesture

Comments are in boldface.
Post-stroke holds are indicated by dots (:...)

1. [ok] / (.4) and it was <was> (.3) a cartoon called Canary Row ♯ (.8)

Beat

2. <and> (.3) it was Sylvester and Tweety Bird ♯ (.3)
3. <and uh> (1.0) / (.1) it starts out with Sylvester sitting in
4. the Birdwatcher's Society
5. whi[ch is way] up in a building several floors up

O-VPT iconic: hands rise up at center to show height.

6. and he looks out with binoculars
7. and he sees Tweety Bird across the street
8. on a [window sill] ♯ (.4) in his little bird cage ♯ (.4)

O-VPT iconic: hand flattens and pats down to show window sill.

9. and Tweety Bird has binoculars
10. and he looks back
11. and ["I tawt I taw a putty cat"]

C-VPT iconic: head shakes back and forth. (voice changes)

12. <and uh> (1.4) ǂ (.7) <uh the> (.4) whole cartoon / (.1)
13. is / (.2) Sylves[ter / (.2) of course]
Metaphoric: hands rotate up and forward to present "of course."
14. trying to get Tweety Bird like he always does
15. and Tweety Bird / (.1) <is> (.5) / (.5) the pet of this old lady
16. called Granny ǂ (.7)
17. and Granny is pretty mean {laughs} for a Granny ǂ (.7)
18. <um> (.6) ǂ (.8) Sylvester tries a number of ways to get him
19. <he uh> (.7) ǂ (.9) tries [going in the front door
   . . . .
20. of the] building / (.1)
   . . . . .

O-VPT iconic and deictic: hand tilts forward and to side for going in, and indicates building's direction. **This illustrates a case where one gesture seems to convey both an event and a location at once and thus belongs to two categories.**
21. there's a little [sign that says [no dogs] or [cats]] allowed
                     (1)   (2)   (3)
(1) O-VPT iconic: hands form sign shape. (2) and (3) are superimposed beats.
22. 'n im[mediately] he's thrown out
C-VPT iconic: left hand throws object to right space.
23. <he> (.5) tries / (.1) climbing up the drainpipe ǂ (1.0) <uh> (.7) / (.5)
24. and he gets all the way up there / (.1)
25. <and> (.7) / (.2) the little Tweety Bird starts screaming
26. and then Granny comes
27. and [throws him] off the window sill down back to the ground ǂ (1.2)
O-VPT iconic: hand tilts forward and to side to show trajectory.
28. <he tries> (1.0) going [up] the in[side] of the [drain pipe]
                        (1)   (2)   (3)   . . . .
(1) O-VPT iconic: hand rises up in loose point.
(2) O-VPT iconic: hand rises further in more precise point.
(3) O-VPT iconic: repeats (2).
29. and Tweety Bird runs and gets a bowling ball
30. and drops it [down] the drain pipe ǂ (.8)
C-VPT iconic: both hands appear to shove bowling ball down. **Note the shift from O-VPT in (28) to C-VPT in (30).**
31. <and> (.4) / (.4) [as he's com]ing up and the [bowling] ball's
                  (1)   (2)

32. coming down
(1) O-VPT iconic: right hand rises straight up from lap into center for Sylvester coming up.
(2) O-VPT iconic: left hand drops down from head level into center for the bowling ball coming down. This iconic is best regarded as a single gesture with two hands performing different roles. By calling it a single gesture we can understand the significance of the center space to which each of the hands is sent: it is here that the crucial interaction of Sylvester and the bowling ball will take place.

33. he [swallows it]
. . . .
O-VPT iconic: left hand moves straight down into center, while right hand moves straight up into center and forms space around left hand, to show the bowling ball passing into Sylvester's mouth. Space is used here in a way consistent with the preceding gesture, and now it is clear that a single gesture exists with the two hands performing different roles. Also note that the meaning of the right hand has slightly shifted: whereas in the preceding gesture it was Sylvester as a whole, here it has become Sylvester's open mouth.

34. and he [comes out the bottom of the drain]pipe
. . . .
O-VPT iconic: left hand arcs down and to right, passing under right hand which is extended to the left at waist level, to show Sylvester coming out. The meaning of the left hand has shifted: whereas it had been the bowling ball, now it is Sylvester with the bowling ball inside him.

35. and he's [got this big bowling ball in side him]
. . . .
C-VPT iconic: both hands press against own stomach, to show the location of the bowling ball. Note the second shift to C-VPT. This shift and the one at (30) occurred, respectively, at the beginning and end of a causal sequence of events: bowling ball into pipe → bowling ball inside Sylvester. The steps in between were presented from the observer point of view.

36. [and he rolls on down] into a
O-VPT iconic: both hands roll over one another, to show rolling down the street.

37. [bowling alley]
Metaphoric: both hands spread open, as if to show completion.

38. and then [you hear a s]trike
Metaphoric: both hands spread open.

39. <uh> (.8) he <tries> (1.0) / (.1) <a> (.9) / (1.6) few other

40. things
41. he∗ / (.2) he tries to <um> (.5) / (.2)
42. set [down] a∗ / (.2) <a∗> (.5) a [crate]]

. . . .
        (1)   (2)
(1) C-VPT iconic: both hands appear to place crate down.
(2) Beat superimposed on the word that refers to the crate gesture in (1). **Note that the scene transition was marked by abundant hesitation, suggesting confusion and memory difficulties, and during this period of confusion all gesture activity ceased. As soon as the next scene was recalled, speech became fluent and gestures resumed.**

43. and put [a board] across it like a seesaw ǂ (.4)
Iconic: left hand moves horizontally, to show board. **The viewpoint of this gesture is indeterminate.**

44. and then he [throws] a five-hundred-pound weight
Dual C-VPT iconic and O-VPT deictic: hands move forward and down, showing throwing motion, and end in points, showing the direction of the weight. **The gesture begins as a character viewpoint of throwing and ends in pointing, which has the viewpoint of an observer. This is a gesture with two viewpoints.**

45. on the [other] end
Deictic: right hand points to left.

46. and that / (.4) [catapults] him up
O-VPT iconic: hand rises up to show catapulting.

47. and he [grabs] Tweety Bird ǂ (.8)
C-VPT iconic: hand grabs something.

48. and as he [comes back] down he [lands on the ground]
        (1)   (2)
(1) dual C-VPT iconic and O-VPT iconic: the hand appears to grip something (the character's point of view) and at the same time falls straight down to show coming back down (an observer's point of view). **Another gesture with two viewpoints. The gestures in (48), (49), and (51) should be regarded as a unit in the sense that they depict a continuous narrative text and utilize a consistent space and combination of viewpoints to do it.**
(2) repeats (1).

49. and he [starts running] away
Dual C-VPT iconic and O-VPT iconic: hand, still gripping something, moves laterally to right, to show running away.

50. and at this time the five-hundred-pound weight comes down
51. [and lands] on him
Dual C-VPT iconic and O-VPT iconic: left hand arcs through air and onto right hand, still gripping something.

52. and [Tweety] Bird gets away
?Metaphoric: both hands spread apart, possibly a metaphor for disappearance.
The difficulty in interpreting this gesture as metaphoric is that the opening of the right hand, the gripping hand, could be a C-VPT iconic for the cat letting the bird go. The right hand in fact did open slightly before the left. It is also possible that there are two gestures, the first iconic.

53. <he uh*> (1.2) you see [him [drawing] up / (.4) [lots of]
. . . .
    (1)   (2)   (3)

54. blueprints and Tweety Bird says ["I wonder what he's up to" ‡ (.8)]
. . . .
    (1 continues)   (4)

(1) C-VPT iconic: both hands appear to hold onto blueprints.
(2) and (3) beats: superimposed on words that refer to the blueprints in (1).
(4) C-VPT iconic: superimposed on continuing blueprints gesture, head tilts, voice changes to play the bird's part. We have two character viewpoints, although only one is active at a time.

55. <and uh> (1.0) / (.1) the next thing] you know
. . . .
                    (1 ends)

End of blueprints gesture (1).

56. he comes [swinging thr]ough on a rope
O-VPT iconic: hand swings across body from periphery to opposite side, showing the cat swinging.

57. and then [he [just] [misses] [the] window]
. . . .
    (1) (2)   (3)   (4)

(1) Iconic or metaphoric: both hands show open space, either for the window or for "just missing."
(2), (3) and (4) beats: superimposed on words that refer to and modify the "just missing" gesture. This is a case where either a metaphoric or iconic interpretation would be appropriate, although the metaphoric meaning of "just missing" seems the more plausible.

58. and he [smashes] into the brick wall beside it ‡ (.9)
O-VPT iconic: flat hand pivots down and to front, to show smashing into the wall from the perspective of an observer looking on at the rear.

59. <um> (.6) ‡ (1.5) then he tries* / (.4)

60. and I wasn't really clear on why he thought [this would work]
Metaphoric: both hands seem to support object for concept of next episode.

61. they've got [streetcars] in this ‡ (.7)
Metaphoric: both hands close around something for reference to streetcars.

This metaphoric is made to contrast to the previous one by an arbitrary kinesic change.

  62. {Listener: uh huh}

  63. <um> (.6) / (.4) no wait [bef* / (.1) before the [street] car

                 . . . .

                        (1)   (2)

(1) Spatial metaphor: finger raised and points to right space for previous episode.

(2) Beat: superimposed on the word that refers to the episode that is going to be postponed.

  64. there's another one

       . . . .   (1 continues)

(1) Continuation of metaphor for previous episode.

  65. <he um*> (.7) / (.2) the old lady calls down

    . . . .   (1 continues)

(1) Continuation of metaphor.

  66. to the desk clerk / (.1) of this] hotel

     . . . .

                       (1 ends)

(1) End of metaphor. **The spatial metaphor in which the right space was set up to be the previous episode continues through the entire introduction of this new episode.**

  67. and says she's checking out

  68. and would / (.1) he please send someone up for the bags

  69. well# (.6) <uh> [Sylves]ter's sitting in the [mail boxes / (.3)

                                          . . . .

                  (1)   (2)

(1) Metaphoric: left hand appears to hold up object, for introduction of character into scene.

(2) C-VPT iconic: both hands clasp together at heart, acting part of Sylvester in the mail box.

  70. [behind] the <uh> (.1) [hotel] desk]# (.6)

       . . . .

       (3)   (4)

(3) and (4) beats: superimposed on words that refer to the small box gesture in (2).

  71. and he hears this

  72. so he goes [scra]mbling up to <um> (.4) # (.8) the room / (.2)

O-VPT iconic: both hands flick forward and up, to show scrambling up.

  73. [dress]ed like a bellhop

C-VPT iconic and deictic: left hand points to own torso.

74. <and> (.5) / (.2) she∗ <um> / (.6) he [knocks] on the door
C-VPT ?iconic and deictic: loose hand moves slightly forward. The direction is that of the door from the character's viewpoint. The hand shape is not appropriate for knocking, and thus the iconic component is dubious; the movement forward, however, is clear.
75. and she's / (.1) [in] transom / (.1) [look]ing down ⌡ (.7)
        (1)   (2)
(1) C-VPT iconic: head tilts forward to show Granny looking down.
(2) C-VPT iconic: both hands move down from own eyes. The second gesture shows 'eidola,' rays leaving the eyes. This could qualify it as a metaphor of vision, but the gesture was classified as iconic since the speaker continues to play the part of the character.
76. <and uh> (.8) she∗ / (.2) he says you know I'm here for your bags
77. and she says on [OK just a minute ⌡] (.4)
C-VPT iconic: head tilts to side, playing Granny.
78. <uh> they're right [behind] the door
C-VPT iconic: head tilts forward, playing Granny.
79. and I'll meet you [down] in the lobby ⌡ (.5) and so-
C-VPT iconic: head tilts forward, playing granny.
The quoted utterances (lines 77–79) were accompanied by head movement gestures, which seems quite reasonable; if gestures were to be made they would have to be the *character's* gestures, since the speaker was enacting the character, and this is the kind of gesture the speaker performed.
80. {Listener: what's she doing in the transom?}
81. she [crawls] up in the transom
O-VPT iconic: hand rises up with wiggling fingers, to show crawling up. Now the speaker speaks for herself and gestures shift to O-VPT, which serves to mark the change of voices.
82. she's [look]ing down at him outside
C-VPT iconic: head tilts forward to show Granny looking down. Cohesive repetition of the earlier gesture for looking down.
83. and he doesn't see her
84. [she's checking I] assume to see that it's Sylvester
Metaphoric: both hands hold object representing the explanation
85. <so he> opens the door
86. and he grabs the bag and the bird cage
87. and the bird cage is covered up
88. and he tosses the bag away
89. and he starts to run off with <the uh> (.4) ⌡ (.5) bird cage
90. and as soon as he gets outside the building ⌡ (.4)
Gestures disappear. Perhaps this stretch had been pre-planned when

the listener asked a question. Unlike the answer, it may have seemed repetitious and this explains the absence.

91. he [opens it] up # (.6)
C-VPT iconic: both hands open in front of body.

92. <and uh> (.9) [she's in the cage [not the bird]]

            ....

          (1)   (3)

93. she [beats] him up # (.4)
     (3)

(1) Metaphoric: both hands flip over with palms up for revelation of Granny.
(2) Beat: superimposed on the metaphoric at the contrasting word.
(3) Metaphoric: new gesture similar to (1) for the denouement.

The metaphoric gestures in (92) and (93), plus the iconic in (91) for opening up the cage, are basically the same; the movements are similar and all were performed with both hands. The repeated use of the same type of gesture may have influenced the way the speaker structured (94) and (95). That is, gesture may have affected speech. Once the two-handed gesture appeared, the speaker kept using it and had to find a semantic thread that supported it. The metaphoric gestures provided the thread but imposed their own effects of shifting the perspective to a metanarrative level. The first metaphor conveys that something was a revelation, the beat highlights a contrasting referent, and the last metaphor comments on something as a predictable conclusion—comments on the narrative as a structure from the outside. The iconic gesture in (91) for opening up the cage thus may have induced the metanarrative conclusion in (94–95).

94. [she beats] him up [a lot] (laughs)
Beats: highlight the words that refer to the predictable conclusion.

95. you know like [any time] [she sees him] she [beats] him up # (.5)
Beats: more of the same as in (94).

96. another thing he does is <um> (.4) # (1.0)

97. [he <see]s> (.5) an organ grinder [with a little monkey # (.8)]
   (1)   (2)

(1) Beat: beginning of episode.
(2) C-VPT iconic: hand rotating, to show working an organ.

98. well he en[tic]es the monkey away from the organ grinder
C-VPT iconic: head tilts back for "come hither."
with a banana

99. and then [mugs] the monkey to get his little [uniform]
          (1)   (2)

(1) C-VPT iconic: left hand appears to strike a blow.
(2) Deictic and C-VPT iconic: hands point to clothes on own body.

100. [little] hat
Deictic and C-VPT iconic: points to own head.
101. and his [little] <uh> (.3) ǂ (.8) <uh> (.2) jacket ǂ (.7)
Deictic and C-VPT iconic: hands point to clothes on own body. **All of these gestures are ambiguous over who is wearing the uniform; there is little in the gesture to indicate if it is Sylvester or the monkey.**
102. <and uh> (.7) / (.1) he goes [crawl]ing up the drainpipe again
O-VPT iconic: both hands rise up for ascending the drainpipe.
103. dressed like the monkey and he's [trying to masquera]de ǂ (.4)
. . . . .

Metaphoric: both hands spread apart and forward with a rotation, to represent the concept of trying. **Rotation is a frequent gestural metaphor for trying.**
104. and he gets in <the uh> apartment / (.4)
105. and he's looking for Tweety Bird
106. and / (.1) you know
107. when[ever] she looks at him he tries to make monkey noises
Beat: summary statement.
108. and scratch himself and all ǂ (.7)
109. <and uh> (.8) she catches on very quickly
110. and beats the hell out of him again ǂ (.9)
111. <uh> (.4) and the last thing he does / (.1) is <um> (.5) ǂ (1.2)
112. he's tight∗ / (.5) like walking on a tightrope / (.3)
Again, gestures largely disappear; the passage is metanarrative, yet does not introduce a new episode until the end, and the lack of novelty on both the narrative and metanarrative levels may explain the absence.
113. on the ∗ / (.1) [the [wires] [that the] [trolley]]
       (1) (2)   (3)   (4)
(1) O-VPT iconic: both hands flat, palms down, point at each other, to show the wires.
(2), (3) and (4) beats: superimposed on wires gesture at words that refer to it.
114. is [connec]ted to / (.5) {with questioning intonation}
O-VPT iconic and deictic: right hand moves back and forth next to head while pointing up.
115. {Listener: uh huh}
116. <um> the street cars {questioning intonation} you know that th∗
117. [where they] / (.2) [connect] above [to get] their power ǂ (.9)
     (1)   (2)   (3)
(1) Deictic: points at "wires" above, next to head.
(2) O-VPT iconic and deictic: hand rises and tilts to horizontal, to show wires as well as location. Also, head tilts toward hand to show wires overhead.

(3) O-VPT iconic: in same position next to head, hand moves backward to describe the form of the connecting wires.
118. and he's [walk]ing on it / (.1)
Beat: resumption of story.
119. and the streetcar comes up behind him / (.7)
120. and he＊ so [he's running] along the wire
O-VPT iconic: left hand moves away while fingers wiggle, to show running away.
121. and every time the [street car] catches up to him
O-VPT iconic: right hand loops forward and back to show the street car catching up. Looping out and back can be explained by the accomplishment semantics of "catches up." This verb implies having reached a goal (Vendler, 1967); the gesture, by reversing direction, deliberately marked the end of its trajectory and this corresponds to the end state meaning of the verb.
122. and he steps on the part where [the / street car's connecting]
O-VPT iconic: the left-hand palm faces down, making a flat surface, while the right-hand index finger repeatedly jabs into this palm from below, to show the trolley connector contacting Sylvester's foot. The gesture conveys more complete information than speech in this example—the shapes of the foot and connector.
123. [he] gets a shock ǂ (.6)
Metaphoric: both hands, loosely curled, move apart with palms facing. The metaphoric aspect of this gesture is the separation of the hands, which represents violent explosiveness, and the loose curvature of the hands, which often appears when a passive transformation is depicted.
124. and the [cam]era moves down
?Deictic: both hands point to own torso and move down. One possibility is that the hands indicate the viewer of the cartoon or the camera and its viewpoint. This mysterious gesture is a fitting way to close the narration, since it shows the kind of puzzle that can remain after the most careful study.
125. and it's Tweety Bird / <uh> (.2) [driving] the street car and
C-VPT iconic: left hand appears to grip trolleyman's control.
126. {Listener laughs}
127. the little ol' lady next to him ǂ (.4) <uh> ringing the bell ǂ (.8)
128. <uh> / (.1) and that's basically it
129. it's really very violent in a way
130. [but] / (.1) that's＊ that's what it is
Conduit: both hands present cartoon as object.

4   *Gestures of the Concrete*

In this chapter and in chapter 6 I will present details about the varieties of gesture: what they look like, how they function, and in general how they are able to express our thoughts. My aim in these two chapters is to demonstrate with numerous examples that gestures and speech are truly integral parts of a single process, with the gesture manifesting the imagery that is inherent in this process at an early stage. (Chapter 5 describes an experiment testing the communicative effects of gestures on listeners.) The present chapter is devoted to gestures that depict concrete objects and events. These are the gestures of the concrete, the ones that we call iconic. Chapter 6 concentrates on gestures of the abstract. By studying gestures of both the concrete and abstract kinds, we can see how speakers represent objects and events in actual and fictive worlds. We will see that speakers reveal in their gestures what they regard as relevant and salient in the context—the "psychological predicate" of which Vygotsky (1962) wrote. At the same time speech may be unable to express fully the shading of relevance and salience that is shown in the gesture, since speech (but not gesture) is constrained by standards of linguistic form, and these standards add their own limits to the speech channel. The first point to establish is that, in performing gestures, the speaker's hands are no longer just hands, but *symbols*.

Gestures Are Symbols

Gestures are not just movements and can never be fully explained in purely kinesic terms. They are not just the arms waving in the air, but *symbols that exhibit meanings* in their own right. They have a meaning that is freely designated by the speaker. The hand can represent a character's hand, the character as a whole, a ball, a streetcar, or anything else; the space likewise can be freely designated—a table top, a street, the side of a building, midair. In other words, the gesture is capable of expressing the full range of meanings that arise from the speaker. Gestures are symbols different from spoken language, however. They are created—in contrast to retrieved—by the speaker at the moment of speaking. They coexist with the words and sentences of speech but are qualitatively different from those words and sentences. They are a separate symbolic vehicle with their own history, and finding their own outlet in space, movement, and form. This coexistence of different *qualities* of symbols—both idio-

105

syncratic and standard—is the fundamental aspect of gestures and speech emerging at the same time from a common core process of meaning presentation.

That gestures are symbols is convincingly demonstrated by comparing the gestures produced by different people when they are describing the same event. The descriptions can be compared because of our method of presenting the same narrative stimulus to all subjects. In the following, five speakers are describing a scene from a cartoon in which one character tries to reach a second character by climbing up the inside of a drainpipe (the sixth speaker did not produce a gesture for this event). The drainpipe conveniently stops at the window ledge where the second character is perched ever so provocatively. The hands are symbols in that they represent something other than themselves: a character rising upward and other specific details, depending on whatever an individual speaker chooses to highlight in the episode. The individually different gesture forms have a common core of meaning, not because of a code or gesture language, but because each speaker separately created her own manual symbol of the event. For each symbol refers to the basic event of upward motion, and yet is unconstrained by standards of well-formedness of the type that hold in linguistic systems.

Speaker 1 (see fig. 4.1):

Figure 4.1. Speaker 1's iconic gesture with "he tries going [up the inside] of the drainpipe." Sylvester is depicted as an undifferentiated blob rising upward. The extended index finger may be an attempt to convey the interiority of the path or simply indicate the destination. The blob hand is not without meaning but highlights no aspect of Sylvester's person (no limbs, etc.).

(4.1) he tries going [up the inside] of the drainpipe

Iconic: hand rises up with the index finger extended, depicting the character rising and possibly the interiority of the pipe.

Speaker 2 (see fig. 4.2 at the top of page 107.)

(4.2) he tries climbing up the [drainspout] of the building

Iconic: hand rises up with first and second fingers wiggling, depicting the character's rising and clambering movements.

Figure 4.2. Speaker 2's iconic gesture with "he tries climbing up the
[drainspout] of the building." This
speaker also shows a blob rising upward and, in addition, she depicts
clambering movements.

Speaker 3 (see fig. 4.3):

Figure 4.3. Speaker 3's iconic gesture with "and he goes [up
THROUGH] the pipe this time." The
gesture shows a differentiated hand
shape depicting the interiority of
the path, combined with upward
movement.

(4.3) and he goes [up THROUGH] the pipe this time
*Iconic: hand rises up in basket-like shape, depicting the character rising up and
the interiority of the pipe.*

Speaker 4 (see fig. 4.4 at the top of page 108.)

(4.4) this time he tries to go up in[side] the rain gutter
Iconic: hand rises with index finger pointing (like speaker 1).

you know [. . .]
Iconic: fist-hand shows barreling.

[barrel]ing up through it
Iconic: fist-hand flexes backward at wrist, showing character rising.

Figure 4.4. Speaker 4's iconic gesture with "you know [...] barreling up through it."
The gesture shows the rotational movement of "barreling."

Speaker 5 (see fig. 4.5):

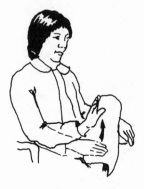

Figure 4.5. Speaker 5's iconic gesture with "he tries [climbing] up
the rain barrel." This is a minimal
gesture for the scene: just ascent
(not even a blob).

(4.5) he tries [climbing] up the rain barrel

Iconic: hand flexes backward, showing the character rising upward.

Although a quantitative comparison of the gestures and speech is not
realistic, there seems to be about as much variation among the linguistic
choices in these examples as among the gestures. The words referring to
the drainpipe include, for example, "drainpipe," "pipe," "drainspout,"
"rain gutter," and "rain barrel." This variation is not obviously less than
the manner of moving the hands upward, pointing or not pointing, in a
basket shape, rotating, or with a backward flexion. Each speaker highlights her own aspects of the situation (this explains much of the varia-

tion) but all retain the core meaning of the character rising upward. Here we have five people, five memories of the same event, and five gestural-verbal descriptions of the event that converge precisely because the hands are performing as symbols. Thus there coexist two linked symbol systems: speech and gesture, products of a single integrated process.

Interpretation of Iconic Gestures

Mind reading

By the title of this section I do not mean anything occult: I mean real mind reading. I mean noticing the gestures with which speakers unwittingly reveal aspects of their inner mental processes and points of view toward events when these are not articulated in speech. In gestures we are able to see the imagistic form of the speaker's sentences. This imagistic form is not usually meant for public view, and the speaker him- or herself may be unaware of it or think that it has been well hidden; but it is visible to those who would look at the gestures.

ICONICS IN A TV DOCUMENTARY. Here is an example of mind reading in which a concrete gesture is the key. I observed this during a BBC film about the Kayapo, a tribe of Indians of the Amazon who have lately come under severe ecological threat. At the time of the film (about 1970) they were still living in their traditional manner. The anthropologist, Terence Turner, was describing the Kayapo mode of life and said, regarding life in the village, that the women don't have a collective focus to their lives. At the same time, he made a gesture in which his hand moved toward his own body. Then he said that the men dominate the political life of the village, and made a gesture in which his hands moved away from his body. These were clearly not self-referring gestures, despite the use of the speaker's own body as a reference point, since they reversed gender roles. The gestures were in fact geographical. They suggest that the speaker was, in his mind, standing at the outer circle of houses in a typical Kayapo village and looking in at the center. Kayapo villages have a circular plan and the houses around the periphery are the exclusive property of the women (see fig. 4.6). At the center is the men's hut, open only to men, which is, in fact, the center of the village political life. Economic power and political power thus are separated and this separation is modeled by the Kayapo themselves in the layout of the village. We get a glimpse into the anthropologist's mind as he spoke. We see a picture of the village with the anthropologist visualizing himself at the outer edge looking in. This

Figure 4.6. Layout of a Kayapo village. The anthropologist imagines
himself on the outer ring where the
women's houses are situated, looking inward to the inner ring where
the men's hut is located.

picture was present even though he was talking about the political life of
the village. He was thinking in terms of the Kayapo's own geographical
metaphor and included himself in it. This image could have been the
primitive form of the sentences whose final forms were about abstract
ideas such as "collective focus" and "political life."

ICONICS IN THE UP-THE-PIPE SCENE. We can perform a similar mind-
reading exercise with other gestures. By looking at the gestures, we can
discover, for each person, what was highlighted, what was relevant and
what not, and from this infer the imagistic side of their utterances. The
five up-the-pipe gestures demonstrate how individual speakers made
their own choices of what was salient. Some of these choices are revealed
in speech but not necessarily all. All five speakers included upward movement and all omitted details of the character's appearance. But each
speaker also emphasized other details that were not emphasized by the
others. Thus, for every speaker we infer that upward movement was salient. For speaker 2 we also infer that clambering was salient; for speaker
3 that interiority was important; for speaker 4 that interiority and manner of movement was important, etc. The following remarks illustrate
how the up-the-pipe gestures can be interpreted.

SPEAKER 1 (see fig. 4.1):
The example was "he tries going [up the inside] of the drainpipe." The
gesture presented a blob hand, upward movement, and an extended forefinger; and each of these features can be interpreted by referring to the
cartoon scene. The upward motion corresponds to the upward trajectory

of the character, the blob corresponds to the character himself, and the extended forefinger corresponds either to the interiority of the path (the character compressed inside the pipe) or to the character's final destination—either way, something connected with the path. We infer that the salient elements of the scene for this speaker were upward movement and something about the path of movement. On the other hand, details about the character's person were unimportant—not even his limbs were hinted at.

SPEAKER 2 (see fig. 4.2):
The example was "he tries climbing up the [drainspout] of the building." Like speaker 1, speaker 2 used a gesture that also presented a blob hand and upward movement, but added wiggling movements of the first and second fingers. The blob was equipped with feet, and we infer that the clambering up the pipe was salient for this speaker, whereas the first speaker had not selected this detail. The speaker, indeed, said "climbing," a verb conveying a clambering manner of movement, while the first had said "going"; thus both speakers' linguistic choices and gestures were coexpressive (as usual, their gestures slightly anticipated the speech in their preparation phases).

SPEAKER 3 (see fig. 4.3):
The example was "and he goes [up THROUGH] the pipe this time." The gesture again presented something moving upward, but in addition strongly emphasized the interiority of the pipe path. This the speaker did with a "basket-hand," made with the palm facing up, the digits extended, separated, and slightly bent; all of this was the hand shape that moved up. The gesture thus included distinct semantic parts: a moving entity, upward movement, and a shape suggesting hollowness. Note that each semantic component was assigned to a different kinesic aspect of the gesture: thus each meaning was symbolized in its own part of the gesture; motion of the entity was conveyed by motion of the hand, direction by direction of the hand, and hollowness by shape of the hand. Yet all three were combined into a single gesture-symbol that presented the elements simultaneously. Such is a synthetic gesture: distinguishable meaning segments brought together into a single symbol-hand. The gesture took the basket form it did because of the immediately preceding gesture by this speaker. It thus shows the influence of previous gestures on later ones. In the cartoon Sylvester makes two attempts to reach Tweety, the first on the outside of the pipe, the second inside. Speaker 3 described the first by

saying: "he crawls [up a pipe]" and simultaneously performed a blob-rising gesture with no additional features for the path, for the manner of movement, or for anything else. Then she went on to describe the event: "and when he gets up to the bird the [grandma hits him] over the head with the umbrella," with a hitting gesture at the bracketed portion. Then she came to our example, "and he goes back and he goes [up THROUGH] the pipe this time," and the basket-shaped gesture. Thus this basket-shaped gesture highlighted exactly what was distinctive about the second ascent: that its path was inside the pipe in contrast to the previous path on the outside. It is true that the first ascent had "exteriority" just as much as the second had "interiority," but at the moment of the first ascent there was nothing noteworthy about the path; the ascent itself was the novelty. These gesture depictions thus spotlight the scene in a way that we can plausibly take to be how the speaker herself was thinking of it, that is, in terms of what is novel and contrastive. The speaker's mind was moving forward on a stream of contrasts and in her gestures we see this process externalized.

SPEAKER 4 (see fig. 4.4):

The example was "this time he tries to up in[side] the rain gutter, you know [. . .] [barrel]ing up through it." The first gesture depicted an undifferentiated blob moving up. The second depicted a rotational movement, coexpressive with (and anticipating) the verb "barreling" in speech. The third gesture depicted an undifferentiated blob moving up and anticipated the rest of the verb phrase, "up through it." Note that the rotational movement, like the clambering movement in the second speaker's gesture, is an inference: in the cartoon itself the character is invisible inside the pipe (see the Appendix for a line-by-line description of the cartoon). Nonetheless, the speaker inferred the manner of movement, and this inference appeared in the gesture.

SPEAKER 5 (see fig. 4.5):

The example was "he tries [climbing] up the rain barrel." The gesture depicted upward movement of an undifferentiated blob, but the speaker's thumb was tucked into her palm as her hand flexed upward, and this could have conveyed interiority; thus the gesture may have supplemented speech, which did not mention that Sylvester was inside the pipe. At the same time, however, there was nothing in the gesture to convey the manner in which Sylvester was moving and so the verb, "climb," included more information than the gesture. This example thus is unusual in that it illustrates speech supplementing gesture as well as gesture supplementing speech. If the primitive version of the sentence was an image of clambering up the inside of the pipe, we have a case where some parts of this image were manifested in speech and others in gesture.

POINTING IN A CONVERSATION. Mind reading is also possible in non-narrative discourse. In the example of this section it is a conversation in which a speaker unwittingly reveals something that he was attempting to conceal. Pointing is really a form of abstract gesture (see chap. 6), but I include it here among the gestures of the concrete as another example of mind reading. I used this conversation in chapter 1 to illustrate deictic gestures, and now we see more of it. The participants were previously unacquainted male graduate students at the University of Chicago. The tape was made as part of a research project on face-to-face interaction by Starkey Duncan (Duncan and Fiske 1977). The two students were simply brought together before a video camera and told to have a conversation. This command typically elicits a series of maneuvers during which the participants try to find a common theme about which they can talk. The example we are considering is from this introductory phase; it ends with the participants' discovering a workable theme, but only after a cat-and-mouse game that is the substance of my example. In conversations no less than narrations the predominant gesture is pointing when a new theme is sought (this is explained in chap. 7). So it was here. One of the participants, H, was trying to find something that could serve as a topic of conversation. In the way of students he asked where the other student, O, had gone to school before. O, however, somewhat mysteriously held back; he did not wish to reveal certain details. In particular, he was avoiding the question of where he had been an undergraduate. His unexpected resistance led to the cat-and-mouse game over this issue. The excerpt begins with two questions by H (see figs. 4.7 and 4.8):

(4.6) H: is this your first year [here]?
Points down to own space.

Figure 4.7. Pointing at the speaker's own space with the question "is this your first year [here]?" The space is for "here," a word used here both for space (the university) and time (one's time at the university). (Also see figs. 4.8–4.11.)

(4.8) H: or [where did you] come from before?
Points into shared interaction space and finger circles.

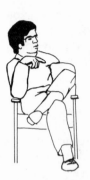

Figure 4.8. Pointing at the shared
space with "or [where did you]
come from before?" Compare the
finger angle to that in fig. 4.7. The
speaker is now setting up a contrasting space for "before," drawing
on the temporal sense of the "here"
in the previous question.

The first pointing gesture in (4.6) marks as "here" the space where H is
located. This "here" clearly means the University of Chicago, where the
experiment was being conducted and where both H and O were students. The second gesture in (4.7) contrasts this "here" with the space it
introduces, the space of "before." The new space was the neutral interaction space shared by H and O (viz., the space where their respective gazes
intersected, H and O being seated at an angle). This use of the neutral
space for "where did you come from before?" fits H's desire to find a
shared topic of conversation. O, however, answers noncommittally:

(4.9) O: um Iowa. I lived in Iowa

The conversation next veered off into a brief exploration of Iowa as a possible topic. However, that eventually petered out and H returned to pro-
bing O's past (see fig. 4.9):

(4.9) H: did you [go to] school [there] or uh?
Points both times into the shared interaction space.

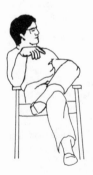

Figure 4.9. Pointing at the shared
space with "did you [go to] school
[there] or uh?" This gesture is consistent with the space in fig. 4.8 and
contrasts with the space in fig. 4.7,
now drawing out the spatial sense
of "here."

Thus H is consistently using the shared space for the meaning "where you came from before." O answers (see fig. 4.10):

(4.10) O: I did go to school [there]
*Points to **upper** level of shared interaction space.*

Figure 4.10. The second speaker pointing at upper layer of shared space with "I did go to school [there]." The speaker uses the shared space, but introduces an upper story. This enables him to differentiate his "there" from the first speaker's dangerous "there."

O uses the shared space, but incorporates a revealing variation. He pointed at a space slightly above the shared space, as if to signal that while his "there" was indeed "where he came from before," it was outside the space that H had marked off as a topic of conversation. This clue is elaborated on in O's next gesture (see fig. 4.11):

(4.11) O: [I went to school] here also
*Points to left periphery (i.e., **away from** H).*

Figure 4.11. The second speaker now pointing outside of shared space altogether. This gesture immediately followed the one in fig. 4.10 and occurred with "[I went to school] here also." The speaker unwittingly maps the contrast between the city of Chicago and the University of Chicago onto space as a center space–left space contrast.

Clearly, this "here" is not the same as H's "here." Indeed, it is as far removed from H's "here" as possible. I do not believe that O was aware of tipping his hand (so to speak), but his gesture reveals that he had dichotomized the space differently from H: the *left* side was to be his "here" and this excluded the "here" of H, which was the University of Chicago.

It apparently arose from an image in his mind that assigned different spaces to the place where he had gone to school (another university in the city of Chicago) and the University of Chicago. Through the gesture we can read his mind to find a meaning which, at this moment, he was attempting to conceal. The drama had a happy ending: shortly after this crucial moment O capitulated and revealed that he had been a student at a Jesuit college; it then marvelously turned out that H also had been a student at another Jesuit college; so they talked about Jesuit education—a topic on which, ironically, O turned out to be the more enthusiastic participant!

The ability to mind read with gestures rests on the close connections of gesture and speech as expressions of meaning, coupled with the potential for gesture to display what is most relevant. That is, the two—speech and gesture—cover the same idea unit in the formation of an utterance, but become distinct in terms of relevance, and this is where the gesture channel can reveal what the speaker thinks is hidden.

Expression of Meaning in Gesture

In this section, I will analyze some of the ways in which gestures express meaning. The focus is semantic. The use of gestures to express pragmatic discourse content has a chapter of its own (chap. 7).

FEATURAL IDENTITY. To compare gestures to speech, Elena Levy and I analyzed each gesture into kinesic features that could be compared to the semantic features of the verbs in the accompanying speech (McNeill and Levy 1982). We defined altogether 44 kinesic features, such as, for example, Fingers Curled or Extended; Index Finger Extended; Palm Down, Up, Right, Left, Toward Self; motion Up, Down, Sideways (left or right), and so forth. This method was the distant ancestor to the current method of gesture transcription summarized in chapter 3. For verbs, we devised a set of 37 semantic features inspired by the semantic analysis methods of Miller and Johnson-Laird (1976). Our list included, for example, Entrance/Exit ("he swallows the bowling ball"); Downward ("he comes down the pipe"); Horizontal ("he runs ahead of it"); and End-State ("it catches up to him" and "he swallows the bowling ball" again). We intended the meaning features to capture the meanings of the verbs in the specific senses in which the narrators used them in the narratives.

There is no necessary reason why the two sets of features, kinesic and semantic, should correspond in any given gesture-speech combination. There is nothing built into the coding method that would force a Downward verb to appear only with a Downward gesture, for example; it could just as well go with an Upward gesture or have no kinesic preference. In fact, however, we found a very good correspondence between the two arrays of features. For example, we found that 54% of verbs with the Downward meaning feature co-occurred with gestures in which there was Downward movement; 0% co-occurred with gestures in which there was Upward movement; 73% of verbs with the Horizontal meaning feature occurred with gestures that included a Left-Right movement feature, compared to only 8% of gestures that moved Downward and 17% that went Upward.

The Downward meaning feature not only went with Downward movements, but also with Curled Fingers more than 60% of the time. Curled Fingers seem to depict passive movement, such as falling under the influence of gravity. The Downward meaning feature did not appear with the contrary feature of Extended Fingers, nor with Both Hands Moving in the Same Direction, nor with Reduplicated arm movements suggesting running. This total pattern of positive and negative associations with Downward suggests a coherent picture in which there is falling, falling under the influence of gravity, only one object moving, and motion other than locomotion. Such a gesture occurred repeatedly in the cartoon narrations. It exhibits a prototypical situation in the cartoon story. The character was constantly falling from great heights, falling alone and involuntarily, definitely not moving in a way he would have been had he been locomoting on his own. The aggregate gesture profile that emerges from the correlations with Downward thus presents a picture that is typical of the cartoon narrative and conveys much more than a single verb could have done. So, even at the featural level, we can see a global picture emerging out of the gestural description.

USE OF TWO HANDS. Many gestures are performed with just a single hand. However, a significant number use two hands, and among the two-handed gestures there are two kinds. In some gestures the hands move in the same pattern but in mirror images. Such gestures do not seem to differ semantically or functionally from their one-handed counterparts. In other two-handed gestures, however, the two hands perform different movements. For example, one hand depicts a character's open mouth while the other hand depicts the bowling ball going inside (see fig. 4.12, for example, which also is line 33 of the narrative in chap. 3). The hands, considered separately, perform different movements but, jointly, create a scene in which there is a single event—the cat swallowing the bowling ball. This is a typical case of a gesture with two differentiated

Figure 4.12. Two-handed gesture for the accomplishment meaning of "[he swallows it]." The left hand enters the space formed by the hollowed out right hand, and this is an accomplishment in Vendler's (1967) sense.

hands. In one hand there is a motionless reference point: e.g., the hand for Sylvester's mouth. In the other hand, active motion: the bowling ball going into his mouth. A similar distinction appears in many ASL signs between a static reference point and an active transformation (Klima and Bellugi 1979). The verbs that went with these gestures, moreover, conveyed what Vendler (1967) termed accomplishments: "they proceed toward a terminus which is logically necessary to their being what they are" (101). Compare chasing and catching up to—the latter is an accomplishment. Two-handed gestures and their verbs thus also illustrate the integration of speech and gesture at the level of meaning. End-State verbs were accompanied with two coordinated hands 68% of the time, and Entrance/Exit verbs 90% of the time. (Verbs lacking the End-State or Entrance/Exit features went with two-handed gestures 40% of the time.) End-State and Entrance/Exit imply actions that reach a goal. This is the "accomplishment" referred to by Vendler. For example, "to swallow" means that something was not merely moving toward the appropriate aperture but that it enters it and goes inside irretrievably; otherwise one has not swallowed. "To catch up to" similarly requires not only movement toward a target but that a certain end state be reached, namely, that the target be reached; otherwise one has not caught up to but just chased. Thus the kinesic form of the gestures co-occurring with these kinds of verbs reflected the logical element of accomplishment. The speech and gesture forms were integrated around the theme of reaching a logical end point.

EXPRESSING THE VIEWPOINT. Another area of meaning where speech and gesture are coexpressive is the point of view, or the feeling of distance from the narrative. Consider the event in the cartoon story where Sylvester climbs up the pipe. This could be conveyed gesturally in either of two ways. One would be to move one's arms up and down, as if climbing a ladder. Here, the viewpoint would be the character's: we imagine ourselves playing the part of Sylvester—the pipe is in front of us and we move our hands up and down as if clambering. Such a gesture has a Character Viewpoint, or C-VPT. With this viewpoint we feel that the narrator is inside the story. A different gesture for the same event would be to make the hand into Sylvester as a whole and cause it to rise upward. We see Sylvester before us, rising upward, but we are not part of the scene. This gesture will be said to have an Observer Viewpoint, or O-VPT. With this viewpoint, the narrator keeps some distance from the story. We have in the viewpoint distinction one of the most readily identified aspects of iconic gestures (Stephens and Tuite 1983 referred to this distinction as iconic$_1$ and iconic$_2$, respectively). A C-VPT incorporates the speaker's body into the gesture space, and the speaker's hands represent the hands (paws, etc.) of the character. Previous C-VPT examples in this book have included the gesture that accompanied "and he bends it way back." The speaker was seeing the event as if he were the person performing the act, rather than taking the viewpoint of an observer of the event. An O-VPT gesture excludes the speaker's body from the gesture space and his hands play the part of the character as a whole. Most of the earlier examples in this book have been of the O-VPT variety (e.g., figs. 4.1–4.5). Overall, in cartoon narratives, 60% of iconics have an O-VPT, 40% a C-VPT (Church et al. 1989).

VERBAL MANIFESTATION OF VIEWPOINT. There are also linguistic manifestations of viewpoint. The C-VPT tends to appear with transitive verbs and single clause sentences; the O-VPT with intransitive or stative verbs and multi-clause sentences. Church and her colleagues (1989) counted 80% of C-VPT event descriptions with transitive verbs and 100% of O-VPT event descriptions with intransitive verbs. In the narrative in chapter 3, 29% of C-VPT gestures were accompanied by multi-clause sentences, compared to 76% of the O-VPT gestures (overall in that narrative 53% of sentences were multi-clause and 47% were single clause). In all of these cases, then, the viewpoint parameter can be incorporated into the utterance's linguistic form. However, this is not at all obvious until the gestural manifestation draws our attention to it.

The viewpoint of the gesture and the form of the sentence achieve equivalent results in terms of distance. In the C-VPT narrators become participants and insert themselves into the gesture space. In the linguistic parallel there is a single clause and a transitive verb. The "he bends it way back" sentence, with its transitive verb and single clause, was thus a typical C-VPT example. Another typical C-VPT illustration is "and drops it [down] the drainpipe." In the gesture the hand appeared to grasp the bowling ball and shove it down the pipe—the viewpoint of the character—and the sentence was again a single clause with a transitive verb. With a single clause there is minimal grammatical separation of the event from the speaker, just as in the gesture the speaker enters directly into an enactment of the story. With a transitive verb the effect on distance is that there is analysis of the event as if under magnification—the role of the character is separated out from the rest of the event. Thus the form of the sentence, along with the gesture, expresses proximity to the story line.

The O-VPT correspondingly appears with complex sentences (multiple clauses) as well as intransitive or stative verbs. A complex sentence, in its own configuration, interposes distance from the action. An example is "he tries [climbing] up the side of the building," where the act of climbing is presented in the embedded clause and the upper clause ("he tries") implies an outside observer of the story who makes the judgment that Sylvester does not succeed. (Trying is an evaluation, not a description; it means trying without success.) In most of the O-VPT examples that we have seen, there is some such implicit distance interposed by the linguistic form of the utterance through the embedding of the action. In (4.12), for instance, the sentence is "he tries going up the inside of the drainpipe," and this was accompanied by an O-VPT gesture. The two clauses of the sentence have different relationships to the story structure. The upper one ("he tries") states an attitude that implies a judgment (the character isn't going to succeed), and this judgment implies narrative distance. The lower clause ("going up the inside of the drainpipe") refers to the actual event in the cartoon. Sometimes the O-VPT is not expressed syntactically in this way, but still there is the speech-gesture coexpression of distance. For example, "and then [you hear a s]trike" (line 38 of the narrative reproduced in chapter 3) was accompanied by an O-VPT gesture even though it is a single clause. But the pronoun "you" in this case codes the distance implied by the O-VPT. It is the general "you" of an unspecified observer.

VIEWPOINT AND EVENT STRUCTURE. The shifts between C-VPT and O-VPT are not at all random; they reflect the causal texture of the episode. More central events in this causal texture are given the C-VPT, while more peripheral ones are given the O-VPT. Statistical confirmation of this difference in centrality and peripherality is contained in the table below from Church and colleagues (1989), which is based on an analysis of three cartoon narrations. They used story grammar categories (Stein

Table 4.1 Gesture Viewpoint and Story Centrality

Event Type	Percentage of Events of Each Type			Number of Events
	C-VPT	O-VPT	Uncodable	
Central	71	24	5	66
Peripheral	6	93	1	72

and Glenn 1979) to classify events as Central or Peripheral. Central meant either (1) initiation of goal actions, (2) main goal actions, or (3) outcomes of goal actions; and Peripheral meant (4) setting statements, (5) subordinate actions, or (6) responses to actions and outcomes (Stein and Glenn had a seventh category—describing the goal—but this was never depicted in gestures and was rarely described in speech). Using these definitions the two gesture viewpoints can be seen to appear in quite different contexts (table 4.1). Seventy-one percent of C-VPT gestures appeared with Central events, and fully 93% of O-VPT gestures with Peripheral events. The examples in (4.12–4.15), successive lines in one speaker's narration, illustrate this association.

(4.12) he tries going [up the inside] of the drainpipe

O-VPT iconic: right blob hand rises up to show character rising up the pipe.

(4.13) and Tweety Bird runs and gets a bowling ball and drops it [down] the drain pipe

C-VPT iconic: both hands appear to shove ball down into open pipe.

(4.14) and [as he's com]ing up and the [bowl]ing ball's coming down

        (1)   (2)

he [sw]allows it and

    (3)

All O-VPT iconics:

(1) right blob hand rises up for ascending character.
(2) left blob hand moves down for descending ball, both into central space.
(3) right blob hand changes shape to form an opening for character's open mouth and left blob hand passes into it.

(4.15) he [comes out the bot]tom of the drainpipe

      (1)

and he's [got this] big bowling ball inside him

    (2)

(1) O-VPT iconic: left blob hand moves down and curves under right flat hand to right side of space (character with the bowling ball inside leaving the pipe).
(2) C-VPT iconic: both hands press bowling ball into own stomach.

The C-VPT and near distance exclusively appeared with the important events in this sequence of cause and effect: the first character's dropping the bowling ball down the pipe (initiation of the action) and the second character's ending up with it inside him (the outcome). These are the main points of the scene. The intervening events supported them but were not the main points, and they all got O-VPT gestures and far distance. All the gestures were iconics and all the clauses were at the narrative level, but the events and the clauses were not equal in terms of their importance for advancing the story line. The difference in centrality motivated the changes of distance, which were depicted in the gesture viewpoint.

VIEWPOINT AND COHESIVENESS. This link up of viewpoint with event centrality or peripherality can be explained as arising from how the narrator keeps up a sense of cohesion in the narrative. Cohesion is automatically produced with central events: each event has its place in the causal sequence of the story and cannot be moved without altering the story. If the speaker is thinking of event G this is automatically cohesive with the other causal events F, H, and so forth. No extra viewpoint is needed to introduce and refer to the chain. When the event is more peripheral, however, this definite location in a chain may be lacking. A peripheral event is precisely one not on the main causal sequence; it is supportive of but not part of the central thread. Thus a secondary chain of comments comes into being to carry its own cohesion and that of the peripheral events. This added chain interposes distance from the story line events. Thus an observer viewpoint appears. This observer, among other tasks, is asked to provide the cohesion that cannot be generated by the peripheral events on their own. In short, one way of explaining table 4.1 is by the need for cohesive consistency: this cohesion is not automatic with peripheral events, and that induces an observer's point of view and distance.

DUAL VIEWPOINTS AND THE IRONIC. The gestures we have seen thus far have had a single viewpoint. This is true even of two-handed gestures, such as "he [swallows it]." However, there also are *dual viewpoint* gestures. These present a scene simultaneously from two viewpoints, for example, a C-VPT and an O-VPT. In cartoon narratives, at least, dual C-/O-VPTs tend to produce an ironic effect, by pitting one viewpoint against the other. This contrast requires, not a *shift* of viewpoint, but a *contrast* of viewpoints. In the example below, an observer is added to a C-VPT gesture at the very moment when Sylvester is presented as if he had captured Tweety, but the observer (the narrator) knows that this moment was in fact a prelude to disaster. The dual viewpoint of the gesture enables the narrator simultaneously to take Sylvester's role and to observe it. Sylvester has used a five-hundred-pound weight to catapult himself up to the window where Tweety is perched:

(4.16) and he [grabs] Tweety Bird
Iconic: grip handshape (a C-VPT).

and as he [. . . comes back] down he [lands on the ground]
Dual VPT iconic: a grip handshape in a downward trajectory (a C-VPT depicting the character gripping the other character, and an O-VPT depicting falling down to the ground). The gesture is then repeated on a smaller scale.

and he [starts running] away and at this time the five-hundred-pound
Dual VPT iconic: grip handshape moves to right.

weight comes down [and lands] on him
Dual VPT iconic: other hand falls on grip hand.

(See fig. 4.13). The downward trajectory is not the movement of the character's hand qua hand but movement of the whole assembly of the two characters plunging to the ground as seen from the outside. The viewpoints are kept separate since each viewpoint has its own kinesic fea-

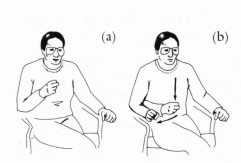

(a)　　(b)

Figure 4.13. A dual viewpoint in two panels. Panel (a) is a single viewpoint (C-VPT) gesture for grabbing with "[he grabs Tweety Bird as he]" and (b) is a dual C-VPT/O-VPT gesture with "[. . . comes back] down." Note that the hand remains in the grip that implies the C-VPT while it descends, which implies a trajectory from the O-VPT. There is an ironic comparison between the observer's view—who knows the upcoming denouement—and the character's—who thinks he has the bird at last.

ture(s) in the gesture, and these are nonoverlapping. The O-VPT had the trajectory in this example and the C-VPT had the handshape. Although there are two viewpoints and just a single hand, the gesture does not mix them up.

Confirmation of the irony implicit in the dual viewpoint gesture was the next step in the speaker's narration. She kept up the dual viewpoint while showing the character run off with the bird and then have the weight fall on him. Having two viewpoints was crucial to showing the character's grip on his (assumed) prize versus the reality of the weight falling on him. The narrator had set all of this up in the first dual viewpoint gesture above. Here we find the gesture channel carrying most of the meaning, for none of these ironic contrasts appears in speech. (This example appears in chapter 3 in the narrative, lines 47–52.)

Another type of dual viewpoint combines the C-VPTs of different characters. Such combinations appear when the speech of one character is quoted. The accompanying example is from the work of Evelyn McClave of Georgetown University (McClave, 1991; see fig. 4.14):

Figure 4.14. A dual C-VPT with "[you] had your doctor go over to check out that person's claim" (McClave, 1991). Two character's viewpoints are represented, one that of the student himself (using his own body) and the other that of his examiner (the pointing hand). A child's dual C-VPT gesture is shown in fig. 11.16.

(4.17) [you] had your doctor go over to check out that person's claim
Dual VPT deictic: hand points to own body.

This is being presented as a direct quote. The speaker, a student, was describing to another student a take-home final exam that he had just written, and was quoting the problem he had been given (in a course in the philosophy of law). Despite the use of the second person pronoun "you," the gesture pointed at the speaker himself; but this is part of the quote. Thus one C-VPT is that of the examiner who says the sentence in (4.17) and points at the trembling examinee; the other C-VPT is that of the speaker himself who is in the role of this examinee. The use of a deictic gesture appears particularly apt in this context. It sets up a consistent use of space where both characters have a locus and provides a diagram of the interpersonal communication that is taking place. So far as I am aware dual C-VPTs are restricted to this context: the gestures are deictics at the speaker himself and the accompanying speech is a direct quote that is addressed to the speaker. We will see in chapter 11 that the dual C-VPTs of children are different in all these respects.

Dual voices were a key concept in Bakhtin's (1981) notion of the dialogic imagination, or hybrid construction, where, for example, "the subordinate clause is in direct authorial speech and the main clause is someone else's speech" (306). Two voices in a gesture present a very similar situation. In the gesture two voices are "heard," or rather seen. As in Bakhtin's analysis, the dual viewpoint enables the narrator to present "two narratives, two styles, two 'languages,' two semantic and axiological belief systems at once" (304).

RELEVANCE. Another manifestation of gesture-speech integration appears when we compare gestures on the dimension of internal complexity. This dimension gives us insight into what is important, relevant, or salient to the speaker in the specific context of the story, and is the basis of the mind reading examples earlier in the chapter. Some gestures are simple: the hand flexed back for Sylvester rising up the pipe. Others are more complex: the bends-it-way-back gesture, for example, had at least these differentiated parts: the character's hand, the character's body, the relationship of the hand to the body, the shape of the hand, the trajectory the hand followed, the shape of the tree, etc. (see fig. 1.1). In between are other iconics, such as the basket hand rising for Sylvester's ascending through the pipe.

At the simplest level, a gesture depicts just a moving blob with only direction as the highlighted feature; this was speaker 5's gesture (see fig. 4.5); it receives a score of 0 on the scale described below:

(4.18) (the same as 4.5)

he tries [climbing] up the rain barrel

Iconic: hand flexes backward, showing the character rising upward.

At a slightly more complex level, the blob can be provided with little feet:

(4.19)

he tries climbing up the [drainspout] of the building

Iconic: hand rises up with first and second fingers wiggling, depicting the character rising and clambering movements.

Also more complex, there can be a differentiated handshape that is combined with the movement (speaker 3, see fig. 4.3):

(4.20) (the same as 4.3)

and he goes [up THROUGH] the pipe this time

Iconic: hand rises up in basket-like shape, depicting the character rising up and the interiority of the pipe.

Finally there is the use of two hands to convey the End-State or accomplishment feature (see fig. 4.12):

(4.21)

and . . . as he's coming up and the bowling ball's coming down
[he swallows it]

Iconic: one hand forms open space for a mouth, and the other hand passes into this space for the bowling ball.

Thus iconics cover a range of complexity. A method for partially quantifying gesture complexity has been devised by Kita (1990). He measured the elaboration of a gesture by adding one point for each of the following:

use of two arms (4.21)
movement of the fingers (4.19)
change of hand shape during the stroke (4.20 and 4.21)
other than a fist or open hand shape (4.20 and 4.21)
other than rest position (4.19, 4.20, and 4.21)

The swallows gesture, for example, involved two arms, a change of hand shape (opening up), a marked shape, and space other than rest; it thus earns a score of 4. The climbing gesture involved only movement of the hand (not even a departure from rest), and earned a score of 0.

This variation in the complexity of iconics suggests a way of determining what is salient or relevant to the speaker. Moreover, we find not only what is relevant, but the moment it becomes relevant. Adding a feature to a gesture implies a relevant detail. The exact moment the feature is added reveals when it is relevant. In example 4.21 (fig. 4.12) the gesture implies that Sylvester's open mouth was relevant. The immediately preceding gesture (not shown) was made with the hands in the same position but with the right hand, rather than being an open space, being a rising blob. The rising blob was Sylvester, and the later open space was his mouth. When his mouth became relevant the hand shape changed. Salience is also important for interpreting the speech. The same linguistic choices have different implications depending on the gesture features that appear with them. In both (4.18) and (4.19) speech included the verb "climbs," but the gestures suggest that different features of the situation were relevant to the two speakers. The simple upward gesture in (4.18) suggests that the manner of moving was not relevant to this speaker, while the gesture with wiggling fingers in (4.19) showed that manner as well as movement were relevant to that speaker. For the speaker in (4.18), the important detail seems to have been the upward trajectory, not otherwise particularized, and "climbs" was used but its implication of a manner was not salient.

Relevance is convincingly displayed in gesture form when we find *sequences* of gestures in which the second gesture contrasts with the first on precisely the dimension that is relevant. Example (4.20), "he goes up THROUGH the pipe," is an illustration of this. The speaker was describing Sylvester's second attempt to climb the pipe; it was on the inside of the pipe, the first attempt having been on the outside. Example (4.20) thus supplied exactly the new factor: that the second attempt was on the inside of the pipe. The prosodic emphasis on "through" likewise highlighted interiority, and gesture and speech were coexpressive. Examining all the narrations of the cartoon, we can see that gestures highlight interiority only if they have been preceded by other gestures depicting the exterior scene. That is, the gestural feature of interiority appears only if it contrasts with an earlier gesture. Two speakers who omitted mention of the first attempt are represented in examples (4.2) and (4.5); neither emphasized interiority in their gestures for Sylvester's second attempt despite the fact that the path was on the inside. In (4.2) the speaker included clambering but no hint of interiority; in (4.5) there was pure ascent and, again, no interiority. The other speakers described both attempts and their gestures for the second ascent did, in every instance, highlight interiority of the path (examples 4.1, 4.3, and 4.4). (No speaker ever mentioned the first attempt and omitted the second.) Sequences of gestures thus demonstrate structuring in accord with a sense of what is relevant, that is, salient, in the momentary context.

The most important implication of the linkage of gestures to the salient and the relevant is that gestures can be used as a tool to infer the speaker's *psychological predicate* at the moment of speaking. In Vygotsky's (1962) use of this term, a psychological predicate (as distinguished from a grammatical predicate, which is not the same thing) is the novel, discontinuous, unpredictable component of the current thought. Thought itself, Vygotsky argued, is the formation of contrasts from the preceding context, and this is the generation of psychological predicates. Consider coming up with the next utterance of a discourse. The gesture singles out what, to the speaker, are the utterance's least predictable, most discontinuous components. The crucial property that identifies gestures with psychological predicates is discontinuity from the ongoing context. Thus, we can infer that the speaker in (4.18) had a psychological predicate that represented only upward movement, while the speaker in (4.19) had one that represented this movement plus the manner of moving. In chapter 9 I will make extensive use of gestures for inferring psychological predicates.

Often, indeed, the gesture appears to be more capable than speech at showing shadings of relevance. I believe there is a good reason for this, which arises from the contrasting natures of gestures and speech. In speech there are obligatory elements, but gestures, precisely because they are idiosyncratic and not subject to a system of standards, are able to select only what is relevant or salient. This disparity between speech and gesture is evident when a complex sentence appears with a simple gesture. In terms of its linguistic structure, "he tries [climbing] up the rain barrel" is more complex than "[he swallows it]," but the first sentence was accompanied by a simpler gesture. In this way, we may *require* the gesture to know what was relevant in the context. This conclusion would apply to efforts to analyze relevance based purely on logical grounds (cf. Sperber and Wilson 1987, which limits the discussion of relevance to verbal contexts).

NEW MEANINGS. Finally, at the most extreme level of the gesture's contribution to meaning, we have gestures that create new meanings. It is possible for gestures to convey aspects of meaning that, in speech, cannot be expressed at all except through elaborate paraphrases. This is not paradoxical if such meanings are part of the initial "growth point" of the utterance (see chap. 8). They can be conveyed over the gestural channel, even if they are lost from the verbal one. In this section I show how gestures can bring out meanings that are quite inaccessible to the linguistic code (they have low "codability"; Brown and Lenneberg 1954). Certain actions, for example, can be referred to linguistically only by means of elaborate paraphrases, but they can be depicted visually in a single gesture. For example, in the following, a long pointed object is shown approaching and contacting a flat horizontal object from below. A linguistic construction can be found that roughly describes this situation (the preceding sentence, for example), but no single verb describes it. A gesture however does convey this action (see figure 4.15):

Figure 4.15. A single gesture with "and he steps on the part [wh]ere [the] [str]eet [car's] connecting." This gesture fuses movement with the shape of the thing in motion (resembling the Atsugewi pattern). The flat hand is the bottom of Sylvester's foot as it bounced up and down repeatedly on the upraised forefinger of the other hand, which is the trolley connector.

(4.22) and he steps on the part [wh]ere [the] / [str]eet [car's] connecting
Iconic: shows flat sole of character's foot stepping on streetcar electrical connector (flat open palm of left hand contacts upward extended index finger of right hand several times).

This gesture fills a logical gap in the English lexicon. It covers the situation in which there is the movement of *a particular shape* of thing: "a flat surface coming down on a pointed object." Verbs of English typically either convey the manner of movement or the cause of movement (for example, "hop" vs. "stride" for different manners; or "the napkin blew off the table" for the implication that moving air was the cause). English has a few verbs where the shape of the moving thing is included in the meaning—for example, "drip" (only something in a droplet shape can be said to drip) and a few others of scatological character—but the vast majority of English verbs tend in the two other directions. Leonard Talmy (1985), from whom this analysis and the verbal examples come, contrasted the situation of the English verbs to another language in which the shapes of moving objects are encoded directly. This is Atsugewi, an American Indian language spoken in Northern California. While Atsugewi does not code the specific motion-shape combination in the example, it does categorize actions by the shapes of the entities in motion, and has different words for distinct motion-shape categories. The above gesture combines shape with motion in the Atsugewi style and extends the coding capabilities of English at a place where the language lacks a linguistic category. To see the speaker's mental representation we must take into account the concurrent gesture and its potential for creating meanings.

ON BEING OF TWO MINDS. Thus far, one meaning divides between two channels. A more extreme case is when a speaker has two *distinct* meanings, yet expresses only one through speech, presenting the other through gesture. Such a phenomenon has been observed with children by Church and Goldin-Meadow (1986) in what they call speech-gesture discordance. Discordance is seen in tests with Piagetian conservation problems, for example, and in solving arithmetic problems. In a Piagetian test (Piaget, [1941] 1965), a subject is presented with two jars of water and watches as one of the jars is poured into a low flat dish while the other jar is left as it is, and is asked which has more—the dish, the jar that was not poured, or do they have the same? The answer, from adults and other children, often delivered in incredulous tones, is that, obviously, the jar and dish have the same amount of water (you just poured it). Preschool children, however, might say that the dish has more water in it, or that the unpoured jar has more, citing the greater expanse of water in the dish or the greater height in the jar. Church and Goldin-Meadow also observed the child's gestures during these tests and found that, in some children, the gestures were discordant. For example a child might say that the dish has more water because it is wider (focusing on the expanse) but, at the same time, make a gesture that depicts the water level being lower (holding the thumb and forefinger close together). Relating height and width is the key for understanding that the amount of water is conserved after it is poured. A discordant child thus seems to have the two halves of this relationship but does not combine them. Rather, one half emerges in speech, and the other in gesture. Concordant nonconserving children, in contrast, have in mind only one dimension (say, width) and perform a gesture that emphasized only it.

Discordant nonconserving children appear to be at a transitional stage of their intellectual development, partway toward achieving conservation. Concordant nonconserving children, on the other hand, are at an earlier stage, not yet having begun the transition. In keeping with this possibility, Church and Goldin-Meadow found that discordant children are much more likely to become conservers after a brief lesson that emphasizes the reciprocal relationship of height and width in pouring water from the jar to the dish. If two nonconserving children are identified by the usual verbal criteria and each receives such a lesson, the one who initially showed discordant gestures is much more likely to become a conserver.

Not only are discordant children more likely to learn from instruction, but an ingenious experiment shows that they do have more on their minds as they solve intellectual problems (Goldin-Meadow, Nusbaum, and Garber, 1991). The children (of school-age in this experiment) were asked to remember short lists of words while they worked on arithmetic problems. The words had no bearing on the problems, they just had to be recalled. A different set of words was assigned with each problem. Arithmetic problems such as "$7 + 5 =$ _____ $+ 5$" (fill in the blank) are usually accompanied by gestures as children talk about them. Again, concordant and discordant gestures can be identified (for example, adding the numbers on the left side of the equation, to get 12 for an answer, might be accompanied by pointing at the 7, the 5 on the left, the 5 on the right, and finally the blank, indicating all positions). The logic of the experiment is that the number of words the child remembers depends on how much spare cognitive "room" the child has while working on the arithmetic problem. The discordant and concordant children had the same number of right and wrong answers, but the discordant children remembered fewer words: they had less cognitive room. They indeed seemed to have more on their minds, and this is what was evident in their gestures.

Anticipation of Meaning by Gesture

A point of interest is where, in the flow of speech, the gesture preparation phase begins. The stroke is integrated into the speech stream in accordance with the phonological synchrony rule: the stroke is timed to end at or before, but not after, the prosodic stress peak of the accompanying spoken utterance (see chap. 1). The preparation phase, in contrast, might appear in a wide variety of speech environments. Table 4.2 shows the variety of utterance positions. This variety, of course, makes sense. The preparation phase, in contrast to the stroke phase, should *not* be associated with specific surface utterance features. At the start of the preparation, any coexpressive concurrent speech has not yet been produced. Eighty-three percent of preparation phases coincide with some grammatical constituent of the same clause that contains the stroke; thus the whole gesture takes place within a single clause. However, there is no special place in this clause where this preparation phase starts. Twenty-one percent start with a discourse marker (Schiffrin 1987) which makes an explicit reference to the discourse, 17% have preparations that occur in nongrammatical locales: pauses, middle of words, or the preceding clause (the bends-it-way-back gesture had such a preparation), and the rest are scattered among various grammatical constituents or single words. In sum, the preparation phase occurs on its own schedule. In contrast, the stroke phase is integrated into the utterance itself, as defined by the synchrony rules presented in chapter 1. The preparations that coincide with discourse markers suggest that the primitive forms of utterances include attempts to establish cohesiveness with previous speech: this is simultaneous with beginning to construct the utterance to come next.

Table 4.2 Speech Segments at Start of Gesture Preparation Phase

Type of Segment	Percentage of Gestures
Grammatical Segments	
Start of Clause	19
Start of Noun Phrase	10
Start of Preposition Phrase	7
Start of Verb Phrase	14
Single Word[a]	12
Discourse Marker[b]	21
Total Grammatical Segments	83
Nongrammatical Segments	
Pauses	9
Middle of Words	2
Previous Clauses	6
Total Nongrammatical Segments	17

[a]A "single word" means any word within a phrase that is not itself a phrase.

[b]A "discourse marker" is any of the small words typically situated at the beginnings of sentences that refer, not to the internal semantic content of the sentence, but to the external context (Schiffrin 1987), such as "well," "so," "now," "then," "I mean," and so forth.

Conclusions

Perhaps the most important fact about iconic gestures is their ability to articulate what, from the speaker's point of view, are only the relevant features in the context of speaking. Thus the gesture lets us actually observe thoughts as they occur. Iconic gestures have this power precisely because they are unconstrained by systems of rules and standards. They are not forced, as is speech, to include features solely to meet standards of form. Thus they can limit themselves to what stands out. Not only are gestures free in this way to incorporate the relevant dimensions in thought, but they also cannot avoid incorporating these dimensions. We ask what forms the gesture, and it is the speaker's construction of meaning at the moment of speaking. The gesture does not manifest kinesic form of its own accord. It cannot *help* but expose the relevant dimensions of the speaker's thought. So we can sum up iconic gestures by saying both that they are free to show only what is relevant, and also are unable to show anything else. For this reason, iconic gestures, together with the accompanying speech, offer a privileged view of thought. They are the closest look at the ideas of another person that we, the observers, can get.

5   Experiment on Gestures of the Concrete

This chapter describes an experiment—the "mismatch" experiment—in which the communication of meaning to listeners by means of gesture is shown. A decisive proof that gestures convey meanings is given by the fact that listeners are able to pick up these meanings when there is no other source than the gesture.

The experiment was set up in such a way that effects could be traced back to the individual gestures to which the listener was exposed. It consisted of presenting a videotaped narration of the cartoon story to a subject and having her retell the story to a listener. The subject did not see the cartoon itself and retold the story only from this videotaped narrative. Unbeknownst to the subject, the videotaped narration was staged by us and included a number of mismatching gesture-speech combinations. These mismatches of speech and gesture were the stimuli. The gestures and speech, taken separately, were in no way strange: only the combination was unusual and we took care that even this was not obvious. Subjects said afterwards that they noticed nothing peculiar about the videotaped narrative, and their assessment of it never mentioned the phenomenon of gesture. The data are the subjects' own speech and gestures during their retelling. It is important to stress that we did not expect the subject to repeat the mismatching combinations themselves. To the contrary, we hoped that they would introduce changes in their own narrations that would remove the mismatches. For one pilot subject, for example, the staged narrator described Sylvester exiting the drainpipe in these words: "and he [came out] the pipe," and performed an up-and-down bouncing movement at the same time. The linguistic choice— "came out"—conveys the cat's movement in relation to a reference point but does not tell the manner of movement, that was shown in the gesture. The listener, in her version, said the following: "and the cat [bounces out] the pipe," thus bringing the verbal and gestural descriptions together and proving that the original up-and-down gesture had been stored in a form to which the speech process could gain access.

It is theoretically conceivable that such mismatches have no effects at all. Subjectively, gestures hardly register in consciousness. But experiments by Feyereisen, Van de Wiele, and Dubois (1988) have shown that gestures can be tapped by viewers as sources of information. Thus a mismatch also might be tapped. Moreover, if speech and gesture are integrated into one system for the speaker, they should also be integrated for the listener. The speaker's full meaning is carried, not by words alone, but by the combination of words and gesture. The verbal part of the message may claim the listener's principal attention but the gesture can still significantly affect the information that is obtained. If the listener not only listens but looks, gestures should affect the listener's account of the story.

The Mismatch Experiment

The mismatch experiment is like the standard narrative experiment except that the stimulus is a videotape of another person telling the cartoon story. The listener (the subject in the experiment) watched this video but did not see the cartoon itself. Then the subject narrated the cartoon story to another person, and we videotaped the performance.

We introduced mismatches of three kinds: manner, anaphora, and point of origin. The first involved a mismatch of the kinesic form of the gesture with speech, while the second and third involved mismatches in space. It turned out that mismatches of space have the more powerful effects. These experiments were carried out by a group of co-workers including Justine Cassell, Karl-Erik McCullough, and Kevin Tuite.

1. Manner (form): verbs that refer to motion but do not convey the manner of motion were combined with gestures that do convey manner. The earlier example where the narrator's hand bounced up and down several times was a manner mismatch. The verb "comes" conveys movement in relation to a reference point but says nothing about the manner of motion—falling, rolling, running, walking, crawling, bouncing, etc. The gesture implies that bouncing was the manner.

2. Anaphora (space): anaphoric pronouns ("he," "she," "it," etc.) were combined with gestures that shift the action to a space already identified with another referent. For example, the right space was established for Tweety and the left for Sylvester; then the narrator said "and he lunges for him" (he = Sylvester) and made a gesture with his right hand lunging to the right. This shift of space implies that Tweety, not Sylvester, did the lunging while the pronoun "he" implies continuity of reference (that the lunger was Sylvester).

3. Point of origin (space): two verbally described actions were combined with gestures whose point of origin in space seemed to shift. For example, the narrator said "and he holds out the cup" and appeared to hold out the cup with himself as the point of origin, and then said "and he takes his hat off" and appeared to remove a cap from Sylvester in front of him with the space in front as the point of origin. Although the character remained the same and there was no apparent shift of reference, the character appeared to leap to a new locus in space.

Procedure

A video of a narration with these mismatches and others was shown to four subjects, who then gave their own narrations. The Appendix gives the full script of the video and its mismatching gestures. The video was presented in three sections and the subjects recounted each section before seeing the next; this was done to reduce memory load and to enlarge the subject's narration quantitatively. The duration of each of the sections was about two minutes and the subject began her own narration immediately after the section was finished.

The listeners were asked afterwards whether anything seemed out of the way in the videotaped narration. No listener commented on anything odd, and none said anything about gestures (their own or the videotaped narrator's). Several subjects in fact admired the videotaped narrator's lively style. The video thus apparently did not draw attention to the gesture channel, and its effects on the subjects' own narratives did not depend on the listeners having paid attention to gestures.

Not every clause on the video was accompanied by a gesture, and not every gesture involved a mismatch, but at carefully programmed points, a total of five anaphor, eight manner, and seven point of origin mismatches were displayed to the subjects.

Results

The mismatches that involved space (anaphora and point of origin) very strongly affected the listeners. Some traceable effects showed up in 80% or more of the subjects' narratives at points where there had been an anaphor or point of origin mismatch in the stimulus. Manner mismatches had effects 25% of the time. So it appears that changes in space are the most potent. When mismatches did not have effects, listeners produced a normal text and performed no gestures or performed gestures normal for the context.

What should be regarded as chance levels of effects in this experiment is hard to say, but the likelihood of the effects on gesture, space, and language that we have observed occurring by chance alone seems very small. For example, rotating the space 90 degrees or switching referring terms are phenomena that almost never occur in normal narrations; yet they occurred after seeing mismatching gestures. Even the 25% effect rate for manner mismatches would be far above chance levels. Subjects never said "bounce" or some other manner verb after having seen nothing in the

Table 5.1 Summary of Mismatch Effects

Type of Mismatch	
Mismatch Type	Percentage of Mismatches
Anaphors	100
Verb manner	25
Point of origin	79

Affecting Element of the Stimulus	
Affecting Element	Percentage of Affected Elements
Speech	0
Gesture	84
Both	0
Unclassified	16

Affected Element of the Narration	
Affected Element	Percentage of Affected Elements
Speech	36
Gesture	43
Both	9
Omission	12

cartoon corresponding to such a manner; yet, after seeing a video narrator's bouncing gesture such words occurred.

Table 5.1 gives the summary statistics from the experiment: first the *type of mismatch,* in terms of the percentage of mismatches in the stimulus that had an effect on the subject's narration; then the *affecting element of the mismatch stimulus* that was responsible for the effect (speech, gesture, or both), in terms of the percentage of effects in the subject's narration that are attributable to the particular affecting element; finally, the *affected element of the subject's narration* that was altered by the mismatch (speech, gesture, both speech and gesture, or the omission of a salient part), in terms of the percentage of mismatch effects that were of the indicated type. (Note that the figures in the latter two cases are calculated on the same basis: they both give the percentage of the affected elements in the subject's narration divided up in different ways.)

In all cases, the affecting element in the stimulus appeared to be the gesture, and it was never the speech. This is apparent in the examples quoted below. In the first example a reference error arose because the gesture had been used in an inappropriate space, in the second a repair and space rotation arose because the gesture emanated from a new and unexplained point of origin, and in the third a lexical choice started from a gesture bouncing up and down. However, this dominance by the gesture in the mismatch does not invariably appear. Subjects in a pilot study did produce examples where speech was the affecting element; e.g., the staged narrator said "Sylvester ingests the bowling ball, comes back out the pipe, and goes rolling down the street"; the subject echoed the unusual verb choice, "Sylvester ate—ingested—the bowling ball," actually introducing it in a repair.

Finally, the affected elements can be the subject's speech, gestures, or both; they are quite diverse. Gestures or speech are also sometimes omitted after a mismatch. "Omission" refers to gestures or verbal descriptions that are reliably present in normal narratives but are missing from a mismatch narration. For example, in one part of the cartoon Sylvester smashes into a wall. Normally this denouement is depicted in a gesture, but in mismatch narrations the gesture was sometimes omitted, perhaps because this was a way of resolving the spatial inconsistency the mismatch had engendered. The omission numbers are the least reliable, however, since inevitably some omissions would have been missed and/or some omissions that occurred were actually due to other causes than the mismatch in the original stimulus tape.

Interpretation of Mismatches

In general the mismatch experiments show that gestures affect listeners to a surprising degree, particularly when the mismatching gesture involves a change of space. It thus seems plausible to claim that gestures play a part in communication even when speakers and listeners are not paying attention to them.

What is the mechanism of this communicativeness? Since the listener reports no particular awareness of gestures as such, it does not work by the gesture's calling attention to itself. This in itself is not surprising. Most listeners are not aware of the phonetic or syntactic structures of what is said to them either, but the speech channel functions effectively without awareness. Nonetheless, a gesture-speech mismatch, even if it does not trigger consciousness of gesture as such, could set off an unusual process of interpretation and memory in the listener. This is precisely because the gesture and speech fail to match, and the listener tries to construct a speech and gesture combination where they do match. Listeners must store the cartoon story in memory, retrieve it later, and build their own version for retelling. If we suppose that a speech and gesture combination cannot be formed in which there are contradictory parts, then the subjects must come up with their own combination that avoids the contradiction. Examples reveal subjects going to quite radical lengths, transforming space and speech in striking ways, to avoid such conflicts.

Example 2 illustrates this dual transformation in a subject whose drive for consistency led her to alter the linguistic and spatial components at the same time.

Examples of Mismatch Effects

I have picked a diverse sample to illustrate the effects of mismatches on listeners:

REFERENTIAL ERROR FOLLOWING AN ANAPHOR MISMATCH (SPA-TIAL). The mismatch was that, in speech, a cohesive pronoun reference was made to Sylvester: "he lunges"; but in gesture this was combined with a shift of space: the lunging was done by the right hand, which had previously been used for Tweety. Thus while in speech there was cohesion, in gesture there was discontinuity.

Although the subject describes the same scene, her description is different from the videotaped narrator's in organization and style. Thus we can be fairly sure that she was recounting the story and creating gestures on her own. The critical detail in her response was an error of reference— saying Tweety for Sylvester—followed by a repair. This error corresponds to the appearance in the stimulus tape of Sylvester in Tweety's space. The speaker's own gestures pointed to the front, and then showed the lunge to the right. When the speaker repaired the reference, saying "I mean Sylvester," she repeated the same gestures, making an identical deictic to the front space and the lunge to the right. Thus the gesture during the repair was the same as during the error, but the speech was now corrected. The repair of "Tweety" by "Sylvester" shows that she detected her error, while the use of the same gestures shows that the gestures themselves were not part of the error; on the contrary, the gestures were held constant while the verbal reference was changed.

On the left below is a description of the event as presented in the stimulus tape, and on the right is the subject's rendition of the same event. The mismatch in the stimulus is identified. The error in the subject's response occurs in the third line, and the repair in the fifth line.

STIMULUS 1	RESPONSE 1
1. next Sylvester decides to climb up	and Tweety's really happy
2. to Tweety's window . . . so he goes	sitting on top of the cage
3. up the drain pipe [Tweety's] *Deictic: right hand seems to hold up Tweety on right side of space.*	and then [Tweet]y goes *Deictic: left hand points to spot in front space.*

4. <u>singing and swinging in his</u> <u>window</u>	down and [tries to climb] *Iconic: left hand moves to* *right.*
5. [and Sylvester's] <u>right near him</u> *Deictic: left hand seems to hold up* *Sylvester in left space.*	—I mean [Sylvester] goes *Deictic: left hand points* *again.*
6. <u>watching him and then suddenly</u>	down and [tries to climb] *Iconic: left hand moves* *right again.*
7. he [lunges] <u>for him and runs into</u> *The mismatch: right hand (now* *Sylvester) lunges into right space.*	up the drain pipe
8. <u>the apartment after him</u>	

LEXICAL REPAIR FOLLOWING AN ORIGO MISMATCH (SPATIAL). The mismatch was that first a gesture in the stimulus appeared to emanate from the speaker's own locus—it was the speaker who was the character performing the action—but then a second gesture depicting the same character performing a second action appeared to emanate from a locus in front of the speaker. The character was the same, and he had not moved from one place to another. Instead, the point of origin of the second action was in a new place, and the character seems to have suddenly materialized in this new place.

This mismatch had a series of consequences for the subject's narrative. The crucial details are a (seemingly) unmotivated repair of verbs—"hijacks" for "kidnaps"—and the subject's own shift of the gesture space—moving the character Sylvester away from herself and into the space in front of her, at the precise moment of the repair, while simultaneously making herself into the victim.

STIMULUS 2	RESPONSE 2
1. <u>he hides around the corner from</u> <u>them</u>	so he hides ab- <u>around the</u>
2. <u>and he gets the monkey to come</u> <u>and</u>	<u>corner and</u>
3.	[lures] the [mon]key over to <u>him</u> .... *Deictic: hand points down* *to own lap.*

4. then he mugs the monkey
and kidnaps [or kidnap]
Iconic: hand reaches to
front.

5. [then he steals his costume]
Iconic: hand grabs and pulls
something to own locus.

6. then Sylvester [dresses up]
The mismatch: both hands put
something on in the center
space, away from self.
[hijacks him and basically]
The repair: both hands grab
own shoulders.

7. in the monkey's costume
[takes his] . . . [outfit] and
Iconic: both hands flip
down from shoulders.
everything and goes back

This example will be revisited and analyzed from a different point of view in chapter 9. It was presented originally in a paper with Nancy L. Dray (Dray and McNeill 1990). I will use parts of our interpretation of it here. The repair of "kidnaps" by "hijacks" is peculiar because the situation being described had few of the usual featural specifications of what might be seen as a straightforward hijacking—there was no vehicle, no path to be deflected from, no movement with a vehicle away from the scene of the hijacking. None of these features existed in the situation of Sylvester's mugging the monkey and taking its clothes. Still, while the speaker seemed to be unhappy with her word "kidnap," she was apparently satisfied with "hijacks." It appears that the subject was focusing on some dimension of contrast in which "hijack" was directly opposed to "kidnap." Her gestures provide a clue to what was taking place. Exactly at the moment of the verbal repair, there was a dramatic gestural repair of who occupies the subject's own space—at first the kidnaper/hijacker and then the victim. In lines (3) and (4), where the speaker's hand reaches to the front, it is either Sylvester or an observer—certainly not the monkey—and in (6) and (7) it becomes the victim, the monkey, and certainly not Sylvester or an observer.

We can explain the new spatial arrangement and repair of "kidnap" as arising from the mismatch in the stimulus. In the stimulus, the first gesture placed Sylvester at the speaker's locus, while the second gesture shifted him to the space in front of the speaker; this occurred without any corresponding linguistic description for movement ("he steals his costume, then Sylvester dresses up"). The subject's spatial shift precisely matches this shift in the stimulus tape. She moved Sylvester from her own locus to the space in front of her. Her verbal repair of "kidnap" by "hijack" in turn can be seen as the subject's maneuver (doubtlessly carried out unconsciously) to provide linguistic coding of the new spatial arrangement that was missing from the stimulus tape because of the mismatch. "Kidnap" focuses on an intruder absconding from a place he has intruded into: "hijack" focuses on the intruder coming into the place. Thus the repair precisely encoded the new space. Whereas "kidnap" fit the space before it was shifted, "hijacks" fit the space after, for by then the monkey was at the center and Sylvester out in front commandeering the clothing. Thus the subject avoided the mismatch in her own narration. It is clear that the shift in the stimulus of the point of origin of action was registered by her, since it was this mismatch that set the chain of events off in the first place.

As this analysis of the subject's speech and gesture space implies, the subject assimilated the mismatch while she watched the stimulus tape. This had wide-ranging consequences for her narration on both the verbal and gestural levels; what occurred in these channels cannot be explained without referring to the mismatch.

LEXICAL CHOICE FOLLOWING A VERB MISMATCH (FORM). Like the "bounce" example mentioned earlier, the mismatch involved a verb that does not convey any manner of motion. The accompanying gesture showed the manner of movement—bouncing up and down. This manner reappeared during the subject's retelling, although not as a gesture but as a lexical choice. She said "goes down stairs" although no stairs had been mentioned in the stimulus at all. Thus, the up-and-down movement originally in a gesture resurfaced as a lexical choice, in which the jagged outline implied in the up-and-down gesture is a dominant feature. At the same time, the subject normalized her own gesture—the character fell straight down and there was no bouncing. Thus the visual contour of the up-and-down gesture in the stimulus had been assimilated but not necessarily remembered in the form of a gesture, or even as a manner of movement. The resurfacing of up and down in a lexical choice implies that to the subject the modality of input—gesture or language—was not clearly distinguished.

STIMULUS 3	RESPONSE 3
1. and swallows it	and Sylvester swallows
2. and falls back down the pipe	the bowling ball

3. [he comes out of the bottom of the pipe]
   The mismatch: left hand bounces up and down three times (no lateral motion)

   and [then goes down stairs]
   Iconic: left hand falls straight down (no bounce and no lateral motion).

4. and goes down the street

   across- back across into

SUMMARY. These examples seem convincing enough. The specific gesture was part of the meaning the listeners were picking up. For the listener, as well as for the speaker, the speaker's gesture and speech seem to form themselves into a single process.

What This Experiment Shows

I have been arguing in these chapters that, for speakers, gestures and speech are aspects of a single process. Each form contributes its own unique level of representation and the total representation is a synthesis of imagistic and linear-segmented modes. The mismatch experiment suggests that the same synthesis occurs in listeners. When you understand someone you, too, form a single unified combination of imagery and speech. The imagery is an integral part of your comprehension. If the speaker provides gestures, they are taken in—unconsciously—and combined with the verbal stream to recover the conveyed meaning. If there are no gestures, as in listening over the radio for instance, the process is not necessarily different. On rare occasions, listeners generate their own gestures. Figure 5.1 is such a case. This is the one case we have found where the *listener* provides the gesture to go with the speaker's utterance:

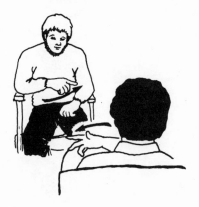

Figure 5.1. Gesture by a listener (the nearer figure) demonstrating image construction during speech comprehension. The listener was not speaking. The speaker was saying "[these are all in order] the way I've described them," and performed a gesture to his left; simultaneously the listener performed the same gesture to *his* left (not imitating the speaker, therefore, but tracking him).

(Speaker): [these are all in order] the way I've described them

Deictic: Points to left to show the temporal order.

(Listener): [_____] ok

Deictic: Points to his own left to show the temporal order. **Note that the direction of this point is the opposite of the speaker's, suggesting that the listener's movement is his own construction.**

Although rare, the existence of even one such example demonstrates that listeners can and do build up matching imagery to accompany the speech they hear.

Gestures of the Abstract

So far we have seen how gestures exhibit images of events and objects in a concrete world (real or fictive). Gesture imagery is not limited to the concrete. Other gestures exhibit images of the abstract—abstract concepts and relationships that are displayed in gesture form. One important class of such gestures I call *metaphoric*. Metaphoric gestures create images of abstractions. In such gestures, abstract content is given form in the imagery of objects, space, movement, and the like. Other kinds of abstract gestures are *beats* and (abstract) *pointing*. Each type of gesture is described in this chapter. But first we should consider the issue of how something as concrete as a gesture can display abstract concepts at all.

Images of the Abstract

There is no lack of means for describing the relationship of imagery to the abstract. I will mention three approaches.

KANT'S SCHEMATA. Kant introduced the term *schema* to refer to a procedure for generating an image of a concept (Kant [1787]1973). A schema for the concept of fiveness, for example, enables us to generate a "sensuous image," such as "| | | | |." Gestures also can be regarded as the products of schemata; this is true of both iconic and metaphoric gestures: Kant's analysis applies to both. Glucksberg and Keysar (1990) have argued that the so-called literal and metaphoric comprehension of words are fundamentally the same. Their argument implies a continuum between the literal and the metaphoric. Invoking Kant's schemata also implies a continuum between iconic and metaphoric gestures. Between the gestures, the homology of an iconic gesture is imposed by external reality, by nature: a blob is homologous to a bounded physical entity and upward movement is homologous to moving up, and we have no power to alter them. In a metaphoric gesture, the homology is one of our own creation. If we *think* of a story as a bounded entity, we can create an image of this kind of thing. The difference between the iconic and metaphoric, from this schema viewpoint, comes down to whether the homology is copied from the world (iconic) or created by the mind (metaphoric). This points up, indeed, one of the major sources of scientific interest in metaphors, which is to identify the constraints on the creation of homologies (see Lakoff and Johnson 1980). Such created homologies could be called "schematic" (in the Kantian sense), but I am calling them "meta-phoric" to emphasize the distinction between metaphoric and iconic gestures, and also for historical reasons (a major type of metaphoric ges-ture, the conduit, was first identified as a metaphor of language; Reddy 1979).

VEHICLE, TOPIC, AND GROUND. A second approach emphasizes the analytic categories introduced by I. A. Richards (Richards 1936) and ex-tended and renamed by Max Black (Black 1962). In the familiar Richards terminology, these categories are the Vehicle, Topic, and Ground. An ex-ample is the expression, "life is a flowing river." Here the Vehicle is "a flowing river." In a gesture, the Vehicle is the gesture image itself. The Topic of the metaphor is the abstract concept that the metaphor is presenting—life or the story genre. The Ground, finally, is the common ground of meaning on which the Vehicle and Topic are linked. In "life is a flowing river," the Ground is something akin to an uninterrupted flow or continuity, and/or confinement to a path. According to Richards, the Ve-hicle alters our understanding of the Topic, the concept of a flowing river altering the concept of life, a process he called "interanimation." Black corrected this to "interaction," since in his view both the Vehicle and the Topic are altered by the metaphor. The concept of a river *and* the concept of life are changed. This interaction is indeed a crucial test of a metaphor and applies to metaphoric gestures as well. The very concept of a story is altered through interaction with the image of a bounded container: a story *becomes* some kind of container. At the same time, our idea of a bounded container is necessarily changed—it becomes some kind of story genre. A reflection of this interaction is our conviction that a story and a container are *similar*. We say, in a Kantian vein, that the homology in a metaphoric gesture has been created. Equivalently, we say that the Topic is altered by the Vehicle and the Vehicle is altered by the Topic.

SIGN, BASE, AND REFERENT. Finally, we can describe metaphoric ges-tures in behavioral terms that lend themselves to empirical analysis. In this approach, we distinguish between Sign, Base, and Referent (Mandel 1977; Cohen, Namir, and Schlesinger 1977). The Sign is the gesture it-self, the handshape, movement, space, etc., that constitutes the gesture. The Base is the objective object or action to which the Sign is homolo-gous. In the case of the bounded object gesture, the Base is, in fact, some bounded object. The Referent is the abstract concept to which the ges-ture refers; a genre, for example. The term Sign reflects the origin of this approach in the study of sign languages of the deaf (see also Kendon 1988b). We employed the Sign-Base-Referent approach in the coding method described in chapter 3. To code a metaphoric gesture we specify all components—the Sign, the Base, and the Referent separately.

Types of Metaphoric Gestures in Narrative

Conduits

Metaphors whereby language, meaning, knowledge, art, genre, etc., are presented as bounded containers have been identified in linguistics under the name of the "conduit metaphor" (Reddy 1979; Lakoff and Johnson 1980). The conduit is actually a family of related metaphors which runs like this: (a) meaning is a substance, (b) the substance is packed into a container, and (c) the container is passed on to a recipient over a conduit. For example, "there wasn't much in it," where the "it" refers to a lecture, implies an image of a lecture as a container and the contents of the lecture as a substance (in short supply, unfortunately). "It's hard getting these ideas across" implies a conduit over which ideas ought to pass. These images of containers, substances, and conduits are only implicit in the words. Conduit metaphoric gestures, however, can depict the imagery directly. Holding up a bounded container creates an image of the container (potentially filled with meaning). Showing this apparition to the listener demonstrates the reality of the conduit.

Most of the uses of conduit metaphoric gestures in narratives are for performing pragmatic references to the text itself or to the interpersonal context of the narrative situation; I will describe these uses in chapter 7. Such pragmatic references mean that the appropriate synchronization rule is pragmatic synchrony. On rare occasions there may also be semantic synchrony, as when someone giving a lecture on linguistics refers to "a linguistic object" and performs a conduit gesture at the same time. But much more frequent are examples where speech and gesture are quite different semantically, while pragmatically they have the same reference. The first of the examples below illustrates this divergence of levels: semantically there is nothing in common between speech and gesture, but pragmatically both channels refer to the cartoon story as a genre.

Not only will we see a large number of conduit metaphoric gestures in this chapter, we will also see languages where conduit metaphoric gestures are systematically absent. This fact suggests that although the conduit metaphor lets us create our own homologies of Topic and Vehicle, it is the product of a certain cultural and linguistic tradition.

IN ANCIENT TIMES. The conduit metaphoric gesture indeed appears to have been a part of Western culture for a long time. The earliest historical reference to it I have encountered is the following by Montaigne (himself fifteenth century), who attributed it to Zeno (sixth century B.C.) in this description of the degrees of knowledge:[1]

> Zeno pictured in a gesture his conception of this division of the faculties of the soul: the hand spread and open was appearance; the hand half shut and the fingers a little hooked, consent; the closed fist, comprehension; when with his left hand he closed his fist still tighter, knowledge. (Montaigne 1958, 272)

BASIC CONDUITS. An example of a conduit gesture is the following, which I have already cited, where the speaker is announcing the genre of his upcoming narrative (illustrated in figure 1.3, repeated here in figure 6.1 with an additional panel):

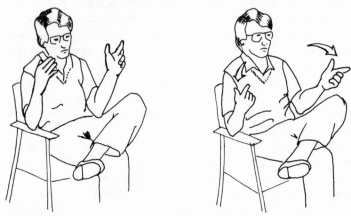

Figure 6.1. Conduit metaphoric gesture with "it [was a Sylves][ter and Tweet]y cartoon" (same as fig. 1.3, with one added panel). The idea of a genre is presented as a bounded supportable object. In the second panel the speaker appears to open the object up.

(6.1) it [was a Sylves][ter and Tweet]y cartoon
        (1)   (2)

(1) Both hands rise up as if holding up an object.
(2) Both hands appear to pull the object open.

The speaker created an object at (1) and presented it to the listener, indicating the conduit. This "object" was the concept of the cartoon

---

1. I am grateful to Josef Stern for bringing this striking passage to my attention.

and/or the idea of the upcoming narration; either way, an abstract concept. The "conduit" was the channel of communication between the speaker and his listener. To conceive of a Sylvester and Tweety cartoon as an object and hold it up to the listener is thinking in terms of the conduit metaphor. There is a created homology between the two orders of things, the Topic (cartoon genre) and the Vehicle (a bounded, supported, and presented object). Indeed, after creating the object and holding it up, the speaker continued with the conduit imagery and proceeded to break it open, at (2); thus he revealed the container's "contents" (the identity of the cartoon).

A very similar type of conduit gesture is the following:

(6.2) I have [a question]

Metaphoric: hand forms a cup for the image of a question (a container) or the hand out to receive an answer (a substance).

The cup is either the question (a bounded supportable object) or the speaker's hand ready to receive the answer (the answer implicitly a substance that can be placed there); either way, the gesture depicts an abstract idea.

These examples illustrate the basic features of conduit metaphoric gestures: the hands create an image of a bounded, supportable object that represents an abstract concept.

VIRTUOSIC CONDUITS. The cartoon-as-an-object gesture led to a natural extension when the speaker appeared to break open the container to show the "substance" inside. The conduit lends itself to this kind of elaboration and the more extreme variations can be called virtuosic. The most spectacular examples often appear during academic lectures; linguists, in particular, create vast structures of conduit metaphoric gestures, and often have I regretted not having video equipment with me at the talks of colleagues who so firmly believe that words, phrases, and sentences are the only substantive parts of language. I have here three other variations on the basic conduit image that can be regarded as virtuosic. The first example occurred during a film narration and is a gesture that presents the meaning of the past subjunctive mood of English; the others come from academic discussions. The past subjunctive—such as "if you had gone to Rome, you would have seen the Colosseum"—carries the meaning of "a potentiality that is not an actuality" (Curme 1931). A potentiality not realized as an actuality is what the gesture in the first example depicts. It was made with two basic conduit cup-of-meaning hands moving outward; then, suddenly, the cups vanished (see fig. 6.2.):

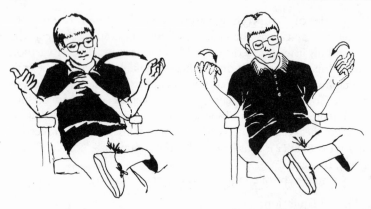

Figure 6.2. Virtuosic conduit with "even [though one might] [have] supposed." The hands spread outward (an image of potentiality) and simultaneously open to form cups of meaning; then they abruptly close. This closure is timed to coincide with the grammatical encoding of the past subjunctive, "have." The image is of an expanding potentiality that vanishes: a fairly good picture of the past subjunctive (Curme 1931).

(6.3)   even [though one might][have] supposed
          (1)   (2)

(1) Cup-shape hands move out from center to side: the idea of potentiality.
(2) Hands snap shut: the idea of nonexistence.

The cup-of-meaning hands conveyed the existence of some meaning; the outspreading is a common image for a potentiality (cf. the gesture for "who knows?"); and the final closure, timed to take place exactly with the linguistic coding of the subjunctive, made the cup-of-meaning vanish. Thus the total effect was that a potential meaning had vanished.

My second illustration was observed during an academic conference and was not videotaped; thus the timing is inexact. The speaker was emphasizing the importance of organization in a certain domain. While he was saying the word "organization," there was a conduit in which the classic cup-of-meaning handshape was modified by rigidly extending and separating the fingers. The image was of the desired rigidity of structure. This was experienced by viewers visually, but would have been felt by the speaker kinesthetically. The concept of organization thus appeared to acquire homology with forceful physical containment and the basic conduit metaphoric gesture was elaborated into an image of rigidity—the quality, the speaker was arguing, needed for bringing order into this domain.

My third example appeared during a NOVA telecast dealing with children's language. The virtuosic touch is that the speaker turns himself into an abstract idea, in this case into the theoretical Language Acquisition Device:

(6.4) he proposed that the Language Acquisition Device
[would simply take in] . . . have a . . . take as its input
Metaphoric: both hands scoop up "input" and appear to shove it into the speaker's own mouth.

A metaphoric use of the body is highly unusual. Most speakers create a bounded entity and offer it to the listener, but rarely do they turn it on themselves and make their own body into a part of the gesture. The gesture, however, was quite effective. The listener, too, is drawn in and finds himself face-to-face with the Language Acquisition Device, swallowing its meal of language data.

Metaphorics in Georgian, Chinese, and Turkana

The conduit metaphoric gesture is not universal. In iconic gestures the direct homology of Base and Referent leads to a high degree of intercultural overlap when the content is the same. In contrast, metaphoric gestures seem to be culturally specific. The schema for producing conduit metaphoric images appears in the gestures of some cultures but not others. We have found excellent conduit examples in English, German, Italian, and Georgian narratives (the latter a non-Indo-European language), but no convincing examples in Chinese or Turkana narratives (also non-Indo-European, but outside of the Western cultural tradition). These latter narratives contain metaphoric gestures of other kinds, but not gestures in which abstract ideas are presented as bounded and supported containers. An odd language in this picture is Japanese. Our Japanese language narrators have performed many conduit metaphoric gestures. I do not have an explanation for the conduit image in these narratives, but all the speakers we have observed have been residents of the United States for a number of years.

The Georgian language narrator commented her narrative by pointing out that she works professionally in the area of film. These remarks were accompanied by numerous conduit metaphorics, of which the following was one (see fig. 6.3 at the top of page 152).

(6.5) i[mas rom me p'ropesio]nali var k'inos dargshi

t[his that I   professio]nal be film's branch-in
'[the fact that I am a professional] in the area of film'

Figure 6.3. Metaphoric gesture (conduit) by the Georgian language narrator as she introduces the film story and says that she is a professional in the field. This very clear conduit appears with a non-Indo-European language. The image of a bounded cup of meaning is not language specific but culture specific.

Metaphoric: hand forms cup, loops to self and then loops out, presenting the image of her profession as film historian to the listener.

This gesture also included a looping movement from the self to the interlocutor, evidently to refer to the conduit itself between the speaker and listener. The English conduit example, "it was a Tweety and Sylvester cartoon," also presented a cartoon-object to the listener, and gestures that highlight this interpersonal aspect of the image seem particularly prevalent at the beginnings of narratives. This not surprising since it is exactly at this stage that the narrator is setting up the channel of communication and thus emphasizes the interpersonal context of the narrative situation.

In a context where an English or Georgian narrator would perform a conduit, the Chinese speaker created a bound*less* substance that she then patted down (this is a metaphoric gesture also used by English narrators, but it is not the conduit). The gesture creates an image of a substance without form. The metaphor is that an abstract idea is a mass of some kind, a concrete substance, but it is not supported in the speaker's hands. In the course of introducing her narrative, the Chinese speaker said (see fig. 6.4; transcription and translation by K.-E. McCullough and C. Wang):

Figure 6.4. Non-conduit metaphoric gesture by the Chinese language narrator as she introduces the film story. The metaphor appears to be that the story is a substance lying in space before her; then she pats on it. In contrast to the conduit there is no container and no support of the substance. English speakers also produce this metaphor.

(6.6) [qianmian yidiar] butai   qingchu
[front-side little]   NEG-too clear
'[the first part is a little] unclear'

Metaphoric: left hand pats up and down in lower center space, beating on "the first part," a substance.

danshi [houmian de   hai ting qingchu]
but   [back-side MOD still quite clear]
'but [the latter part was still quite clear]'

Metaphoric: left hand presses down on "the latter part" contrasting with the (pressure motion of the first gesture).

In an anthropological film of the Turkana people in northwestern Kenya (MacDougall and MacDougall 1977) there are examples of metaphoric gestures of a completely different type. The Turkana are traditional warrior-herdsmen who had been little influenced by Western culture at the time of the film (early 1970s). (For a modern grammar of Turkana, see Dimmendaal 1983.) The following occurred while the speaker was explaining the difference between "Europeans" (viz., the film makers) and the Turkana. He said that the Europeans want to extract every drop of Turkana knowledge (see fig. 6.5; transcription and translation by R. Dyson-Hudson):

Figure 6.5. Non-conduit metaphoric gesture from a Turkana language speaker as he said "these Europeans want to extract all our knowledge—every drop!" The metaphor, while hard to interpret, is clearly different from the conduit image. Knowledge may be a living thing or smoke or vapor rising up.

(6.7) toditarite   ngitunga [lu   na   kilna   yoka . . .
they-extract people   [this-here knowledge our-inclusive . . .
nith!]
pft!]
'these Europeans want to extract all our knowledge . . . pft!'

Metaphoric: hand plucks "knowledge" from brow and releases it into the air.

An abstract concept is "entified" but there is no boundary or container. The image seems to be that something is plucked from the forehead and then released—"knowledge" rises up on its own and disappears (perhaps it is a puff of smoke or a bird). The image is not the Chinese speaker's picture of an inert substance lieing flat on a surface or the conduit image of a bounded container, and definitely not the conduit but an image of something capable of motion on is own. Similar images of things moving up and dispersing appear in the gestures of other Turkana speakers. Figure 6.6 illustrates a different speaker performing a gesture for the concept of having nothing—only your body, as she says:

Figure 6.6. A non-conduit metaphoric gesture by a second Turkana speaker for the idea of having nothing ("he had only his body"). Again, there is the image of something rising up. The final handshape resembles a conduit but the movement is quite different. This opening up of space to exhibit nothingness may be universal.

(6.8) la   lowang kaye abuni   kaye [akwan]
       from side   over he-brought over [his-body]
'from over there he brought only his body'

Metaphoric: something rises up and disappears—her image of nothingness.

To understand these metaphoric gestures fully we would need much more insight into the cultural beliefs of the Turkana people. But we can at least say that Turkana metaphoric gestures suggest an image of abstract concepts very different from our own. In this image abstract concepts are not manipulated, as they are in the conduit, and may not be controlled by the individual personality, but are entities capable of moving on their own.

Metaphors Utilizing Space

There are cohesive uses of space where characters are assigned their own spatial regions and subsequent references to the characters are accompanied by gestures in "their" specific space (see chap. 7). Space also can be given semantic content; in this it is used metaphorically. The speaker can conceive of the plot line, its dramatic content, and the characters as objects with a layout in space. Thus one part of the story can be set aside in space A and a contrasting part in space B. The following is an example where space is dichotomized to represent the relative moral statuses of three characters. The speaker places the actors according to his moral evaluations (see fig. 6.7). There is an opposition between the left space for the actual moral status of the characters, and two non-left spaces for their ascribed moral status. The speaker further subdivided the non-left space (ascribed, not real, morality) into the "bad guy" to the front and the "good guys" to the right. As Kevin Tuite writes about this example, "The speaker has in effect represented the plot of the discourse as a spatially-extended object, with distinct loci corresponding to distinct plot components" (Tuite, to appear):

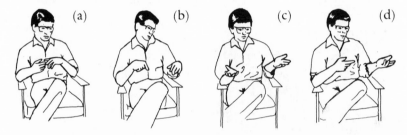

Figure 6.7. Spatial metaphors setting up contrasting spaces for moral statuses. Panel (a) shows the right space for ascribed status of "good guys." Panel (b) shifts left for actual status of "really did kill him." Panel (c) returns to the center for ascribed status of "bad guy." Panel (d) goes back to the left for actual status of "really didn't kill him." The four gestures diagram the moral oppositions of good and evil and true and false in a space endowed with abstract meaning.

(6.9) everyone's morals are very ambiguous

(6.10) 'cause [they're sup]posed to be the good guys

Metaphoric space 1: left hand points right for "good guys."

(6.11) [but she] really did kill him

Metaphoric space 2: right hand moves left into center and head turns left for actual act.

(6.12) and [he's a] bad guy

Metaphoric space 1: hands move to front for "bad guy."

(6.13) [but he really] didn't kill him

Metaphoric space 2: hands and head move to left again for actual act.

The moral ambiguity the speaker found in the film was visualized as space, then, and laid out like a map with spatial regions for the moral conflict. The absolute spatial assignments (left versus non-left or front versus right) had no significance in themselves: what mattered was the oppositions.

A metaphoric use of space appears in narratives regardless of the language being spoken. I can't say if the spatial metaphors are the same in every language, but there are no obvious interlinguistic differences in the use of space metaphorically.

Metaphors Based on Beams and Auras

In addition to the conduit image of language, knowledge, genre, etc. as substance in a container, a number of gestural metaphors present concepts of translucence, shadows, and mental states. A system of schemas provides images of these concepts by playing on the idea of a beam or

Figure 6.8. Eidola in a poster that appeared around the University of Toronto in the summer of 1990.

aura. Some of the gestures embody ancient physical theories, which continue to live on secretly in gesture form.

METAPHORS OF TRANSLUCENCE. The ancients were puzzled by how we are able to see objects that lie at a distance. Various theories were offered, one that the eye sent out beams that contacted the objects; seeing was thus likened to the familiar process of touching. The beams were called "eidola." (Figure 6.8 illustrates a recent example from a poster that appeared around the University of Toronto in the summer of 1990.) A common metaphoric gesture for vision has the hands depict beams leaving the eyes in the direction of the thing being seen. The ancient eidola theory lives on, in gesture form. A variation of this eidola gesture is the following where a speaker describes a scene from a Hitchcock film in which there are superimposed images. This situation is depicted with eidola leaving the viewer and passing through translucent people. Thus, beams passing through an object also present the concept of translucence (see fig. 6.9):

Figure 6.9. Eidola in a gesture for transparency. This accompanied "you can see through the people [into her]." The right hand moves past the plane of the left and rotates as it moves. The metaphor for transparency is eidola passing through the target.

(6.14) people are walking by her and you can
see through the people [into her]

One hand held up for "the people" while the other hand for "seeing" moves past the first hand.

One hand thus represents the translucent people and the other the eidola passing through them. The question is not whether the speaker believes in the ancient theory of eidola; he certainly does not. But, unwittingly, he reinvoked it, and in some sense the old theory was present, giving the visual process an active role of penetrating objects to reach the target of sight behind them.

METAPHORS OF MENTAL STATES. Beams or auras also are used to refer to mental states and mental operations. In the following, the gesture depicts wonderment emanating from the head (see fig. 6.10):

Figure 6.10. Beams emanating from the head for a psychological state. This gesture accompanied "flying into the area [wondering] why all the animals are running away." The state makes itself known by an aura around the head.

(6.15) so uh . . . she's flying into the area [wondering] why all the animals are running away

Metaphoric: hands radiate away from head for beams of "wondering why."

This movement of the hands away from the face or head is a quite frequent gesture for manifestations of all kinds. In films of Japanese speakers I have seen gestures depicting beams that radiate out from the stomach. This corresponds to the traditional Japanese metaphoric locus in the gut for feelings, thoughts, and mental activities in general. Thus, the source of the beams may differ as a specific cultural property but beams themselves seem to be a widespread image of mental states.

METAPHORS OF SHADOWS. A gesture depicting a shadow makes use of the same theory of outward radiating eidola, but now it is the shadow that departs the body and moves off through space (the expression, "to cast a shadow," embodies the same metaphor). In the following, again from the Georgian narrative, a shadow is depicted as detaching from a person and moving through space and finally hitting a wall (see fig. 6.11; only the English translation is provided)

(6.16) [you see a shadow . . . the shadow of a man in a top hat]

Right hand is at arm's length, with the palm to self for the wall. Left hand

Figure 6.11. A shadow being "cast off" to contact a surface. This accompanied (in Georgian) "[you see a shadow . . . the shadow of a man in a top hat]." The left hand—the shadow—moves slowly up to the plane of the right hand which faces the speaker (it is the wall). This gesture was immediately followed by another where the left hand—the shadow hand—drew an outline at the plane locus of the top-hatted figure.

slowly moves forward to line of right hand, with the palm to front for the moving shadow.
Left hand then outlines shape of man in top hat.

The right hand faces the speaker to show the location of the wall; the left hand faces away from the speaker and is the shadow. The moving hand goes out to the plane of the other hand but is aimed to the side of it, which shows that the wall was the plane, not just the hand. The two palms are oriented toward each other, the palm in general being the business side of the hand, and this is the image of the shadow as an entity gliding through space to the wall. The slow pace of the hand is a further significant feature. In the film the shadow is shown ominously creeping forward and upward onto the door as the shadow-caster slowly approaches. The gesture presents the low speed of this approach as a slow moving shadow itself. All of these images play with the basic eidola image.

Metaphors of Change

Finally, we reach gestural metaphors of dynamic processes. Gestures are particularly expressive in this domain since the gestures themselves are dynamic. Gestures of change are among the most elaborate that one finds. In the second example below, the metaphor turns into a whole system of gestures.

TRANSITION. Metaphors for transitions or processes in general always seem to include some element of rotation: the gesture conveys the transition as repetitive and/or cyclic, an image that appears to be based on rotating wheels or gears, although there are no wheels or gears. In the following, the speaker refers to a transition in the film (see fig. 6.12)

Figure 6.12. A metaphoric gesture
for transition or process. This accompanied "and now [we get] into
the story proper." The metaphor
for a process is something rotating
cyclically/repetitively.

(6.17) and now [we get] into the story proper

Metaphoric: hands supporting an object (conduit image) rotate (3×) and move forward (spatial image).

This was in fact a multi-metaphor gesture. There is a conduit object, for the concept of the film as an entity; forward motion in space, for the concept of entering; and rotation for the process—the whole is the speaker's image of a transition into the main part of the movie.

TRANSFORMATION. The next example employs space metaphorically to present a highly complex transformation. The Georgian speaker was describing a scene from the film in which Hitchcock had cleverly joined two scenes through the use of form, space, action, and time. One character (Alice) has killed another (the artist). In terror after her act she wanders the streets of London, reexperiencing scenes of the murder. She comes across a drunk lying on the street with his hand extended, in the same posture as the dead man. Then Hitchcock transforms the image of Alice in the street into a second image of the artist's landlady when she discovers the dead man. This was described by the narrator as follows (giving only the English translation): "At this point a scream is heard from her, but this scream changes suddenly. The scream continues but the face changes and you see that landlady, who is standing exactly the same way as this woman stood in the street, and she is looking at a hand, but this is really the dead person's hand."

Repeatedly gestures leave the left space, which is the scene with Alice, and enter the right space, which is the scene with the landlady (see fig. 6.13). The gesture space was divided into old scene/new scene from the first, and the transformation of the first scene into the second was visu-

Figure 6.13. The Georgian speaker's transformation of one scene into another. This movement was repeated several times, once for each partial changeover. The metaphor is complex: the left side is the first scene; the right side is the new scene; and the movement is the transformation of the first scene into the second.

alized as a piece-by-piece shifting of the left gesture space over to the right gesture space. The space was thus divided, and the visual and acoustic lines with which Hitchcock linked the scenes became successive gestural shifts from one space into the other. The speaker first shifted the scream, next the face, then the posture, and finally the hand itself. (Comments are in boldface; brackets omitted.)

(6.18) at this point a scream is heard coming from her

Left hand points = scream. **She sets up the scream on the left.**

(6.19) but this scream changes suddenly

Left hand holds in midair.
Right hand swings forward and to the right. **She continues the scream on the left, and contrasts it to the space on the right, which is the transformation of the scream.**

(6.20) the scream continues

Right hand holds in midair.
Left hand beats. **This reactivates the scream on the left while preserving the transformation on the right.**

(6.21) but the face changes

Left hand holds in midair.
Right hand swings forward and right again. **Again, a transformation is accompanied by a gesture toward the right space, while the scream is held at the left.**

(6.22) and you can see that landlady

Left hand holds.
Right hand moves down and forward. **This introduces one of the results of the transformation—the landlady—into the right space for transformations.**

(6.23) who is standing exactly the same way

Left hand holds in midair.
Right hand moves up and back. **This is a spatial gesture depicting the landlady standing in the transformation space. Meanwhile, the scream hand is continuing on the left.**

(6.24) as this woman stood in the street

Right hand held in upright position
Left hand loops down and to the right. **The right hand is held in its position to be the landlady standing and the left hand, which had been the scream in the first scene, is now transferred to the right space, the space of transformations, and this space now has become the transformed scene in its entirety.**

This first scene has now been totally transformed into the second scene. From now on, in perfect accord with the basic left-right division of the space, all gestures with either hand are performed in the right space, the space of the new scene, back at the artist's flat.

(6.25) and she's looking at a hand

Right hand held in upright position.
Left hand points down to right.
The landlady is standing (right hand) and looking down (pointing by left hand); all of this is in the right space.

(6.26) but this is really the dead person's hand

Right hand held in upright position
Left hand again points down to right. **The right space is still used since the transformation is complete.**

This gestural solution to the problem of describing an extremely complex cinematic transformation was completely spontaneous. The successive shifts took place fluently as the links between scenes came up in speech.

Conclusion of Metaphors in Narrative

An implication of the phenomenon of metaphoric gestures (of any kind) is that the abstractness of an idea is no barrier to its receiving a concrete reality in gesture form. Movements of the hands are perfectly capable of expressing abstractions. Conduit and spatial metaphors are instantly available. Metaphoric gestures are outnumbered by iconics in narratives, but this is because of the content of the narrative, not any inaccessibility of the gesture itself. On the contrary, metaphorics are among the most frequent of all gestures in other genres, especially conversations and lectures.

Concepts That Take Shape

Metaphoric gestures differ not only culturally, but also individually. Each speaker may come up with his or her own images of the abstract. This follows from the nature of metaphoric gestures. They create homologies between concepts and image schemata, and this creativity leaves room for individuality. The images are idiosyncratic but share a core of meaning. The same core schema, such as the conduit or investing space with abstract meaning, can give rise to quite different looking gestures. Nonetheless, the gestures that present these images could arise from the same schema.

The title of this section is taken from Rudolph Arnheim's book, *Visual Thinking* (1969). In one chapter, Arnheim presented drawings by college students who had been asked to depict in graphic form such abstract concepts as past, present, and future, or a good marriage and a bad marriage. Figure 6.14 shows drawings of past, present, and future done by students of my own, who were assigned some of Arnheim's concepts. The drawings are, in effect, metaphoric gestures on paper. Arnheim indeed referred to such drawings as metaphors: "This spontaneous use of metaphor demonstrates not only that human beings are naturally aware

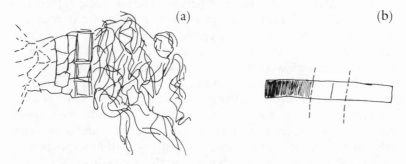

(a)   (b)

Figure 6.14. Drawings by two students for the concepts of past, present, and future (collected following Arnheim 1969). The drawings depict different images either of which could be exhibited in gesture form. Panel (a) shows the future as chaotic, (b) as empty.

of the structural resemblance uniting physical and non-physical objects and events; one must go further and assert that the perceptual qualities of shape and motion are present in the very acts of thinking depicted by the gestures and are in fact the medium in which the thinking itself is taking place" (118). Drawing (a), for example, was described by the student who created it in these words: "Past: solid, yet fading in memory; present: concrete and vivid; future: unknown, chaotic." We would expect a metaphoric gesture for the past by this student would also highlight solidity—for instance, a solid object moving out of sight over the shoulder. Conversely, his idea of the future would suggest a gesture in which the depiction is of chaos—the hands wiggling or flopping, for instance. Drawing (b), from another student, was described as follows: "Past is filled; present is occupied with one thought, action; future is empty because it is not known." Her gesture for the past might also highlight solidity, but her gesture for the future should look quite different— a quiet openness presented, perhaps, in the hands parting to create an empty space. Such drawings, like metaphoric gestures themselves, are idiosyncratic images of past and future. Yet the two students' very different images of the future share a common opposition to the past which they portray as something solid and locked up. Though superficially different, both are component images of a system with a common thread. Such images are comprehensible to others since they capture "structural resemblances" or homologies. The "very acts of thinking" of the subjects are sharable and communicable in this way even though idiosyncratic.

Gesture of Mathematicians

I next describe a specialized type of conduit gesturing that accompanies the technical discourse of mathematicians. In certain respects these gestures are unlike the narrative gestures that we have examined so far. The same gestures appear with different speakers and appear in much the same form in a range of different contexts; a gesture with a certain meaning has a more or less constant form; and the gestures cover single concepts. In all these respects mathematicians' gestures depart from the global-synthetic plan of narrative gestures. Yet, mathematicians' gestures resemble ordinary gestures in co-occurring with speech, being apparently unconscious, not combining with other gestures, and being themselves not composed out of parts. The gestures are thus somewhere on the road to a gesture language, but are not all the way there.

Jacques Hadamard, himself a mathematician, published in 1945 a slim volume entitled, *The Psychology of Invention in the Mathematical Field,* in which he claimed that mathematicians think primarily in terms of images, both visual and kinesthetic, and only secondarily in terms of symbols (including mathematical symbols). This was his own experience and was also the experience of many other mathematicians who responded to a worldwide survey that Hadamard conducted. Hadamard gave an example (76–77) from his own reasoning to show how images carry mathematical meaning, which is repeated below. He is proving that there is a prime number greater than 11 (I cannot say if this is at all interesting from a mathematical point of view, but the psychology of it is interesting; the "I" in the following is Hadamard):

Steps in the Proof	Hadamard's Imagery
A. I consider all the primes from 2 to 11, say 2, 3, 5, 7, 11	I see a confused mass.
B. I form their product: $2 \times 3 \times 5 \times 7 \times 11 = N.$	N being a rather large number, I imagine a point rather remote from the confused mass.
C. I increase that product by 1, say N plus 1.	I see a second point a little beyond the first.
D. That number, if not a prime, must admit of a prime divisor, which is the required number.	I see a place somewhere between the confused mass and the first point.

It is not surprising that there should be gestural manifestations of these kinds of images. The images are mathematical in their references, but visual-kinesthetic in their presentation. In the Kantian framework, we can suppose that the images are products of schematas for mathematical ideas, just as "| | | | |" was the product of the schema for the concept of fiveness. We could call Hadamard's imagery *metaphors* of mathematical concepts of sets, products, divisors, and the like. Thus thinking in terms of images imbued in this way with mathematical significance, mathematicians could generate gestures that also are metaphors of mathematical ideas.

Some years ago I made a videotape of a technical discussion between two mathematicians (Robert A. Morris and Michael P. Anderson).[2] These speakers did indeed perform gestures in which mathematical concepts were realized as visual-kinesic forms, as will be described below.

2. This recording was made in 1975. At the time we all were members of the Institute for Advanced Study at Princeton.

DUALS. For example, the concept of a mathematical dual was accompanied by gestures in which the hand rotates between two positions (in a dual, a relation is replaced by its converse). The following is an illustration (from McNeill 1987; see fig. 6.15):

Figure 6.15. A mathematician's gesture for the concept of a dual with "this gives a [complete duality]." Typically, duality gestures involve a rotation.

(6.27) this gives a [complete duality]

Metaphoric: right hand presents the idea of a dual by looping upward.

The key feature in this gesture was the alternation. Other references to duality were accompanied by the same key feature although details might be different (rather than looping up, the hand might flop sideways, for example).

LIMITS. Other gestures also focused on particular key features that were appropriate for their particular mathematical concepts. The idea of a direct limit was accompanied by straight-line trajectories followed by "end-marking" (a tensed stop). A straight line with an endpoint appears to be an appropriate picture of a direct limit. An inverse limit, in contrast, was made by looping the hand downward and then upward. It is hard to say whether this is an appropriate image of inverseness, although such is possible I am told. It is also possible that the inverse limit gesture was constructed to contrast with the direct limit gesture. Here are two examples, first a direct limit and then an inverse limit:

A direct limit (see fig. 6.16 at the top of page 167):

(6.28) so the continuous linear dual is gonna be a [direct] limit

Metaphoric: hand depicts a straight line with an endpoint.

An inverse limit (see fig. 6.17):

Figure 6.16. The mathematician's gesture for the concept of a direct limit with "so the continuous linear dual is gonna be a [direct] limit." Direct limits involve straight-line movements with end marking (such as an abrupt halt).

Figure 6.17. The mathematician's gesture for the concept of an inverse limit with it's an [inverse limit] of pro-Artinian rings." The downward loop is typical of this concept.

(6.29) it's an [inverse limit] of pro-Artinian rings

Metaphoric: hand shows convoluted downward and then upward line with an endpoint.

SPEECH ERROR. Another example of a limit gesture appeared during a speech error in which one of the speakers said, "this gives an inverse limit," but performed a direct limit gesture. The other speaker corrected the mistake and replied, "a direct limit," and also made a direct limit gesture. The first speaker then accepted the correction, made a third direct limit gesture, and repaired the words, "I mean a direct limit." The error was therefore confined to the speech channel, and was a purely verbal error, while the gesture proceeded in terms of the appropriate metaphoric image. What took place in this error demonstrates Hadamard's claim that thought in mathematics is more closely connected to imagery than to language. The error also points to the theory that the gesture (and the imagery behind it) is the initial form of the utterance and that lexical processes come later.

(6.30) is an [inverse limit] . . . of . . .
Metaphoric: hand shows a straight line with an endpoint.
(6.31) (Listener) it's a [direct] limit
Metaphoric: hand also shows straight line with endpoint.
(6.32) I mean a [direct] limit
Metaphoric: hand again shows straight line with endpoint.

OTHER CONCEPTS. The mathematicians had distinctive gestures for other mathematical concepts, such as quotients, factoring, maps, flatness, and compactness/finiteness; each was distinct from the others, constant in terms of the key features preserved over different occurrences, and similar between the two speakers. Finiteness and compactness, for example, were a tightly bounded space, flatness a flat plane, factoring and quotients a vertical separation of space, etc.

MATHEMATICIANS' GESTURES AS "WORDS." An observation that suggests a somewhat specialized gesture mode is the linguistic segments with which the gestures coincided. As the examples suggest, the spoken text included: "complete duality," "direct," "inverse limit," and so forth; there were no gestures coinciding with phrases or clauses, let alone with complex sentences. Moreover, the gestures tended to coincide with nominal referring terms rather than with verbs. The narrowed temporal locus plus the tendency to associate with nouns suggests gestures that are not global and synthetic, but rather are segmented more like words. Thus it may be appropriate to think of these gestures as imagistic words that take the place of linguistic words, at least within the confines of this particular interaction, and in this respect gestures with uses quite different from anything found in spontaneous narrative discourse. When Hadamard insists that mathematicians do not think with linguistic words, we should ask if instead they are thinking with gestural words.

Other Kinds of Abstract Gestures

The ability of gestures to refer to abstract meanings is not limited to metaphorics. In particular, besides these imagistic gestures, beats and abstract uses of space greatly add to the expressive power of the gesture channel. Finally, there are abstract uses of gesture repetition.

Beats

The semiotic value of the beat is that something is significant, not for its normal referential value, but because of its relationships to the overarching discourse. It is somewhat akin to using a highlighter in a written text. The marked word is made to stand out of its normal context, and this highlighting sends us, the reader, in search of a different context for the word. Extra emphasis on a word when it is in a normal context induces us to seek or invent a different context for it, and beats function in a similar way. Beats, in analogous fashion, signal that the word they accompany is part of some other context than the one that it is immediately presented in. Very often the external context is the larger discourse. Although beats are simple as movements, they are cognitively complex. They do not emerge in children until age 5 and are not abundant until age 11 (chap. 11). The limiting factor appears to be whether the child has developed the *narrative structures* in terms of which discontinuities and relationships to the external context can be defined. Young children have not yet developed them and thus have no basis for beats, despite the motoric simplicity of the gesture.

The following examples illustrate typical contexts in which beats appear during narratives by adults and older children; in every example, the beat marks the relationship of the word it coincides with to the larger context.

REPAIRS. The speaker mentioned one of the characters and decided to use a more specific referring term:

(6.33) and the bird . . . the ca[NAR]y . . throws a bowling ball
                                  Beat.

The beat marked the word that was the repair itself, not the word deemed in need of repair (bird). With a repair, clearly, the relationship of the repairing word to its context, the word it is replacing, is crucial, and the beat highlights this relationship.

NEW CHARACTERS. When a character is introduced into a narrative, the mention of the character is important for its relationship to the story as a whole, not for anything the character is then doing. For example, this was the first mention of Granny in one narrative:

(6.34) and [the old] woman who keeps Tweety
             Beat

The reference is not to the character performing an action in the story, but on a different level to her being introduced as a character.

ADDITIONAL INFORMATION. In the following, the introduction of a new character is accompanied by a conduit presentation gesture, but when her two names are mentioned, each is accompanied by a beat. Moreover, the second beat accompanies exactly what was the added information, viz., her family name, even though the first name was also repeated:

(6.35) his [girl]friend . . .
Metaphoric: presenting the character

(6.36) [Al]ice . . . Alice [White]
     Beat   *Beat*

SUPERIMPOSED ON OTHER GESTURES. The above examples of beats all occurred alone, when the speaker was departing briefly from the main story line to repair something, to introduce a character, to add further details, etc. It is also possible to highlight words in relation to other gestures. In these cases an iconic or metaphoric gesture has beats superimposed on it. Each beat signals that the word it accompanies should be interpreted in relation to the gesture image. The following is such a case, where beats are added to an iconic gesture in the Chinese narrative of the film story:

(6.37) yi   kan ba   [limian you [yige   tiao]
                                 (1)   (2)
       once look you know [inside have [a-classifier slip]
'as she looks in you know, [there's [a slip]'
(1) Iconic: shows hands holding a slip of paper.
(2) Superimposed beat (a).

(6.38) nei [tiaoshang] jiu xiede ba,   ah shi
          (3)
       that [slip-on]   just write you know, ah be

[ling   yige   ren]   gei ta] xiede
(4)
     other a-classifier person] give her] write
'[on that slip] there's writing you know, ah written to her by [another man]]'

(1) Iconic for holding slip of paper continues.
(3) and (4) superimposed beats (b) and (c).

This example was analyzed with Nancy L. Dray (Dray and McNeill 1990) in the following way. Throughout the passage, paperholding was central to the scene, but first (beat a) it was a piece of paper regarded as paper (a physical object), then (beat b) it was a piece of paper regarded as a note (with writing on it), and finally (beat c) it was a piece of paper regarded as a message-bearer (transmitting a message from the other man). Each of the points of reanalysis of the role of the paper was indicated by a beat superimposed on the iconic gesture of paper holding. Maintaining the iconic gesture throughout, the speaker was maintaining a focus on the paper (which corresponds to its importance in the scene of the movie), and at another level, marking contrasts within that continuity, corresponding to the different ways the paper was being represented. Thus, we find superimposed beats when narrators are presenting events on multiple levels and relating words to an ongoing iconic gesture.

Bearing in mind the constant temporal relationship of gestures to speech, we can say from the phenomenon of superimposed beats that, in their primitive stages, utterances are already organized on both narrative and metanarrative levels (see chap. 7).

Abstract Uses of Space

Gesture space itself can be endowed with abstract meaning. For example, a part of space can be identified with a particular character or place in the story. Then subsequent events involving that character or place may be accompanied by gestures in the same space. This produces a cohesive linkage, and often there are linguistic reflections of the cohesion in choices of words and sentence structures, and these might change when a new space is entered or the meaning of the space itself changes. This "endowed space" motivates both abstract pointing—the pointing finger aimed at a concept—and an axial division of space into different roles or meanings. The first example here shows this axial division where two slices of space represent two roles in the story.

SPLITTING THE GESTURE SPACE. My illustration comes from another of the full-length film narratives. The speaker was setting up a new scene (the characters had already appeared in earlier scenes), and said:[3] "she

3. The null sign is used to indicate the locus in speech of deleted grammatical subjects—sometime referred to as "null subjects."

[picks up a] palette of his [and Ø attempts to do a painting] which she does not do very well and then [what he] does is [he steadies her hand to complete] just a- a line sketch and [then she] signs the painting and Ø sits down and [he gets] her a drink and [Ø starts to play the piano] as artists of that time y'know were wont to do." The linguistic references to the two characters are thoroughly interleaved. However, gesturally, the references were separated into two spaces (only the utterances accompanied by gestures are represented):

(6.39)

Center Space (male character)	*Right Space (female character)*
	she picks up a palette
	and Ø attempts to do a painting
then what he does is	
he steadies her hand	
	then she signs the painting
and he gets her a drink	
and Ø starts to play the piano	

Speech and gesture are coexpressive in this passage in two ways. The linguistic forms referring to the two characters show a progression from more explicit to less explicit, and this progression is defined separately for each space. Moreover, entering or reentering a particular space was the occasion for upping the explicitness of the referring form.

In the female character's space, the references are, successively, "she"— Ø—"she." The first pronoun declines to a zero, thus a relatively more explicit referring form is followed by a less explicit one. These were successive references within the same space, with the male character's space not intervening. The zero subject then was followed by "she," an increase of explicitness, and this was because the male character's space had intervened.

Similarly with references in the male character's space. The sequence was: "then what he does is"—"he"—Ø, that is, a steady decline of explicitness. The overmarked reference, "then what he does is," in which the referring form gets its own clause, creates a major discontinuity at the first mention of the male character and the first time his space was used (cf. Levy 1984). This was just after a double use of the female character's space. The speaker was thus introducing the spatial dichotomy as well as the male character. The highly explicit marking of the referring form, which at first seems so excessive, in fact was appropriate for coexpressivity with the gesture. The rest of the references to the male character followed a steady decline within his space and are quite orderly in expressing, with gesture, the continuation of the artist's space.

ABSTRACT POINTING. Concrete pointing in a narrative uses space iconically. The left-right, up-down axes are homologous to the equivalent axes of the space occupied by events of the story. An example of such a referential use of pointing is this:

(6.40) and [throws him off] the window sill
Pointing: right hand points to lower right space.

The gesture depicts the trajectory and final destination of the character. The path and destination iconically represent the layout in the cartoon itself.

Pointing also has an abstract function in narratives, and it is this kind of pointing—abstract pointing—that we will focus on. This is a gesture where the speaker appears to be pointing at empty space, but in fact the space is not empty; it is full of conceptual significance. Such abstract deixis implies a metaphoric use of space in which concepts are given spatial form, and this space can be indexed by pointing. The objects are not actually present, but the compulsion to point at their space remains. In the following two examples, the speaker is at a point of transition in his narrative and is introducing a new character and new development in the plot:

(6.41) and in fact a few minutes later we see [the artist]
Pointing: right hand points to left side of space.

The gesture was synchronous with mentioning the artist for the first time. Orienting to the artist was paramount. This character is referred to again in the following clause and there is again a pointing gesture indicating the same space, but now the gesture is timed with the reference to an action. The space has been revalued and indexed as the space of the scene itself. These abstract uses of pointing perform major discourse functions (chap. 7).

(6.42) and uh she [looks over] Frank's shoulder at him
Points to left side of space again.

SHIFTS OF ORIGO. Thus far we have defined pointing in terms of the target of pointing. Pointing, however, is more complex. It is inherently orientational. The speaker orients toward a target and a region of space.

A pointing finger iconically depicts a line that runs from an "origo" to the target (the term "origo" is from Bühler 1934; also see Jarvella and Klein 1982). A pointing gesture is thus complicated, it consists of three parts:

$$\text{Origo} \rightarrow \text{Referent} \quad \text{Object}$$

where the gesture proper depicts the line that connects the origo to the target. The origo implied in the gesture can be identified by tracing back the line to its starting point; this is not always the speaker himself. For example, in the following, from a conversation, a speaker contrasts two kinds of pointing, the first with an origo not at himself, the second with the origo shifted to his own locus, and these correspond to an attempt to shift the thematic content of the conversation (fig. 6.18 and 6.19):

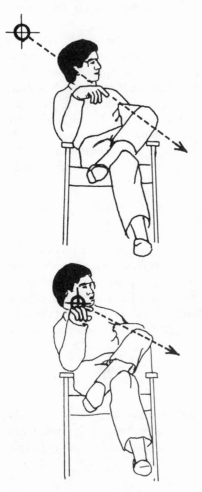

Figure 6.18. Pointing gesture with origo not at self with "did you [go to] school [there] or uh?" The speaker is orienting the listener to the listener's space for "there," and this favors the origo to the side. (Compare with fig. 6.19.)

Figure 6.19. Pointing gesture with origo at self with "oh an' you went to undergraduate [here]?" The "here" in question is where the speaker is located. The speaker is orienting himself to the space and the origo shifts to reflect this. (Compare with fig. 6.18.)

(6.43) did you [go to] school [there] or uh?
Points with an origo off to the side: orienting from someplace other than self.
(6.44) (Interlocutor: I did go to school there, I went to school here also, um so I came back kind of I wa-)
(6.45) oh an' you went to undergraduate [here] or?
Points but with origo now at self: orienting from self.

The gesture at (6.43) had an origo not at the speaker and implied that the speaker was establishing someone, not himself as the origin of the space for "there." The gesture at (6.45), when the origo swung to himself, implied that he was now orienting for himself. This self-origo was in fact the first to be used by this speaker. The preceding pointing gestures, including the one in (6.43), had origos not at himself. The complete meaning of (6.43) thus seems to have been: in relation to you, did you go to school "there?" In contrast, the meaning of (6.45) was: in relation to me, did you go to school "here." The first space left it open to the listener to define "there," but the second space could only be a "here" defined by the speaker. These examples are from the cat-and-mouse interaction that I presented in chapter 4 to illustrate gestural mind reading. The speaker of (6.43) and (6.45) was attempting to find out where the listener had gone to school, and the listener had merely said, "at Chicago." The new origo at (6.45) can be seen as part of the speaker's attempt to pin down the listener. By insisting on his own person as the origo, he could exclude the ambiguous reference to Chicago that had been the listener's way of avoiding disclosure. The gesture at (6.45) could only be the University of Chicago, while the gesture at (6.43) and earlier could have been anywhere the listener imagined himself to be. The word selection, "undergraduate," in (6.45) had the same effect of excluding the city meaning as the referent of "here," since only a university has undergraduates. Thus the origo shift and the word choice (through its implications) were the coexpressive elements in this situation.

Gesture Repetitions

Sometimes gestures are repeated but rarely is the second gesture an exact repetition of the first. If a contrast is implied, the second gesture may be enhanced. The enhancement conveys the contrast. On the other hand, if a gesture is repeated without an implied contrast the second gesture is usually a diminished version of the first. The diminution conveys the lack of contrast. Thus we have two opposite situations, gesture enhancement (for contrast) and gesture diminution (for lack of contrast). The following are two illustrative examples.

ENHANCEMENT. The contrast is between uses of space on two levels. The first gesture is pointing that sets up a locus in the narration itself ("that's my father's newsstand"). The second gesture is also pointing but now it sets up a repair of the speaker's own speech ("not newsstand, news SHOP"). The values of the spaces are quite different—one part of the story line, the other part of the speaker's own discourse—and this contrast is marked with enhancement (forward movement is added) (see fig. 6.20):

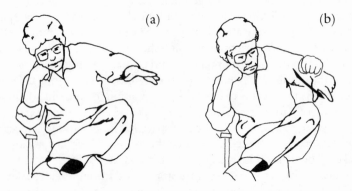

Figure 6.20. Gestural enhancement of meaning. Panel (a) shows the gesture with "that's [my father's news]stand"; this sets up the news stand in the left space. Panel (b) shows the enhanced point with the correction, "not [newsstand] [news SHOP]." The pointing indicates a further space on the left and marks the difference between referring to the news stand (first gesture) and referring on a metalinguistic or metapragmatic level to the speaker's own discourse (the point).

(6.46) that's [my father's news]stand
                        (1)

(1) Deictic: hand swings to left.

(6.47) not [newsstand] [news SHOP]
              (2)   (3)

(2) Deictic: hand swings forward and to right.
(3) Deictic: hand swings forward and left.

The gesture at (1) is to the left; that at (2) is to the right (contrast of negation); the one at (3) is the enhancement and conveys the speaker's metalinguistic repair.

DIMINUTION. The following example again includes a metalinguistic comment, but in this case the comment belittles the concurrent utterance (with the word "whatever") and doesn't bring in contrasting information (see fig. 6.21), and the second gesture is about half the physical size of the first.

(6.48) oh and then you see him trying to get into the apartment again over some wires and [it's the the trolley car . . .]
Iconic: shows moving trolley connector (fig. 6.21a).

(6.49) [wires whatever]
Iconic: repeats showing the connector, but much smaller (fig. 6.21b).

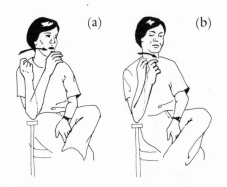

(a)   (b)

Figure 6.21. Gestural diminution of meaning. Panel (a) shows an iconic gesture with "over some wires and [it's the the trolley car . . .]. Panel (b) is a reduced repetition with "[wires whatever]." The disparagement of the word choice "wires" by "whatever" is conveyed in the diminution.

CONTINUATION. A different type of gesture repetition is the following. In this case, the same iconic handshape is maintained throughout a series of descriptive statements, each of which occurred with its own gesture performed with the other hand. The maintained handshape created a cohesive link uniting all the statements and other gestures. At the end of the string of statements, the speaker referred to the entity that had been depicted all along in the continued gesture, and utilized for this a definite referring noun phrase (implying that the entity was an established referent; Chafe 1976).

The speaker was describing a scene in the movie in which a character is shown lying in bed holding a newspaper. The narrator's left hand performs a gesture for holding the newspaper, and this was preserved throughout the description. Simultaneously, the right hand performed a series of different gestures for the successive clauses:

(6.50) he's [in his bed]
Iconic: holding the "newspaper" with his left hand.   ←

(6.51) and he can see [the door]
Iconic: holding the "newspaper" with his left hand.   ←
Points to right with right hand.

(6.52) from [a mirror] which is on the other side of the room

Iconic: holding the "newspaper" with his left hand.   ←
Points to front with right hand.

(6.53) he just [sees him] in the mirror

Iconic: holding the "newspaper" with his left hand.   ←
Iconic: right hand wipes across "mirror" surface.

(6.54) and uh he's [trying]

Iconic: both hands hold the "newspaper."   ←

(6.55) [to put down the paper slowly]

Iconic: both hands slowly move the "newspaper" downward.   ←

The narrator refers to the newspaper verbally for the first time only in (6.55), but the reference is made with a definite noun phrase, "the paper," not "a paper." To the speaker, the newspaper was an established, recoverable object in the scene and he presents it as such to the listener (cf. Chafe 1974, 1976). The newspaper in fact had been present in the scene all along, but only as an image, not as a verbally designated entity, and this image was enough to bring out definite reference to it.

SELF-GENERATION OF OPPOSITIONS THROUGH REPETITION. The forward movement of the hand with "news SHOP" conveyed nothing about news shops or the location of the news shop in relation to the newsstand (since they were one and the same thing); it conveyed only the existence of a contrast between two levels of meaning. The "newsstand" of (6.41) was normal language, referring to something in the story, whereas the "news SHOP" of (6.47) was metalanguage, referring to language itself (in fact, to (6.46)). Many metaphoric gestures can be seen to form chains in this way in which mini-systems of opposition briefly emerge. The diminution in (6.49) contrasted on the parameter of extent of movement, and this also had no iconic significance; the content of the diminution was coexpressive with the spoken form "whatever." These mini-systems are not structures derived from the spoken language, but temporary structures, good only as long as these specific contrasts are at the forefront of the speaker's thoughts (see chap. 9).

Conclusions

Metaphors, including metaphoric gestures, provide us with the power to think of the abstract in concrete terms—in images of space, form, and movement that are not just concrete images but that become abstract concepts. Many psychological studies have demonstrated the efficiency of human thought in concrete contexts, and conversely, the striking lack of efficiency of thought forced to deal with abstract modes of representation such as the symbols of formal logic (Johnson-Laird 1983). Metaphoric images thus can be said to play a crucial role in the effectiveness of human thought; and gesture images, because they are ubiquitous and readily available, can be claimed to play this crucial role with great frequency. This fact explains why metaphoric gestures are such a common accompaniment of speech in narrations and conversations and why apparently all cultures provide schematas for constructing homologies between abstract content and concrete imagery. Metaphoric images are the culture's way of influencing individuals' thought. Society cannot directly control thinking, but it does influence it by providing schemata for creating metaphoric images.

What can we conclude about the metaphoric process itself? The creation of homologies depends on an ability to consider space, movement, etc., in a new light. It is not just space, movement, etc., but these qualities imbued with abstract content. The important thing about metaphoric imagery is that it is simultaneously concrete and abstract, and this is what the efficiency of thought requires. There is therefore a meta-level capacity inherent in metaphoric thinking. Philosophers such as Max Black (1982) and I. A. Richards (1936) have emphasized the "interanimation" of the Topic and Vehicle; the psychologists Glucksberg and Keysar (1990) emphasize the formation of new categories by combining the Topic with the Vehicle. But, in addition, the Vehicle is used for conveying, not just an image, but an image felt to be homologous with abstract content. This image *is* the abstract thought. The meta-level process indeed forms a new category, as Glucksberg and Keysar maintain, and depends on interanimation, as Black and Richards proposed, but it also reveals a capacity to think about one thing in two ways. Without this capacity, we would be confined to concrete levels of thought or to assaults on the abstract that are painfully inefficient and prone to error. Young children in fact do seem to have a limited capacity to adopt meta-level perspectives, even though they are not limited in their ability to see the world in terms of novel or fanciful imagery. The almost total absence of metaphoric gestures in children until a late stage of development thus emphasizes the importance of meta-level thinking in the creation of gestures of the abstract (see chap. 11).

Part Three

Theory

7   *Gestures and Discourse*

At the gesticulation end of Kendon's continuum gestures differ from
sign languages precisely in that they are not constrained by codes. Languages (including sign languages) provide certain conventional packages of meaning that speakers cannot avoid. It is often the case that if we
mark one feature, the code forces us to mark another feature whether
we intend to or not. But since gestures are not constrained by language-
like conventions, the gesture needs to mark only those features that are
relevant and is free to leave other features unspecified. This expressive
freedom implicit in gestures is most apparent when gestures express
pragmatic content. English is a language particularly weak in systems for
marking the structure of discourse. Swahili, for instance, has specific particles, "ka" and "ki," that indicate whether a statement belongs to the
main story line or to the subsidiary background (Hopper 1979). English
has no equivalent devices for drawing this distinction, nor for marking
many other pragmatic distinctions. However, gestures, unconstrained
by a code, are free to express pragmatic content.

My purpose in this chapter is to to examine the relationship of gestures to ongoing, real-time storytelling. The method of collecting gestures during cartoon and film narrations makes this examination feasible.
The original purpose of the method was to have a standard situation in
which to study gesture performance, but now we can reverse direction
and use gestures to study narratives. I will argue the following: that gestures reflect the discourse functions of the sentences they co-occur with.
Thus, gestures can be used to study this discourse, and how the speaker is
construing the discourse structure as he or she proceeds through the narrative. Very often a gesture reflects a discourse function while the sentence does not, or does not clearly enough for an onlooker to notice it
without having the function revealed in the gesture first. Thus, gestures
show something about the process of narration that would be missed if
only the speech channel were regarded as the vehicle of narrative.

Moreover, while gestures refer to discourse structure they also are integral parts of the utterances they appear with. From this we can infer
that utterances themselves include references to discourse as an integral
part of their being. Even though the linguistic code does not enable the
speaker to express these references in words, the gesture channel does express them. A speaker creates his own context through discourse but he

also includes in each utterance a reference to the discourse, and this reference may be at the forefront.

The kinds of discourse relationships that gestures reveal include succession, voice, point of view, distance, and level; also, they reveal the property called "communicative dynamism"—the property whereby utterances push the communication forward (Firbas 1964, 1971). Such discourse references are built into utterances as fundamental properties shown, first and foremost, in the gesture channel of the utterance.

I have organized this chapter into three main parts plus a conclusion. The first part analyzes the *structure of narrative discourse*. The second deals with the *functions of gestures* in narration and how the different kinds of gesture specialize in different levels. The third looks at *communicative dynamism* and how discontinuity in discourse determines when gestures occur and the degree of elaboration they receive.

Structure of Narrative

Introduction

To explain the discourse shaping of gesture types, it is necessary to have a general theoretical picture of narrative structure as such. The different kinds of gesture can be shown to favor one part of this structure over others. The following is one such theoretical picture.[1]

"Storytelling" or "narrating" refers to the entire set of events that make up the conveying of a story by one person to another. Each of these events may be referred to by the storyteller, and this provides a way of tracking the narrative structure as it is built up on multiple levels for all the parties concerned.

Storytelling is not just a succession of events or episodes, one after another. It is structured on multiple levels, with subtle shifts of time and space, perspective, distance between narrator and narrated, and integration of the sequential with the nonsequential—these are its fundamental dimensions. Gestures track these dimensions. From one gesture to the next, depicted imagery is partially the same and is partially changed: the changes become the highlighted oppositions in the structure of the narrative, strengthening our understanding of the parallels and repetitions that make up the "poetics" of the narrative (cf. Silverstein 1984). Narrative language is thus not a two-dimensional affair with only intersecting

1. Much of the text that follows first appeared in a paper with Justine Cassell (Cassell and McNeill, to appear). Because so many references to this paper would be needed if I were to acknowledge each point individually, I use this footnote to acknowledge the paper as a whole. It goes without saying that Cassell's contribution to this chapter has been vital.

syntagmatic and paradigmatic axes: it has a full, rounded, three-dimensional structure, one dimension of which is imagistic (both visual and kinesic, and either holistic or analytic). Many of the parameters of the basic structure of literary art are conveyed in gesture in spontaneous storytelling.

The context of the narrative may be conceived of as a set of interlocking "participation frameworks" (Hanks 1991) or "mental spaces" (Fauconnier 1985), where actors participate in a given act. One important frame is viewing the cartoon or film. The "actors" in this frame are the narrator and the TV screen. Another frame is the telling of the story, and the actors are the narrator and the listener. A third frame—generally more complex—is the world of the story itself, in which, for example, a woman retrieves a note from her handbag and surreptitiously reads it. The units of this participation framework are represented events, any one of which may be selected and referred to by the narrator.

References can be defined in all of these frameworks on several levels. Stories generally refer to incidents or occurrences that follow one another in the real or fictive world (e.g., a character climbs up a drainpipe to reach an upper story). In addition, narratives recounting cartoons or films also contain references to the event of observing the visual text itself, the film or cartoon story ("it was a Sylvester and Tweety cartoon," or "it didn't start out a talkie, it started out just music in the background"), and/or to the event of the storytelling ("I'm going to tell you about a cartoon I just saw"). References to these "metanarrative events" and "paranarrative events" often act to indicate junctures between the parts of a story. This narrative structure is provided on the verbal and the nonverbal levels, but is often more apparent on the nonverbal level.

Narrative, Metanarrative, and Paranarrative Levels

THE NARRATIVE LEVEL.   This consists of references to events from the world of the story proper. The defining characteristic of sentences at this level is that the listener takes them to be a faithful simulacrum of world occurrences in their actual order. This temporal constraint is what determines the narrative level (Labov and Waletsky 1967; Hopper 1979; Hopper and Thompson 1980). Thus, the narrative level must be somehow distinguished, so that the listener will understand that the order in which the sentences on this level appear is itself part of the story. Film and cartoon narrations invariably have a story line in which events occur in a certain order, and thus the narrative level is at the core of the narrators' concern in recounting the stimulus. Gestures play a crucial part in marking sentences whose order is a simulacrum of the story line.

THE METANARRATIVE LEVEL. Not only do narrators tell the story plot line, but they also may make explicit references to the structure of the story as they build it up. Clauses presenting the story about the story are interwoven with the narrative level and constitute the metanarrative level. Unlike narrative clauses, metanarrative clauses are unconstrained by the order of events in the real or fictive world. It is precisely for this reason that it is crucial to mark narrative and metanarrative clauses; one kind is a simulacrum of the world order, the other kind is not. Any reference to metanarrative events requires the ability to manipulate the story as a unit and to objectify it, and to comment on the story as an event in itself.

THE PARANARRATIVE LEVEL. Storytellers also make references to their own experience of observing the film or cartoon and/or to the event of storytelling itself; this introduces the paranarrative level. At the paranarrative level, narrators step out of the official narrator role; they speak for themselves, as their own personality, and their emphasis is on the relationship of narrator to listener. Each of these levels is illustrated in the following excerpt from a narration (Cassell and McNeill, to appear).

(7.1) um have you seen any of the uh Bugs Bunny   [PARA]
cartoons?

(7.2) (Listener: yeah like)

(7.3) right, ok, this one actually wasn't a Bugs Bunny   [META]
cartoon

(7.4) it was one of the- the series   [META]

(7.5) (Listener: oh, ok)

(7.6) and it had Tweety Bird and Sylvester   [META]

(7.7) (Listener: alright {laughs})

(7.8) so so so you know   [PARA]

(7.9) (Listener: the cat right?)

(7.10) right uh huh   [PARA]

(7.11) (Listener: ok)

(7.12) and uh the first scene you see is uh   [META]

(7.13) this this window with Birdwatcher's Society   [NARR]
underneath it

(7.14) and there's Sylvester peeking around the window   [NARR]

Event Lines

The sequence of events that comprises the story proper is only one of a number of sequences of events that comprise the total narrative. The sort of storytelling that appears in our studies is composed of five "event lines."[2] These make up the three narrative levels. The concept of an event line gives us a way of analyzing the ongoing discourse from the vantage point of each individual sentence. The narrator of a film or cartoon story does not fill the role of narrator throughout the storytelling process. The "narrator" is at first a viewer, looking at a TV screen on which is displayed the visual text—the representation in images of a particular story. After first receiving the narration, the recipient then becomes the supplier of a narration, telling the story to someone who has never seen the cartoon or movie. Any given sentence may include a reference to one of these event lines, and this reference places the sentence on the corresponding narrative level. The events lines that we can identify in cartoon and film narratives are the following:

1. First there is the sequence of events in the story. References to this event line dominate the narrative level. In the cartoon, a character climbing up the pipe to a window is preceded by the two simultaneous events of this character looking at a second character through binoculars, and the second character looking at the first character through binoculars.

2. This story is made available by way of a visual text which is the cartoon or film. In the cartoon the event of one character climbing up the pipe is preceded by that of the second character looking through binoculars which is preceded by the first character looking through binoculars. References to this event line appear in the metanarrative level.

3. The viewing of the cartoon also has its own temporal sequence of actions: first the person watches the TV screen, and then sees the character with binoculars in his paws. This event line also appears at the metanarrative level.

4. The person watching the cartoon forms a representation in memory of the visual text that is more or less complete with respect to the sequence of events depicted in the visual text. And this event line also occupies the metanarrative level.

5. Finally, there is the sequence of recounting the cartoon to a listener: the interpersonal narrative. At this point the viewer becomes a speaker and may say, "It was a cat and bird cartoon—you know the kind." References to these kinds of interpersonal events occur on the paranarrative level.

2. An insight due to Michael Silverstein.

These narrative event lines are important because all of them may equally well form the subject of the narrative that the listener hears. That is, not only the events of character 1 chasing character 2 are conveyed in a narrative, but also the events of watching the cartoon and then describing it. The event sequence of the story plot (1) is the narrative level of the discourse. The visual text event line (2), the viewing line (3), and the representation line (4) form the metanarrative level of the discourse: the part of the narrative that is about narrating. The interpersonal event line (5) is what we are referring to as the paranarrative level of the discourse: the part of the story where the narrator steps out and speaks in his or her own voice to the listener.

Given all of this, it is not enough to say that the order of the story follows the order of events unless we also specify which narrative events are being referred to, and the level of the discourse on which the reference is made (narrative, metanarrative, paranarrative). In speech there is rarely a clear-cut distinction between reference to a character's actions, and references to the narrator's own actions. The same linguistic devices perform both functions. In gesture, however, distinctions are drawn between these levels of the narrative. Likewise, distinctions are drawn between the point of view of the narrator and that of the characters (Cassell and McNeill, to appear).

Function of Gestures in Narrative

Different kinds of gesture appear depending on where in the narratological structure the speaker is operating at any given moment. These gestures thus embody specific information about the discourse structure. The major associations of gestures and narratological structures are summarized in figure 7.1.

The chart shows the gesture situation reached by traversing the different combinations of narratological features. Note that there are missing combinations, e.g., there are no iconics and no perspectives at the metanarrative or paranarrative levels. However, there are different voices throughout the chart: a character, an observer, the narrator as a narratively created role, or the narrator as participant in the experimental situation. Thus the different gesture occurrences are genuinely distinctive additions to the narrative structure, and by tracking them, along with speech, we can uncover the narrative structure exactly as it is being unfolded in real time.

Formally speaking, the gestures at the different nodes of figure 7.1 are nicely adapted to the pragmatic functions being performed there. Iconics

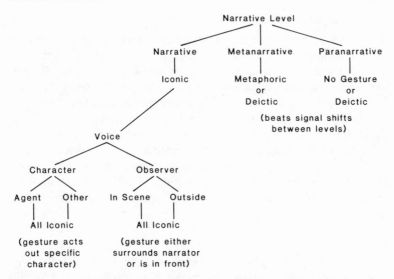

Figure 7.1. Narratological structure of gesture. Each branch leads to a specific type of gesture that is the gesture for that combination of narratological features.

appear at the narrative level, where the content consists of emplotted story events; iconic gestures exhibit these events. Metaphorics appear at the metanarrative level, where the content consists of the story structure itself viewed as an object or space; metaphoric gestures present the story as an object or an arrangement in space. Pointing appears at all levels when orientation or change of orientation is the focal content; pointing conveys a relationship of an origo to the gesture space. Finally, beats appear when there are rapid shifts of level; beats indicate the temporal locus of the shifts without having to convey the content on either of the levels involved.

In this section, as in Cassell and McNeill (1990, to appear), I discuss the relationship between speech and gesture in terms of the diagram in figure 7.1. The gesture categories and relationships already introduced in previous chapters will be related to the storytelling relationships summarized in that structure. I will concentrate on how gestures mark the various elements of a story: that is, how gestures participate in the depiction of action, person, space, and time (narrative events); and also how gestures participate in the articulation of the discourse (metanarrative and paranarrative events): that is, the role of gestures in narrative phenomena such as voice, perspective, order, etc., that take a given set of abstract story components and realize them in a particular way in a particular story.

Gestures at the Narrative Level

The narrative level is not an undifferentiated recounting of descriptive clauses. It presents events, real or fictive, in a text order that is taken by the listener to be the same as the order of world events. Within this general iconic sequence, however, variations can and do appear. Gestures have their part to play in this enrichment of the narrative line. Iconic gestures are the chief accompaniments of the narrative level, but they change depending on narrative voice and perspective and the distance of the narrator from the narrated event that is implied by the different options within these parameters. In parallel, the grammatical forms of speech also changes, and we see in speech, as in gesture, a further illustration of distance, since multiple clauses can be used to depict distance of the observer from the story.

Voice

Voice—who is speaking at the moment—is inferred from the viewpoint of the iconic gesture.[3] We infer the character as the voice when the depiction is dispersed over the narrator's body in an appropriate way: in the C-VPT the narrator's hand plays the part of a character's hand, the narrator's body the part of the character's body, etc. The gesture enacts the character and we infer that this character is the one who is narrating at the moment. Conversely, in the O-VPT the depiction is concentrated in the hand, the character shown as a whole the hand, and the voice accordingly is that of an observer/narrator. The narrator's body is an onlooker and the voice is this onlooker, possibly the "omniscient observer" of fiction (Brooks and Warren 1959) or the narrator replaying his or her earlier role of observer of the video screen. The use of space also differs for these voices, and this provides another clue to differentiating them. With the character voice the space envelopes the narrator—it is a space for the enactment of the character, and includes the locus of the speaker at its center. With an observer's voice, in contrast, the narrative space is localized in front of the narrator—as if it were an imaginary stage or screen—and in this space the narrator moves the relatively undifferentiated figures (blobs). The following example illustrates both the observer and character voices, and the points at which the speaker shifts between them. The extract begins with the observer voice, shifts to the character, then back to the observer, and ends with the character once more. The voices shift

3. The term "voice," in the way I am using it here, comes from narratology (e.g., Genette 1980). It is of course quite different from the familiar linguistics usage of the word, such as "in the passive voice."

back and forth in this manner and the shifting is neither arbitrary nor random, as I will explain below:

(7.15) he tries going [up the inside] of the drainpipe and

O-VPT iconic showing blob rising up.

(7.16) Tweety bird runs and gets a bowling ball

(7.17) and drops it [down] the drainpipe

C-VPT iconic showing Tweety shoving bowling ball down.

(7.18) and . . . [as he's com]ing up and the

O-VPT iconic with the right hand for a blob rising up while the left hand for the bowling ball is floating motionlessly in the upper periphery.

(7.19) [bowling] ball's coming down
. . . .

O-VPT iconic with the left hand for the bowling ball coming down while the right hand for the character floats in the lower periphery

(7.20) he [sw]allows it
. . . .

O-VPT iconic with the left hand (bowling ball) passing inside the space formed by opening the right hand (character's mouth).

(7.21) and he [comes out the bot]tom of the drainpipe
. . . .

O-VPT iconic with left hand (now Sylvester with the bowling ball inside) coming down and under the right hand (now the pipe).

(7.22) and he's [got this] big bowling ball inside him
. . . .

C-VPT in which both hands place round ball into own stomach.

The narrator began with O-VPT, shifted immediately to C-VPT, reverted to O-VPT for four more gestures, and ended with another C-VPT. In terms of distance, the narrator was at first remote from the fictive world, then inside it, then remote, and finally inside again. These alternations are not random but are motivated movements of the speaker closer to or farther from the narrative line. A given event may be portrayed as if it were being experienced, or as if it were being seen from a distance. This is manifested directly in the form of the concurrent gestures. The functional separation of voices suggests that the character voice appears when events are salient. The narrator begins to play the part of the characters directly, and this shifts the gesture mode to the

C-VPT, altering the meaning of the hands, limbs, movement, and space. As we saw earlier (chap. 4), this alternation respects the causal texture of the episode. The character's voice appears when the event is central to this texture, the observer's when it is more peripheral. Both voices are on the narrative level, but within this level a distinction between central and peripheral is drawn. The more central events are automatically cohesive: just by remembering the main outline of the episode—Tweety drops a bowling ball; it ends up inside Sylvester—the narrator finds that the events at (7.17) and (7.22) cohere automatically with the story line, and they are given C-VPT. The remaining events support this outline but are not automatically cohesive either with respect to it or each other, and they are described with an observer's voice whose comments form their own cohesive chain.

Perspective

Perspective is a separate question from voice; it is not who is speaking, but where the observer stands. Where the observer stands is also revealed in gestures (all necessarily with an O-VPT). The gestures described above for the bowling ball scene had *outside* perspectives. A second perspective is common among children but infrequent with adults. This is an *inside* perspective, where the observer is a kind of resident eye that sees but does not act. Below are two examples from adults, the first an outside perspective, the second the rare inside perspective:

Outside perspective:

(7.23) and he tries to swing from an upper story window of one building [right] into Tweety's window

    . . .

Blob hand moves from right side to left side.

This is the perspective of an observer looking on as Sylvester is swinging in front of her, apparently matching the experience of the narrator watching the cartoon (the right-to-left direction of the gesture was the same as the trajectory in the cartoon). The syntactic structure of the utterance is again multi-clause, with the upper clause implying an observer ("he tries" is the narrator's evaluation of the character's lack of success, not a description of his goals).

Inside perspective:

(7.24) and you see him swinging down [across] the rope

        . . . .

Both hands clasped together, move from a location near the narrator's shoulder across the front, and to the side.

From the starting point of this trajectory (next to the speaker's head), we infer the perspective of an observer who is standing in the middle of the space that the character is swinging through. The narrator was thus inside the fictive world. The inside observer's perspective—by bringing the observer into the scene—may enhance the contrast of the character's confident swing with the observer's awareness of an upcoming disaster (the character smashes into a wall).

Distance as a Narrative Strategy

As a dimension, distance subdivides references at the narrative level of storytelling. Distance underlies both the voice and perspective parameters. Distance is least with the character voice, intermediate with the inside observer voice, and greatest with the outside observer voice. The effect of these changes is to classify events in terms of importance, and the more significant the event, the smaller the distance. Small distance implies greater detail in the representation, and thus the character voice is appropriate for events of the greatest importance. The narrator in this voice is inside the narrative event and in contact with the greatest amount of detail. An observer voice is used for events of lesser importance and the outside observer is the most remote. Thus, such a perspective should appear with events of peripheral significance. As Church and her colleagues have shown, this is the case (see chap. 4). The inside observer perspective adds further flexibility to distance. By indexing the listener with "you" and bringing the observer into the narrative space at the same time, the speaker of the final example above implied shared knowledge, and shared knowledge can be used for rhetorical effects. The inside voice is also a film strategy when the camera becomes a resident observer to heighten dramatic effect. Not surprisingly, for stories based on films and cartoons, we see a cinematic strategy in our narratives. With the speaker who said, "you see him swinging down across a rope," with an inside observer voice, there is something of the quality of setting the listener up for the denouement, which is lacking from the more matter-of-fact description with the outside observer voice ("and he tries to swing from an upper story window of one building").

The primitive form of these utterances, we infer, incorporates distance and, correlatively, greater or smaller amounts of imagistic detail, as a function of the importance of the event. Sentences with more distance and less detail are unpacked with multi-clause sentences, in which an extra grammatical level above the event is added to simulate the distance of the observer (see chap. 4).

Movement to Other Narrative Levels

Choices as to voice and perspective are made within the narrative level proper, but a story is very rarely entirely narrated at that level (except perhaps by young children). In the same way that a narrative would be barely comprehensible if it was entirely composed of reported speech without framing clauses, a story is easier to understand when parts of its structure are made explicit. Thus, narrators move from the narrative to the metanarrative (and the paranarrative) level throughout the discourse. The shifts of level can be seen most clearly through two different gestural phenomena: the use of beats to mark movement, and the semiotic value of deictic gestures found within levels.

GESTURES THAT MARK NARRATIVE MOVEMENT. The following excerpt is from examples (7.1)–(7.14). I now add the gestures that occurred with each example to indicate the kind of narrative information that is given in the clause that they accompany.

(7.25) um have you [seen any] of the uh Bugs [Bunny] cartoons?
                        Beat   *Beat*

(7.26) [right] [ok this one] [actually wasn't] a Bugs Bunny cartoon
         Beat   *Beat*   *Beat*

(7.27) it was one of [the– the] series
Metaphoric: hands rotate to depict object in a series of objects.

(7.28) and it had [Tweety Bird and Sylvester]
                      Beat

(7.29) [so so so you know]
         Beat

(7.30) right un huh

(7.31) and uh the first [scene you see] is uh
Iconic: hand depicts flat surface of window ledge

(7.32) this th[is win]dow with [Birdwatcher's] Society underneath it
                    (1)   (2)

(1) Iconic: depicts window ledge
(2) Iconic: depicts rectangular sign

(7.33) and there's [Sylvester] peeking around the window
Iconic: enacts Sylvester peeking over ledge

The first clause (7.25) of this narration does nothing to describe the story, but does function to involve the listener; it has a paranarrative function. This participation frame is signaled by two beats. The second and third clauses (7.26 and 7.27) still do not describe the story but classify the visual text (cartoon) as an example of a genre: the event line indexed at (7.26) is metanarrative, and it is signaled by three beats. The first introduction of the protagonist of the story is again metanarrative and is also indexed by a beat, at (7.28). At (7.29) the level is paranarrative, and there is again a beat. The narrative level is finally reached at (7.32) and (7.33), and here appear the first iconics.

As we saw in chapter 6, in the flow of a narration, beats tend to take place when the narrator withdraws momentarily from the narrative plot line and enters another participation frame either to repair a lexical item (a metalinguistic function), to introduce a new character (a metanarrative [representational] event), or to add new information about an already introduced topic in the narration (also a metanarrative function). That is, beats can be said to signal a momentary increase of distance between the narrator and the narrated event.

One concern that has been put forth is that to interpret the function of beats we must rely on words to identify where there is a shift of levels. If words were the crucial index of the discourse function there would be a risk of circular reasoning: mistakenly thinking that the beat signals the discourse function when really it is the words that do. However, beats accumulate at episode boundaries (40% of all beats occur at these junctures). This observation is independent of words, since we know that there is an episode boundary from the story itself (see the section on Communicative Dynamism below). This is an objective reference point that establishes the function of the beat without circularity. Other beats appear with verbal repairs, first mentions of character, summaries, etc., and these too have a function that can be recognized from objective sources of information that avoid circularity.

Beats thus reveal that a movement away from the temporal axis of the story is taking place in order to present some of the discourse-pragmatic content that also is part of storytelling. This step-off can occur within a single word. Thus a clause in which a beat is found often performs, not the referential function of describing the world, but the metapragmatic function of indexing a relationship between the speaker and the words uttered. The relationship indexed in the previous example was one of objectification: the story was being described not in terms of a series of events in the world, but as an object with external contours. The remaining gesture, the metaphoric in (7.27), then, appropriately depicts the story-as-object. Thus beat gestures can signal movement between narrative levels, and between participation frames within levels, even when this movement is not consistently marked in the speech channel.

THE VALUE OF NARRATIVE SPACE. The gesture space in front of a listener is an active arena where the actions of characters in a story are enacted, and where a narrative observer may be depicted as watching those actions. Another feature of the gesture space, however, is its changing semiotic value. That is, the same physical space can be, at different points during the narration, occupied by the characters from the story, by a television screen and a viewer, or by the actual narrator and his or her listener. These changes in value are marked by deictic gestures, which point out the participants in the current frame of interpretation.

The excerpt given below comes from a narration of the full-length movie.

(7.34) [it- it's sort of a fade-out]
Metaphoric: fade out (curl and uncurl hand).

(7.35) [y'know Frank obviously mad] [stalks off]
          (1)   (2)

(1) Deictic: over right shoulder.
(2) Iconic: stalks off.

(7.36) and then the next time we see [anyone] [involved . . .]
Two deictics: point down right.

(7.37) Frank and Al- [not Frank]
Metaphoric: negation (closing hand).

(7.38) [the artist] [and Alice] are [walking by]
          (1)   (2)   (3)

(1) and (2) both deictics: speaker points towards right and then center.
(3) Iconic: walking from center to left (away from Alice's space).

Several deictic gestures are found in this segment of the narration, but although the deictics look morphologically identical, their semantic value is different with each occurrence.

The metaphoric gesture in (7.34) performs the metanarrative function of making explicit the scene transition. The first deictic gesture in (7.35) indicates the location of a character in the story, and this is at the narrative level proper. Frank, whose previous position has been shown by an iconic gesture made in the center space, directly in front of the narrator, is now shown to be leaving the stage rightward in the first deictic gesture. The next two deictic gestures, occurring in (7.36), also point towards the right (this time front and down rather than up and back), but this time the points occur at the metanarrative level, indicating in space the position of a new scene (or new focus space; Grosz 1981). The metaphoric gesture for a fade-out in (7.34) had been made by moving from the left to in front of the narrator; by contrast the new scene is introduced to the speaker's right. Thus the gestures in (7.34) and (7.36) jointly describe an invisible time line in front of the narrator, with events moving forward into time from left to right. The deictic gestures in (7.38), although they indicate the same place in space, refer back to the narrative level, and to the position of two new actors, the artist and Alice. The spatialization of their position is used in the subsequent iconic in (7.38), which shows the two of them leaving from the right and walking left. Thus two cohesive chains are established utilizing space: that on the narrative level, involving (7.35) and (7.38); and that on the metanarrative level, involving (7.34) and (7.36).

Deictics occur at the paranarrative level as well, as shown in the next excerpt from the very beginning of a cartoon narration.

(7.39) well [it was one of the ahm Tweety Pie and ahm] the cat
       Beats.

(7.40) [cartoons]
Metaphoric: hands present cartoon to listener.

(7.41) (Listener: Sylvester)

(7.42) [Sylvester] right
Deictic: points at listener.

In this example, after metanarrative beats and a metaphoric, a deictic gesture serves to link the participants of the interpersonal participation frame, who share a common piece of information, namely the name of a cartoon character.

Deictic gestures are part of the way in which narrators seems to diagram the plot structure of their story. Physical space becomes a space of referential possibilities, and any refocusing of the referent space brings out pointing. In terms of the narrative model, this abstract pointing marks new characters, at the narrative level proper; new events, at the metanarrative level; and a relationship between speaker and hearer, at the paranarrative level. All are threads interwoven in the construction of the narrative. In terms of the generation of the utterances of the narrative, part of the primitive stage of the utterance is the sense of where the narrator stands in relation to the participants in the various event lines that are being entwined.

Gestures at the Metanarrative Level

Beat and deictic gestures may signal the narrative function of accompanying speech and the referential space that is in play at any given moment in the narration. Within each narrative level, in addition, there are characteristic patterns of gesture occurrence. Table 3.7 showed the frequency of the different gesture types in narrative and extranarrative contexts (extranarrative combined metanarrative and paranarrative). Important for present purposes is the distribution of the non-iconic gestures: beats, metaphorics, and deictics. Beats, which have a metapragmatic function, occur both in narrative and extranarrative contexts. They accompany metanarrative speech, but they also accompany repairs, reported speech, and metalinguistic comments, which can occur as frequently in narrative as in extranarrative clauses, and they are superimposed on iconic gestures, which occur only in narrative speech (see below for discussion of superimposed beats). The two other categories of gestures associated with extranarrative comments were metaphorics and spatializing gestures, including deictics. The capacity of metaphoric thinking to create new homologies between gesture forms and abstract meaning relationships explains the selective presence of metaphoric and spatializing gestures at the metanarrative level.

METAPHORIC GESTURES IN METANARRATIVE. The function of metaphoric gestures is generally representational for ideas expressed in the accompanying speech that do not have a physically depictable form. This function is most often called into play in metanarrative speech, where the cartoon or film narration may be objectified and commented on in the verbal channel, and presented as an object in the gestural channel. The prototypical example has been the statement at the beginning of a cartoon narration ("it was a Sylvester and Tweety cartoon"). A similar example from a different speaker is this:

(7.43) and . . . of course the next [develop]ment in the plot is
Metaphoric: both hands present object to listener.

The metaphoric is again a conduit in which the narrator raises his hands from his lap towards the listener. In this example, speech and gesture work together to make clear the metanarrative level at the transition to the next episode. The speech presents the episode as an example of a type ("the next development"), while the gesture represents the narrator, not as an observer (as in a narrative level gesture), but as the conveyor of this object which is the episode. Conduit metaphorics are frequent at these episode junctures. In such uses of metaphoric gestures, time is instantiated as a bounded entity, the time of the next event in the plot line, the time of the viewing of the cartoon (as manifested in speech in the past tense verb "was"). Thus narrators localize the various narrative times in the gesture channel.

Process metaphorics are also fairly common in narratives. One of the examples cited in chapter 6 was, "we get into the film proper," accompanied by a metaphoric gesture in which the hands rotated around each other and moved toward the listener. Here the narrator was concentrating on the continuity between the events leading into the film.

SPATIALIZING GESTURES IN METANARRATIVE. The other characteristic use of gesture at the metanarrative level is to spatialize, or locate in the physical space in front of the narrator, aspects of the story being narrated. In these examples, contrasts and differences between characters, events, or themes are set up as contrasts in space. The illustration of this metaphoric use of space cited in chapter 6 was splitting the gesture space between two characters. Although the verbal references for the characters were interleaved, their gesture spaces were distinct. In effect, there were two reference spaces unfolded and laid out like a map.

Although conduit gestures are not found in narrations in all languages, there is in every language some use of metaphoric gestures at the metanarrative level. These non-conduit narratives—the Chinese especially—do contain abundant metaphoric gestures of other kinds, and often they are used where in English or Georgian a conduit would appear. However, the gestures do not depict abstract ideas as bounded containers. On the other hand, the use of spatializing gestures appears in all narratives we have recorded, regardless of the language spoken.

Gestures at the Paranarrative Level

The striking characteristic of gesture use at the paranarrative level is how reduced it is. When narrators speak as themselves, outside of a necessarily narrative situation but adopting the role of a participant in a socially defined situation of speaker and hearer, they make only a small number of gestures of a restricted kind. Iconic gestures are virtually absent. Deictic gestures are found, as described above, when these index knowledge shared by speaker and hearer. The role of deictic gestures here is to indicate the participants of the event. Beat gestures are also found when they mark the inception of a paranarrative portion of the discourse, or when they signal repairs or other metalinguistic relationships. This is not to say that the nonverbal channel is inactive at the paranarrative level. In conversations, for example, the participants perform mainly metaphorics when they are not searching for a new topic, at which time they perform deictics (see below). And research by Goodwin and Goodwin (to appear) shows that gaze plays an important role in structuring the participation of a speaker and hearer in a narrating event. Thus the reduction of gesture in paranarrative contexts seems to be a specific clue for this level of narrative organization, opposing it to the narrative and metanarrative levels, and does not necessarily occur in other genres.

Gesture and Ground in Swahili

Narratives are often considered to subdivide into foreground and background—what the story is about, and the supporting material, respectively. The foreground can be equated with the narrative level, and the background with the metanarrative and paranarrative levels. This identification remains problematic, however, chiefly because the linguistic means for marking foreground and background are minimal in English speech. English has repeatedly been the subject of discussions of ground: in contrast to other languages, such as Swahili, there is not a systematic way in English of distinguishing foreground from background. Hopper and Thompson (1980) describe a number of criteria for foreground clauses (such clauses tend to emphasize perfective aspect, differentiate the participants in the action being described, highlight the affectedness of the object of the action, and so forth), but these are semantic criteria, not form criteria (Cassell and McNeill, 1990). In Swahili, however, there is formal marking of foreground and background. The segment *ka-* replaces the tense marker of the verb and signals a continuation of the tense of the previous clause: during narratives, *ka-* therefore occurs in foreground narrative-level descriptions where continuity of the theme is coded. The segment *ki-*, in contrast, replaces the tense marker of the verb when there is interruption of thematic continuity by background information of some kind (the meaning of *ki-* is conditional: "if such and such" corresponds to English "as such and such"; the effect is to remove the clause from the ongoing description of events in the narrative event line). Thus to examine the Swahili Tweety narrative offers a way of comparing gesture types within a system of formal ground marking. This narrative was by a young Tanzanian woman, and was recorded and analyzed by Karen Peterson.

In English narratives, iconics accompany narrative level statements and metaphorics and beats accompany metanarrative level statements. What of the Swahili narrative, where the speaker obligatorily marks the narrative level with *ka-* and the nonnarrative level with *ki-?* The result is clear for the narrative level: the Swahili narrator's iconics invariably accompanied *ka-* verbs. Where she had *ki-* verbs, she systematically avoided gestures. Her metaphorics and beats appeared with clauses that contained neither *ka-* nor *ki,* but were still clauses with a metanarrative function (it is beyond my meager knowledge of Swahili to explain how they could be metanarrative without conditional marking). An example of *ka-* marking with an iconic gesture is "i-ka-" in the following example of dropping the bowling ball down (called a tire):[4]

(7.44) i-ka-chuku-a li-mpira [fulani i-ka-]

       take   tire   [certain]

'and found a certain tire'

Iconic: appears to grasp object.

  . . . tumbuk- iz-a

  . . . push down

'and pushed it'

An example of *ki-* marking with a lack of a gesture is "if (= as) it sings beautifully" (and no gesture). An example of a metanarrative level statement accompanied by a beat, and without either *ka-* or *ki,* is "[therefore] he searched for all possible means of being able to get the bird." Thus, where there is a formal linguistic indicator of ground, we find that narrative-level gestures pattern themselves in the same way as in English speech. The nonnarrative-level beats also appear as in English, but the exact role of *ki-* in gesture performance remains unclear.

Gestural Inertia

Inertia refers to the continued use of the same gesture over and over through a series of semantic and pragmatic transformations. Though the meanings are changing, the form is retained. The gesture is being recalibrated. An example is given below where the transformations are used to create layering in the discourse.

4. I am grateful to Karen Peterson for locating the gestures and for giving me a tutorial on Swahili grammar.

LAYERS OF DISCOURSE. The phenomenon of subdividing the ground into layers was described for purely verbal texts by Reinhart (1984). Gestures achieve this kind of subdivision on an even more extensive scale. Gesture inertia creates such hybrids as fore-foreground and back-foreground. The process is recursive and an embedded layer can have other layers tucked away inside it and so forth. Which is foreground and which background soon becomes obscure, but the layers are clearly separated in the gestures. This kind of discourse situation evolves with a rich sense of the embeddedness of each utterance within the overall discourse structure.

Gesture inertia marks the highest layer and the various recalibrations mark out the units on lower levels. In the following example, the speaker had skipped several episodes of the cartoon, belatedly discovered this, and broke off the story to insert a quick summary of the missing scenes. This summary was presented as a background comment to the overall story structure. But embedded within the summary were other narrative and metanarrative references to the missing scenes. Thus, the summary was background to the main storyline, but within this background were other narrative and metanarrative statements.

The example begins with a crisscross gesture depicting overhead wires. This gesture was part of the story event that was interrupted when the speaker realized there were missing scenes. The speaker broke off the crisscross and shifted to an unusual gesture space, far to the left and high up and to the rear, near her head. At the same time, she said "part of the problem is that Tweety Bird's inaccessible." The new gesture appears to have been both an image of the concept of inaccessibility and of the structural significance of a metanarrative level, literally a "side" comment.

This "inaccessibility" gesture was the inertia gesture that now persists through the entire summary to come. This particular continuing gesture, with its side comment and inaccessibility meanings, reflected the meta-narrative background character of the entire summary. Using the same inaccessibility hands arrangement, the speaker performed a series of iconics that depicted the events of the missing scenes. Thus, the arrangement of the gesture space and the confinement of the iconics to a highly marked space with a distinctive hand formation established the dominance of the metanarrative event line over the narrative details being given. At the same time, the gesture provided a gloss that the summary detailed the effects of Tweety's inaccessibility. The whole production implies that the core idea was a metanarrative comment on the character's inaccessibility and the subsidiary details were illustrating this generalization about the story. The example demonstrates a reversal of the usual order of importance in narratives, where the narrative event line is the foreground and metanarrative comments the background. Here the main points were the events on the metanarrative event line.

To diagram the discourse structure created during this summary, we can use the format of numbered paragraphs:

1.0   the last one he tries is to walk across . . .
1.1   part of the problem is that Tweety Bird's inaccessible
1.11   so he has to climb in the window somehow
1.12   so he's devised several different ways of getting in—
1.121   climbing up the rain barrel
1.122   trying to swing across by a rope
1.0   and finally the last one he decides to try is to walk across

The cohesive crisscross gestures with which the example began also appeared at the end when the speaker resumed the interrupted episode ("and finally the last one decides to try"). These beginning and ending statements are at level 1.0; they are the same event line on the plot level (the same event in fact). The format of paragraphs makes clear that the "inaccessibility" gesture (the hands in the far left space and back next to the head) was preserved as long as the 1.1 level was preserved; this is all on the metanarrative level and is a separate event line in which the events are the narrator's own representation of the story and these representational events are referred to. At the same time, the iconicity of the gestures increased as the degree of story events embedded within level 1.1 increased. Thus at 1.11 and 1.12 (representational and story level event lines) the new gestures were mixes of metaphorics and iconics, while at 1.121 and 1.222 (story events) they were pure iconics. Thus we are shown quite graphically in gestures the narrator's multilevel organization of discourse.

Once we have discovered this multilevel structure, we can see that it also had an effect on the choice of verbal expressions. These verbal manifestations of the layering are quite obscure without taking into account the gestures, but by looking for recurring surface linguistic patterns we find the same hierarchical structure:

Level 1.0 (story event line) was marked by use of "the last one" in both of its occurrences.

Levels 1.11 and 1.12 (mixtures of representational events and story events embedded under 1.1) were marked by use of "so he," semantically implying that what is coded is a result (cf. Schiffrin 1987).

Levels 1.121 and 1.122 (story events embedded inside 1.12) were marked by "verb-ing" forms, which simultaneously convey that actions are being carried out and that there is a continuing process (which we know is in progress on another level, the representational event line of 1.1).

Level 1.1 (representational event line) was marked by "part of the problem."

The passage including the gestures is the following. The lines in this excerpt have been numbered according to the above system for easy reference:

1.0 the last one he tries is [to walk] across

Iconic for wires: both hands form crisscross in center gesture space.

1.1 part of the problem is that Tweety [Bird's inaccessible]

Metaphoric for inaccessibility: left hand in far left space, up next to ear, right hand on left side down at lap.

1.11 so he has to [climb in] this window somehow

Iconic within metaphoric for climbing in: left hand flips down then back up next to ear.

1.12 so he's devised several different ways of [get]ting into the window

Iconic within metaphoric for getting in: both hands flip down then up to ear.

1.121 [climb]ing up the rain barrel

Iconic within metaphoric for climbing up: left hand flips down and then up next to ear.

1.122 trying to [swing across] by a rope

Iconic within metaphoric for swinging across: both hands arc through gesture space and up to ear.

1.0 finally the last one he decides to try [is to walk across]

Iconic for wires: both hands form crisscross in center gesture space.

Superimposed Beats

While the inertia example is remarkable for its size and complexity, it is not the only way to achieve layering of discourse levels; nor is it unusual in terms of its principles. A simpler (and much more frequent) illustration of layering is the superimposition of beats. The beats are added to iconics or metaphorics with the effect of signaling a discontinuity, a relationship between the word the beat accompanies and the narrative level of the gesture rather than the relationship between the word and the other words in the sentence. Here, too, layering occurs, but very quickly, within the span of a single word or syllable. For example, the narrative quoted in chapter 3 includes a statement when the speaker said "you see [$_{iconic}$ him [$_{beat}$draw]ing up [$_{beat}$lots of] blueprints . . .]" (lines 53–54). In this statement she simultaneously marked events on two event lines. An iconic gesture of holding the blueprints belonged to the narrative level, while the beats marked brief shifts in which the speaker was uttering words that referred to the blueprints, that is, to the gesture—what was being done to them ("drawing them") and their quantity ("lots"). This achieves a layering of the narrative and metanarrative in that the iconic gesture presents the narrative event, while the words indexed by the beats provided comments on it. Superimposing beats was this particular narrator's favorite use of the beat gesture, and many other examples are to be found in the narrative in chapter 3.

Using Voice to Shift Narrative Levels

Sometimes a shift of level is marked by a new gesture "voice," from character to observer or vice versa. The operative factor is probably the change of distance that comes from this. An example of such a shift also appears in the narrative in chapter 3 (lines 75–82). The listener intervened with a question and the narrator answered by repeating part of what she had said before. At the same time, she shifted to the O-VPT. What is striking about this example is that the story content is exactly the same in the two versions (7.45 and 7.51). Only the voice changes, the more distant observer voice emerging when the narrator addresses the listener's question. The passage begins with a series of C-VPT enactments:

(7.45)   and she's . . . [in] transom . . . [look]ing down
      (1)   (2)

(1) C-VPT iconic: head tilts forward to show Granny looking down.
(2) C-VPT iconic: both hands move down from own eyes to show "eidola."

(7.46)   and uh she- . . . he says you know I'm here for your bags

(7.47)   and she says oh [OK just a minute]

C-VPT iconic: head tilts to side, squeaky voice, playing Granny.

(7.48)   uh they're right [behind] the door

C-VPT iconic: head tilts forward, squeaky voice, playing Granny.

(7.49)   and I'll meet you [down] in the lobby and so-

C-VPT iconic: head tilts forward, squeaky voice, playing Granny.

This quoted speech was accompanied by head movement gestures that are the *character's* gestures; that is, the speaker was enacting the character, and this included her gestures. Now, the listener asks:

(7.50) (Listener: what's she doing in the transom?)

(7.51) she [crawls] up in the transom

O-VPT iconic: hand rises up with wiggling fingers, to show crawling up.

The answer was accompanied by an O-VPT iconic. This reply is close to being a repetition of the earlier description with the C-VPT (7.45). This shift of voices was shown only in gesture and was specifically for the paranarrative level reply, since the speaker immediately returned to C-VPT enactment.

(7.52) she's [look]ing down at him outside

C-VPT iconic: head tilts forward again to show Granny looking down.

Conclusion and Summary

The narrative and metanarrative event lines have distinct gestural manifestations, and there is further differentiation within the narrative event line by "voice" and perspective. The two event lines also can be combined, in which case one of them dominates the other, and this too is registered in gesture. In contrast to the spoken texts that we have been analyzing, a written text may include hints of its underlying discourse structure, but in a written text the narrative structure is an implied structure and often cannot be isolated in specific language forms as such. Rather, the underlying narrative structure of the text must be inferred from a pattern of usage that is inherently imprecise as to locus. A spoken text, through its gestures, makes the imagery of discourse structure explicit. Gestural distinctions show the exact moment at which narrators shifted voice and perspective and change distance between themselves and the narrative text; when they shift between levels of narrative structure, and embed levels within levels; and the details of these narrative structures, including which voice is speaking and whether there is more than one. We can thus use gesture occurrence to investigate the dynamic process of narrative construction in "real-time," and from this observe much of the richness of discourse structure that is incorporated into utterances.

Gestures and Communicative Dynamism

The discourse structure not only has a highly differentiated effect on the types of gesture that a speaker performs but it also is a major determinant of when a gesture is likely to occur, and of how complex it is if it does occur. The crucial variable here is "communicative dynamism," or CD, which Firbas (1964, 1971) defines as the extent to which the message at a given point is "pushing the communication forward."

We can conceive of the CD variable defined separately on each of the event lines described earlier. A reference to an event provides a momentary focus and this focus can be on any of the event lines. As the speaker moves between levels and event lines, at any given moment, some element is in focus and other elements recede to the background (cf. Grosz 1981). This focal element will have the effect of "pushing the communication forward" on its event line and will provide its own local peak of CD. Thus a reference to a story event focuses on the narrative event line and creates a peak of CD on that level; a reference to structuring the story proper focuses on the metanarrative event line and creates a peak of CD there. Several CD peaks can thus be developing simultaneously and, from the gestures, we can figure out which particular peak of CD is active at the moment. For example, does the narrator choose to focus on a character, or on the story structure itself: these are different event lines and either could be the discontinuous element, but the speaker usually chooses one, and this choice we can infer from the gesture output.

We see this kind of choice in the following example, taken from Elena Levy's (1984) dissertation: "so the next main scene you see with [Sebastian] is um [Sebastian] and some of his friends are carousing in a courtyard." The second mention of the character is unexpectedly explicit (his name rather than a pronoun) and accompanied by a gesture. The two Sebastians belong to different levels of the narrative discourse structure. The first is part of a metanarrative reference to the narrative structure itself, while the second begins a new episode of the narrative story line proper. From this point of view, there is a separate peak of CD on each level, and the second Sebastian is explicit and accompanied by a gesture because it is being used to refer to the character for the first time on its level (also see Levy and McNeill, to appear).

Variations in CD have a decisive effect on the occurrence of gestures. Gestures appear at the peaks of the CD on their level; points of low CD tend to be devoid of gestures of any type. I will present next the arguments that gesture occurrence is determined by CD at every level. It is important to show that different narrative levels have their own peaks of CD. To do this I will organize the discussion into two parts: CD where references are to the story line (the sentence level) and CD where references are to large segments of the story (the episode level). I will begin with the sentence.

Dynamics at the Sentence Level

If there is no gesture at all, the sentence as a whole is low in CD. If there is a gesture, then the gesture picks out the specific sentence elements with the highest CD in the sentence. Moreover, more complex gestures reveal higher peaks of CD, and the details identify what, in the flow of the narrator's thought, is adding to the CD.

Some indication that this hypothesis may be true is that the theme of the sentence—the element that is usually lowest CD—does not receive a gesture in normal cases, except when it is itself being introduced (i.e., it is high in CD). Gestures usually accompany the elements of sentences that are not the theme but plausibly contribute information about the theme, and thus are high in CD.

To provide a rationale for my argument, I will begin with a principle of grammatical coding given by Givón (1985), who wrote: "The less predictable/accessible/continuous a topic is, the more coding material is used to represent it in language" (197). Thus, CD should directly correlate with the quantity of linguistic substance devoted to the linguistic segment. Insofar as gesture-speech is a unified system, we should expect that Givón's principle would apply to gestures as well. The quantity of coding material should increase either with additional linguistic material or gesture material, or both. Thus, a gesture should occur exactly where the information conveyed is relatively unpredictable, inaccessible, and/or discontinuous, viz., where CD is increasing, and with what Vygotsky regarded as the psychological predicate (Vygotsky 1962). A psychological predicate (not necessarily a grammatical predicate) is the thought element least predictable and most discontinuous from the preceding context. In general, the greater the CD the (a) more probable the occurrence of a gesture, and (b) the more kinesic complexity the speaker will devote to it, if a gesture occurs at all. The least complex gestures are beats and abstract pointing, and they might occur with the first step of rising CD, signaling that some discontinuity has occurred. There might also be a correlation of CD with gesture voice. In a narrative, the voice of a character seems to push the communication forward more than the voice of an inside observer, and an inside observer might push it more than an outside observer. Thus, I would expect the following *progression of gestures* as a function of increasing CD:

(highly thematic references)

> no gesture
> beats, pointing (on the narrative level)

> O-VPT iconics with one hand and some highlighting
> O-VPT iconics with two differentiated hands
> C-VPT iconics

(highly "rhematic" references, where the rheme is the added information about the theme; Halliday 1967).

Moreover, among iconics, the gesture should reveal what the specific contribution to CD is. Adding informational specificity adds dimensions of contrast and multiplies the avenues of departure from the existing context. Moreover, using two channels at once doubles the effect. Others have proposed contrast as a driving force for processes of lexical differentiation in children's language learning (Clark 1988), and we are proposing the idea for the structuring of ongoing discourse (cf. Gathercole 1989).

Examples suggest that gestures are in fact triggered by peaks of CD. In the familiar example of "he goes [up THROUGH] the pipe this time," the occurrence and semantic content of the gesture were determined by the high CD elements of the sentence. Here is the full context of that example:

(7.53) and so he tries to get in the building again

(7.54) he crawls [up a pipe]

(7.55) and when he gets up to the bird the [grandma hits him] over the head with the umbrella

(7.56) and he goes back

(7.57) and he goes [up THROUGH] the pipe this time

The gesture in (7.54) was simply the hand rising upward with the palm flat; in other words, it encoded only the trajectory. Likewise the linguistic choice was "crawls up," which encodes trajectory and manner. The gesture in (7.57) also presented a rising hand but the hand was formed into a kind of hollow basket shape. The gesture and speech in (7.57) thus encoded not only the trajectory but the fact that the trajectory was interior to the pipe. The two versions of going up the pipe illustrate the place of contrast with the preceding context in increasing the quantity of coding material. The gesture and the lexical choice of "through" each introduced the dimension of interior-exterior, and set the value as "interior." The added gestural and linguistic quantity in (7.57) thus differentiates it from the version in (7.54). On the other hand, in the first version, there was no contrast in terms of the dimension of interior-exterior at all and exterior was simply the assumed default value. In contrast to "up THROUGH," the other components of the utterance in (7.57), "and he goes" and "the pipe this time," are lower in CD and the gesture avoided them. That these elements were lower in CD seems a correct judgment, since both were carryovers from the preceding sentences in the narrator's description of the scene (7.56 and 7.54).

Two-handed gestures with differentiated roles also plausibly mark high CD. When one hand becomes a character's mouth, and the other hand a bowling ball passing into it, the communicative impulse of the accompanying speech ("he swallows it") is enhanced; the syntactic starkness of three words would normally signify little CD, but the sentence gains prominence with the gesture.

To test if gestures mark peaks of CD, we need to correlate gestures with some other, non-gestural indicator of CD. Since word order is insufficient as an index of CD in English, we need some other measure. I have chosen the *amount* of linguistic material used to make the reference (Givón, 1985). In the up-through-the-pipe example, the gesture stroke coincided with a reference to the character's path that was supplemented with extra stress. This marked reference contrasts with the references in the previous utterances where contrast was not implied. Givón provides this *scale of linguistic quantity* for nominal referring forms:

(most continuous/predictable)

> zero anaphora
> unstressed pronouns/verb agreement
> stressed pronouns
> full NPs
> modified full NPs

(least continuous/predictable)

A similar scale was proposed by Levy (1984). However, gestures are not coexpressive with just nominal referring forms, but with a wide variety of other sentence segments. The linguistic scale can be supplemented with the category of predicates and independent clauses. Predicates and independent clauses present more linguistic quantity than any of the above nominal referring forms, and plausibly a gesture stroke that coincides with a full predicate or clause marks the highest degree of discontinuity and unpredictability. Levy (1982) showed that new thematic

Table 7.1 Gesture Variety and Degree of Linguistic Encoding

	Linguistic Form Used for Reference			
∅	Unstressed Pronoun	Noun Phrase	Modified Noun Phrase	Clause or Verb Phrase
included in 1 iconic that covers the clause	excluded from 3 adjacent iconics			
		1 beat with the NP included in 3 iconics that cover clause or VP		
			1 O-VPT iconic with the NP	
				4 deicitcs with the clause or VP
				3 O-VPT iconics (one hand)
				3 O-VPT iconics (two differentiated hands)
				3 C-VPT iconics

references in discourse tend to appear in predicate positions when they are first mentioned, and then shift over to subject positions upon subsequent mentions. This is because it may be necessary to provide descriptive content in order to identify a new theme, and the predicate can more readily include this. Later mentions, in contrast, need only to index the reference, and this is appropriate for the subject. Thus, I will regard full predicates and clauses, when they are accompanied by gesture strokes over their full extent, as having higher CD than any nominal form—zero, pronoun, or full noun phrase.[5]

Table 7.1 presents the iconics, beats, and pointing gestures (narrative level) in one narration, sorted out according to the grammatical

5. There are obvious exceptions where nominals can be shifted into a designated high CD position; for example, one can say "sweetbreads I don't like," and highlight sweetbreads before other elements in the sentence—a transformation that in fact is called focus movement (Prince 1981). However, such constructions are totally absent in the narratives we have collected.

categories with which the gesture stroke coincided in speech. I have not counted gestures and sentences that introduced scenes (these will be described in the later section on CD at the episode level). We see that no gestures specifically accompanied the zero and unstressed pronoun references (a gesture could accompany a zero reference if a processing pause occurred at that point). With simple noun phrases, only a beat specifically accompanied the reference. With modified noun phrases, an iconic gesture accompanied a reference; it had an O-VPT and was simple in form. Finally, with clauses and verb phrase predicates, for the first time, C-VPT and complex O-VPT iconics accompanied the references. That is, the complexity of the gestures increased when the quantity of linguistic material in the concurrent referring forms increased. As the table also reveals, the probability of a gesture also increased. As noted, no gestures accompanied zero and unstressed pronoun referring forms. On three occasions, indeed, gestures occurred in sentences with unstressed pronouns but precisely excluded the pronoun. At the other extreme, gestures occurred thirteen times with clauses and verb phrase predicates. Both the complexity and the probability of gesture occurrence increased, therefore, at places of where we infer CD was heightened.

An example of the converse process is declining CD. This can occur when the speaker forgets the next step of the narration. In the following, the forgetting seems to take place in stages, the gestures running down in complexity, and ending in total cessation. The series starts with an iconic, shifts to a metaphoric, then to a beat, and finally to no gesture at all, as the speaker's memory also declines:

(7.58) [and jumps in the window]
Iconic: hand shows character jumping in.

(7.59) and [this] way he can [fool] [Granny]
       Beat   *Beat* *Beat*

(7.60) who is [of course] [Tweety Bird's] protector
        Beat   *Beat*

(7.61) uh and . . . let's see what happens he . . . tries to . . .
(No gestures.)

The speaker then recovered from this nadir, again in stages. Her gestures first reappeared in the form of several beats, then a metaphoric, and finally a full C-VPT iconic enactment of a concrete event:

(7.62) to [find out] where Tweety Bird is hiding in [the house]
       Beat   *Beat*

(7.63) and when the [grandmother sort of catches on] to him
Beat and metaphoric for "catching on."

(7.64) [she's apparently] been .. [caught on]
       Beat   *Beat*

(7.65) [has caught on] all along
       Beat

(7.66) [that this] [is] [really] [Sylvester] [the][cat]
     Beat   *Beat Beat*   *Beat*   *Beat Beat*

(7.67) [after] [Tweety Bird]
     Beat   *Beat*

(7.68) [but she's sort of playing along]
Metaphoric for "playing along."

(7.69) [and she says . . . here's a nice new penny for you little monkey or something like that and she]
C-VPT iconic: Granny holding out the penny.

The different gesture types in this series, both its fall and rise—iconic, beat, metaphoric—fit the principles of discourse shaping described earlier: the whole succession can be pictured in terms of declining and then rising CD, as the speaker drifts away from the narrative event line and then back again, with beats appearing while she shifts levels and the metaphoric when she can do no more than view the episode as a whole ("she's sort of playing along").

Dynamics at the Episode Level

To demonstrate peaks of CD on the text and representational event lines, we can look at narratives when the speaker is introducing new episodes.[6] At such junctures the discourse structure of the story comes into focus and one finds peaks of certain types of gesture. On each level there is a separate peak of CD, and gestures accumulate at the metanarrative level

6. Much of the material in this section is the work of Elena Levy and is taken from an article with Levy (Levy and McNeill, to appear) and an earlier article with Levy and Laura Pedelty (McNeill, Levy, and Pedelty 1990). I use this footnote as an inadequate acknowledgment of Levy's great contribution to the discussion of communicative dynamism in this section.

in accordance with the quantity of material principle. Often the episode boundary is marked linguistically with statements like "and the next thing we see . . . ," or "now the scene shifts to . . . ." With these meta-narrative level references, gestures specialized for discourse come into play, specifically metaphorics, pointing, and beats. Thus the types of gesture associated with high metanarrative CD are the opposite of gestures with high CD at the narrative level. As we have seen, gestures associated with high CD on this level tend to be complex iconics, while beats and pointing manifest lower CD.

POINTING IN NARRATIONS. Marslen-Wilson, Levy, and Tyler (1982) had a narrator telling a comic book story from memory. As the subject spoke, however, he held a copy of the comic book on his lap. This arrangement generated a large number of pointing gestures, since the speaker used the picture that appeared on the comic book cover to point to figures of the two central characters in the story. Although the picture was constantly available, pointing was not uniformly spread out through the narrative. One hundred percent of the episode-initial references to the characters were accompanied by pointing, but only about 40% of the within-episode references were. This distribution suggests that pointing was used to establish the referents that would be the theme in the subsequent discourse. The following extract from the narrative occurred when the speaker was reintroducing after a lapse the two main characters for a new episode of the story. It shows that the first mention of the characters was accompanied by a pointing at the comic book cover (the preparation phase coinciding with "the Hulk" and the stroke with "the Thing"); in contrast, the immediately following references to the same characters were gestureless ("the Hulk is getting stronger"; "the Thing keeps catching him off guard"):

(7.70) so then it cuts back to [the Hulk **and the Thing**]
                                                 (Prep)   (1)

Prep: raises right hand to prepare for pointing.
(1) Stroke: points at comic book cover.

(7.71) and they're still battling and knocking down chimneys

(7.72) and nobody's really getting any temporary advantage and

(7.73) the Hulk is getting stronger but the Thing keeps catch-

(7.74) ing him off guard and tripping him up

BEATS AT EPISODE BEGINNINGS. In Levy (1984) beats appeared in a narrative with the function of introducing new information as potential discourse topics (see also Levy and McNeill, to appear). More recently, Cassell (1991) has confirmed that 40% of all beats in the narrations of adult speakers occur at episode boundaries—the site at which new topics are brought into play. In Levy's dissertation, subjects narrated a full-length film. She divided the resulting half-hour-long narratives into episode units using such formal criteria as explicit references to scene changes, e.g., "they show one scene," and so forth. Of 37 episode-initial references to characters made with full noun phrases (e.g., "the central character figure"), 22 were accompanied by gestures; most of these were beats. Of 64 references to characters with full noun phrases that appeared later in episodes, only 17 had co-occurring gestures of any kind. Thus, again, gestures—in this case, beats—accompanied the introduction of discourse themes. Levy counted only gestures that coincided exactly with the referring term in speech (as in the beat example cited earlier; within episodes gestures occurred with other than references to the character, e.g., with verbs, verb particles, clauses, etc., and were frequently combined with them).

POINTING AND BEATS IN THE GEORGIAN NARRATION. The use of gestures to introduce themes also appears in non-English narrations. The Georgian narrator whom I described in chapters 4 and 6 used many metanarrative linguistic devices for scene changing. It is clear that her gestures—both deictics and beats—occur more often at those points where the scene explicitly changes than in later parts of scenes. Table 7.2 shows the first two coreferential chains in this narrator's presentation of a

Table 7.2 Coreferring Chains in the Georgian Language Narration[a]

Coref. Chain	Position in Coref. Chain	Referent	Referring Expression	Pointing Gesture
1	1	"young woman"	es axalgazrda kali (=this young woman)	yes
	2	"	es kali (=the woman)	
	3	"	es kali (=the woman)	
2	1	"man"	es k'aci (=this man)	yes
	2	"	es ka- k'aci (=this m- man)	yes
	3	"	es k'aci (=this man)	
	4	"	es k'aci (=this man)	

[a]Table prepared by Elena Levy; translation by Kevin Tuite.

new scene (in the middle of the overall narrative), their referring expressions, and the occurrence or nonoccurrence of gestures. Again, the gestures are limited to the initial references to the characters in the scene. The gestures included are those that exactly coincided with the referring term, gestures later in the scene coincided with other parts of the sentence.

This example is from a passage that begins and ends with explicit scene-changing devices (at the start: "the next scene is . . . "; and at the end: "and the whole scene gives us the impression that this woman is doing something wrong"). In between are two animate coreferential chains, one for the "young woman" and the other for the "man." As in English-language narrations, the Georgian speaker's gestures specifically accompanying referring terms appeared with episode-initial references, suggesting that in her narrative system, too, gestures help to create and introduce thematic referents. Thus, the results are the same in the narrations of two quite different languages.

POINTING IN CONVERSATIONS. Finally, in a different genre—a conversation—there also is an accumulation of pointing while the speakers are negotiating potential topics of conversation. Abstract pointing gestures accompanied these initial efforts during which new information was the dominant discourse relationship. Subsequent coreferences (i.e., old information) were not accompanied by gestures of any kind. The use of pointing is parallel to the narrations described above. Table 7.3 summarizes the first two coreferring chains of a conversation (the same conver-

Table 7.3 First Coreferring Chains in a Conversation[a]

Coref. Chain	Position in Coref. Chain	Referent	Referring Expression	Pointing Gesture	Other Gesture
1	1	"Mary"	Mary	yes	—
	2	"	we	yes	—
	3	"	she	—	—
	4	"	she	—	—
	5	"	Mary	—	—
2	1	"Cindy"	Cindy	yes	—
	2	"	she	yes	—
	3	"	zero	yes	—
	4	"	we've	—	—
	5	"	Cindy	—	—
	6	"	her	—	—
	7	"	we've	—	—

[a]Table prepared by Elena Levy.

sation between two graduate students, H and O, that has provided previous examples; in this table, the contributions of the two participants have been combined).

Pointing was used, then, as an accompaniment to the introduction of potential conversational topics. The rest of the conversation confirmed this pattern. Following these initial coreferential chains, pointing gestures continued to accumulate until the conversational topic was firmly established, which was the theme of Jesuit education (see chap. 4). Once this topic was successfully negotiated (and this took many clauses), the amount and density of pointing subsided, to be supplanted by mostly metaphoric gestures. This conversation points toward the role of deictic gestures in fulfilling a particular discourse function: that of orienting both speaker and listener toward new material *as potential discourse topics*. Similarly, beats signal transitions to other levels of structure, some of which also introduce new material.

Conclusion

We see that gestures, free from the constraints of the linguistic code, are able to express the discourse functions of the speech with which they co-occur. Often these functions are shown more clearly in gesture than in speech. Gestures exhibit such narratological features as voice, perspective, narrative distance, and narrative level; they are able to show what is significant in the immediate context and exclude what is irrelevant; the more developed the gesture, as a symbol, the more discontinuous the current utterance from the preceding discourse. Gestures occur with the specific sentence elements that mark the peaks of CD. English grammatical systems generally do a poor job at marking such pragmatic variables and it is to gesture that we turn to make the discourse structure clear.

Remembering that while it is the gesture *stroke* that singles out peaks of CD and marks level, voice, perspective, etc., the preparation for the stroke started somewhat earlier, and we can say that the speaker foresees in fine detail the discourse role of the utterance-to-come from the earliest stages of its evolution. In this sense, discourse information is part of the core of the utterance without which the utterance could not come into being. Moreover, it is the gesture and its image that carries this pragmatic content. In the next two chapters I will consider how gestures can have an effect on the speaker's thought.

8   Self-Organization of Gesture and Speech

My general argument in this book so far has been the following: gestures and speech are closely linked in meaning, function, and time; they share meanings, roles, and a common fate. They are related in such a manner that the gesture and the utterance can be said to cover the same idea unit (Kendon 1980). Thus, in explaining gestures and speech and how they co-occur, we are concerned with the interaction of two modes of representation. Gestures and speech, considered jointly, reveal a process in which holistic and imagistic representations interact with analytic and linguistic representations. Gestures (global and synthetic) and speech (linear and segmented) co-occur and are coexpressive in acts of speaking. From this co-occurrence during the same linguistic act, I posit an interaction of imagery and socially-constituted linguistic systems during utterances. The theory to which we are committed emphasizes that speech and gesture arise from an interaction of mental operations of opposite character—imagistic and linguistic. In this chapter, I attempt to describe more exactly the process of this interaction, including how gestures and speech are related in time.[1]

Microgenesis

The viewpoint I adopt is microgenetic. An utterance is regarded, not as a static sentence presented in speech or on a page, but as a process that has an internal development and has this sentence (or other surface linguistic constituent) as its final stage. It is the internal development that we highlight with the term microgenesis. We view the utterance as something that emerges and focus on the emergence. A microgenetic approach demands its own unit of analysis which is quite different from the units familiar in information processing psychology. In the latter the units are the smallest elements into which a psychological process, such as utterance formation, can be *decomposed* (Palmer and Kimchi 1986). In a microgenetic approach, on the other hand, the unit of analysis is the smallest component that has *a capacity to grow,* to develop into something else—the final utterance. The two kinds of unit are nonoverlapping, even incompatible, in their definitions and reflect quite different assumptions concerning the goals of explanation (see McNeill 1987, for comparison of "C-type" to "D-type" explanations).

1. I am grateful to Nancy L. Dray for discussing this chapter with me.

The deepest insights into defining the types of units needed in microgenetic analysis come from L. S. Vygotsky (1934, 1962, 1986), the great Soviet psychologist and semiotician of the 1930s. Vygotsky argued that to analyze consciousness psychologically *the unit of analysis should be the smallest unit that has the properties of the whole.* In the case of verbal thought, the minimal unit must retain properties of both language and thought. To decompose this unit into components—lexical retrieval, syntactic formulation, etc.—would not produce more minimal units but would actually destroy the minimal unit. The minimal unit is irreducibly composite. This is necessary because the unit should be *unstable.* Instability is the crucial property that enables a microgenetic unit to change and grow into something else. Vygotsky wrote about the internal dynamism of thought as follows:

The relation of thought to word is not a thing but a process, a continual movement back and forth from thought to word and from word to thought. In that process, the relation of thought to word undergoes changes that themselves may be regarded as development in the functional sense. Thought is not merely expressed in words; it comes into existence with them (1986, 218).

In this process of continual movement back and forth, speech has specific semantic functions: (1) what Vygotsky called "sense" dominates "meaning" (i.e., the context-specific aspects of thought dominate the generalized context-independent aspects); (2) a single linguistic sign can designate all the separate elements of thought active at the moment; (3) different elements of thought flow into one another and congregate in the linguistic sign. (These functions we recognize as the qualities of gestures.) The tension between thought and word (the continual movement back and forth in Vygotsky's description) enriches both sides of the minimal unit. Linguistic signs are not in themselves units of consciousness. Instead, the role of linguistic signs is to *mediate* consciousness (Zinchenko 1985; Tul'viste 1989). In this view, the linguistic component (a) gives consciousness a concrete anchor in the system of language and (b) brings new material into consciousness.

Growth Points

THE CONCEPT. The concept of a growth point arises from the realization that a given utterance does not just "snap on" with all its structural details fleshed out. It develops in a certain order. This order is not necessarily the order in which the words appear in the surface utterance, and the starting point is not necessarily the first word to be uttered. The underlying starting point of the sentence is what I refer to as the *growth point.*

What does the growth point consist of? It is, theoretically, the utterance's primitive stage, the earliest form of the utterance in deep time, and the opening up of a microgenetic process that yields the surface utterance form as the final stage. The growth point is the speaker's minimal idea unit that can develop into a full utterance together with a gesture. In keeping with Vygotsky's conception of the minimal units of a microgenetic process, growth points must retain properties of the whole. The whole, as observed repeatedly in this book, is an integrated performance of speech and gesture; it is an image and a linguistic construction. These are integrated into a single process. The growth point then should be a combination of image and word, of image and linguistic meaning category.

A plausible hypothesis about the growth point is that it is the peak of CD, the equivalent of what Vygotsky called the psychological predicate (Vygotsky 1962). That is, the content of the growth point tends to be the novel departure of thought from the presupposed background. It is the element in thought that stands out in the context and may be the point of greatest relevance.

The concept of the growth point unites image, word, and pragmatic content into a single unit. In this way it is a unit with the properties of the whole and could initiate the microgenetic process of the utterance formation. It is also a unit that encompasses properties of an opposite character—both imagistic *and* linguistic, idiosyncratic *and* social, global *and* segmented, holistic *and* analytic—and this is a source of instability (the instability of the growth point is the foundation of the dialectic developed in chapter 9).

INFERRING THE GROWTH POINT. The growth point is a theoretical concept. However, the theory of the growth point itself suggests a way of empirically inferring growth points. An excellent observable clue of what the growth point is in any given utterance is obtained from observing how speech and gesture combine.

The following is how the growth point is inferred from gesture: We assume that the image and the linguistic segment(s) with which the stroke coincides have *always* been together in the microgenesis of the sentence. They come together at the beginning of the utterance in deep time (a few seconds back), are jointly constructed during the preparation phase (marking the beginning of the gesture), and remain a unit as the rest of the utterance and gesture develop around them. The combination is then presented intact, as a unit, along with the rest of the utterance. This assumption is consistent with the synchronization rules for gestures described in chapter 1. We saw there that strokes and their coexpressive words coincide on the semantic, pragmatic, and phonologic/kinesic levels. The preparation phase of the gesture, in contrast, appears in a wide variety of verbal contexts (see chap. 4) since it is associated, not with the current speech, but with speech to come.

In using gestures to infer the growth point, the coinciding stroke and speech could be used mechanically; viz., assume that precisely the linguistic segment with which the stroke coincides is the growth point. But this would be too rigid and would lead to errors. It is necessary to follow a more heuristic approach and make allowances for the possibility that the stroke has anticipated speech. Such anticipation would place the stroke ahead of its linguistic partner in the speech stream. The extent of anticipation could amount to a syllable or word. Thus we have this recognition procedure for the growth points of utterances: *the growth point is seen in the gesture stroke, together with the linguistic segment with which it co-occurs, plus a word that follows this segment if this word preserves semantic and pragmatic synchrony.* That is, words that follow the stroke are potentially part of the growth point if they have the same semantic and pragmatic content as the gesture. On the other hand, words that precede the stroke are never counted as part of the growth point. Even if there is this small uncertainty over the precise words that belong in the growth point, there is never any ambiguity over whether the growth point is the CD peak, as the examples below show.

The linguistic side of the theoretical growth point is not necessarily the full linguistic segment which we see in the surface utterance. We must rely on the full linguistic segment empirically to infer the growth point, but this does not mean that the theoretical growth point includes the phonological signifier. A more appropriate description would be that it is a linguistic meaning category. That is, it is a semantically interpreted segment based on the categories of the speaker's language. This is already a socially-constituted, coded, segmented linguistic form, even if the phonological signifier is not yet activated. The theoretical growth point is a combination of two meaning systems, one idiosyncratic and created at the moment of speaking, the other socially-constituted and created by the culture.

GROWTH POINTS IN SPEAKERS OF DIFFERENT LANGUAGES. If the growth point is a unit of thought, it should show uniformity among speakers of different languages while speech itself shows great diversity. A remarkable thing about iconics is their high degree of cross-linguistic similarity. Given the same content, very similar gestures appear and accompany linguistic segments of an equivalent type, in spite of major lexical and grammatical differences between the languages. This resemblance suggests that the gesture emerges at a level where utterances in different languages have a common starting point—thought, memory, and imagery. Any cultural differences in semantic category are minimal. The utterance structure builds up around the growth point and unpacks it into a hierarchical, linear-segmented linguistic structure. Depending on the language, however, this unpacking process proceeds in different directions. The differences arise from the requirements of the language system. Each language has its own rules for utilizing segmentation and grammatical forms, but the gesture remains part of the growth point and appears in the same temporal relation with equivalent linguistic segments in the different languages.

The following examples compare gestures produced by speakers of four languages: Georgian, Swahili, Mandarin Chinese, and English, all describing the same scene. This demonstration takes advantage of the fact that we had shown the cartoon stimulus to speakers of different languages. In the scene that is being described, a character drops a bowling ball into a pipe and onto a second character who is climbing up the inside of the pipe. Most people, after viewing the cartoon, remember this scene and describe it with one or more accompanying gestures. The gesture that depicts the character's dropping the bowling ball is synchronized with the particular expression in each language that most specifically refers to this act. First, the Georgian speaker's version (transcription and translation by Kevin Tuite; the first line is the Georgian text, the second line a gloss, and the third line idiomatic English):

GEORGIAN (see fig. 8.1):

Figure 8.1. The Georgian speaker's gesture showing Tweety dropping the bowling ball. The stroke coincided with the Georgian verb "cha[agdebs]" (throw-down). "Chaagdebs" and the downward image are the implied growth point.

(8.1) da uzarmazar rk'inis burts . . . cha[agdebs]

　　　and enormous iron　　ball . . . [throw-down]

'and throws down this enormous iron ball'

Iconic: both hands at head level push down on what appears to be a large round object.

The speaker appears to grasp a large round object and push it down into the space before her. This movement synchronizes with the verb meaning to throw something down (a single word in Georgian), which is the segment of the sentence most specifically describing the motion the gesture also depicts.

An essentially identical gesture appears in the Swahili narration (even though the narrator took the bowling ball to be a pliable substance, namely, a tire):

SWAHILI (see fig. 8.2):

Figure 8.2. Swahili speaker's gesture showing Tweety dropping the bowling ball. This stroke coincided with the root "tumbuk" (push down") of the much longer polymorphic verb. This root and the downward image are the implied growth point.

(8.2) i-ka-chuku-a li-mpira fulani i-ka-

　　　take　　　　tire　　　certain

'and found a certain tire'

[. . . tum]buk- iz-a

[. . . push down]

'and pushed it'

Iconic: hands push thing down.

(recorded in Tanzania by Karen Peterson, who also provided the transcription and translation). The hands move down, and this movement is timed to coincide with the verb root "push-down" (again, a single element). As in the Georgian gesture, the downward thrust coincides with the segment that most specifically expresses the downward motion that the gesture also is depicting.

The Mandarin speaker's description of the bowling ball episode produced an interesting difference (transcription and translation by Karl-Erik McCullough with the assistance of Chuan Wang):

CHINESE (see fig. 8.3):

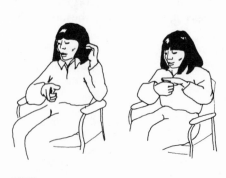

Figure 8.3. The Chinese speaker showing Tweety dropping the bowling ball. This stroke coincided (ending in an audible pop) with "gei," marking a result. The speaker had interpreted the bowling ball as a plug with which Tweety was trying to seal the drain pipe. The gesture and the "gei" signifying the accomplishment coincided. "Gei" and the downward image are the implied growth point.

(8.3)

jiu ba	neige eh da hei qiu, jiu ba	neige gar
just as for	that eh large black ball just as for	that cover

ah shangmian
ah over-side

'with you know that ah big black ball, with it (he) covers the top'

neige ba	neige jiu [gei] du shangle
that as for	that just [result] plug over-complete

'that plugs it completely'

Iconic: left hand arcs down and contacts cupped right hand with a popping sound.

The speaker interpreted Tweety's motivation for shoving the bowling ball into the pipe to be to plug the pipe, rather than to drop it down the pipe, and her gesture showed this achievement of the plugging. This is the only case where the growth point reveals a different conceptual understanding of the cartoon episode. The downward thrusting of the hand accordingly concluded with the coexpressive linguistic segment under this understanding, which was the word *gei,* a particle marking the achievement of the result (an End State meaning). The impact of the left hand on the right—the moment of plugging—made an audible pop, and this sound occurred exactly when she said *gei*. Thus, while the downward thrust of the gesture did not coincide with a word for downward movement (there was in fact no such word in the sentence), the stroke coincided with the word that expressed the chief idea of the sentence: achievement of an outcome. If this is the correct explanation, the rule still holds that the word with which the stroke coincides is the word that expresses the same idea unit.

Finally, here is an English-language speaker's rendition of the same scene (speaker 1, above):

ENGLISH (see fig. 8.4):

Figure 8.4. The English speaker's gesture showing Tweety dropping the bowling ball. The stroke coincided with the verb particle "down." "Down" and the downward image are the implied growth point.

(8.4) and Tweety Bird runs and gets a bowling ball and drops [it down] the drainpipe
Iconic: both hands push down a large round object.

This narrator also seizes a large round object and appears to shove it into the space in front of her. The movement coincides with "it down" (and excludes "drops"), which is the segment of the English sentence ("down") that specifically conveys the downward motion exhibited in the gesture.

Thus, three languages: one gesture, and a fourth language (Chinese) differing in a way that is entirely explained by the speaker's interpretation of the cartoon. A character is depicted as pushing a large round object into a space in front the speaker. Looking at the video tapes it is quite easy to follow this part of the story with no other information than the gestures. The differences that appear, such as the Swahili speaker's showing a pliable tire or the Chinese speaker's regarding the ball as a plug, arise from their interpretations of the cartoon, and not from a kind of speech-gesture integration that lacks growth points.

The gestures are similar despite the radically different linguistic systems in which the speakers were couching their verbal descriptions. In English the sentence structure was the standard SVO transitive verb sentence pattern; in Chinese it was again SV; in Georgian it was an OV pattern with an elided subject; in Swahili there was a single polymorphic verb into which was built a subject marker, a continued tense marker, a verb root (with which the gesture stroke coincided), a causative suffix and a final vowel that signaled the indicative mood. Thus, even though each language required its speakers to construct sentences widely divergent from the sentences of the other languages, the combination of gesture and speech in each case was essentially the same. In English, Swahili, and Georgian the gesture coincided with the segment of speech that also conveyed the idea of downward motion. This was true even in Swahili, where this idea unit was embedded in the middle of a long polymorphic word and had to be, as it were, sought out by the gesture. In Chinese the stroke of the downward gesture coincided with the segment that conveyed the idea of a result, and this resultative segment, rather than a verb for downward motion itself, was the coexpressive segment with the gesture.

Although the surface locus in speech of this coexpressive segment varies greatly among the languages, the gestures teach us to look at the underlying development of sentences and the source of speech in a growth point that coincides with the imagery. The gestures suggest that in each language the image exhibited in the gesture is constructed with the one linguistic segment that is equivalent to the gesture in meaning. In three of the languages the gesture lined up with the word that best encodes downward motion. The linguistic meaning category corresponding to this word together with the downward image would be the growth point from which the rest of the sentence developed. In the Chinese sentence, the segment was for the meaning of a result, and the growth point would have been the image of closing the pipe and the End State meaning of the segment *gei*. None of the growth points were to be identified with the first occurring grammatical elements in the spoken sentence. Rather, the growth point was held in the speaker's memory while she constructed a sentence structure around it.

THE VARIETY OF GROWTH POINTS. When the contexts are the same, speakers of different languages show impressive similarities of growth points. However, within a language, when contexts and discourse situations are different, one is impressed, rather, by the variety of growth points.

Some likely growth points in English speech are illustrated in the following examples. I have purposely selected examples to demonstrate as wide a range as possible. I have also picked examples that show how growth points can be inferred from both iconic and non-iconic gestures (metaphorics, beats, pointing), and also how a series of interdependent growth points can develop through a discourse. Empirical growth points—just those suggested in these examples—include verb particles ("down"), proper names ("Tweety"), pronouns ("he," "she," "they"), an adverbial ("of course"), and verbs ("decides"). Other examples show full noun phrases. This tremendous variety suggests that grammatical sentences can emerge from growth points that may appear virtually anywhere in the final structure of the sentence.

The speakers of the examples are different in all of the cases. The transcriptions show stroke phases only (which are in brackets); the preparation and retraction phases are not shown.

In the following the growth point is an adjectival plus the image of a cage from an observer's point of view:

(8.5)   and uh the bird [is cov-] the bird cage is [covered] with a cloth
             (1)   (2)

(1) O-VPT iconic: both hands start to arc downward to outline the bird cage, but the gesture is aborted.
(2) O-VPT iconic: large downward arc in full.

We infer that "covered" was the growth point, together with the image of the bird cage and its cover. The interesting point here is the speaker's false start and repair, and what seems to have triggered it. The false start occurred during "covered," but the repair was of "bird," which the speaker corrected to "bird cage." She then proceeded with the rest of the sentence, repeating "covered," which was not repaired. Also, the verb and gesture combination was repeated as a unit. The false start was triggered by the lexical error of "bird" rather than "bird cage," not by the growth point, as we infer it. The source of the false start could have been the too-early surfacing of the growth point, "covered," which then interfered with the activation of "bird cage" and was cut off as soon as it attempted to reach the surface. This suggests that errors can be triggered by the growth point when it is itself included in the flow of the utterance. In turn this is consistent with the assumption that the growth point is constructed in advance and held in abeyance while the rest of the utterance is built up around it.

In the following the growth point is an adverbial combined with the conduit image:

(8.6) and uh the whole cartoon is Sylves[ter . . . of course]
<u>trying to get Tweety Bird like he always does</u>
Conduit metaphoric: hand rotates up to form cup.

The growth point, we infer, was the unlikely element, "of course," plus the metaphoric image of the cartoon as an object exhibited in the gesture. That is, the speaker's thought was focused on the pragmatic content of "of course" (viz., something that is following a predictable pattern) plus the image of the cartoon story as an object seen from the outside. This unit was the focus of the speaker's thought. It's not necessary to include Sylvester in the growth point, since phonological anticipation could have produced the partial overlap of the stroke with the reference to that character. The implication of this example is that growth points can incorporate discourse information and refer to non-narrative contexts. "Of course" implies confirmation of an expected event or pattern (the well-known pattern of Sylvester trying to get Tweety Bird). The gesture was a metaphor of the cartoon as a whole, presented as an object. Thus the growth point referred to "the whole cartoon," and added that it lived up to an expected pattern. This growth point evolved into "the whole cartoon is Sylvester of course trying to get Tweety Bird like he always does," an articulation and specification of the meaning of the inferred growth point. I will return to this example below with a more detailed analysis to show how the components of the surface utterance could have arisen out of such a growth point.

The growth point in the following is a verb combined with a highlighted event on the metanarrative level:

(8.7) <u>the last way he [decides] the-</u>
                    Beat.

The level is metanarrative and the gesture is a beat. Even a beat, and the highlighting it provides, can be part of a growth point. The growth point seems to have been "decides" plus the relationship of the act of deciding to the story structure beyond the immediate utterance. Such pragmatic awareness would have been in the speaker's idea unit. The rest of the utterance, "the last way he decides," expands on the growth point by referring explicitly to this larger context.

In the following there are several growth points. Each refers to an individual and is combined with a locus in space, and each is linked to the other growth points to form a series:

(8.8) everyone's morals are very ambiguous
'cause [they're sup]posed to be the good guys
Metaphoric: points to right.

[but she] really did kill him
Metaphoric: points to left.

and [he's a] bad guy
Metaphoric: both hands move to front.

[but he really] didn't kill him
Metaphoric: both hands move to left again.

This example (repeated from (6.9)–(6.13)) illustrates a series of growth points and dependencies between them. The speaker metaphorically divided space into two spheres: one for the actual morality of the characters (the left) and the other for their apparent morality (not the left). The gestures designating these spheres suggest that the following were the growth points: "they're supposed," "but she really," "he's a," and "but he really." These include pronouns and appear to be the themes of their respective sentences. However, I will argue that they are not themes when the meaning of the gesture space is taken into account; they are, in fact, rhemes—high CD psychological predicates of their utterances (Firbas 1964). This analysis will also enable us to see how the growth point of each utterance made essential reference to the other utterances of the series.

First, the argument that the pronouns were the rhemes of these utterances: the structure of the series is a systematic alternation of plus and minus values in which, in each case, the new information becomes the referent of the pronoun. The first sentence announces the plus-minus situation itself ("everyone's morals are very ambiguous"). Starting with the second sentence, the grammatical predicate asserts a "+" moral value ("supposed to be the good guys"). The not-left spatial assignment however marks it as apparent morality. The next sentence asserts a "−" moral value ("really did kill him") while the left space marks it as real. The third sentence asserts another "−" moral value ("he's a bad guy"), but the not-left space marks it as apparent. Finally, the fourth sentence asserts a "+" moral value ("really didn't kill him"), and the left space marks this as real.

The apparent versus real morality gesture distinction alternates between the "+" and "−" moral value predicates in such a way as to create the following symmetrical dichotomization of moral evaluations:

Sentence in series:	2	3	4	5
Pronoun reference:	they	she	he	he
Morality in predicate:	+	−	−	+
Right: Apparent morals	+		−	
Left: Real morals		−		+

The schema of "+" and "−", combined with the alternation of real and apparent morality spaces, was the overarching structure for the series of sentences as a whole. Given this structure the only varying factor was the identity of the character in each sentence, and this the pronouns provided. In this way, a case can be made that the pronouns were the *high* CD elements of these sentences, despite their inexplicitness and initial position.

As this analysis makes plain, successive growth points can be linked to one another. The growth point in any one utterance referred to the position of the utterance in the series as a whole. These utterances cannot be considered in isolation, but must be considered jointly as members of the series.

Since similar growth points can appear in quite different languages, it seems that growth points are capable of evolving in a variety of different directions that depend on the specific resources and standards that exist in the language. Moreover, words that enter into similar grammatical structures can be part of different types of growth points. There is no necessary association between the type of grammatical structure and the kind of growth point. The growth point is not a stimulus that leads automatically to a final surface sentence structure. The sentence structure is the end product of heuristics and compromises, a kind of self-organization or mutual evolution. I will consider a model for this kind of process later in the chapter.

Another important conclusion is that growth points incorporate discourse relationships, perspectives, narrative distance, successions, and levels. The inferred growth points suggest that discourse references are built into utterances from the start. That is, discourse references are not extra factors added into sentences during their generation, but are intrinsic parts of them, without which sentences would not exist at all.

ANALYSIS OF THE UNLIKELY EXAMPLE. Empirically identifying the growth point is quite useful for a theoretical analysis of utterance formation. If we know the starting point we can say something about how the whole developed. To illustrate this type of analysis I have picked the example in (8.6). The inferred growth point was "of course" plus the image of the cartoon as an object, and the utterance that evolved was "the whole cartoon is Sylvester of course trying to get Tweety Bird like he always does." I have picked this example precisely because "of course" seems, on the face of it, such an unlikely starting point for any kind of utterance. Nonetheless, the utterance can be explained as arising around this adverbial expression (i.e., its semantic-pragmatic value) plus the gesture image. Thus the example has the additional role of demonstrating that it is crucial to take into account gesture information to see growth points.

The example also illustrates the evolution of utterances that refer to discourse structure. The growth point, "of course," plus the image of the cartoon as an object, refers to the cartoon narrative as a predictable pattern. The development of the growth point specifies and amplifies this metanarrative reference by activating further knowledge about the cartoon and its genre.

Starting from the growth point of "of course" plus the gesture image, we find two developments of the utterance: (1) "trying to get Tweety" specifies what this predictable pattern actually is; (2) "like he always does" articulates the predictability factor itself. The lead-in, "and the whole cartoon is Sylvester," also could be unpacked from the "of course" plus conduit growth point, since it is a reference to the domain of the prediction. However, there is no positive evidence for this part of the utterance coming from "of course," inasmuch as the preparation phase of the gesture did not start until after the start of "the whole cartoon." While the onset of the preparation phase shows the last moment at which the deep time evolution began, we have no way of knowing whether or not it began sooner. These utterance components—"the whole cartoon," "trying to get Tweety," and "like he always does"—together expressed the growth point. We can therefore conceive of the microgenesis of the utterance as the unpacking of the, on the face of it, unlikely growth point of "of course" plus the conduit image.

Other Approaches to Growth Points

The linguistic analysis of a sentence structure typically portrays a hierarchical tree. If there is a dominant point in this kind of tree it is the root of the tree, the S node, which stands over the sentence as a whole. In the early days of psycholinguistics, S nodes were in fact proposed as growth points (e.g., Miller and Chomsky 1963), but this approach was abandoned after extensive criticism by Fodor, Bever, and Garrett (1974). The concept of a growth point remains, however, and in more recent psycholinguistic theories growth points have been proposed that are not at the S node. W. J. M. Levelt (1989), in his book *Speaking*, presents a linear model of speech production in which the basic components are (a) a conceptualizer, or source of preverbal "messages," (b) a formulator, and (c) an articulator. The growth point is the first chunk of information to be handed over from the conceptualizer (Levelt doesn't use the term "growth point," but the concept is the same). This growth point is the theme of the utterance, viz., the reference (real or fictional) about which the utterance provides further information and tends to be the first word to be uttered. Related views have been put forth by others, in particular, MacWhinney (1977), Delancey (1981), and Du Bois (1987). These authors differ from Levelt on what constitutes the starting node of the sentence—instead of the theme, they suggest the perspective of the sentence, or the starting point of the flow of attention—but agree with him that the growth point is the initial grammatical element of the sentence.

However, empirically inferred growth points require a quite different kind of theory. Gestures imply a much wider assortment of surface realizations of growth points than would be allowed in the left-to-right theories of Levelt, MacWhinney, and others, where only the first grammatical element is the growth point. Far from being presupposed topics about which utterances provide information, or themes, empirically inferred growth points are *rhemes*—high CD psychological predicates. A psychological predicate may be the first element activated in deep time but it is held in abeyance while a linguistic structure is built up around it. Then, in surface time, it may come out later (indeed, the psychological predicate usually surfaces as the grammatical predicate, but this too is not a hard and fast rule, as we saw in example (8.8), where the subject slot realized the psychological predicate).

Self-Organization

If language alters thought, that is, if the conceptualization of thought and the formulation of language are allowed to develop *interactively,* the evolution of the utterance can have an influence on its own development by calling for reconceptualizations. The various grammatical slots of the utterance can be worked out later, as the refinement and specification of the growth point goes on, and these formulations may call for additional conceptualizations. That type of interaction is a fundamental quality of the self-organizational model of utterance and gesture generation to be presented in this section.

The framework of the model describes thinking/speaking as a self-organizing process. Self-organization means that the formation of utterances does not depend on conscious control of the process itself, nor on a specific source of inputs to trigger successive steps. The utterance structure and conceptualizations built into it emerge without executive control, of their own accord as it were. The aim of the model is to provide a sketch of how this self-organizing process could take place, starting from growth points that are inferred from gestures. I emphasize the word "sketch": it is not a complete model by any means, but presents an interesting alternative to the usual type of linear, step-by-step information-processing model in psycholinguistics.

The model is inspired by self-organizational models in developmental neurobiology (von der Malsburg and Singer 1988). Self-organizing systems exist as physical models (water coming to a boil, for example, embodies self-organizing systems of rising columns of hot water) and as models of nervous system growth (for example, the growth of fibers from the retina into the brain, as proposed by von der Malsburg and Singer, is a self-organizing system). Such a model seems appropriate for the creation of gestural-linguistic utterances since self-organization has biological meaning, as has been argued persuasively by von der Malsburg & Singer. However, I will point out areas where, in my view, a biologically based model makes unrealistic assumptions in its psycholinguistic applications.

General Properties of Self-Organizational Systems

Von der Malsburg and Singer give five properties of self-organizational systems in general. These properties can be recognized in the formation of utterances as well:

1. *Organization takes place in a system of fragments that initially is in a relatively unorganized state.* In the speaking system, imagery and language themselves provide the fragments usable for potential new utterances when the speaker is shifting from one idea unit to the next. It is at such points of change that the speaker's ideas are likely to be most fragmented and open to new developments. In narrative discourse it is possible to recognize in subsequent utterances fragments of earlier utterances. For example the repetition of "down" in a succession of utterances appears to be such a case: "Sylvester falls back down the drainpipe . . . rolls down the street into the bowling alley." In between the first idea unit and the second

idea unit, we can posit, theoretically, a relatively disorganized state in which different images and linguistic forms are simultaneously active but not structured. These might include the appearance of Sylvester, how he moved with the bowling ball inside him, and so forth. Other speakers mention these details but this speaker did not; nonetheless, they could have been among the fragments that ushered in the next utterance cycle. Unlike in physical or neurobiological systems, however, in the utterance system the number of fragments is small and the degree of structuring high, even at the start. Still, a case can be made for a crucial role of fragmentation in speaking.

2. *Small deviations in this system self-amplify, compete, and cooperate.* The "small deviations" in the utterance system are the growth points. For self-organization to take place a growth point is essential. It then enters into processes of self-amplification, competition, and cooperation. Examples illustrating each of these processes can be found:

a. *Self-amplification* is analogous to reproduction in Darwinian evolution. An example is how the conduit image and "of course" growth point drew in more conceptualizations ("the whole cartoon is Sylvester," "trying to get Tweety," and "like he always does").

b. *Competition* can be found on several levels (cf. Bates and MacWhinney 1982). There can be, first of all, competition among growth points. Competition ensures that what is selected is the most vigorously growing (the "fittest") growth point at the expense of others. In the boiling water model, upward movement in one place requires downward movement somewhere else. In utterances, one growth point can defeat rivals by incorporating new information at a greater rate, making better use of imagery and language fragments, and so forth. Competition appears in this rococo example where five separate growth points duel over which is to set up the subject slot: "because it . . . the uh . . . well actually what happens is he- I- you assume that he swallows this bowling ball" (that is, competition over introducing "it," "the . . . ," "he," "I," and "you"; with "he" finally winning).

There is also competition on the level of rival formulations stemming from a single growth point. Again the "of course" example provides an illustration. There was, theoretically, either of two versions: (the actual choice) "Sylvester of course trying to get Tweety Bird like he always does" or the opposite, "Sylvester of course, like he always does, trying to get Tweety Bird." The victory may seem small, but it had to be won.

c. *Cooperation* with other fragments enhances the fitness of a growth point. "He" in the example above was first rejected, but its final fitness was enhanced by the metanarrative reference of "you assume," originally one of its rivals. This reference set up a framework in which "he" also could get into a subject slot ("you assume he swallows").

3. *Global order arises from local interactions among fragments.* Global order fixes the overall orientation of the emerging structure. In example (8.8), a symmetrical pattern of sentences and gestures reveals a global orientation.

4. *"Participating forces" and "boundary conditions" set the stage for self-organization.* Although such words are unusual for describing utterances, there are analogies in sentence processes. Participating forces would include the semantic and pragmatic values that guide the process of utterance formation. Boundary conditions would include the speaker's affective-volitional tendencies (Vygotsky 1962), preceding utterances (Bock 1986), preexisting context, rhythmical patterns, and many other such limiting factors.

5. *There may be several equivalent organized patterns, and these compete during organization.* We have already considered competition under property (2). Here von der Malsburg and Singer (1988) consider how competitions are won. They speak of "slightly deforming" the boundary conditions to break the symmetry of rival organized patterns. In utterance formation rhythmical patterns can have this effect and there may be still other sources of asymmetry. In the "of course" example, the clause that came just before "of course" had a strong-weak alternating stress pattern ("AND the WHOLE carTOON is SylVESter"). The rest of the utterance continued the strong-weak pattern ("TRYing to get TWEEty bird like he ALways does"), whereas the rival but unrealized choice would have changed it to weak-strong ("like he ALways does TRYing to get TWEEty bird").

Thus all of the general properties of self-organizing systems can be found in the process of forming utterances. We see in utterances, no less than in other self-organizing systems: a starting point of fragments; small deviations (growth points) that develop through self-amplification, competition, and cooperation; global order that fixes the overall orientation of the structure; forces and boundary conditions that limit the development; and biasing tendencies that resolve competitions.

Self-Organization of Gestures and Speech

The model is dynamic, incorporates the structure of a social interaction, is internal, multirepresentational, and operates in terms of contrasts from the existing context. It incorporates discourse structure, is automatically cohesive, uses linguistic signs as mediators, has a growth point consisting of imagery and a linguistic category, starts with a unit that has properties of the whole and shows how linguistic structures transform meaning as this unit develops into a new form. It seeks to characterize the utterance's growth point, how it evolves and changes into a surface linguistic form, the relationship of the utterance to the discourse, and how consciousness changes as this process takes place (see fig. 8.5).

The model constructs the spoken utterance *and* the gesture as an integral whole. The spoken utterance and the gesture arise as a single unit with two parts—the gesture being a presentation to the outside world no less than the spoken part of the utterance. They both arise out of the imagery-verbal growth point: as the syntactic structure of the spoken utterance works itself out, the gesture is also being constructed.

A gesture is potentially always available from the imagistic component of the growth point. However, as we have seen, in some contexts there are no gestures at all, while in other contexts gestures appear but with minimal complexity; in still others more elaborate gestures take place. The absence of a gesture for the utterance is itself a meaningful fact. We have seen that the complexity and frequency of gestures increases with the CD, so the degree to which the growth point departs from the existing context is one factor in producing the gesture. The lack of a gesture signifies the lowest degree of CD. This can be explained by the low CD growth point being completely transformed into linguistic format. Another factor in the self-organization of utterances and gestures is time. If there is no way to bring them together in time, the gesture could not

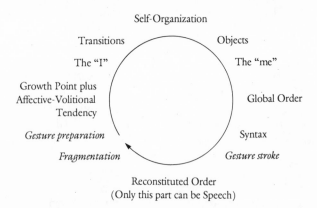

Self-Organization

Transitions   Objects

The "I"   The "me"

Growth Point plus
Affective-Volitional   Global Order
Tendency

Gesture preparation   Syntax

Fragmentation   *Gesture stroke*

Reconstituted Order
(Only this part can be Speech)

Figure 8.5. The self-organizational cycle. The next utterance and gesture arise out of the fragments of the previous utterance/gesture. Various aspects of the self and consciousness can be localized during self-organization, and these are shown at the appropriate places. The anticipation of outer speech by the preparation phase of the gesture and the integration with outer speech of the stroke phase are explained by their respective places in the cycle.

occur in synchrony with the linguistic segment, and thus could not be combined with speech.

The model posits a continuous cycle of Self-Organization that leads to Global Order, followed by a Reconstituted Order; this Reconstituted Order undergoes Fragmentation; the Fragments then Self-Organize into a new Global Order, are Reconstituted, and so forth endlessly. Such cycles must repeat indefinitely over the course of a lifetime, and are interrupted only in trauma. From an early stage of life onward, an endless chain of self-organizational cycles provides continuity of mental life. From this continuity it follows that utterances never exist in isolation. The dream of experimental psycholinguistics, to have isolated sentence "stimuli" to which subjects respond, is not only a methodological impossibility, it is a conceptual phantom.

AN EXAMPLE OF THIS PROCESS. Even though we can posit a lifetime succession of cycles, we are only able to analyze short sequences. Nonetheless, the model allows us to conceive of the verbal expression of thought as an endless braid and thus to identify the moment of thought in relation to the context that has preceded it. The production of CD in such a model is accordingly an inherent activity. To illustrate how an utterance might self-organize, I will give the following example in which a speaker struggles to introduce a concept of nurturing while avoiding the implications of linguistic transitivity (from a conversation between two close friends; see chap. 9 for the gestures with this example):

(8.9)　the fact [that she's /][she's nu- uh][/ she's somehow / she's]
　　　　　　　(1)　　　　(2)　　　　　　　(3)
[done this nurtur][ing] [thing and here you-]
(4)　　　　　　　(5)　(6)

you were feeling sort of like she was this person that you didn't want to nurture in any way

The gesture at (4) is the critical one. Here the speaker started rotating her hands round one another vertically and then came out of this rotation by extending her right hand to the right as if presenting an object; however, the object went, not directly to the interlocutor, but to the side. This appears to be an image of a process leading to a product, a product that is deliberately separated from the locus of the listener. To view this utterance and gesture as the outcome of a self-organizational cycle we must begin in the previous cycle or cycles. At (2) and (3) there is a conveniently overt fragmentation which, in our model, is an essential part of the next cycle at (4). The key utterance, "she's done this nurturing thing," began in the fragments "she's nu- uh" and "she's somehow." From such phonetic and semantic fragments, we want to see how a self-organizing process could have taken place.

The growth point from which (4) emerged was an image of some mechanism that was churning around and yielded an object off to the side; this added the image of separation from the interlocutor. Thus it was a mechanism producing a product as opposed to an inherent quality or direct action with a character perspective and the mechanism was linked to the referent of "she" and the category of nurturing. The question now is: what conventional oppositions from the linguistic system would be recruited by this growth point? "She's done this nurturing thing" was the result. This structure could have self-organized since "do NP" is favored by the idea of a product and would have had a competitive advantage over "nurture," the transitive verb. Also, "nurturing," the adjective modifying a noun, is favored by the spatial separation of the interlocutor from the nurturing product, since this adjective is stripped of the presupposition of an agent responsible for the nurturing or an object receiving the nurturing. The competition in the self-organizational process is over creating the intended oppositions already established by the growth point image and linguistic meaning category. In this case, the opposition is between objects and actions, with the first the intended pole. In such a competition, "do NP" and "nurturing thing" easily rise to the top over their rivals. (Various implementations of this kind of competitive sorting out are conceivable: ATNs [Wanner 1980], demons and logogens [Selfridge and Neisser 1960; Lindsay & Norman 1977; Morton 1969], and modules of various kinds [Marcus 1980; Frazier and Fodor 1978]. These details occupy much of the attention of experimental psycholinguists, but I think almost any choice among the various alternatives that have been proposed and battled over would work equally well in a self-organizational model.)

Order Out of Disorder

The model posits that each new cycle begins with the disintegration of the preceding cycle in the context of an Affective-Volitional tendency, which Vygotsky described as follows:

We come now to the last step in our analysis of the inner planes of verbal thought. Thought is not the superior authority in this process. Thought is not begotten by thought; it is engendered by motivation, i.e., by our desires and needs, our interests and emotions. Behind every thought there is an affective-volitional tendency, which holds the answer to the last "why" in the analysis of thinking. (Vygotsky 1986, 252)

The basic source of change is disruptive forces—motivation, emotion, and a future orientation—whose systematic role is explained by the self-organization model. These forces activate linguistic segments as particularly relevant or interesting or emotionally appropriate.

The critical importance of disorder in the cycle is that it builds semantic cohesion directly into the process. If the fragments of the preceding cycle are used to start the next cycle, there is inevitably a partial continuation of the preceding stream of speech and thought, ensuring coherence. We see this directly in such examples as (8.8), where growth points were dependent on earlier growth points.

The discourse context also is related to the self-organizational cycle at the initial stage. All the event lines are treated in the cycle in a uniform way. Self-organization may take place on any event line, or on several at once with one event line embedded in another, as we saw in chapter 7. Explicit discourse references to the metanarrative and paranarrative levels (such as "the next scene you see is"), when they appear, can be built into the cycle directly and in essentially the same way as references on the narrative level.

The formation of fragments could work something like the following. In any given context, some aspects are of more interest than others. Shifting the focus of interest enhances new contrasts and defines what contrasts with what. Affective regulation would be a major source of such shifts. Often a contrasting gesture is added to the next cycle just to highlight an opposition. Emotion changes the meaning of contrasts and can add wholly new ones. One easily recognized situation is humor. When narrators find particular scenes amusing, as shown by their actually laughing, there is a major discontinuity in speech accompanied by a shift of narrative level. In the following example, the laughter itself became the growth point (English gloss from the Georgian narrator): "then he tries to climb up on the outside of a drain pipe—{laughs} oh [this is funny!]." In terms of self-organizational cycles, there is a new growth point not traceable to the fragments of earlier cycles. The linguistic segment "funny" refers to the laughter and an emotion of amusement itself was the source. The gesture was deictic, a paranarrative pointing at the listener. Thus a new growth point was constructed around amusement plus an interpersonal orientation that included the listener.

One of the early discoveries of experimental psycholinguistics, made by Robert Jarvella (1971) and by others, is that people have partial involuntary amnesia for the surface details of speech that they have only recently heard. The extent of verbatim memory is about one sentence; thereafter, memory for surface detail is poor. Listeners are quite successful at retaining the gist of what they have heard (Fillenbaum 1966), but unable to remember details of the form. This amnesia makes sense in terms of the cycle of Order and Fragmentation. The previous sentence breaks up naturally to make way for the next cycle.

At the same time, previous cycle(s) provide fragments to the new cycle. Bock (1986) carried out an experiment in which she could alter the probability of a subject's utilizing a particular sentence form in speech by presenting, in an unrelated framework, a sentence of the same type just prior to the test. This effect was due specifically to the subject's having experienced the form, not having remembered the content of the sentence (see also Levelt and Kelter 1982).

"Order" is the general term in the self-organizational model for the structuring process that follows and depends on the disorder of the Fragmentation phase. It would include microprocesses of retrieval, pattern formation, and construction, which are, perhaps, entirely automatic and unconscious. The term "module" is often used to refer to such automatic processes, implying a package of operations that can be applied as a unit to perform a preprogrammed task. The details of microprocesses and their modularity (which remains controversial) have been investigated by numerous psycholinguists (e.g., Altmann and Steedman 1988; Bock 1982; Bock and Warren 1985; Clark and Clark 1977; Crain and Steedman 1985; Dell 1986; Ferreira and Clifton 1986; Frazier and Fodor 1978; Fromkin 1971; Garrett 1980; Levelt 1983, 1989; Marslen-Wilson 1975, 1984; Stemberger 1985, and many others). The final stage of the self-organizational process is Reconstituted Order. It is the Reconstituted Order that can actually be spoken. I will give a refinement of the self-organizational model in the next chapter that illustrates how the Order phase could proceed.

Consciousness and Awareness of the Self

The self-organizational cycle can be related to the stream of consciousness which William James ([1980]1961) described as alternating between two phases, "transitive" and "substantive." The former is the unintrospectable relational part of the stream of consciousness and the latter the objectlike part of which we can become aware. The self-organizational model links the flow of consciousness to cyclicity. The transitional phase is the dynamic transformation of thought during the cycle, the substantive phase is the final linguistic articulation of a global idea unit. Introspection cannot reveal the dynamic transformation, since, as James himself said, to stop the process is to turn it into an object. In our terms, to stop the cycle is to transform it linguistically, and this brings the dynamic transformation to an end.

The cycle also provides a natural place for the social, interpsychic mediation of verbal thought. This interpsychic side arises from the linguistic component. If we think of the cycle in terms of an inner voice, this can appear as the voice that "I" actively offer to a social other; or it may appear to be a voice that the other is offering to "me," the passive recipient (to use the terms proposed by Mead 1974). In either case, thinking is mediated by a linguistic category and this implies a social other in the context of thought. The very process of self-organization thus implies a dialogue or narrative in which there is social interaction. This is because the growth point is constructed with a linguistic segment at its core.

In the self-organizational cycle the "I" dominates the growth point; as the utterance structure evolves the "me" takes over. There is this continuing oscillation of the active and passive sides of the self, with the more structured side of the utterance being the sphere of the passive "me." This passive self corresponds to the feeling that syntactic parsing is automatic, a point that some psycholinguists regard as crucial (cf. Ferreira and Clifton 1986). It is conceivable that Mead's impression of the self as having two sides, the "I" and the "me," arises from self-organizational cycles of verbal thought. In his writings Mead characterized the "me" as the self of which we are most aware. The "I" is the self that we are uncertain about. It is the "I" that acts, and this action always carries with it an aura of unpredictability. These polarities correspond to phases of the self-organizational cycle. When it seems that we address the other in our inner dialogue, it is the "I," the unpredictable fellow in our identity, that appears to address the inner speech symbol to the other. When the other appears to speak to us, it is the passive "me" who listens. In both situations there is a social model of consciousness, but there is a difference in the phase of thinking, whether it is active or passive, whether we feel we are pushing into the unknown or sitting back and receiving dictation. This could be a powerful source of self-awareness and, because of its cyclic nature, of the sense of the self as possessing a duality, the "I" and "me."

The Role of Periodicity

A model devised by Kevin Tuite (to appear) explains how gestures and coexpressive linguistic segments can come together in time. This provides the motor for driving the self-organizational cycle. Tuite advocates several points: (1) speech consists of the presentation of signs—gestural and spoken—accompanied by a rhythmical pulse; (2) more complex gestures result from the superimposing of semantic features upon an intonational/rhythmical base; (3) more gestural complexity corresponds to more contrast and differentiation.

Since the stroke of a more complex representational gesture usually coincides with the intonation peak, just as the stroke of a simple kinesic pulse does, it seems not unreasonable to view gestures of the former type as being the kinesic enactment of semantic features superimposed upon an intonational/rhythmical base. The simplest class of gesture corresponds to the intonational pulse, without an additional content. Efron's (1941) baton gestures (beats) are of this type. . . . "Ideographics" (spatial gestures) are basically beats with one additional feature—spatial locus—added onto them, enabling them to meaningfully contrast with one or more gestures of the same kind. . . . The class of gestures termed "iconic" corresponds to Efron's physiographics. . . . Iconics differ from simple and ideographic beats both in terms of their semiotics and their motoric complexity. Nonetheless, the stroke portion of an iconic gesture tends to coincide with the nuclear syllable of the accompanying tone group, just as is the case with beats. This leads me to believe that iconic gestures are built upon an underlying pulse as well, but with different types of features extracted from the speaker's internal representation. (Tuite, to appear)

A rhythmical pulse could control the periodicity of the self-organization. The cycle inherently is repetitive and thus naturally would have a certain periodicity. A rhythmical pulse would guide the process so that at the final moment integration of the spoken utterance and the gesture could be achieved. This rhythm is measurable when speakers perform gestures continuously (viz., when G-phrases contain successive G-units; see chap. 3). In these circumstances gesture strokes follow one another at fairly regular intervals that can be measured. These measurements show an interval of 1 to 2 seconds (this is true of both English and Georgian speech). One to 2 seconds can thus be taken to reflect the periodicity of the average self-organizational cycle (as opposed to the much longer periodicities that correspond to paragraph-sized chunks of information; Butterworth and Beattie 1978). Average speech rates also show a periodicity of about 1 proposition per 1.5 seconds, which fits reasonably well with the rhythmical pulse. This 1.5 second period appears, moreover, both in spoken languages and sign languages, such as ASL, where the linguistic code requires only about half as many words per clause (Klima and Bellugi 1979, 187). Thus, the same period appears in different languages, different modalities, and across a 2:1 range of word densities. It is striking that the interval in ASL is the same. The periodicity suggests that the same self-organizational process applies in that language as well.

In table 8.1 I demonstrate the periodicity of gesture output by presenting an excerpt from one of the cartoon narratives with the timings indicated. I give the verbal transcription and locate with brackets every kinesic event, however small (see column two). Only some of the kinesic changes thus bracketed are gesture strokes; the others are small finger ex-

Table 8.1 Temporal Intervals between Movements and Strokes

Frame Number	Kinesic Event (* = stroke)	Interval between Movements	Interval between Strokes
7498	so he *[dresses] up like		----------------------
		70 frames = 1.17s[a]	
7568	a [doorman]		76 frames = 1.27s
		6 frames = 0.10s	
7574	goes *[up] there		----------------------
		40 frames = 0.67s	
7614	... and um ...		
		(pause for 176 frames = 2.93s)	
7790	and the *[grand]ma		----------------------
		56 frames = 0.93s	
7846	[shouts]		70 frames = 1.17s
		14 frames = 0.23s	
7860	out *[oh]		----------------------
		40 frames = 0.67s	
7900	the [bags]		56 frames = 0.93s
		16 frames = 0.27s	
7916	*[are] ...		----------------------
		18 frames = 0.30s	
7934	[right]		
		20 frames = 0.33s	74 frames = 1.23s
7954	[beneath]		
		36 frames = 0.60s	
7990	*[behind] the door		----------------------

[a]s = seconds

tensions, adjustments of shape or space, and the like. All such minor events are indicated, however, since they are necessary to reveal periodicity. With each such movement (bracket) the 4-digit number recorded on the video frame at the end of the movement is also given (see column one); these numbers are in 1/60ths of a second.

Among the kinesic changes, those that are gesture strokes are indicated with an asterisk (*). Comparing the rhythmicity of the strokes to that of the minor movements provides a simple but effective experiment. If there is an underlying rhythmical pulse, we should expect the intervals between asterisks to be stable while the intervals between brackets not related to the underlying pulse to be unstable (Kozhevnikov and Chistovich 1965). Thus, we expect the intervals between strokes to be more stable than the intervals between minor kinesic events. The latter intervals are not entrained by a rhythmical pulse and would vary depending on many factors.

The third column shows the intervals between all movements, including the minor kinesic events that are not regarded as gestural. The final column gives the intervals just between the successive gesture strokes. The intervals between all the movements, including the non-gesture minor ones, average 0.53 seconds. The intervals between the strokes average 1.15 seconds. (The 2.93 second pause has been excluded from these calculations.) Individual stroke intervals vary somewhat around this average but the amount of variation is small (0.93 to 1.27 seconds, or 30% of the average interval). The succession of all the movements including the minor kinesic events, in contrast, vary much more (0.1 to 1.17 seconds, or more than 200% of the average interval). Thus, the more stable interval, by far, is that between the successive strokes, which we identify with the rhythmicity of the synthesis of image and word during the self-organization of the utterance.

Other passages show similar average periodicities and stabilities. One speaker, for example, gave an average interval between movements, including minor ones, of 1.04 seconds and between strokes of 1.88 seconds. The between-strokes interval ranged from 1.3 seconds to 2.5 seconds, or 63% of the average interval, compared to 0.2 seconds to 2.05 seconds for all movements, or 180% of the average interval. This speaker produces gestures at a slower rate than the speaker behind table 8.1 (1.88 seconds compared to 1.15 seconds), but the stability of strokes is very similar.

According to our explanation, both the gesture stroke and the spoken utterance are performed together at more or less regular intervals. These intervals turn out to be between 1 and 2 seconds.

9   *How Gestures Affect Thought*

We are now ready to consider the following proposal: gestures do not just reflect thought but *have an impact on thought*. Gestures, together with language, *help constitute thought*.[1]

Since gestures carry both semantic and pragmatic content, and speech is often silent on the dimensions of content that the gesture presents, can we conceive of gestures as actually having an effect on thought? Is such a thing itself thinkable? Or must we assume a model whereby the full content of thought is worked out and translated into a mixture of speech and gesture? I will argue that the first alternative is more than feasible; it is demanded by the facts: gesture can affect thought; this is particularly so for thought as it is shaped by its context.

Such an argument helps to explain why gestures occur in the first place. Gestures occur, according to this way of thinking, because they are part of the speaker's ongoing thought process. Without them thought would be altered or incomplete. The argument also explains why gestures get more complex when the thematic discontinuity from the context is greater. Discontinuity implies the inauguration of a new dimension of thought; since each aspect of the gesture is a possible departure from the preceding context, the gesture can bring in new dimensions by adding complexity.

Dialectic of Gesture and Language

My first concern is to outline the kind of system that would enable gestures to help constitute thought. If we take seriously the concept that speech and gesture are two aspects of one process—not that gestures are paralinguistic features or added kinesic emphasis, but that gestures and speech really *are* parts of one process—the best theoretical approach is to regard this process as a dialectic of gesture imagery and verbal/linguistic structure.

The gesture side of this dialectic is a global-synthetic image. It is idiosyncratic and constructed at the moment of speaking; and it does not belong to a systematic code. The linguistic side is a linear-segmented hierarchical linguistic structure. This utilizes a grammatical pattern that embodies the language's standards of form—"the way we do it"—and

1. I am again grateful to Nancy L. Dray for extensive discussion of the issues presented in this chapter.

245

draws on an agreed-upon lexicon of words. What a dialectic of these two forms of representation could be like is the subject of this chapter.

The slight anticipation of speech by gesture implies a microgenesis of utterances over brief intervals of time. This interval I have called *deep time*. It is crucial to realize that the gesture also is evolving over this same interval. The gesture is, at the beginning stage in the growth point, an image. It is schematic, reflective of context and a psychological predicate at the moment of speaking, but lacks an outer kinesic form. At the final stage, when there also is speech, the gesture takes on its kinesic form— the movements that we usually take to be the gesture. Thus, the two channels evolve together. At the final stage, the gesture stroke and speech are integrated into a single performance in which there is a synthesis of gesture and a specific utterance form. If we make the assumption (which is in no way unusual) that thought is multidimensional, a dialectic of speech and gesture means that some dimensions of thought are presented in the gesture and others in linguistic form. There is a synthesis, and at the moment of synthesis language and gesture are combined into one unified presentation of meaning. This is an act of communication, but also an act of thought. Not only the listener but the speaker is affected. That is, the speaker realizes his or her meaning only at the final moment of synthesis. Only at the final synthesis is there the joining of a linear-segmented, analyzed representation with a global-synthetic and holistic representation. The synthesis—its analytic and holistic qualities—is a single mental representation for the speaker which did not exist until the instant of fusion at the rhythmical pulse. Thus a dialectic implies that the speaker's thought evolves through the course of the utterance-gesture formation and comes, as Vygotsky said, into existence with it. This synthesis is possible since (a) speech and gesture have the same referent (fictive or real), and (b) speech and gesture, when they differ, complement each other rather than clash with each other, each providing the other with dimensions of the same thought.

In a dialectic, imagery and language forms can be activated but parts of them not used; not all parts fit into the synthesis. Such fragments of image and language do not necessarily vanish. They are available to later cycles of self-organization and might have a long-range effect on the discourse as it unfolds. Since the constraints on form are far more stringent on the language side one would expect that such unused orphans affecting later cycles would most often be linguistic, but fragments of images also in fact appear (a case is described below).

An underlying rhythmical pulse is essential for synthesis. It provides the point of convergence that completes the evolution of the utterance.

At this instant there is synthesis of the image with the linguistic structure, integrated into one performance of speech and gesture. Kevin Tuite (to appear) writes: "The kinesic base which underlies both gesture and the gesture-like component of speech (i.e., the intonation) is represented as a rhythmic pulse. If expressed gesturally, the pulse peak corresponds to the stroke portion of the gesture. If expressed vocally, the pulse peak is represented by an intonational peak, which—presumably because of the more elaborate processing required by speech production [viz., self-organization of the utterance]—may be somewhat delayed relative to the gestural stroke."

A dialectic invites us to regard the temporally extended process of utterance formation and gesture creation as a continuous transformation of thought. Thought changes from an image that is essentially idiosyncratic to an articulated structure consisting of a gesture integrated into a performance that has a linguistic form. This new whole has a social component (the verbal side), yet retains individuality. A dialectic is between opposites: opposites are unstable and this produces a transformation by initiating and then overcoming conflicts: idiosyncratic and social, image and word, instantaneous and successive, holistic and segmented, global and linear. All of these qualities, although opposed, coexist in gesture and speech. The final effect is to combine, at one moment, one's personal imagery (one's personal context of thinking) with a linguistic structure constructed for the situation. The analytic mode, namely language, is joined to the holistic mode, which is the gesture.

Since the gesture contribution to this synthesis carries specific pragmatic content, we can also see how the full synthesized utterance (gesture and speech combined) can be adjusted to its context even though one channel cryptically and partially conveys pragmatic content. It is the synthesis of image and language that has this function.

Rather than finding an impenetrable cutoff between conceptualization and formulation, as in modular information-processing theories (Levelt 1989), we see an interpenetration of thought and language: there is speaking in thought and thinking in speech. In this dialectic the formulation process changes thought from holistic with analytic elements to analytic with holistic elements. Gestures add individually conceived distinctiveness to the socially regulated linguistic structures.[2]

2. Not all speakers agree that thought is transformed by the process of speaking. Some speakers feel subjectively that they first have a completely formed thought which they then revamp into speech. Speech, to them, is a more or less mechanical process of expressing what is already an articulated structure of ideas. It is possible that there are two kinds of people after all: but it also is possible that these speakers undergo a very rapid self-

Propositions on a Dialectic

The concept of a dialectic can be summed up in a few propositions. Laying them out may make the whole concept clearer:

1. Thought, language, and gesture develop over a temporally extended interval.

2. Their structure changes during this interval from internal to external.

3. Thought, language, and gesture (image) coexist throughout their lifespans.

4. Language and gesture have different impacts on the formation of thought. Gestures provide the differentiation of the thought from the existing context at the moment of speaking, and the contribution tends to be idiosyncratic. Language causes this idiosyncratic thought to meet standards of form for social communicativeness ("the way we do it").

5. Language and gesture have a changing relationship in deep time. At the primitive stage thought is largely imagistic and minimally analytic; at the final stage (the utterance itself) thought is both imagistic and analytic and is a synthesis of the holistic and analytic functions.

6. This synthesis is achieved at a specific rhythmical moment. The synthesis is the integration into a single performance of the gesture stroke and the coexpressive linguistic segment, both presenting the same meaning in two combined forms.

It was this kind of dialectic that Vygotsky had in mind when he wrote about the relation of thought to word as "not a thing but a process, a continual movement back and forth from thought to word and from word to thought." (1986, 218). Although Vygotsky did not recognize it, his conception of verbal thought implicitly invokes something like gestures as elements of thought. The tension between imagery and word (the continual movement back and forth in Vygotsky's description) enriches both image and speech. The spoken utterance is a transformation of the image. It is a linear-segmented version of the image plus those obligatory linguistic elements required by the standards of good form in the language. (Examples of this transformation are given below.) The mean-

---

organizational dynamic which first remains tacit and then is expressed. They first speak internally and then produce speech overtly for the listener. It is still possible that, even for such a speaker, gestures have an impact on thought. That is, the evolution of the thought is not finished until the gesture has made its contribution, and this can occur later. I have noticed in my informant on this style of speaking small gestures during utterances that spatialize oppositions. It seems that the movements make the oppositions more distinctive to the speaker and this is why they occur, which is an influence of the gesture on thought, even assuming that the thought was fully articulated in advance.

ing of the gesture also is transformed by the spoken utterance. Language generalizes the gesture and assimilates its context-specific meaning to the conventional categories specified in the linguistic system.

So, in a dialectic, we envision two quite different modes of thought becoming integrated into a single unified presentation of meaning. Time is the key for this integration. The utterance and the gesture begin as an idiosyncratic growth point. Always kept together on the basis of rhythm, they are united in the final performance of the utterance where both the personal and the socially regulated coexist—as a gesture and a linguistic form. This presentation is the speaker's experience of thought, the phase of self-organization where there is an object of consciousness (James [1890]1961). The gesture's contribution is to be context-specific and language's is "the way we do it"—an analytic linguistic form. The crucial insight is that both the imagistic and the linguistic are the elements of the person's thought.

Example of a Dialectic

An example of a dialectic is the following, where the syntactic form of the utterance embodies the imagery of the gesture. The synthesis of two modes of thought is particularly clear in this example. The whole syntax of the utterance was an unfolding of the meanings implicit in the gesture. The speaker was a precocious eight-year-old boy, and he was narrating from memory a film in which he had watched the antics of a spider named Anansi (a character taken from Ashanti folklore). The boy explained at one point (see fig. 9.1):

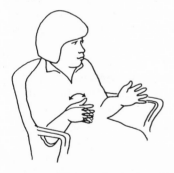

Figure 9.1. Gesture showing the idea of pursuit plus inaccessibility with "and so [they wanted] to get where Anansi was." The use of two hands and the motion of the one and the stasis of the other are the equivalent, in images, of the two clause structure of the sentence with the verb "want" and the nominalized location "where Anansi was."

(9.1) the fish um had taken Anansi
and he went in his stomach right now
and / so [they wanted] to get where Anansi was

Left hand held motionlessly with the palm turned towards center, while right hand performs spider-walking movements without approaching: an image of

*Anansi in the fish (the stationary left hand) while Anansi's sons (= "they")
seek him (the moving right).*

The basic image suggested by this gesture was that of two objects one of
which was moving and the other of which was motionless and confined;
yet, despite this movement, the objects didn't get any closer to each other.
This image could have the meaning of approach yet inaccessibility and be
unpacked into the utterance "they wanted to get where Anansi was."

According to our dialectic hypothesis, the gesture actually affected the
child's thinking. The sentence structure is the verbal version of the gesture thought. The sentence can be seen as segmenting, rearranging and
linearizing the gesture to fit the canons of English speech. Only by referring to the gesture can the structure of the sentence be explained. The
sentence, in its turn, provided a whole set of linguistically meaningful
categories for the gesture. The sentence had two clauses corresponding
to the two objects in the gesture; one clause centered on the right-hand
object ("they") and the other on the left-hand object (Anansi). Moreover, the verb "want" provided a linguistic structure and meaning
category to match the gesture's lack of closure. "Want" also implies that
the achievement referred to as "getting" has not taken place and this too
enters into a synthesis with the gesture, generalizing the gesture while
the gesture grounds the linguistic category. "Want" and "get" together
unpack the motion exhibited in the gesture that, despite this motion,
could not produce closure of the objects. Again this is a dialectic synthesis in which the gesture is related to a general category while the linguistic structure is grounded in specific images. Finally, the reference to
Anansi was in nominal form, "where Anansi was," which is a form of NP
that encapsulates Anansi grammatically just as he had been encapsulated
in space (the image of Anansi in the fish).

In a number of details, then, the gesture and the utterance are alike;
yet they also are different, and each makes its own contribution to the
whole. The total dynamic of the utterance is understandable as a transformation of the contrasts implicit in the image into the more systematic
contrasts of the linguistic system, and this is in microcosm the process of
thought in general. In this process, the gesture is an essential part of the
content of speech.

The Contribution of Gesture

According to our hypothesis, gestures, regarded as microgenetically
evolving representations, are an actual part of a person's construction of
thought and meaning in a given context. In this section I will attempt to

analyze this contribution by gesture. A key concept is that of contrast, or opposition in a field of oppositions. This is because contrast provides a way to understand the contribution of both gesture and language in a common framework. Gestures and language then can be compared in terms of the contrasts they add, this concept being a common ground that offers a way for them to synthesize and which makes it possible for us to see where gesture and language make similar and unique contributions to thought.

Contrasts in Fields of Oppositions

The concept of contrast is a basic tenet of modern linguistics. Saussure ([1916]1959) said that in language there are only differences. However the contrastiveness of gesture is not the same as the contrastiveness of language, and the way the two kinds of contrastiveness differ is crucial for explaining how gestures affect our thoughts. At any moment in the progression of discourse, the participants have a knowledge, awareness, and focus that are specific to that moment: this is what Nancy L. Dray and I referred to as contextual thinking (Dray and McNeill 1990). Context in this sense is something internal to the speaker-thinker, and dynamic. To this internally constructed context gestures add contrasts. The thought, that is, its contrastive component, is formed against the backdrop of the person's contextual thinking. Language's contrasts and the individual's contextual thinking must form a rapprochement, but they are not by any means the same. Language provides conventional packages of meaning that one cannot avoid. Marking one feature of meaning often obliges us to mark another. Precisely because gestures are not constrained by language-like conventions, the gesture needs to differentiate only those aspects of meaning that are significant. This is why the nonconventional and momentary creations of gestures play a role in thought. This process would extend through the full cycle of self-organization of the gesture-utterance. Language is the system of regulated contrasts; gestures are outside of this regulation. Since they are unregulated, integrating them with language allows free play to idiosyncratic imagination in the midst an act of social standardization—the agreement that we must all reach with the standards of form of the speech community. The gesture is the injection of personality into language.

A mechanism by which gestures can affect thought is adding, dropping, or changing contrasts. An example of adding a contrast is the cartoon narrator's description of Sylvester climbing up the inside of the drainpipe. She said, "he goes up THROUGH the pipe this time," and made a gesture in which her hand rose up in a basketlike shape—a kind of image of upward rising hollowness. Part of the thought unit was referential (referring to Sylvester, the pipe, the climbing) but another part was oppositional, and this was the part that expressed relevance—the path was on the inside as opposed to the outside the pipe, as it had been previously. The gesture's part of the idea unit is an image of the current attempt and how it differs from the former one. In this case gesture and speech combine forces to introduce the same contrast. The stress on the word "through" also highlights the relevance of the interiority of the path.

A contrast, moreover, can be understood only as pertaining to a certain field of oppositions. Without this field no contrast is possible. (An electron and a syllogism are different but they do not contrast because there is no sensible field of oppositions.) In this example the underlying field was ways of going up a pipe and the gesture opposed the inside pole of it to all other ways. The gesture thus made two contributions to thought. One is that it marked an opposition; the other is that it introduced a field of oppositions within which the inside path was meaningful.

This process of contrast in a field of oppositions thus provides a mechanism whereby gestures can bring the context into the person's thought. In the example, thought is analyzed as a field of oppositions of ways of going up a pipe. In this context inside versus outside made sense, and that opposition was the person's thought. The gesture contributed both contextual relevance in the form of the field of oppositions, and added meaning by introducing the opposition within the field that was the focus of the idea unit at the moment of speaking.

Another aspect of opposition is creativity. Gestures create their own fields of oppositions and define their own oppositions within them. This depends on the existence of gestures outside a system of regulated contrasts. The process could be the following, one in which the gesture raises itself up by its own bootstraps. The gesture introduces a field of oppositions such that it, the evolving gesture itself, is the principal opposition. We automatically complete the gesture by finding a field in which the gesture occupies one extreme. The field is understood in such a way as to make the opposition meaningful. Only such a field, where the gesture is in opposition to something else, is invoked. The other pole of the field of oppositions is what the gesture is not. The example of going up the pipe illustrates this process nicely. The upward-moving, basket-shaped hand created a field in which it—this rising hollow shape—opposed something that is not like itself. The gesture repeated the rising of the earlier gesture but added the feature of hollowness. This hollowness was contrasted to not-hollowness, and the field of oppositions was such as to make this contrast meaningful. The contrast existed at the moment of speaking. The previous blob-like rising gesture did not create a field in which shape had a meaningful role of any kind. Then there was a different field of oppositions. The speaker's thought during the second gesture was thus focused on hollowness and was structured in the context as an opposition of hollowness versus not hollowness, corresponding to the image of an inside path, whereas previously this opposition did not enter into her thought at all.

There is evidence that a process of contrast within fields of oppositions is possible for babies before the end of the first year (Kolstad and Baillargeon 1990). Thus the mechanism of contrast in the gestures of thought could be involved in acquiring the language-gesture system from the start.

In my final comment on oppositional thought, I will compare it to treatments of thought more commonly invoked in psychology. An opposition derives its meaning from *differences,* whereas retrieval and association—concepts that psychology commonly invokes—rely on *addition.* If concept A retrieves B, the sum, A + B, is the meaning. In an opposition, however, the meaning of A depends on its *difference* from B in a field of oppositions that contains both A and B. Both addition and opposition generate meanings, and they cannot be reduced to each other. Both sources of meaning must be assumed and, here, I have been emphasizing the contribution of opposition.

The Contribution of Language

In a dialectic synthesis, as we are envisioning it, language and gesture combine at a rhythmical pulse to provide a single presentation of meaning, both imagistic and verbal. The process begins in a hypothetical growth point consisting of a linguistic category and an image, as described in the preceding chapter, and comes to fulfillment, as also argued there, in a self-organizational cycle. In this section I will sketch some possibilities for the linguistic modules that come into play during this process of synthesis. The addition of language modifies the speaker's thought processes as they pass from the primitive, internal form at the start of the cycle into a fully social articulatable utterance.

The first question we face is to choose an appropriate linguistic formulation. There is a range of possibilities, but one concept that fits well into the analysis of growth points and their unpacking is that of a frame (Fillmore 1977, 1982, 1985; Fillmore and Atkins 1991). To quote Fillmore (1982), "By the term 'frame' I have in mind any system of concepts related in such a way that to understand any one of them you have to understand the whole structure in which it fits; when one of the things in such a structure is introduced into a text, or into a conversation, all of the others are automatically made available. I intend the word 'frame' as used here to be a general cover term for the set of concepts various known, in the literature on natural language understanding, as 'schema,' 'script,' 'scenario,' 'ideational scaffolding,' 'cognitive model,' or 'folk theory'" (111). An important addition to the frame concept is that different frames are associated with certain lexical and syntactic patterns. This is the aspect of the frame that makes it such a natural part of the self-organizational cycle in the Global and Reconstituted Order phases (see fig. 8.5). Each constellation of words in a frame is attached to a set of other words and also, crucially, with sentence patterns such that, when a word is chosen, there is also added to the cycle a possible grammatical pattern. The frame is fundamentally a meaning structure, with a range of possible syntactic structures attached. This provides both avenues for expanding the growth point and, inevitably, requirements which select parts to develop further and parts left behind as orphans. As Fillmore and Atkins (1991) say, "grammatical and semantic information come packaged together. Each lexical item, or idiomatized phrase, can be associated with what can be called its valence description, a description which specifies, in both semantic and syntactic terms, what the expression requires of its constituents and its context, and what it contributes to the structures which contain it" (5, original emphasis omitted).

A frame thus possesses the dual attributes that we require of a module for generating a synthesis of imagery and linguistic form. The frames most explicitly worked out by Fillmore and his colleagues never seem to appear in the cartoon and film narrations—which is not surprising, since cartoon narrations are not designed to address questions of interest in the theory of linguistic semantics. This lack of overlap does not, however, prevent us from seeing the relevance of this approach or how the general concept of a frame would apply to our texts.

I will illustrate such applications with one of the frames analyzed by Fillmore (1977) and described in Fillmore and Atkins (1991); this is the "commercial transaction" frame. To quote Fillmore and Atkins again, "In such theories [viz., frame semantics], a word's meaning can only be understood with reference to a structured background of experience, beliefs, or practices, constituting a kind of conceptual prerequisite for understanding the meaning. Speakers can be said to know the meaning of the word only by first understanding the background frames which motivate the concept which the word encodes" (3). In the commercial transaction frame the needed background knowledge includes understanding what is meant by property, ownership, money, a contrast, transfer and exchange, and other factors. Understanding these kinds of things is prerequisite to reaching into the frame and finding the kinds of syntactic patterns that are "the way we do it" for unpacking an image having to do with economic transactions.

Table 9.1, based on a chart from Fillmore and Atkins, shows a major part of the frame (the rows and columns are labeled to bring out the role of the frame in producing a synthesis, a detail not found in Fillmore and Atkins). The items in the first column at the left are verbs that apply to commercial transactions. We assume that they represent language categories and could appear as parts of growth points. The rest of the entries in the row describe a syntactic pattern. To complete this pattern it may be necessary to obtain more information: this information is indicated at the top of the table in the columns. The extra information may be extractable from the image or may require further conceptualization (thus a return to conceptualization from formulation). In either case, the columns show how the growth point must be elaborated on, operated on, enriched, and possibly simplified as it is transformed into the syntactic pattern given in the body of the table. For example, assume a growth point in which the image part is motion from the front toward the speaker; assume further that this motion is combined with the verbal category of buying. That growth point would lead to the pattern in the

Table 9.1 The Commercial Event Frame (Based on Fillmore and Atkins, 1991)

Linguistic Category in Growth Point	Elements Unpacked from Image or Added from Background Knowledge			
	Buyer	Seller	Goods	Money
Buy	Subj	(from)	D-Obj	(for)
Sell	(to)	Subj	D-Obj	(for)
Charge	(I-Obj)	Subj	(for)	D-Obj
Spend	Subj	∅	for/on	D-Obj
Pay	Subj	I-Obj	[for]	D-Obj
Pay	Subj	(to)	for	D-Obj
Cost	(I-Obj)	∅	Subj	D-Obj

Note: D-Obj means direct object, I-Obj indirect object, Subj subject, parentheses indicate optionality in general, square brackets show optionality only if the goods are identifiable in the context, the ∅ symbol that the particular verb does not have a slot for a seller, and the prepositions signify the type of prepositional phrase that begins with that preposition.

first row. This row defines what is implicit in the verbal category of buying and how to unpack the image into a syntactic pattern. The image provides some of the required information. There is a representation of the
goods or seller (the point in front) and the idea of transfer (the motion).
The pattern tells the cycle to unpack this information and where to place
it. One may also have to return to conceptualization to find other information called for in the pattern. For example, to fulfill the preposition
(for) option, reconceptualization may be necessary. Thinking thus is
driven, in part, by the requirements of the frame and its syntactic pattern.
At the same time, some aspects of the image may not fit into the frame
and may be left in the gesture or may be orphaned perhaps to be taken up
in later cycles of self-organization. For example, the hand may slant down
as it moves, and this does not have a place in the frame. Such an image
might convey the relative locations of the source and recipient of the
goods; or, in a metaphoric interpretation, their relative statuses. The
frame provides no way of transforming this aspect of the image into linguistic form. If it is left in the gesture, the gesture thus complements the
verbal formulation. The end result is a new synthesis of image and language in which some aspects of thought are segmented and transformed
into a hierarchical structure, other aspects are recruited to complete the
frame, and still others remain unsegmented and untransformed in the
gesture. The speaker's thought is thus changed, enriched, and divided
into speech and gesture. Changes also proceed in the reverse direction.
The abstract frame, which on its own is a decontextualized and relatively
static component of one's linguistic competence, is grounded in the form
of a concrete image that embodies the speaker's context of speaking.

One interesting implication of this analysis is that different languages,
insofar as they invoke different frames, will create other thought patterns
during the course of self-organization, even if the growth points are similar; the growth points themselves may also be different (as in the example
of the Chinese speaker's description of the bowling ball scene). The
Whorfian hypothesis of linguistic relativity (Whorf 1956; Lucy 1987)
thus formulates one implication of this approach to meaning.

Three Examples

In this section I will analyze three examples to show how they achieve a
dialectic synthesis. The linguistic contributions in these examples have
almost never been analyzed in frame terms; so we will be rather ad hoc on
this side of the synthesis.

"NURTURING." This example was first presented in chapter 8 to illustrate the operation of self-organizing cycles (ex. 8.9). We can use it now to illustrate a dialectic. It comes from Dray and McNeill (1990) and is taken from a videotaped conversation between two close friends:

(9.2) the fact [that she's /][she's nu- uh][/ she's somehow / she's]
           (1)   (2)   (3)
[done this nurtur][ing] [thing and here you-]
(4)   (5)   (6)

you were feeling sort of like she was this person that you didn't want to nurture in any way

(1) Left arm moves slightly up then down.
(2) Both hands move towards each other and up into the central gesture space with palms facing down.
(3) Slight wiggling of hands, still maintaining same configuration.
(4) Hands rotate around each other with palms facing body.
(5) Right hand comes out of rotation to far right side (palm up), presenting the "thing," while left hand holds facing body.
(6) Retraction: both hands move to armrest of chair during the word "thing," and the left hand continues to slide forward on the armrest during the phrase "and here you," coming to a complete stop precisely when this phrase ends.

The speaker started out with a simple transitive verb, "nurture" ("she's nu-"), but rejects this and comes out with a much expanded construction: "she's done this nurturing thing," which encodes the nurturing in a more oblique way. Why was this elaboration pursued? The explanation leads us to see the contribution of gestures to thought.

Here is the way that Nancy L. Dray and I analyzed these gestures:

The first three gestures correspond to three false starts. Gesture (1) never gets off the ground at all—it is aborted immediately, along with the speech. Gesture (2) starts to form what presumably would correspond to an image of nurturing, but because the gesture is aborted we cannot really see what this image would have been. Gesture (3) appears to be altering or manipulating the incipient image; this corresponds to the linguistic choice "somehow," which, along with the gesture, may be interpreted at the level of discourse (modifying the manner of nurturing), or metadiscourse (commenting on the current state of the discourse, which is in flux as the speaker tries to reformulate it). Gestures (4), (5), and (6), which accompany the expanded construction, display an image not of nurturing itself but rather of a process leading to an entity, and the entity is presented not to the interlocutor but off to the far right side of the speaker. The linguistic construction also reflects this "process-leading-to-an-entity" image: it represents nurturing as a quality ("nurturing") of an entity ("thing") that is the product of a process performed by the subject ("she's done"). The speaker thus contrasts this particular case of nurturing with the kind of nurturing that would have been an inherent quality of the action (in which case the transitive verb—"she's been nurturing you" or "she's nurtured you"—would be predicted), of the person performing the action ("she's been nurturing$_{ADJ}$"), or even of the result ("she's done this nurturing$_N$"). With the observed construction, the act is merely the default act "doing" and the nurturing just a modifier of the default entity "thing." The effect is to maximize the separation of nurturing from the other components of the situation (viz., the action, the participants). (Dray and McNeill 1990, 476)

Each gesture provides a new potential opposition within the emerging thought. The fields of opposition also are shifting. The false starts and aborted gestures at (1), (2), and (3) imply a search for a meaningful opposition. The fragments are the source of the next cycle. The overt breakdown with *nu-* is an essential part of the next phase according to the self-organizational model. Likewise the slight wiggling of the hands at (3) was a gesture fragment that grew into the far more dynamic rotation at (4). The first frame called up a transitive verb paradigm (not unlike the "sell" row in table 9.1 above), but this was rejected because of the implications of this frame and its distortion of the speaker's meaning. The dialectic of image and word gets a new lease on life and the two modes finally reach a rapprochement at (4), (5), and (6). The image involved is some whirling process that goes around and around, and then issues a product—an object of some sort; moreover, the product pops out to the side, away from the listener. This object is contrasted to the previous aborted gestural image of presumably a quality of an act or person. To state the field of opposition, then, it is a field in which something like Mechanical Products and Natural Qualities are the primary contrasts, with the gestures at (4) and (5) marking the presented meaning as being at the mechanical end of this field. The gestures most directly express the contrast. At (4) the hands rotate around one another: an image of a process of some kind. At (5) the hand comes out of the rotation and into a palm up orientation off to the side, the process produces its product: the image of a presented object which is deflected from the listener. The gestures at (4) and (5) are *themselves* the speaker's meaning in the context. Until she generated this image of an object emerging out of a process, she was unable to proceed with speech or gesture. She could not speak, precisely because she did not have a clear image of where to go. Once she created this image, the rest of her utterance followed directly without hesitation. Thus we have this analysis of the speaker's saying "she's done this nurturing thing": the speaker was herself striving to *understand* the relationship between her listener and the act of nurturing (the hearer was, as we can tell from the previous discourse, the object of the nurturing act). There was a challenge in this to her understanding because she was attempting to use the abstract concept of nurturing in a special way. The act being referred to was characterized as a nurturing act; but at the same time the speaker did not want to express any commitment to believing that this act was a sincere act or a characteristic act of the agent, or actually succeeded in nurturing the listener.

All of these elements, conceptual and pragmatic, were floating around until the gesture provided the image that could gather them together. The fragments then congregated into the image of a process that produced an entity, with this entity being the act of nurturing which itself was presented as an object off to the listener's side. Thus the speaker could understand *in the form of a gesture* how to describe nurturing without implying that it was sincere or that the listener was a willing participant, and the words promptly followed. The new and successful semantic frame had some connection with processes and outcomes of processes, such as "carry out" or "make" (although we have no analysis of these frames). The solution formulated by the speaker is very neat. My point is that it was an *image-solution* that existed in the gestures. These gestures were the speaker's thought in this context. This illustrates why gestures must be regarded as cognitive necessities, particularly when thought faces complexities and obstacles.

"NEWS SHOP." Examples in which successive gestures include minimal changes of form or space from the preceding gesture are particularly pure illustrations of the importance of contrast. In the following, the second gesture presents a spatial opposition to the first gesture that corresponds to a shift from one event line to another. The gesture marks this shift simply by adopting the opposite space. The space does not have meaning in itself: the opposition is the important thing. The third gesture then presents an opposition to the second gesture within the same event line, and again simply adopts the opposite space. The space of the third gesture is nearly the same as the space of the first, and this also has an appropriate impact on thought, since it establishes cohesion with the first space—the correct discourse relationship at this point. None of the gestures convey semantic content, but they trace out in spatial form specific types of pragmatic content and, on the hypothesis of a dialectic, represent this content in the speaker's thought:

(9.3) that's [my father's news]stand
                   (1)

(1) Deictic: hand swings to left.

not [news stand]
      (2)

(2) Deictic: hand swings forward and to right.

[news SHOP]
(3)

(3) Deictic: hand swings forward and left.

The gesture at (3) is much like the one at (1), but has shifted the semiotic value of the gesture from the event line of the story, at (1), to an event line where a metalinguistic correction takes place, at (3). Such gestures suggest that the speaker's thought was indeed structured around contrasts. The linguistic contribution to this example would have been a general rule of parataxis: juxtaposition of parallel phrases unpacks the contrast.

"KIDNAPS." A particularly dramatic case of a rapprochement of two fields of opposition—gestural and linguistic—comes from the mismatch experiment described in chapter 5. The example involved the sudden repair of "kidnaps" with "hijacks," accompanied by a sudden reorganization of the gesture space. This example is also used in the paper with Nancy L. Dray (Dray and McNeill 1990); comments are in boldface.

(9.4) he hides ab- around the corner

and [lures] the [mon]key over to him
        (1)   (2)   . . . .
and kidnaps [or kidnap] [HIJACKS him and basically]
                    (3)   (4)
[takes his] . . . [outfit]
(5)   (6)

(1) O-VPT iconic: right hand shows path of monkey in front of speaker.
Note: at this point the monkey is located in front of the speaker.

(2) O-VPT iconic: right hand points further down into space and closer to the speaker.

(3) O-VPT iconic: right hand reaches to front to indicate grabbing of monkey.

(4) C-VPT iconic: both hands suddenly grab own shoulders.

Now the monkey is located at the speaker's locus and the speaker's hands are Sylvester's hands.

(5) C-VPT iconic: both hands flip down from shoulders.

Again the monkey is at the speaker's body and the speaker's hands are Sylvester's hands.

(6) C-VPT iconic: left hand flips down again.

This continues the arrangement started in (4).

The first three gestures show the monkey being lured over to Sylvester, who is at the speaker's locus: the monkey is in the gesture space before the speaker. Then, all of a sudden at (4), the monkey appears at the speaker's locus and Sylvester is turned into two disembodied hands grabbing the speaker's shoulders from the space in front. This new arrangement of space is preserved for the remaining gestures. What should our analysis be of the speaker's thoughts?

The mismatch stimulus tape had presented the listener with a sudden shift of position: whereas Sylvester had previously been at the videotaped speaker's own locus he at this point in the narration suddenly appeared, as if rematerialized, in front of the speaker. The subject retelling the scene resolves this spatial inconsistency of the stimulus tape by placing Sylvester in front and the monkey at her own locus, even though the monkey was the one character that had never occupied the speaker's locus in the mismatch stimulus tape. The combination of the monkey at the self and the word change from "kidnap" to "hijacks," focuses on an intruder coming into a place. The gesture with "kidnap" at (3) showed Sylvester grabbing the monkey in the space before the speaker. This was immediately replaced at (4) by Sylvester's disembodied hands grabbing at the speaker herself. The space shift was in perfect synchrony with the verb shift. This combination removes the unsettling inconsistency of the mismatch tape by adopting the mismatch tape's final arrangement with the intruder (Sylvester) ending up in front of the speaker. Linguistically, too, the verb shift could have provided an appropriate frame that would guide the rest of the evolution of the utterance.

The new spatial arrangement seems to reflect a change in the subject's thinking about the episode. Once this spatial arrangement was introduced at (4) it was maintained through the rest of the example (and beyond). The synchronization of the shift to the new spatial arrangement with the lexical repair suggests that the speaker's thought was simultaneously formed of the new image and word. It was the speaker's new thought of the cat as an intruder rather than a tempter that resolved the inconsistency in the stimulus tape. This new thought was contained in neither the word "hijacks" nor the image of the monkey located at the self. It was the result of the interplay, the movement back and forth between them. The idea of an intruder was constructed through the *combination* of the new space and "hijacks." Thus the speaker brought together two fields of opposition and found a way to make the oppositions in both coincide. The new imagery field was Sylvester grasping at the speaker's locus versus not grasping at it; the new linguistic field was, equally roughly, commandeering versus absconding. The rapprochement of these sets of oppositions came together at the moment the speaker said "hijacks" and made the self-grasping gesture. A detail confirms this interplay. The word at (3) was not completed: the speaker said "[or kidnap]," stripping the verb of its expected third-person -s, as if the old space and the verb were already removed from the speech cycle. Dying on the vine, "kidnap" was no longer related to the subject, "he," and so the basis for -s disappeared. This is fragmentation again, and such fragmentation was a necessary part of the next step. "Kidnap" appeared while the gesture still had the monkey in the front space and immediately before the introduction of the new space. It also presented the old verb just before the appearance of the new. The old space and verb thus set the stage for the new space and verb. The new choices were, in both cases, opposites to the old: space was turned inside out and "hijacks" was apparently the opposite word on the relevant dimension of what is being done to the victim (commandeered rather than absconded with).

Some Relationships

Such examples suggest that gestures themselves and the imagery out of which they develop have an effect on the speaker's thought at the moment of speaking. What does this imply for other descriptions of thought?

Relation to CD

The contrastive nature of thought explains one of the major facts about gestures and discourse: why gestures sometimes don't occur. When the CD is minimal, gestures do not occur. One explanation runs as follows. A gesture implies differentiation in a field of similarity. For this reason, the gesture, in itself, would tend to create heightened CD. Thus, when CD is low, gestures *cannot* occur. In this low CD state there must be no contrast, no differentiation from the preceding context. A gesture here would fly in the face of a discourse structure based at this point on minimal CD. Conversely, when there is discontinuity with the context and CD is high, a gesture can carry this contrast forward by creating a field of similarity that embodies the context and cuts a new opposition through it. Thus, when the CD is high, gestures are likely to occur; and the greater the discontinuity the more elaborate the gesture, since this multiplies the avenues of contrast. So, if thought is a process of differentiation within fields of opposition and the cyclic creation of new fields and oppositions, gestures with minimal CD cannot occur, and gestures with peaks of CD actually can amplify the thought and drive the cycle forward.

Relation to Metaphor

Basically, metaphoric gestures permit thinking in terms of concrete objects and space when the meaning is abstract. While the human mind may prefer imagistic content, it also has the crucial complementary metaphoric capacity to think of the abstract in terms of the concrete, and this capacity we observe at work in metaphoric gestures. From the point of view of contrastive thought, metaphoric gestures add fields of opposition and distinctiveness, and this contribution of new oppositions provides a major role for metaphoric thought. The high frequency of metaphoric gestures in narratives and conversations can be explained as a concrete mode of thinking that may be more accessible than abstract propositional thought (Johnson-Laird, 1983). Instead of thinking only of being About-to-Deliver-an-Account-of-a-Tweety-and-Sylvester-Cartoon, we can think of a physical container—we create a homology between this container and the abstract idea. Thus the quite abstract idea is presented as an object in space (see fig. 6.1). The gesture contributes to this whole pattern of thought. The crucial human ability that such metaphors reveal is the forming of homologies between imagery and abstract concepts. That different cultures specify their own imagery schemas testifies to the crucial importance of metaphoric images. Just as physical needs dictate cultural standards in how the body should be fed, adorned, defended, etc., mental needs dictate standards in thought; and these are provided by metaphors that are no less culturally specified. Thus metaphoric gestures display cultural specificity, although they are universal in that they occur in some form everywhere.

Lakoff and Johnson (1980), jointly, and more recently Lakoff (1987) and Johnson (1987), separately, have developed extensive arguments in favor of the central role in the mind of metaphoric thought. I can quote the following from Johnson (1987) to illustrate: "We structure and understand a domain of one kind (here, the psychological/perceptual) in terms of structure projected from a domain *of a different kind* (here, the physical/gravitational). What is unusual (i.e., not recognized by standard theories) about this dimension of metaphorical activity is that it is an actual structuring operation *in our experience*" (Johnson 1987, 80–81, emphasis in original). This view also implies a favoritism for concrete thought, and the ability to create homologies—the "projection" of which Johnson speaks. Psychologists interested in metaphor have not dealt with the projection of imagery to abstract thought. A typical metaphor in a psychological experiment is, for instance, "Lenny is a blimp," where Lenny is a person of some obesity and a blimp is the metaphoric image (Glucksberg and Keysar 1990). The metaphor uses one concrete entity (blimp) to describe another concrete entity (Lenny). The relevance of concrete-to-concrete metaphors to forming concrete images of the abstract is unknown. Concrete metaphors of the already concrete are very rare; they are almost totally lacking from the narratives that I have collected.

Relation to Categorization

Conceptual categories are embedded in contexts and this has an effect on the semantic value of the category. Categories are not fixed entities but show what Barsalou (1987) has called "the instability of graded structure":

> Graded structures do not represent invariant structural characteristics of categories. Instead it is proposed that instability in graded structure occurs because different concepts temporarily represent the same category in working memory on different occasions. Rather than being retrieved as static units from memory to represent categories, concepts originate in a highly flexible process that retrieves generic and episodic information from long-term memory to construct temporary concepts in working memory. (P. 101)

An example of such instability is the relationship of cows, goats, horses, and mules to the category of animals. In the context of milking, cows and goats are the typical animals, more so than horses and mules, but in the context of riding, horses and mules turn into the typical animals, more so than cows and goats (Roth and Shoben 1983). Such instability, as Barsalou argues, is characteristic of human concepts. Instability in this sense is, in the model I have been describing, a part of self-organization. In this section I propose a mechanism for the contextualization of categories.

In the cows, goats, horses, and mules example, the animals that best typify the animals category change from context to context. When milking makes cow and goat seem like typical animals at the expense of horse and mule, what is happening? In the mechanism I am suggesting, the formation of contrasts is the essential feature. The word "cow" has a certain reference, but what contextualizes it is not this reference but how the reference contrasts with other things. The set of contrasting things is controlled by the individual. The person thus creates a field of oppositions in which a cow is a maximal contrast. This is the mechanism: a word in a context induces a field of oppositions such that the referent of the word maximally opposes the rest of the field. The field of oppositions and how it is carved up is the embodiment of the context. The field of oppositions includes the referent and its opposites: both extremes of the field are needed to represent the context; this, as far as the mechanism is concerned, *is* the context. Cows oppose horses in the field of oppositions of barnyard creatures suitable for harvesting milk, and this is how "relevance to milking" affects the category of animals. That is, cows are at the positive end of this opposition and horses are at the negative end. Goat does not oppose cow in *this* field of opposition, but goat does oppose cow in a different field of opposition, e.g., animals suitable for making wineskins. Thus, the same word has different relations to the category of animals in different fields of opposition.

In a discussion of markedness, Bosch (1988) emphasized that markedness (such as extra stress on a word) can "switch off a default interpretation of a definite referential expression" (214). In (9.3) the speaker said "news SHOP," and this signaled that the word "shop" was metalinguistically contrasted with the word "stand." The default interpretation of "shop" is reference to a certain kind of small business, but this was switched off or placed lower in a hierarchy of importance. The effect of the stress is to call attention to the word in one context, and this sets us looking for a different context, which we find as a contrasting word choice.

The gesture, with its contrast to the preceding gesture, worked in a parallel way. The spatial opposition became an image of the metalinguistic opposition. In narratives the categories invoked and manipulated are highly ad hoc (Barsalou's term). For example, moving up on the inside versus the outside of a pipe is a distinction within an ad hoc category; it is not a standard category of English. Similarly, a flat object stepping on a pointed object accentuates contrasts only within an ad hoc category, not one that is standardly entrenched in English. Narrators create these ad hoc categories with great ease. One factor in this flexibility would be thinking that is, at a fundamental level, contrastive. With such thinking, the content of thought is under-determined until it has been differentiated from other contents.

Relation to Narrative Thought

Metaphoric gestures and other abstract gestures illustrate how gestures add contrast to thought, as I described earlier. Such gestures particularly make thinking about narrative structure possible in visual terms. Jerome Bruner in his recent books, *Actual Minds, Possible Worlds* (1986) and *Acts of Meaning* (1990), has put forth a theory of thinking in which the narrative mode is a separate kind of thought, a peer to propositional thought, but not the same thing. The narrative mode is concerned, not with picturing the world of objects and events, but with the "vicissitudes of human intention." As Bruner writes, "There are two modes of cognitive functioning, two modes of thought, each providing distinctive ways of ordering experience, or constructing reality. The two (though complementary) are irreducible to one another. Efforts to reduce one mode to the other or to ignore one at the expense of the other inevitably fail to capture the rich diversity of thought" (Bruner 1986, 11). The narrative mode is truly a form of thinking, extending even to perceiving; "It is possible to arrange the space-time relationship of simple figures to produce apparent intention or 'animacy.' We plainly *see* 'search,' 'goal seeking,' 'persistence in overcoming obstacles'—we see them as intention-driven" (18). Furthermore (assuming a positive result from a proposed experiment), "we would have to conclude that 'intention and its vicissitudes' constitute a primitive category system in terms of which experience is organized, at least as primitive as the category system of causality" (18).

We can go a step further and conceive of gestures playing a role in thought in this narrative mode. Particularly inasmuch as the gesture, more directly than the speech, can reflect the mind's own narrative structure, the breaking edge of our internal narrative may be the gesture itself; the words follow. This status of gestures in narrative thought would be consistent with the temporal relations of gesture and speech, the gesture foreshadowing the speech by its typical brief interval. A written text may include hints of this imagistic structure, but it is an implied structure that often cannot be located in specific linguistic forms. A spoken text, through its gestures, in contrast, makes this imagery and discourse structure explicit. And the mental text has this imagery as its foundational element.

Relation to Visual Thinking

Rudolph Arnheim (1969) described with great insight the role of images as a medium of thought. He gave this example among many others: a supplicating suitor appears as the flash of a bent figure (taken from a description by Edward Bradford Titchener: Titchener wrote a century ago, which accounts for the quaintly bent knee). To Arnheim such imagery is the very medium of thought, and it is by no means limited to concrete thoughts. The first thing we notice about Titchener's image is its extreme economy. It selects just a bent figure, there is nothing else. This selectivity is actually an essential quality in thought, as Arnheim says, and distinguishes these images of thought from eidetic imagery, so-called photographic memories. The latter is imagery without thought. An eidetiker can look at a complex picture and pay attention to only part of it and later recall the image and scan it for new details that he had not noticed before. Some eidetikers can actually superimpose their memory image onto a current perception and obtain depth perception in random dot stereograms (Stromeyer and Psotka 1970). The imagery of thought is of quite a different kind, selective, elusive, and existing only as part of intelligent thinking. Arnheim comments that this sketchiness "is a quality invaluable for abstract thought in that it offers the possibility of reducing a theme visually to a skeleton of essential dynamic features, none of which is a tangible part of the actual object. The humble suitor is abstracted to the flash of a bent figure" (108).

Arnheim also thought gestures revealed the imagery of thought. (The gestures were ones we would classify as metaphorics.) A gesture in the form of a bent hand could exhibit the concept of humble-suitorhood. Arnheim wrote that "the gesture limits itself intelligently to what matters. . . . The abstractness of gestures is even more evident when they portray action. One describes a head-on crash of cars by presenting the disembodied crash as such, without any representation of what is crashing. . . . The bigness of a surprise is described with the same gesture as the bigness of the fish, and a clash of opinions is depicted in the same way as a crash of cars" (117). In Arnheim's view, then, concepts are formulated in terms of perceptual images and gestures reveal them in overt performances.

However, Arnheim felt compelled to combine this approach with a kind of glottophobia. He doubted that language could in any way be a vehicle for thought. He saw verbal thought as the rival of visual thinking, rather than as an integral part of it. He wrote, "In order to evaluate the important role of language more adequately it seems to me necessary to recognize that it serves as a mere auxiliary to the primary vehicles of thought, which are so immensely better equipped to represent relevant objects and relations by articulate shape. The function of language is essentially conservative and stabilizing, and therefore it also tends, negatively, to make cognition static and immobile" (243–244). What I disagree with in this position is that while images are the medium of thought as we have seen, *images and language also coexist as a single system.* Arnheim discussed gestures and was one of the first to observe that they are a special window onto the mind. But he did not consider gestures in relation to discourse or language in any form. Thus he did not observe the close temporal, semantic, and functional linkages of gestures and language that has been the message of this book.

Arnheim's glottophobia is unnecessary even from his own point of view. Renunciation of language is not an inherent step in the argument that imagery is the medium of thought. As far as I can see, this problematic conception of language is one that Arnheim shares with gestalt psychology in general, and which was inherited from this tradition. He writes of language in the narrowest possible terms, for instance, in the following, "Since language is a set of perceptual shapes—auditory, kinesthetic, visual—we can ask to what extent it lends itself to dealing with structural properties. The answer must ignore the so-called meaning of words, that is, their referents" (229). With perception defined as the interplay of internal psychological forces, as in gestalt theory, and language stripped of all but its outer form, there is no way to incorporate language except as a second sensory system. The indispensable component of linguistic meaning is regarded as an alien gloss that has no intrinsic connection to language: "Language turns out to be a perceptual medium of sounds of signs which, by itself, can give shape to very few elements of thought. For the rest it has to refer to imagery in some other medium" (240). This view leaves no room for linguistic and cultural modulations of thought. The way out, paradoxically, is precisely to integrate language into Arnheim's theory of visual thinking. This shows the way to extend imagery to the structure of discourse and narrative—an impossibility for pure perception which can know nothing other than the "patterns suppliable by the senses."

Relation to Mathematicians' Thinking

In a recent best-selling book, yet another doubter that language mediates thought writes to deny that mathematical thought is verbal. Roger Penrose (1989), a mathematician and physicist, argues that mathematical thought cannot be reduced to language (joining Jacques Hadamard, 1945, and many others). There is no reason to doubt this claim, so far as it goes. If mathematicians detect no role of verbal symbols in their mathematical reasoning, we cannot refute them. (For that matter, they detect no role for mathematical symbols either.) In the 1930s Hadamard conducted a survey of the then active mathematicians and one of his respondents was Einstein. Einstein's description of his own thought processes is often quoted, but bears repeating; he wrote,

The words or the language, as they are written or spoken, do not seem to play any role in my mechanism of thought. The psychical entities which seem to serve as elements in thought are certain signs and more or less clear images which can be "voluntarily" reproduced and combined.

The above mentioned elements are, in my case, of visual and some of muscular type. Conventional words or other signs have to be sought for laboriously only in a secondary stage, when the mentioned associative play is sufficiently established and can be reproduced at will. (Einstein, quoted in Hadamard 1945, 142–143)

Penrose himself describes similar experiences. He writes, "almost all my mathematical thinking is done visually and in terms of nonverbal concepts, although the thoughts are quite often accompanied by inane and almost useless verbal commentary, such as 'that thing goes with that thing and that thing goes with that thing.'" (424). This is not completely nonverbal, since all those "that things" (even though unvarying in form) could play a role in pointing to the references in an intricate line of thinking. But the mathematicians' point seems clear: "words or language" are not agents of mathematical thinking. The question I wish to consider is whether we should take this to mean that mathematical thinking must be considered as a different kind of thought altogether from the human dialectic of thought that is mediated through image and word or, rather, as an illustration of this dialectic in a different form.

This is not an issue of whether mathematicians use linguistic signs in their thinking. The process could be structurally a dialectic with image and signs of a different kind; visual and muscular signs created out of images for example, of the kind Einstein mentioned. In chapter 6, I described gestures that mathematicians perform in technical discussions. These are spontaneous presentations of images corresponding to mathematical concepts. They are not elements from a sign language; yet they are language-like in several ways: they are more stable than the gestures of narrators, more repeatable, more shared by other speakers, and refer to single concepts rather than global ideas. The mathematical gestures in fact have some characteristics of the rightward (sign-language) end of Kendon's continuum. Thus it is conceivable that thoughts in mathematics include imagistic signs that carry mathematical significance. The example in chapter 6 of a speech error that was combined with a correct direct limit gesture implies that the *gesture*, not the word, was the medium of thought. A key fact about mathematics gestures is that they stand for nominal type concepts not event type concepts; thus they could function as recurrent signs with fixed referents. Such symbols could enter into a dialectic with more holistic imagery. This would explain the employment of gestures by mathematicians. Gestures, or rather the segmented images they exhibit, could be the instruments of mathematical thinking and perform a job analogous to linguistic symbols during narrative thinking. The dialectic of mathematical thought would involve the combination of two kinds of image, then, the more segmented and fixed with the more holistic and context-specific.

The perception of music by performing musicians also might seem to offer examples of a different kind of thought process, but Bever and Chiarello (1974) found evidence that while melodies are registered by the right hemisphere by nonmusicians, they are received by the left hemisphere of performing musicians. Sophisticated listeners appear to treat music in the same hemisphere they would use for the analytic segmentation of thoughts into linguistic form, and something similar could be happening with mathematical thought. One of Penrose's observations is that, after concentrating intensely on mathematical problems for a time, he finds it difficult suddenly to switch to speaking (musicians have told me of similar lapses into speechlessness after they have been performing for a long period). This implies, not a separate form of consciousness, but overlapping use with language of the same resources. A dialectic explains this as follows: mathematical (and musical) thinking shares with verbal thinking the same kind of primitive stage but is unpacked in different directions (stable segmented images for mathematics, something else—still uncertain—for musicians). When the mathematician (or musician) must suddenly switch from mathematics or music to speech, he has to reimpose onto the self-organization of thought a linguistic system of unpacking; and this is what is difficult.

Relation to Nonverbal Thought (Odors)

Although mathematical and musical thought may be similar, structurally, to thought with language, there are other kinds of thought that seem to be truly different from verbal thought. The synthesis of language and image accounts for only a part of thought, perhaps the most distinctively human part, but surely not all that we are capable of. Vygotsky (1962) visualized thought as two intersecting circles: one circle nonverbal, the other linguistic, and the intersection is what he called the verbalization of thought and the rationalization of language. The intersection is where the synthesis of image and word takes place, and where the transformation of thought into a linear-segmented hierarchical form occurs. Outside the intersection there may be language without thought and thought without language. A case of thought without language may be the experience of odor (some may balk at calling experiencing odor thought, but this is undeniably a form of cognition). Odors are, as we say, ineffable, and that is because odors lie within the nonverbal circle. If you describe an odor, you encounter obstacles, and what will your gestures be like?

In 1990, at the University of Toronto, I had a chance to observe two people in this situation. The experiment was carried out by Ms. Silja Ikäheimonen-Lindgren in my class on gestures at the 12th International Summer Institute for Semiotic and Structural Studies. She presented each subject with an assortment of odors—some pleasant, some bad. There were many different sources: cosmetics, household chemicals, natural things like food and spices, and others. Describing these odors with words that refer to the odors themselves is extremely difficult, and both subjects invented ingenious strategies for escaping the limits of language. Their strategies were conveniently opposites. One subject described objects in the world that were sources of odors resembling the one she was experiencing. This led her to create little narratives in which the objects appeared as if they were the characters of the story. She then identified the odors with these characters. Her gestures were thus mostly spatializations not fundamentally different from the uses of space that appear in film and cartoon narratives. The other subject concentrated on the effects of the odors in his own respiratory tract. The references were to his own nose and mouth and occasionally chest. Gestures were what he termed "snout gestures," where movements seemed to radiate out from the tip of the nose—weaker smells affected only the nostrils, stronger ones the area next to the nose, and overwhelming stenches the whole face (the subject had spent many years in the professional theater, and was extremely good at this kind of facial expressiveness).

We learn from this exercise how the linguistic-gesture system copes with the circle of thought outside of the intersection with language. We have found at least two strategies: look for accompaniments from the outside world and describe them, with gestures to match; or look for accompaniments from the inside world and describe them, with quite different gestures to match. In other words, a process of image-language synthesis can still take place, despite ineffability.

Conclusion

The examples I have presented in this chapter could be joined by battalions of others. All would suggest that thought is image *and* word. This picture of mental life, as the dynamic combination of opposite modes of representation, is fundamentally different from the linear, mechanical picture of thought and language that has been the mainstay of information-processing ideology for psychologists. Conceiving of thought as a dialectic lets us glimpse into the creativity within ordinary human acts of speaking, thinking (including visual thinking), and storytelling. Gestures are part of this creativity.

10   Experiments on Self-Organization

I describe here five experiments on gesture production. They were carried out over several years and for a variety of original purposes. Nonetheless, all can be given an interpretation in terms of attempts to manipulate the self-organizational cycle and to change the timing and balance of imagery and language as they interact during the process of speaking and gesturing. This approach to experimentation is rather different from that often taken in the gesture field. In earlier experiments, following a tradition more developed in social psychology than in cognitive psychology, the goal has usually been to recreate daily experiences in which gestures figure and obtain data about those experiences. For example, Jacques Cosnier and Bernard Rimé have tested whether gestures occur when talking over the telephone, and found, perhaps surprisingly, that gestures are no less frequent when the speaker cannot see or be seen by his listener (e.g., Cosnier 1982; Rimé 1982). The experiments in this chapter lean more to cognitive psychology in that they follow an opposite kind of strategy, namely, attempting to use experimental methods to probe the mental processes involved in gesture performance.

Five Experiments on Gesture Production

Delayed Auditory Feedback

We have carried out experiments where we observe the gestures that occur under conditions of delayed auditory feedback (DAF)—the experience of hearing your own voice continuously echoed back. DAF markedly impedes speech performance. The question is what does it do to gestures and their temporal relationship to the disrupted speech? We found that gestures become more frequent under DAF but they do not lose synchrony with speech. This suggests that DAF lessens the extent to which the speaker translates thought into speech, leaving more of it in gesture, but the dynamic relationship of image and language remains unaffected. In a second DAF experiment the speakers repeated gestures and speech verbatim. Thus they did not have to construct meanings from scratch, as narrators do. In this case, and only in this case, timing also changed, with gestures leading speech. This result suggests that storing gestures and speech in memory and repeating them enables speakers to alter the internal dynamics of the utterance formation process. There is no longer a synthesis of gesture and speech at a rhythmical pulse but in-

273

stead two somewhat independent chains of behavior that remain together only very loosely.

The echo of DAF can be produced by an audio tape recorder or by a computer equipped with a speech digitizing system and a delay program. The first experiment below was performed with a tape recorder, the second with a speech digitizer. The advantage of the digitizer is that a much greater variety of delays is possible. However, the two experiments differed in other ways that are more important for interpreting the results in terms of the dynamics of formation. The tape recorder version was performed as a cartoon narration; it shows how the relative balance between image and language changes under DAF although the timing does not change. The digitized version was performed with speech and gesture recalled from memory; it shows how the timing of speech and gesture does change when there is not construction of meaning.

FIRST DAF EXPERIMENT (BALANCE). The experiment was carried out with Laura Pedelty and Karl-Erik McCullough, and the idea for it was suggested by Nobuko B. McNeill. DAF might have an effect on gesture. If gesture and speech are two sides of a single integrated process, then the difficulty of speaking under DAF could tip the balance of informational complexity toward the gesture and away from speech. We showed the cartoon stimulus to subjects and asked them, as usual, to recount the story to listeners. To produce delays with a tape recorder the subject speaks and as he speaks his voice is recorded; he listens to this recording as it is made (over earphones). The amount of delay is determined by how long it takes the tape physically to move from the record head to the playback head of the tape recorder. At the distance and tape speed on our machine, the delay was about 0.2 second. According to Lenneberg (1967), such a delay, roughly the duration of a syllable, should produce the maximum disruptive effect on speech. The subjects were asked to wear earphones during the whole narration, but for the first half of the narration there was no delay (the subject could hear his voice but it was instantaneous); then we turned on the DAF.

The effect of DAF on speech is indeed dramatic. Speech slows down; the subject stammers and stutters. There are surprising mispronunciations of a Spooneristic kind (the effects of DAF are so impossible to suppress that the technique can be used for detecting malingering in claims of deafness). Subjectively the experience of DAF is that your voice is lagging behind itself. The tendency is to slow down, to let it catch up—but to no avail, since it slows down just as much.

In contrast to the devastation of speech, DAF has no effect on gesture performance except to enhance it. Gestures become more frequent and more complex. In one notable case, which I describe below, gestures went from zero presence with normal speech to frequent occurrences under DAF. At the same time, linguistic complexity dropped. This enhancement of gesture combined with a diminution of language is what suggests that DAF changes the balance between image and word in the formational process, with gesture representing more of the thought. Viewed as a dialectic, the difficulty of speaking under DAF discourages a full synthesis of language and image, so the image remains the principal avenue of expression. At the same time, the temporal relationships of gesture and speech are preserved. Despite the slowing down and consequent disturbance of rhythm, the gesture is still synchronous with the coexpressive part of the utterance.

To present the effects of DAF on both speech and gestures, I will describe an unusual speaker who performed virtually no gestures under normal speech (no delay) conditions. With DAF he suddenly started to make gestures. These gestures, moreover, were specifically linked to sudden collapses of sentence complexity that took place under DAF. So long as the subject could maintain the degree of complexity that characterized his normal speech there were no gestures, even though he was under DAF. Thus, to tie this finding to the model of self-organizational cycles, the occurrence of additional gestures appears to be linked to incomplete linguistic transformations of growth points.

Speech output was phonetically severely disturbed by DAF. The disturbances were in speech rhythm and in undesired repetitions of the initial sounds of words. This was the speaker's first experience with DAF: "S-s-st-i-i-ll s-stubbornly pursues the Tweety Bird uh (laughs) all right the next s-s-scene h-has . . . the front desk of the ho . . . tel . . . and the . . . the phone rings at the front desk and the . . . desk attendant answers then it's the lililolady c- calling do-w-n."

To measure sentence complexity I counted, for each sentence, the number of *recursively* embedded clauses. This gives the "depth" in Yngve's sense (Yngve 1960). A single-clause sentence ("Sylvester climbed the pipe") was given a score of 1; a sentence with one embedded clause ("Sylvester, still pursuing Tweety Bird, climbed the pipe") would have a score of 2; a sentence with two embedded clauses, one inside the other ("Sylvester climbed the pipe which led to the ledge where Tweety was in his little cage"), would have a score of 3, and so forth. Conjoined clauses do not increase the depth. "Sylvester was determined to get Tweety, and climbed up the pipe" has two clauses but would still be depth 1, since there is no recursive embedding.

When there was no DAF, this speaker's average depth was an extraordinary 3—two recursively embedded clauses *on average!* An example of his average sentence complexity is this (recorded without DAF):

(10.1) oh, (*Clause 1*) then he tries to- then he proceeds
(*Clause 2*) to clamber up inside . . . a drainp- spout
(*Clause 3*) which . . . eventually will lead up to Tweety's window

The syntactic structure of his speech under DAF was disrupted only some of the time. At least part of the time the speaker could maintain his average depth of 3, but at other times the sentence structure collapsed, apparently without warning. On these occasions, and only these, gestures would take place. Looking at the sentences that were accompanied by gestures under DAF, we could see that the sentences were much less deep. The average score of those sentences was in fact just 1 (a single clause). The following are sentences with and without gestures, both recorded under DAF:

No gestures, score = 4;

(10.2) and she r-r-requests the b-e-llhop to get her bags and bird cage . . . because she's planning on checking out

This sentence can be visualized as an inverted tree in the usual way, and this exhibits four clauses:

Clauses	Depth
S(she requests the bellhop)	1
S(to get her bags and bird)	2
S(because she's planning on)	3
S(checking out)	4

In contrast, the following illustrates the collapse of syntactic structure when there was a gesture:

Several gestures, score = 1:

(10.3) the next s-s-[scene] . . . ha-a-as the [f-f-front] desk of
                    (1)   (2)
(1) Deictic: left hand points forward to "next scene."

(2) Iconic: left hand slides from right to left for shape of the desk.

a [ho . . .]tel [. . .]

  (3)   (4)

(3) Left hand rises up and down slightly.
(4) Left hand rises farther.

The tree diagram for (10.3) has but a single S:

Clause	Depth
S(<u>the next scene has the front desk of a hotel</u>)	1

Gesture (1) was abstract pointing corresponding to the scene transition and was followed by an iconic at (2). The gestures at (3) and (4) are difficult to classify. They may have been beats; nonetheless, they definitely were gestures. When there was not a syntactic collapse, in contrast, no gestures at all occurred.

DAF has its effects primarily on the articulation phases of the speech cycle—disruptions of rhythm and phonetic sequencing. At the stage of constructing growth points, on the other hand, the process appears to be much less affected. Why do gestures occur just at the moment when DAF induces a syntactic collapse? The answer, in terms of self-organizational cycles and the dialectic of imagery and word, is that the growth point is intact but its transformation into a grammatical linear-segmented form is impeded. What should have been a linguistic structure is blocked. However, in a dialectic there is a dynamic balance of image and word and the underlying idea unit does not disappear but remains as a possible gesture. Such a process is dramatically revealed in the case of the present speaker, since he ordinarily suppressed all gestural manifestations of information complexity. This interpretation in terms of a dynamic balance between image and word also suggests an explanation for how this speaker was able to avoid gestures under normal conditions. He did it by tipping the balance in the other direction, toward pure verbalization. That is, he avoided gesture by speaking more (or he spoke more by avoiding gestures). A tendency to perform gestures could have been present, but every emerging gesture was returned to the self-organizational cycle to be transformed into another utterance segment. We can see what might have been such a process of recycling in example (10.1), when the speaker added yet another relative clause, "which . . . eventually will lead up to Tweety's window." Other narrators of the same episode left this particular spatial relationship in the gesture channel. This speaker uniquely translated it into linguistic form. The lengthy pause (. . .) provided time for sending the image back for further translation into linguistic structure. For whatever reason, this speaker routinely suppressed gestures and elaborated on linguistic structure. Hesitations such as the one just demonstrated seemed quite prominent in his speech under normal conditions and suggested that feedback of gestures could have been taking place. Under DAF, however, with its many disruptions of timing, this recycling process was more difficult and gestures could sneak out.

Other subjects performed gestures under both normal conditions (0 delay) and DAF. For those subjects, also, DAF impeded speech and increased gestures. Under DAF, they nearly doubled their output of gestures from 0.78 to 1.30 gestures per clause (see table 10.1). At the same time, their syntactic depth and number of words per sentence declined. However, the effect on sentence complexity was small, in part because sentences not under DAF were already so very simple and close to the theoretical minimum that there was little room left for a DAF effect (depth declined from 1.31 to 1.22 clauses; words from 6.59 to 5.22).

It has been proposed that gestures *aid* speakers in the process of executing speech (Feyereisen 1987; Barroso et al. 1978); this is so in normal cases, but with DAF the reverse was true. Far from helping speakers to reach their usual level of sentence complexity, gestures occurred precisely with simpler sentences. There was an inverse relationship between speech complexity and gesture occurrence, not a direct one.

Under normal conditions, when the cycle is not artificially impeded, gestures add distinctiveness to thought and speech. Speech and gesture develop together. Gestures may alter the structure of thought and, in this way, lead to better articulation in language as well. That is, the positive correlation involving gesture occurrence may be, not with language as such, but with *thought:* more elaborate gestures going with more elaborate cognitive processing in general.

SECOND DAF EXPERIMENT (TIMING). The relationship of gestures to speech in time is ordinarily firmly fixed. So it was in the first DAF experiment. In a way, however, this is surprising. We could have expected the

Table 10.1 Density of Gesture Output in Normal Speech and under DAF

	Average Number of Gestures per Clause	Average Depth of Sentence in Clauses	Average Number of Words per Sentence
Normal Speech	0.78	1.31	6.59
DAF Speech	1.30	1.22	5.22

reverse, that under DAF the normal synchronization of speech and gesture would break down. Asynchronies of speech and gesture have been induced in experiments where the hands have been unpredictably loaded with a weight while they were in motion (Levelt, Richardson, and La Heij 1985). In this circumstance speech gets ahead of gesture. In DAF the reverse interference takes place: speech is unpredictably impeded while the gesture can proceed normally. Thus we might expect the gesture to get ahead of speech. However it is clear in the first DAF experiment that such a breakdown of synchrony did *not* occur. The speaker said in (10.3) "ha-a-as the [f-f-front] desk" and performed an iconic stroke at the place indicated for the shape of the desk. The gesture slightly anticipated the word "desk" but this is not enough to be considered a breakdown of synchrony. The gesture coincided with a word that overlapped the gesture in meaning in this context. The growth point, in other words, remained intact, despite the surface disruption of speech. This shows that speech and gestures can be constructed together over the full cycle and remain a unit even though speech output is being grossly disturbed. What must we do to produce the type of asynchrony that would be the counterpart to the asynchrony observed in Levelt, Richardson, and La Heij's experiment? The key is to remove meaning from the cycle.

When a speaker is able to control his own rate of speech and gesture, it is possible for him to hold the gesture in abeyance until he senses that he can say the corresponding word. In this way he can remain in synchrony. In the first DAF experiment, the narrator's gestures could have been held back while he waited for his slowed-down speech to catch up. Crucial for making these kinds of adjustments, however, is the speaker's sense of speech and gesture developing together, as a single process, from a growth point into an external presentation of symbols. This inner sense of dialectic was evidently not disrupted by the DAF. But what if there is no need to incorporate meaning in the cycle? According to our hypothesis, the synthesis of image and word is a rapprochement of two forms of meaning representation. If meaning is diminished in importance, however, there is less of a basis on which to bring the speech and gesture forms together. Then gesture and speech may become disconnected in time. However, the cost for doing this is to undo the normal dialectic of image and gesture in structuring thought.

One procedure for draining the cycle of meaning would be to make sure the utterance and gesture are not constructed from scratch. Ironically, the time-honored psycholinguistic technique of having subjects recite utterances from memory verbatim can be recommended as a good method for draining meaning from utterances. If both gesture and utterance can be exactly remembered (whereas in a cartoon narrative only the episode is remembered) it is possible for the speaker to lose touch with the sense of a developing single entity that consists of the utterance and gesture. Rather than refer to each other, each form of symbol can refer to its stored standard. Thus repeating utterances and gestures from stored templates could produce asynchrony under DAF.

An experiment conceived and carried out at the University of Ottawa by Richard Mowrey and William Pagliuca has three methodological features that address the question of timing under conditions where a normal dialectic of image and word is unlikely:

First, the subjects had to perform a continuous series of linked gestures. Since the gestures were continuous and linked, it was less likely that the subject would hold back a gesture since there were others to come.

Second, the gestures and speech were set up in advance and recited in the same form over a large number of trials.

Third, rather than responding to DAF in a spontaneous manner, which is by slowing speech down and waiting (in vain) for the echo to catch up, Mowrey and Pagliuca forced themselves to vocalize continuously, no matter how strong the impulse was to slow down (the subjects were Mowrey and Pagliuca themselves). The effect of this "talking through" DAF is an astonishing amount of involuntary stammering. The speaker finds himself saying the same words or parts of words over and over in chains that may last several seconds. Then, unexpectedly, he produces the next segment, which again he repeats over and over. The result is that the speaker never knows when he will actually be able to utter the next linguistic segment. Thus it is unlikely he could hold back the gesture until speech is ready for it. (The bits of speech that are repeated might become greater with longer DAF delays but this observation is tentative, for a reason to be explained below.)

These aspects of the experiment make feasible testing for the breakdown of the speech-gesture synchronization rules. The gestures were predetermined iconics that went with the following text. This same text was used many times during the experiment:

(10.4) [you take the cake out of the oven]

Hands remove cake.

[you put the frosting on it]

Swirling gestures with single flat hand while holding cake in other hand.

[then you put the berries on it]

Downward gestures with single closed hand while holding cake in other hand.

[then you cut it]

Up and down gestures with single vertical flat hand while holding cake in other hand.

[and you serve it]

Both hands present cake.

Mowrey and Pagliuca said this text and performed the gestures with echoes of 0, 0.5, 0.10, 0.20, 0.30 and 0.45 seconds (a syllable in continuous speech without DAF normally takes about 0.20 seconds). The experiment was performed with a speech digitizer and computer controlled delay (using equipment in the Phonetics Lab at the University of Ottawa). There is, however, one methodological disaster to report. The experimenter identified the delay condition for each trial by announcing a code number and this was recorded directly on the sound track of the videotape. This was part of an effort to achieve blind responding, an effort that was all too successful. The code by which to convert the recorded numbers to the time delays has been lost! Only one time delay is known, and this by another error. On one trial the experimenter inadvertently gave the actual delay instead of the code, and the delay on this trial was 0.20 secs. Despite the loss of the code, we can still draw the critical conclusion that under conditions of prescribed speech and gestures DAF can disrupt synchrony. It causes gestures to precede speech by a much wider margin than normal.[1]

To give an idea of the magnitude of the effects of DAF on gesture timing, I have constructed the diagram in fig. 10.1. It represents the kinesic landmarks in the gesture that depicted placing the first berry on the cake (going with "then you put the berries on it"). Two gesture phases are represented: preparation (the fingers start to curl in; the hand rises up), the stroke (the hand starts down; the hand reaches its lowest point)— easily recognized landmarks that occurred in every berry-placing gesture. Landmarks provide a way of comparing gestures under different delays. The lines in the diagram show the phonetic segment that the speaker was articulating at the moment of the gesture landmark. In the 0-second delay, the preparation phase started with the beginning of the corresponding clause ("then you put"), and the downward stroke slightly anticipated its coexpressive word "put." But in the 0.20-second delay, preparation began during "frosting" and the stroke coincided with

1. The first trial in each block of trials was always a normal, non-DAF run; thus, there is no danger of mixing up non-DAF with DAF trials, even though the amount of delay on the DAF trials is lost.

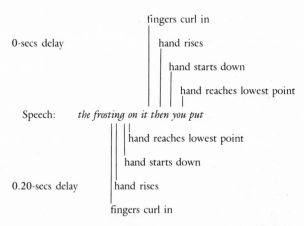

Figure 10.1. Forward displacement of gesture in relation to speech under 0.2 secs DAF when both speech and gesture are reproduced verbatim from memory. Gesture landmarks are used to relate the two delay conditions. There was extensive repetition of speech fragments under DAF that is not shown in the diagram; to represent this would push the landmarks much farther apart.

the juncture between "frosting" and "on it," words pertaining to the preceding gesture.

THE TWO DAF EXPERIMENTS COMPARED. One way of viewing these experiments is that they manipulate the dialectic of speech and gesture. Making speech itself difficult can shift the balance in this process away from the linguistic side to the imagery side. But to interfere with synchrony it is necessary to intervene at a more basic level. If the need to construct meaning itself is removed from the process (by having the subject recite speech and gesture from memory), then a temporal decoupling of speech and gesture is possible, with the gesture preceding the speech (the reverse asynchrony from that produced when the gesture is unexpectedly impeded; Levelt, Richardson, and La Heij 1985); this effect is quite reliable. Thus a hierarchy of effects is suggested; speech itself is relatively easy to disrupt; the dialectic of image and speech is much harder. When the dialectic is foregone, synchrony disappears. Another way of stating the same phenomenon: in the second experiment there was no growth point for the utterances and gestures (they were just replays from memory); in the first experiment there were growth points, and they survived DAF and preserved speech-gesture synchrony.

In terms of self-organization cycles, then, DAF has little or no effect on the construction of growth points, but it does have an effect on the linearization and segmentation phases of the cycle that grows more radical the closer to the speech output that one gets. This differential effect of DAF on gesture and speech brings out the underlying microgenesis of utterances.

Inhibiting Gestures

DAF interferes with speech. What happens when gestures are artificially blocked? Restraining gestures should have no effect on growth points, but suppressing a gesture that could otherwise have been part of a gesture-speech synthesis might have a detectable effect on speech. Extrapolating from our unusual subject who did not gesture at all, we should expect that sentence complexity will increase. In a sense, an inhibition of gesture experiment is the opposite of a DAF experiment. DAF impedes speech and gestures become more prominent: if we inhibit gestures speech should become more prominent, in the sense of more complex. The two experiments together would suggest that conceptual complexity can be shifted between speech and gesture in a fluid exchange.

One kind of trade-off in fact may occur. For example, at one point in the cartoon story, the cat masquerades as an organ grinder's monkey and gets into the bird's sanctuary. But then he is unmasked or, more exactly, unhatted, by doffing his monkey's cap, and he is exposed as a cat. When gestures are allowed, the hat doffing is typically demonstrated in a gesture. The accompanying speech may refer to the act of raising the hat but rarely if ever includes a description of the spatial relationship of the hat to the cat. Narrators who are restrained from gesturing, however, describe specifically this spatial relationship. Here is a speaker describing the scene under restraint (balancing a broom stick in both hands while delivering the narrative):

(10.5) and . . . then sh- I think she lifted
up his hat and slammed it back on his head

For comparison, here is a different narrator describing the same event while free to gesture:

(10.6) [and he takes off his hat to her]
Iconic: hand appears to remove hat from own head.

We can see the possible effects of gesture suppression in how the first speaker (10.5) identified vertical motion as "lifted up," whereas the second speaker (10.6) provided only "takes off." This latter is neutral as to direction. The vertical movement of the hat was conveyed in the gesture. Also, the non-gesture narrator in (10.5) specifically mentioned the relationship of the hat to the head ("she lifted up his hat and slammed it back on his head"—which happens to be inaccurate, but the point of mentioning the relationship remains valid). The gesture speaker in (10.6) did not refer to the cat's head in speech at all but did refer to it in the gesture. Thus, the referential specification of the event shifted to speech when gestures were not allowed.

Such effects, however, do not increase linguistic complexity enough to show up statistically. We cannot demonstrate a general increase in linguistic complexity when gestures are inhibited—only this kind of local shift. To express the shift of complexity to language quantitatively, we can count the number of clauses used to describe each scene and compare the scenes where gestures are allowed to those where they are inhibited. The raw frequencies almost double when gestures are suppressed, seeming to show a massive effect of gesture inhibition on verbal complexity (see the first column of table 10.2). However, if we also take into account the length of the scenes being described in the two situations, it turns out that in the experiment the scenes where gestures were inhibited were also longer. The difference in length is just enough to account for the increased number of clauses. A line-by-line description of the cartoon was prepared by Elena Levy (see the Appendix) and the number of lines in this description for each scene was divided into the number of clauses the subjects produced for the scene. This division exactly cancels the difference between the inhibition and non-inhibition situations (see the second column of table 10.2).

Experiments by others have found that inhibiting gesture performance leads to verbal amplifications but these experiments do not necessarily conflict with table 10.2. Graham and Heywood (1976), for example, found that speakers who were given the task of describing drawings to listeners (who in turn had to reproduce these drawings) included fewer demonstrative pronouns ("this," "that," etc.) and more spatial references ("to the left of," "on the right-hand-side of," etc.) when they were blocked from gestures. This result is not surprising. Given that the instructions to the subjects were to inform their listeners about spa-

Table 10.2 Average Number of Clauses for Scene Descriptions with and without Gesture Restraint

	Average Number of Clauses per Scene (Raw Frequency)	Average Number of Clauses per Scene (Corrected)
With restraint	8.4	3.0
Without restraint	4.5	3.0

tial relationships, gestures could have been part of a conscious communicative strategy and suppressing them could have called out a compensatory strategy of shifting references to the language mode. In narratives, however, gestures are typically unwitting accompaniments of language and gesture suppression would not have given the speakers the idea of having to compensate by shifting references over to language.

Shifting the Type of Gesture

If gestures give insight into thought, then we should find gestures changing with redirections of thought. We attempted to demonstrate this kind of congruence by one of the classical means for shifting the focus of consciousness, viz., controlling the speaker's attention: this was the independent variable. And we were able to show that, along with the shift of attention, the type of gesture also changed from beat to metaphoric or iconic: this was the dependent variable. Thus attention and gesture both changed. We can infer that some change in the focus of consciousness is involved when there is a shift of attention and gesture.

In one situation we encouraged subjects to focus on story events at the narrative level; in two other situations we got them to focus on the meta-narrative level or on a subpropositional level of lexical repair. We found that we could induce either iconics or beats by shifting the focus of the subjects' attention in these ways (Pedelty and McNeill 1986).

We first let the subjects watch the cartoon stimulus in the usual way; this was so that they would know the story line. Then we showed them brief excerpts from the cartoon a second time. The excerpts were nine transitional sections where one scene changes to the next. There was enough detail in the excerpts for the subjects to recognize its place in the cartoon. We picked transitional sections since it is plausible to focus attention on different narrative levels at these points. Thus we could keep the propositional content the same while the narrative level was being shifted. (However, we did not repeat the sections in their original order.) After each of the excerpts we asked the subjects questions designed to direct their attention either toward or away from the narrative plot line. The following are examples of the questions we used:

a. *To focus attention on the plot line:*
"How does the cat get up to the window in this episode?"

b. *To focus attention on relationships with other parts of the narrative:*
"At what point in the cartoon did this occur?"

c. *To focus attention on relationships with alternative linguistic items:*

"The cat's foot gets smashed by the weight" (specifying the wrong body part). The subject was asked to correct the word, e.g., "no, it was his head."

The subjects gave their answers to each question, and we videotaped the process. The logic of the method is that answers to questions like (a) would tend to be accompanied by iconics, since to answer this kind of question requires focusing on narrative level cartoon events. Answers to questions like (b) would tend to be accompanied by beats or metaphorics, since to formulate an answer at this level the subjects must think on the metanarrative level about the cartoon as a whole and the relationships of events to other events. The corrections required by questions like (c) also should be accompanied by beats, since the emphasis is on the differences between words which downplay the grammatical context of the word and highlight its relationships to other words. The metanarrative focus of question (a) and the lexical focus of question (c) jointly comprise what I called in earlier chapters the extranarrative level. Table 10.3 shows the results, grouping together the two kinds of extranarrative focus. Subjects performed beats, iconics, metaphorics, and abstract deictics. They produced iconics mostly with a narrative plot-line emphasis. Beats appeared in all situations, including the narrative and the extranarrative focus. Metaphorics and deictics favored the extranarrative emphasis. Thus the extranarrative level of questions like (b) and (c) effectively blocked the tendency to produce iconic gestures and brought out a tendency to produce beats and metaphorics.

Table 10.3 Gestures at Two Levels

98 Experimental Gestures Induced through Emphasis (Pedelty and McNeill, 1986)

Frequency (Percentage) of Gestures at Each Level

Level of Emphasis	Iconic	Beat	Metaphoric	Deictic	Total
Narrative	28 (65)	12 (28)	2 (5)	1 (2)	43
Extranarrative	4 (7)	38 (69)	10 (18)	3 (5)	55

600 Spontaneous Gestures in Narrative Discourse (McNeill and Levy 1982)

Frequency (Percentage) of Gestures at Each Level

Level of Emphasis	Iconic	Beat	Metaphoric	Deictic	Total
Narrative	226 (57)	134 (34)	12 (3)	25 (6)	397
Extranarrative	35 (17)	134 (66)	31 (15)	3 (1)	203

There is a striking similarity between this gesture distribution, created experimentally, and the distribution of spontaneous iconics, beats, metaphorics, and deictics in narratives. The similarities suggest that the gestures in the experiment are of the same kinds as the natural gestures. In the spontaneous and experimental cases, respectively, 57% and 65% of narrative gestures were iconic, 34% and 28% were beats, 3% and 5% were metaphorics, and 6% and 2% were deictics. On the extranarrative level, 17% and 7% of the gestures in the spontaneous and experimental cases were iconics, 66% and 69% were beats, 15% and 18% were metaphoric, and 1% and 5% were deictic. (The spontaneous gesture data are shown for comparison in table 10.3.)

From the remarkably close similarities between the spontaneous gestures and the elicited gestures, we can say that the experiment involved normal self-organization: an elicited iconic is not something different from a spontaneous iconic, etc. Thus we can confirm that when iconics, beats, and metaphorics occur spontaneously in discourse, the focus of attention differs. We can say that the gestures change their form when there is a redirection of thought. In terms of self-organization, this shows the interpenetration of gesture and language and how the evolution of the gesture is linked to the focus of attention.

Utterance Formation in Two Languages

I cited examples in chapter 8 of similar growth points in Georgian, Swahili, English, and Chinese utterances when speakers were describing the same episode in the cartoon story. The conclusion I emphasized there was that growth points can be similar despite wide variations in the linguistic system. Another implication of a dialectic of imagery and language is that similar growth points can lead to different dynamics: starting from the same growth point, if the grammar is different the interaction of image and language must also be different. The kinds of questions we are interested in here are, for instance, what kinds of internal dynamic differences are permitted in the formation of referentially equivalent utterances in different languages? Do some aspects of utterance formation vary, while other aspects do not?

The experiment in this section is another cross-linguistic investigation, but differs from the earlier one in several crucial respects. Here bilingual subjects are involved: each person was compared to himself when describing the cartoon story in two languages. In the jargon of experimental design, the person, the cartoon, and the gestures were held constant while the language varied. Such a design makes possible a precise comparison of the construction of utterances in two linguistic systems.

The experiment was devised and conducted by Sotaro Kita (1990). It is bold in concept. Kita found two nearly perfect bilingual Japanese/ English speakers, both young men, who had grown up with roughly equal exposure to each language and culture. The subjects were shown the carton stimulus as usual, and asked to retell the story to a listener. The critical methodological innovation was to have each speaker tell the story twice, in Japanese (to a listener fluent in Japanese) and in English (to a listener fluent in English). The order of the versions was counter-balanced.

Kita located episodes where the same information was narrated in each language. Then he compared the gestures and identified all the scene descriptions that were accompanied by the same iconic gestures. Those descriptions with the same gestures were the critical comparisons. There were about 300 utterances in each language where speech referred to the same events and the same iconic gestures were performed.

To illustrate a comparison, the following is the same subject's rendition of a scene first in English and then in Japanese:

(10.7) he [runs across] the street
        . . . .

(10.8) [miti o] wata te
        . . . .

      streeet go-across
'goes across the street'

Iconic (both languages): hand moves laterally (the stroke) and then holds (shown by the dots).

The gesture in both versions depicts a character running across the street. This covers the phrase that means in each language "goes across the street." The inferred growth points are thus equivalent in Japanese and English, namely, "miti o wata te" and "runs across the street" (that a phrase should be the growth point does not seem impossible in such simple cases). However, the dynamics of utterance formation are not the same.

The post-stroke hold (the dots) shows a continued semantic activation of the iconic gesture. It implies that the speaker felt that some of the words that went with the gesture had not yet been said when the stroke phase ended. This hold was a way of extending the gesture to cover these other words. In effect, it expanded the moment of the gesture-speech synthesis. But the active part of the gesture reveals in each case a different semantic focus, or primary gesture-speech synthesis. In English this focus was on the identity of the movement image itself. The primary synthesis of speech and gesture meant the following: this lateral movement is of the type, "runs across." In Japanese the focus was on the locus of the action. Here the synthesis meant: this lateral movement is located on the street, "miti." The other language's focus was then what was added and covered by the post-stroke hold. So both languages regarded the two components—action and locus—as an idea unit, but differed in how they ordered it in terms of focus. Viewed as a dialectic, the organization of the English utterance grew up primarily around the idea of lateral movement combined with "runs across," and then subsequently added the detail of the location. The organization of the Japanese utterance was just the opposite: it grew up primarily around the idea of lateral movement combined with the idea of a location (the street) and added as the detail the type of movement. In this way, the internal dynamics of English and Japanese utterances were quite opposite to each other, even though the same individual was describing the event and performing the same gesture while doing it.

Moreover, such a difference corresponds to the intuitive experience of fluent bilinguals when they are shifting from English to Japanese or vice versa: in English the focus feels like it is on changes of state, while in Japanese it seems to be on static states and arrangements of objects (I am told this by Nobuko B. McNeill). This kind of intuitive contrast is what the above difference in focus would produce. How images of motion are preferentially linked to linguistic segments is presumably a characteristic enduring part of the language: in one case the language (English) links the image to the segments that identify and classify it, while in the other the language (Japanese) links it to segments that refer it to a locus. This shift is palpable and can be experienced by speakers equally at home in each language as they move between linguistic systems.

Thus from these post-stroke holds we can deduce a difference in the dynamics of forming utterances in the two languages. This is not the only point where Japanese and English imply different dynamics of how utterances are formed. Again, the difference is in how the languages deal with actions. Japanese de-emphasizes verbs for this purpose. Instead Japanese has a system of onomatopoeic words that often seem to provide the growth point for Japanese sentences. The actions themselves are identified by the verb, as in English, but the actions are not linked to the verb but to the onomatopoeia dynamically. Thus English and Japanese differ in where the image of the action is connected to linguistic form and in whether there is identification of verbs with action. This identification is closer in English than in Japanese. Some examples of onomatopoeias (with Kita's glosses):

ba:n to (intensive collision)
do:n to (collision of heavy objects)
pon to (collision of light objects)
dondon to (progression without hesitation)
kaki:n to (collision of metallic objects)

These onomatopoeias are attested linguistic forms, integrated into their sentences. Their grammatical role is that of an adverb, as shown by the postposition attached to them, *to*. Since they are adverbs they are free to appear in a variety of sentence positions before the verb but not in the final position (which is where the verb goes). Kita found that such onomatopoeic adverbs are strongly associated with iconic gesture strokes (98% of them occurred with strokes) and are used to initiate the stroke. In terms of self-organization, the association with the stroke implies that the onomatopoeia plus the gesture image was the growth point. Gesture strokes in English, in contrast, but rarely appear with adverbs.

This fact again implies a different dynamic for dealing with actions. In English, images of actions have a natural counterpart in the verb, which can enter into the growth point along with the image. In Japanese, however, the language does not dynamically link the verb to the action; the verb may not be in the growth point at all but must be added later to fulfill a structural role. (In this respect it seems similar to such semantically unmotivated verbs of English as "do" when it functions to carry tense but has no semantic content; e.g., "where did you go last night?" which really means "where *went* you last night?") Because of the verb-final SOV pattern of Japanese, onomatopoeia permits the speaker to have a growth point early in the surface flow of speech. The structural difference between Japanese and English in the placement of verbs (SOV versus SVO) could be a factor inducing characteristic growth points— onomatopoeia in one, verbs in the other—and the resultant different dynamics in the two languages for forming sentences.

The results so far have shown that Japanese and English differ in how utterances are formed internally. Another situation is when there is a pre-stroke hold for an iconic gesture. Here the two languages behave identically. The hold extends the preparation phase of the gesture by freezing the hand in midair before the stroke phase begins. Kita looked at pre-stroke holds and the co-occurrence of discourse connectors—words that refer to cohesive relationships with the discourse, such as English *so*, *at the same time*, *as*, and the relative pronouns (*that*, *who*, etc.); and Japanese words such as *dakedo* 'but', *soiste* 'and then', and the pronoun-like heads of relative clauses (*toki* 'when', *tokoro* 'where', and others). Pre-stroke holds were particularly likely when there were such words. The hand freezes until the discourse word is over and then goes on to perform the stroke (these are, recall, iconic gestures: if a specific gesture were to accompany such a discourse word, it would tend to be a metaphoric or a beat). The speaker apparently feels that the discourse word prevents him from integrating a single speech-and-gesture performance; so he holds back the gesture until the discourse word has been uttered. Kita points out that such freezes could imply either of two facts. One is that the speaker looks back into the discourse for a cohesive connection before providing anything new; thus he holds back the stroke (which is the new) until the discourse connector has presented the cohesive linkage. The other is more dynamic: discourse cohesiveness itself is a factor that freezes gesture production; the transformation of the image into a gesture cannot proceed until the place of the utterance in the discourse has been made clear. In terms of self-organization, Kita's alternatives are different perspectives on how utterances are related to discourse.

Putting the three sets of observations together—the different semantic focus implied by post-stroke holds, the equally different focus implied by the phenomenon of Japanese onomatopoeia, and the similarity of Japanese and English in how they hook utterances to the discourse during their primitive stages of development—we can say that languages become more divergent the farther along we go in the dynamic process of utterance formation. The study of Georgian, Swahili, Chinese, and English utterances also showed similarities at the early phases of utterance formation to be followed by differentiation into the quite distinct patterns of the different languages.

The goal of teaching a second language is, as is often said, to produce a capacity to use the sentences of the new language; not only to use them grammatically and with the right words and pronunciation, but in the right contexts as well. The observations described here about the internal dynamics of sentence formation suggest another dimension of language that a learner would have to master. Utterances in the new language might have quite different internal dynamics from those in the language the student already speaks. One practical reason for teaching gestures as well as speech patterns (cf. Wylie 1985) is that gestures could help the learner master this crucial but hidden dimension of language. Teaching gestures would also provide a point of contact between the learner's preexisting linguistic abilities and the abilities to be learned, since gestures would expose the similarities of the primitive stages of utterances in the old and new languages as well as providing a vehicle for their dynamic differences. In general, a much more dynamic method of learning might be feasible. Laurence Wylie had this kind of learning in mind, I believe, when he wrote: "If language teachers want to teach language in the context of communication, they must help students to be knowledgeable about the cultural and psychological implications of the process of communication for which their words serve mainly as an excuse. . . . [Communication] through words, yes, but also through paralanguage, body movement, facial expression, proxemics, above all through rhythm. . . ." (784–785)—especially rhythm, the essential vehicle for the synthesis of image and language in utterance formation.

What the Experiments Show

The experiments described here can be placed in relation to each other in terms of the self-organizational cycle. The first DAF experiment suggests that the initial growth point phase of an utterance remains temporally a unit despite the major slowing-down imposed on speech itself by DAF. On the other hand, the second DAF experiment suggests that when the growth point has meaning drained from it by use of verbatim recall, gesture and speech may split apart in time. The experiment on the effects of redirecting attention implies that speech and gesture change together when thought changes its focus. The inhibition experiment suggests that gestures and speech divide referential specifications of events. Finally, the two-cultures experiment shows the possibility of unearthing dynamic differences between languages. That is, Japanese and English progressively diverge from each other the farther from the growth point we go; but at the growth point the differences are minimal—differences in which elements in a situation are to be emphasized, characteristically the action for English, the locus of the action for Japanese—a contrast that probably reflects the basic typological possibilities of the two languages (SVO and SOV, respectively).

Part Four

Topics

As children acquire their language they are also constructing a speech-gesture system. Gestures and speech grow up together. We should speak not of language acquisition, but of language-*gesture* acquisition. This idea was put forth by Riseborough (1982), and I believe the evidence described in the present chapter strongly supports it. In general, gestures and speech emerge together, implying that a linkage of gesture and speech exists from an early stage. However, the nature of the linkage changes; the speech-gesture system itself must develop. A striking illustration of this development is that when a child seems to have mastered a linguistic form this form may not yet be properly integrated with gesture. An example of such lack of integration is given in example (11.13). Examples of these kinds imply a dimension of language development that in certain cases continues long after the child has become able to generate grammatically complete sentences. In such cases we cannot get a true picture of children's linguistic achievements if we focus exclusively on the development of verbal skills.

The growth of children's gestures also provides some of the best evidence that in performing gestures the hands are, in fact, symbols with meanings in their own right. This is because we can observe the formation of the symbols as a process. Moreover, the different kinds of gesture do not develop at the same time; iconics and the various gestures of the abstract follow quite different developmental paths. Thus, when we see the fully developed gestures of adults, we see symbols that may have taken ten years or more to develop and whose path of development was specific to its type.

Gestures and Speech Develop in Parallel

That children's speech and gestures develop together suggests that they are components of a single system from the earliest periods. From age two or so onwards, the two never seem to be separate. This is one argument for considering speech and gesture to be two aspects of a single process (chap. 1). A broad and I trust uncontroversial characterization of the development of language is that it passes through three overlapping stages, each of which has its own typical gesture patterns:

1. There is an initial emphasis on denoting concrete objects and situa-

tions. This is possible with very simple expressions—provided there is sufficient context shared by the child and others, as there invariably is, to infer the child's meaning. This stage typically occupies the first two years and part of the third. During this same stage, concrete pointing and the initial emergence of iconics are the gesture events. At least initially, it is not the case that gestures and speech co-occur. Typically the young child (between one and two years or so) either gestures *or* speaks, but not both at the same time.

2. There are gains in flexibility, particularly in the construction of sentences for the expression of relations (spatial, temporal, causal, interpersonal, etc.) between objects and persons. At this stage it is possible for the child to sort out the linguistic ways in which different semantic relations are coded, but he doesn't yet understand how to code the relationships of sentences to the larger discourse (Karmiloff-Smith 1979a). This stage typically occupies the third, fourth, and fifth years, approximately. The gesture accomplishments include further development of iconics and the beginning of beats. Gestures by this time co-occur with speech, a yoking that is henceforth never broken.

3. The emergence of discourse coding is the final stage, and this occupies the remainder of the primary language acquisition period, until adolescence (see Karmiloff-Smith 1979a). During this time the rest of the gesture system develops: beats, abstract pointing, and metaphors.

Symbol Formation

The emergence of gesture and language is a process of increasing symbolicization, of *symbol formation,* as this term was employed by Werner and Kaplan in their classic book of that title (Werner and Kaplan 1963). I will use this section to analyze the emergence of gestures in terms of symbol formation, including the growth points of children's utterances which the gestures imply.

Within a symbol there is an overt sign, the physical presentation of the symbol, such as a gesture or spoken word. This physical side was called the "signifier" by Saussure ([1916] 1959). The concept to which the signifier is connected was called the "signified." Together, signifier and signified jointly comprise the "symbol." The term "symbol formation" refers to the development of this kind of structure. For adults, gestures are symbols in the sense that the hands can be freely designated to take on different meanings. The same hand configuration can be hands, entire people, inanimate objects, abstract ideas, etc. Thus there is a distinction between signifier and signified. For children this freedom is less developed, and the gestures are less symbolic in the sense that they remain closer to enactment. Young children act as if the form of the signifier has to have some necessary connection to its signified. One of Vygotsky's examples was a child who was told that in a game a dog would be called a cow. Then the following dialogue took place:

Does a cow have horns?
Yes.
But don't you remember that the cow is really a dog? Come now, does a dog have horns?
Sure, if it is a cow, if it's called cow, it has horns. That kind of dog has got to have little horns. (Vygotsky 1962, 223)

Symbol formation thus means that signifiers come to have flexible links to signifieds and that arbitrariness increases. This applies to gestures as well as words (Werner and Kaplan 1963). With lessened arbitrariness, children are not free, as are adults, to change the meanings of their gestures without changing, at the same time, their form. Symbol formation thus means that the speaker can realize different meanings with the same physical display.

Another symbol property is the relationship of symbols to other symbols. Adult gestures are often parts of series of gestures in which relationships of cohesion, contrast, or diminution help determine the form that the next gesture takes. Children also add features to gestures, often more than adults do, but add them to make the gestures into a more realistic simulation of the event, not to distinguish one event from other events. Symbol formation thus also means that the signifier tends to include only those properties that reflect meaningful contrasts.

During development there is a gradual symbolicization in terms of arbitrariness, flexibility, and contrastiveness. This process manifests itself in many areas of gesture performance—the size of the gesture, the use of space, the timing, the setting of gestures in relation to other gestures, and so forth.

WERNER AND KAPLAN'S THEORY. An explanation for the development of form and the growth in use of symbols by children can be found in a principle to which virtually every developmental psychologist has subscribed. Piaget (1954), Werner (1961), Bruner (1966), and many others have recognized that objects and events in the world are, for little children, represented in the form of the actions that the child himself performs on the objects, or in the form of the actions the thing itself performs (simulated by the child). Broad categories, that is, whether a referent is alive or is an artifact, are understood by preschool children (Carey 1985), but to differentiate within these categories children appear to use enactments and animistic thought (Piaget 1929). To take a homely example, a spoon is mentally represented by a child—not only with respect to a taxonomy of cutlery or contrasting shapes or metallic instruments (various ways an adult might choose)—but also in terms of the actions the child himself performs with the spoon: picking it up, putting it in his mouth, licking it, pounding with it, etc. The child doesn't see himself presenting meanings so much as enacting them, and in this state he *is* what he is symbolizing: "At the beginning stages of symbolic play, where play sphere and reality sphere are little differentiated, we may assume that from the child's viewpoint he *is* what he represents; there is little awareness of the body as a *medium* of representation" (Werner and Kaplan 1963, 95, emphasis in original).

The age at which such action representations disappear is quite indistinct. In some circumscribed areas they may never disappear. Many adults, I suspect, represent the layout of familiar environments in terms of the paths they follow to get from one place to the next, not in terms of the objective arrangement of space. To them what they *do* as they trudge along, **is** space. Thus they can be much amazed when they find out, at long last, that two rooms they had always thought of as being at opposite ends of a roundabout path are really contiguous and separated by just a wall.

In their book Werner and Kaplan described the process of symbol formation under the heading of "distancing." At an early stage of development the signifier and signified have little distance between them. This appears in children's use of onomatopoeia. A French-speaking child said, for example, *boom-er*—the sound effect of something falling plus the French verb ending, *-er*. A German child said, for the act of going down a slide, *whee-en*—the sound one makes going down a slide plus the German verb ending, *-en*. We have found that in nearly every case of onomatopoeia during children's narratives there is a gesture at the same time, a co-occurrence that supports the linkup of gesture and onomatopoeia as two faces of an underlying lack of distance between signifier and signified. All of this restriction of symbolization by lack of distance makes the gestures of children less flexible, less able to take on other meanings without changing form, less able to contrast with other gestures, and more burdened with characteristics that arise from their being actions but that are not needed for them to be symbols.

CHILDREN'S GROWTH POINTS That distance and symbolization increase with development explains one important developmental fact:

children's gestures are less frequently combined with speech at younger ages. Most utterances are not accompanied by gestures. There is a major increase in gesture frequency with speech around age five, at which time adult levels are attained (see table 11.1). In terms of Werner and Kaplan's theory, as long as children are using their own bodies as the medium of representation there is little reason for gestures and speech to co-occur. The key fact is that when the body as a whole is the medium of representation neither speech nor gesture stands out and there is no basis for a division of function between them. Each has the same function with respect to the body. Either may express the child's meaning; they do not differ, and thus do not co-occur. Only with increasing distance is there a definite relationship between gesture and utterance, and with distance the two channels are able to acquire different functions.

Around the beginning of school (and of literacy) distance seems to become established once and for all and these modes differentiated. The theory thus suggests that little children's growth points are necessarily unlike those of older children and adults. At a young age growth points do not resolve themselves into imagery and linguistic segments but are bodily states where action, imagery, and word are fused syncretically. Many indications can be cited of qualitatively different growth points in little children. Vygotsky's little subject, above, did not give up the image of the cow when he tried to switch the words "dog" and "cow." The image of a cow was not sharply distinguished from the pronunciation of "cow." Gestures are less frequent, as noted, and when they occur resemble actual actions both in time and space. The earliest iconics (during the second year) often do not accompany speech at all. Later iconics, although now accompanying speech, do not necessarily synchronize with speech and often lack clear-cut temporal boundaries. Thus synchrony itself must develop. The gesture space is also unique, and is like the space of actual actions—large and centered on the child's own locus. In Werner and Kaplan's terms, the gesture and the utterance are aspects of a larger medium of representation involving the child's actions. Immersed to-

Table 11.1 Percentage of Clauses with Gestures
at Four Ages

Age	Percentage of Clauses with Gestures	Number of Clauses
2–3	28	98
4–5	68	109
8	58	164
11	58	200
Adult	67	134

gether in this medium, speech and gesture do not form their own separate areas of mental processes. That step awaits distance and symbol
formation.

Protogestures

The First Year

Even in the first few minutes of life there is an association of hand movements with vocalization (De Casper and Fifer 1980; Meltzoff and
Moore, 1977). Within a few weeks there are "protogestures" and "pro-
tospeech" (Trevarthen 1977, 1986, to appear)—that is, motions of the
hands and arms, such as raising the hand above head level, that appear in
the company of speech articulatory movements of the tongue and lips,
although there may be no sound. The linkage of the manual and vocal at
so early an age suggests a biological connection of the two systems in
what Trevarthen argues is a capacity for intersubjective communication
between infants and caretakers. The infant is endowed with the raw materials with which such communication is effected—including the impulse to make communicative movements of the hands and arms along
with speech.

By 12 months of age, or so, gesture movements with definite referential significance have emerged in the form of concrete pointing (Bates et
al. 1983; Lock 1980). A convincing demonstration of the referential significance of this early pointing is when a child reaches out in the direction
of a desired object, and *looks away from the object and to the adult* who is in
a different direction (Bates et al. 1983). Such a gesture could still be in
part reaching, but the child clearly includes the adult in a communicative
loop with the gesture. Pointing has captured a great deal of attention
among developmental psychologists (e.g., the papers in Lock 1978),
since it has been regarded as a precursor of speech developments. It is
striking that none of these observers of little children has ever described
anything that could remotely be called an iconic gesture. Pointing at concrete targets seems to be the only meaningful gesture at this age.

The Second Year

Protogestures develop further in the second year. The discovery that
children invent their own gesture "words" and even combine them is of
recent origin, although many parents have seen their own children doing
such things. These gestures function like spoken words, and may appear
in linguistic development before spoken words (Acredolo and Goodwyn, to appear). They are like iconics, in that they depict actions and ob-

jects, but are different from iconics in a fundamental way, since they do not occur with speech (pointing combines with speech but depictive gestures do not; Morford and Goldin-Meadow to appear). Most of the gestures between 12 and 18 months are whole-body enactments with a C-VPT (see table 11.2, based on observations of one child by Acredolo and Goodwyn, to which I have added the gesture viewpoints). Examples are sniffing for "flower," putting a finger to the nose and raising it for "elephant," putting the palm of the hand to the mouth and making a smacking noise for "Cookie Monster," and so forth. Of the 29 gestures in table 11.2, 19 are whole-body enactments. Moreover, the first 9 gestures are exclusively whole-body enactments.

Table 11.2 First Iconic Gesture "Words" of One Child (based on Acredolo and Goodwyn, to appear).

Viewpoint	Referent[a]	Gesture	Age of First Appearance (months)
Body enacts C-VPT	Flower	sniff, sniff	12.50
"	Big	arms raised	13.00
"	Elephant	finger to nose, lifted	13.50
"	Anteater	tongue in and out	14.00
"	Bunny	torso up and down	14.00
"	Cookie Monster	palm to mouth plus smack	14.00
"	Monkey	hands in armpits, up-down	14.25
"	Skunk	wrinkled nose, plus sniff	14.50
"	Fish	blow through mouth	14.50
Hand O-VPT	Slide*	hand waved downward	14.50
Body enacts C-VPT	Swing*	torso back and forth	14.50
"	Ball*	both hands waved	14.50
Hand O-VPT	Alligator	palms together, open-shut	14.75
"	Bee	finger plus thumb waved	14.75
"	Butterfly	hands crossed, fingers waved	14.75
Emblem	I dunno	shrugs shoulders, hands up	15.00
Body enacts C-VPT	Hot	waves hand at midline	15.00
"	Hippo	head back, mouth wide	15.00
From a game	Spider	index fingers rubbed	15.00
Body enacts C-VPT	Bird	arms out, hands flapping	15.00
"	Turtle	hand around wrist, fist in-out	15.00
"	Fire*	waving of hand	15.00
"	Night-night*	head down on shoulder	15.00
Unclassifiable	X-mas tree	fists open-closed	16.00
Body enacts C-VPT	Mistletoe	kisses	16.00
Hand O-VPT	Scissors	two fingers open-closed	16.00
Body enacts C-VPT	Berry*	"raspberry" motion	16.50
"	Kiss	kiss (at a distance)	16.50
Hand O-VPT	Caterpillar	index finger wiggled	17.50

[a]An asterisk (*) marks a gesture that appeared spontaneously with the child; all others, including the first nine, were directly taught or were imitations of adult actions.

There are also O-VPT gestures. The 6 such in table 11.2 all emerged late in the period covered by Acredolo and Goodwyn. In these gestures just the child's hand depicted the event or object (e.g., the hand waving downward for a slide). The almost 5:1 C-VPT to O-VPT ratio is much higher than in older children and adults.

Gesture words, like spoken words, reflect the semantic relationships that are emerging in the child's structuring of the world during the second year. Although the length of the utterance does not change (viz., it is always one word) there is a development of new semantic relationships, and these are expressed in both speech and gesture. The semantic relationships in the early gestures are agents and objects. For example, the gesture for "flower" was sniffing: in this case the referent was the object of the action. The gesture for "anteater" was the tongue going in and out: the referent was the agent. Both of these examples appeared quite early, by 14 months. Later on, gestures began to include more oblique relationships. For example, a gesture referring to a hot object was the hand waved at the midline, as if enacting the experiencer's movement. In single-word speech, as well, Greenfield and Smith (1976) found that initially only agent and object relationships appeared and the more oblique relationships, such as experiencers, emerged later (see Fillmore 1968, for definitions of these terms).

The protogesture period is dominated initially by pointing, then by C-VPT whole-body enactments, with O-VPT manual iconics making a late appearance. Children at this age combine pointing gestures with speech but not iconics with speech. The emergence of speech-accompanying iconic gestures is the next development.

True Gestures

Iconics

The youngest child we have observed narrating the cartoon story was two and a half years old. This child clearly produced iconic gestures with her speech, although not in huge numbers, and had both O-VPT and C-VPT gestures. An example of a C-VPT is the following, in which she depicts Sylvester climbing up the pipe (this is the same scene for which I described adult gestures in examples (4.1) through (4.5)). The child showed this event by actually leaving her chair to demonstrate climbing (see fig. 11.1):

(A 2¹/₂-year-old)

(11.1) [and he . . . cl- climbed up]

C-VPT iconic: child leaves chair and moves to other chair (to climb up).

Figure 11.1. A C-VPT iconic gesture by the 2½-year-old illustrating enactment with a greatly expanded gesture space, with "[and he . . . cl-climbed up]." The child was on her way to climb up another chair just off camera. This is part of the gesture and offers a dramatic illustration of the expanded gesture space of young children which matches the actual space of action for the child.

We can infer that somewhere around the second birthday, when children start putting together simple sentences and undergo the famous vocabulary explosion, they begin to produce iconic gestures along with speech. Among iconic gestures, however, there are major changes. In little children the gestures are essentially *enactments,* as Werner & Kaplan (1963) pointed out. If the child is describing someone running, he might make a gesture with his feet as in (11.1). The iconic gestures of children are not diminished gestures, like those of confused speakers. On the contrary, they are very robust. This robustness, indeed, is part of what children must overcome in the development of iconics, for it is a continuation of the enactment of the protogesture period.

General Features of Early Iconics

In this section I present examples of children's iconic gestures organized to demonstrate that their gestures lack full separation from action. All of the gestures clearly are used to refer to objects or events that are present in memory, not in the physical environment. They are in no sense attempted manipulations of existing objects, but they have many qualities in common with physical actions performed on the external environment. No single gesture will display all of these features, but the features are common in samples of gestures collected from children of six years or so and younger.

GESTURE SPACE IS ACTUAL SPACE. Children's gestures are immature with respect to their use of space. While space represents something in the narrative, it remains the physical space in which the child is carrying out his actions. A partial symbolism results, a mixture of representation with real physical constraints, and this manifests itself in several qualities of children's gesture space: it is full-sized, it centers on the child and moves about with him, it has local orientation, and all parts of the body are equally privileged to move in it, and it may incorporate extra movements.

1. *Iconics are large.* The gesture space of children fills a larger volume and seems to lack any definite boundaries. We have seen an example of this already in (11.1), and the following is another (see fig. 11.2):

Figure 11.2. A 6-year-old's over-sized C-VPT iconic gesture with "[it's a whole bunch of boxes]." The child is moving his hands as if stuffing letters into adult-sized mailboxes. This is another demonstration of the expanded gesture space of young children. The scale approaches that of the actual action space.

(A 6-year-old)

(11.2) th- this mail- [it's a whole bunch of boxes]

Iconic and deictic: both hands overhead at arms' length and moving forward and backward as if stuffing letters.

This is the posture, movement, and amount of stretching a child his size would require for the real action of reaching up and placing letters into mailboxes.

Another illustration is from the two-and-a-half-year-old where she depicts punching on a grand scale (see fig. 11.3). The large size of children's gestures is clearly part of the gestures' being enactments: the gesture is the size of real reaching up to mailboxes, real climbing, real punching, etc.

2. *Iconics are centered on the child.* Like real actions, gestures revolve around the position that the child occupies; and this is true even of the O-VPT iconics. Adult gestures are located in the space in front of the speaker, and the space is a flattened disk in which the horizontal and vertical dimensions are exploited, but the dimension of depth is truncated

Figure 11.3. A giant-sized C-VPT gesture from the 2½-year-old when she said "and they [punch]." Again, the space of the gesture approximates the space of actual actions.

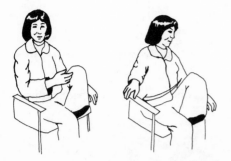

Figure 11.4. An adult's iconic gesture with "and [rolls down the] street." As is typical of adults the gesture space lies in front of the speaker and the gesture is a horizontal movement through this space. Compare with the 2½-year-old's gesture for this event in fig. 11.5.

and no action takes place behind the body's frontal plane. This is true even of adult C-VPT gestures (the action still takes place in front of the body). In contrast, the gesture space of young children is more nearly spherical and centered on the child's own position, and gestures may take place behind the body. The accompanying examples will illustrate the difference. The same scene from the cartoon was being narrated, and the adult performed a wide sweeping movement that remained within the disk and never crossed the frontal plane of the body (see fig. 11.4). The child, the two-and-a-half-year old, also performed a sweeping gesture, but her gesture ended up with the child turning completely around in her chair to indicate the room behind her (see fig. 11.5).

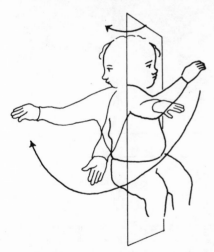

Figure 11.5. The 2½-year-old's gesture for the same scene as the adult's in fig. 11.4. The gesture extended to the room behind her, with "and it went away with that . . . [in there]," showing again that the space of gestures is not distinct from the actual space of the room. (See fig. 11.14 for another rendition of this gesture.)

(An adult)

(11.3) and he comes rolling out of the bottom of the rain barrel and [rolls down the] street

Iconic: arm swings to far right.

(The 2¹/₂-year-old)

(11.4) and it went away with that . . . [in there]

Deictic: turns around in the chair and points to the room behind her for Sylvester's final destination.

3. *Iconics have local orientation.* To adults the layout of space implies a

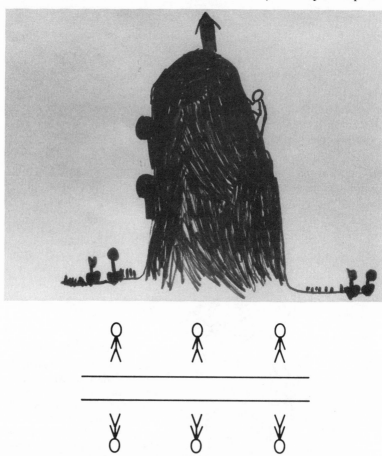

Figure 11.6. Local orientation. The mountain was drawn by the child whose gesture is illustrated in fig. 11.7. Local orientation implies that the artist does not make use of uniform coordinates for uprights and horizontals, such as the sides of the page. The people next to the road are upright with respect to their own side of the road but not to the other. The mountain is only partly structured by the page. The trees are glued to its side, showing that the child could not figure out how to attach them, although they are not sticking directly out from the side of the mountain either.

coordinate structure that is external to the actions that are performed in the space: the walls of the room, the sides of a page, and so forth. Adult gestures reflect such coordinates. Facing upward in gesture space is facing upward regardless of what the hands are doing. Children's gestures, in contrast, imply a reference grid that arises from the child's own movements. This is a further indication that their gestures lack full separation from their own actions. A similar lack of external coordinates appears in children's drawings (Arnheim, 1969). Children will draw a mountain or road on the page and orient the trees, houses, people, etc., by reference to the sides of the thing drawn. This leads to such drawings as those in figure 11.6. The mountain in this case was drawn by a child whose gesture space also showed local orientation. The following is how she depicted the movements of Sylvester pacing back and forth (see fig. 11.7):

Figure 11.7. Local orientation in a 7-year-old's gesture space with "this way . . . [an' this way]." This is the child whose mountain is shown in fig. 11.6. As she moves her hand to the back she rotates it, so that the character won't fall off.

(A 7-year-old)

(11.5) n' then he was walking around y'know . . . this way . . . [an' this way]

Iconic and deictic: hand moves from far front to far rear for the walking character, and rotates so that palm remains upright.

The orientation of the character was defined in relation to the child's own palm, as if the character were standing on it. As she showed Sylvester's pacing moments, she moved her hand to the rear and rotated it in an awkward way so that her palm remained upright (thus Sylvester wouldn't fall off). Adult speakers describing this pacing perform the gesture in a horizontal left to right direction, honoring the flat disk shape of their gesture space and having the upright defined in relation to the larger space of the room.

4. *Iconics use appropriate body parts.* Another action-like property is that gestures are executed with the same moving parts as real actions. For example, a child uses her entire body to show the cat leaving the drainpipe (see fig. 11.8):

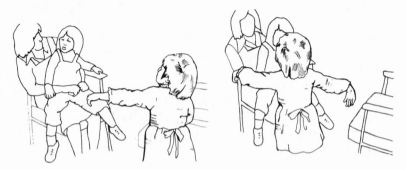

Figure 11.8. A dynamic whole-body C-VPT gesture by a 4-year-old with "[and he rolled out]." The panels show two stages of the gesture. Again, the implied space and movement approximate a real action.

(A 4-year-old)

(11.6) [and he rolled out]

Iconic: skips forward two steps, one arm extended to the front, the other to the back.

This is similar to example (11.1). The gesture in (11.6) is particularly revealing of the process of gesture formation since the motion was the child's *conception* of the event, not a direct imitation of the cartoon. In skipping, she matched the cat's high-speed trajectory, but her dancer's arm posture must have been her own invention. She was not merely reproducing what she had seen in the cartoon, therefore, since her actions had a life of their own in a way not modeled in the cartoon. She was enacting the cat, becoming it and acting for it. Another example is shown in figure 11.9. The child was describing Sylvester hiding in a mailbox and made her whole body into the gesture.

5. *Iconics incorporate extra movements.* In addition, a child might incorporate extra movements into gestures to simulate the look and feel of real actions. Even when a gesture is performed by the hands, it may contain extra movements that have this function. Adult speakers add details to gestures in order to convey contrasts with other gestures, but the extra movements that children add do not have any evident relationship to contrasts. In the two-and-a-half-year-old's gesture (fig. 11.14) for the cat

Figure 11.9. A stationary whole-body C-VPT gesture by a 5-year-old with "[Sylvester the cat was hiding in the mailbox]." The child represents Sylvester with her own body crouched as if inside the mailbox.

exiting the pipe, for example, the hands opened and closed repeatedly, and this reproduced the appearance of the character with the bowling ball inside him. In the example where the child was demonstrating the location of the mailboxes (fig. 11.2), there were repeated little jabs—stuffing the letters into mailboxes. Another child showed a character looking through binoculars. To convey that the character's eyes were, in the cartoon, tremendously magnified, he opened up his ring-hands in front of his eyes to show the magnification (see figure 11.10):

Figure 11.10. A 6-year-old's eidola gesture executed with an extra movement to create the appearance of magnification with "well [y'see] uh Sylvester Johnny, he was lookin'." The scene in the cartoon showed Sylvester's eyes magnified through binoculars.

(A 6-year-old)

(11.7) well [y'see]   uh Sylvester Johnny, he was lookin'
            · · ·

Iconic: both hands form rings in front of eyes and then open.

To sum up, the space of children's gestures shows the characteristics of the space of real actions. While the gestures are symbols, in that the hands depict things and actions other than themselves, they are not completely separated from the child's own actions. Gesture timing also shows characteristics of real actions.

GESTURE TIMING IS LIKE REAL ACTION. Adults iconics generally have clear-cut temporal boundaries. The gesture comes on at a definite moment, lasts, and then disappears, often abruptly. This timing marks the symbolic function: the gesture is active only while it is relevant, and disappears as soon as it is not relevant. With children, however, gestures are not organized so much as symbols as like actions, and this causes them often to blend together syncretically (Werner 1967). A lack of definite temporal boundaries has a number of effects. For example, it is unclear where one gesture ends and the next begins. Gestures emerge gradually, start to change, and evolve into new gestures; the transitions are difficult to locate. Lacking definite temporal boundaries, a gesture can line up with one word in speech, even though it is coexpressive with a full clause—a kind of gestural holophrasis. Again lacking a definite temporal locus, a gesture can recur several times during a coexpressive clause. In these respects, gestures are like real actions performed with speech.

1. *Iconics blend together.* An example that illustrates gesture symbols coming gradually into view and then fading away is the following from a six-year-old. The speaker was describing one character in the cartoon looking at another character through binoculars:

(A 6-year-old)

(11.8) [and he was looking out from his building]

Iconic: hand opens and closes twice for eyes opening, and at the same time the hand rises up.

(11.9) [on all the windows] on the other building across the street

Iconic and pointing: the hand still opening and closing now points to other building in front.

In (11.8) his right hand opened and closed twice while he described looking at something (probably for the eyes opening and closing). Simultaneously the preparation phase of the next gesture was taking place in the same hand (the hand rising up). Thus the idea of the other buildings across the street was beginning to emerge during the gesture for looking, much as it would, in fact, if the child were turning to point at something while still looking at it. The overlapping of ideas continued in (11.9) when he pointed to the next building, while the gesture from

(11.8), the opening and closing of the hands, continued. These gestures—the character looking and the building being looked at—are not unconnected semantically, and the .child's presentation smoothly combines them in time. An adult speaker describing the same layout, in˙ contrast, precisely shifts gestures between the successive meanings by briefly relaxing the hands after each one:

(An adult)

(11.10) [he's looking out]

Metaphoric: both hands show eidola beaming out.

(11.11) [over] across the uh

Beat, then rests.

(11.12) [w- what l- looks appears] to be a row between two (etc.)

Metaphoric: hand sweeps back and forth, then rests.

The child's depiction of looking in terms of opening the eyes (fig. 11.8) is itself the product of representing an event in terms of action. The adult subject, again in contrast, depicted the event deictically, by showing the line of regard. That is, the adult gesturally depicted the abstract geometry of the scene, whereas the child exhibited a concrete action that was potentially an occurrence in the scene.

The child's absence of clear-cut boundaries suggests a semantic process in which, rather than combinations of distinct meaning segments, there is something more like a continuous modulation of meaning through time. Yet this continuous modulation of meaning is combined with a grammatical construction of words ("and he was looking out from his building on all the windows on the other building across the street," etc.). Another manifestation of a different method of combining meaning with verbal structure is the following.

2. *Iconics are holophrastic.* Since gestures lack distinct temporal boundaries, they can line up with a single word, even though the gesture is coexpressive with the whole clause and would be expected to cover this clause. Thus, children can seemingly violate the semantic synchrony rule. Here is an example in which a six-year-old described dialing a phone (see fig. 11.11):

(A 6-year-old)

(11.13) [Granny] . . . called up this man

Iconic and deictic: pointing hand goes around in circles at ear.

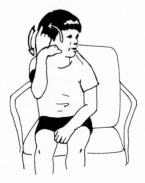

Figure 11.11. A 6-year-old performing a holophrastic gesture
with "[Granny] . . . called up this
man." The dialing motion at the ear
refers, not to Granny, but to the
whole event of Granny calling up
the man. The gesture implies, in its
timing, that the word "Granny"
holophrastically encoded this total
event.

While the gesture refers to the same action as "Granny called up," it
was synchronous with just "Granny." Such a word, accompanied by a
gesture that depicts more than the word conventionally does, can be
called holophrastic. To judge from the synchronous gesture, "Granny"
referred to both a part and the whole—the performer of the action as
well as the total event. The word "Granny" was thus not associated with
just the analytic component.

What is striking about this example is that we seem to have a holophrastic word *within* a grammatical context (see McNeill 1985a, for other examples). It thus reveals an undeveloped gesture masked behind a well-formed
surface utterance. If this word with a complete propositional meaning had
occurred during the single-word period of development, in the speech of a
much younger child, it would be described as holophrastic. But in this case
the word was part of a grammatical sentence. The sentence unpacked the
image, but then the image also remained attached to one of the words as if,
for the child, the growth point had not been exhaustively reformatted by
the sentence. The concept that children are building a language-*gesture*
system applies here, then, to reveal a dimension of language acquisition
still undeveloped, even though the surface linguistic structure is complete
and meets standards of good form.

One implication of such holophrastic gestures is that when children,
appropriately and seemingly successfully, segment and organize surface
sentences, this fact does not necessarily imply a parallel dynamics of
thought. Many developmental psycholinguists believe that language
rests upon a cognitive base. Lois Bloom (1973) wrote, for example, that
"children learn syntax as a mapping or coding of their underlying cognitive representations" (20). If a child says "drink milk," or some other such
transitive verb-and-direct object expression, this suggests that the child is
capable of subdividing its thought into two components: an action

(drinking) and an object of this action (milk). Bloom's argument was to deny that children can learn syntax without such parallels of meaning differentiation, but the phenomenon of holophrastic words within grammatical structures implies an ability by children to build up sentence structures without parallels in the underlying meaning structures. In other words, there may be a phase of linguistic development whereby syntactic structures emerge at least in part autonomously. Superficially complete utterances may mask undifferentiated and primitive growth points. This points to an unsuspected further dimension of children's language development in which the relationship of growth points to the linguistic code is changing. Developing an adult type growth point may continue for a number of years.

3. *Iconics recur.* The same gesture can recur during a stretch of speech with which it is coexpressive without change of meaning. This is not the repetition of gestures with amplification to add contrast or with diminution because the speaker has lost the thread; it is a second or even third presentation of the same gesture meaning. The child thus attaches the same meaning to different words, one after another, and does not treat each word as a separable component of the meaning. Here is an example from a six-year-old who made three successive upward movements performed by different parts of the body (see fig. 11.12):

Figure 11.12. A 6-year-old's triple iconic with "[he climbed] [up] it [from the outside]." First a finger rose, then an elbow, and finally a foot: each conveying holophrastically the event of climbing up.

(A 6-year-old)

(11.14) [he climbed]
Iconic: hand rises up.

(11.15) [up] it
Iconic: elbow rises up.

(11.16) [from the outside]
Iconic: foot rises up.

As in the holophrastic example, single words continued to be associated with the same image that was also unpacked by the sentence and the segmentation of the image was not complete. This example also illustrates in a charming way children's readiness to use body parts to perform gestures—the elbow and foot—that adults do not usually employ.

To summarize the timing of children's iconics: their gestures (1) fade in and out, and overlap; (2) focus on single words, rather than covering coexpressive phrases or clauses; and (3) occur in multiple bunches without changing meaning. These are qualities of gesture that could arise from an incomplete separation of gestures from real actions.

Reverse Chronological Sequence

The above listing of the features of children's iconics does not give a clear picture of how gestures develop over time. Changes through time can be conveyed better by comparing speakers of different ages who are describing the same scene from the cartoon. In general, as we move to younger and younger ages, the gestures become increasingly actionlike. I will present the examples in the reverse chronological order, starting with an adult and ending with the two-and-a-half-year-old child. The scene is when Sylvester rolls out of the drainpipe with the bowling ball inside him.

(An adult)

(11.17) and he [comes out]

Iconic: both hands form the pipe and move in shallow arc down and right.

(11.18) [n' you see him rolling down] a street

Iconic: points to front and rotates (4X).

The adult speaker highlights just what seems relevant in the situation: in (11.17) the hollowness of the pipe and the cat's trajectory; in (11.18) the bizarre movement of the bowling ball inside the cat.

(An 8-year-old)

(11.19) an' [it went like this]

Iconic: lifts up both legs and extends them to front and side, while both hands form round space between legs for the bowling ball.

(11.20) a- an' then um he- he came [down]

Iconic: hand moves down.

(11.21) 'n' then he went [rolling down] the (unintelligible)

Iconic: lifts up legs again.

The child involves his entire body in (11.19) to demonstrate how the bowling ball ended up inside the cat. In (11.20) he performs an adultlike downward iconic (O-VPT) for the cat's trajectory, but in (11.21) reverts to use of the whole body again for the rolling. Thus the child had a mixture of mature and immature features.

(A 5-year-old)

(11.22) an' then he [rolled down]

Iconic: hand flips (2X) and moves to right, ending in a point to the front.

(11.23) w' a [barrel on 'im on] his bottom

Iconic and deictic: hand grasps own bottom.

(11.24) there's a big [bump] on his bottom

Iconic and deictic: touches own bottom again.

This child demonstrates the rolling ball in (11.22) with an O-VPT gesture not unlike an adult's, but in (11.23) and (11.24) invokes his own anatomy to demonstrate the appearance and locus of the ball inside the cat (see fig. 11.13). He thus relies on corresponding moving parts to depict the ball and its appearance.

(The 2¹/₂-year-old)

(11.25) an' it went [d-o-w-n]

Iconic: hand plunges from above head to below chair.

Figure 11.13. A 5-year-old's iconic gesture with "w' a [barrel on 'im on] his bottom there's a big [bump] on his bottom." The locus of the ball and its appearance inside Sylvester are shown with the child's own corresponding body parts.

(11.26) and uh . . . [he went away with that]

Iconic: hand sweeps from above head to far right, and opens and closes several times to show the rolling bowling ball.

(11.27) [in there]

Deictic: turns around in the chair and points to the room behind her for Sylvester's final destination.

In all three gestures by this child the space is enormous in absolute terms; in (11.25) there is an O-VPT with a scale considerably larger than the child's own body size; in (11.26) there is an O-VPT for the cat rolling with the bowling ball inside, again on a huge scale; and in (11.27) she turns around and encompasses the whole room. Also, the manner of depicting the rolling ball in (11.26) is unusual since she does this by opening and closing her hand several times (see fig. 11.14). Her gesture depicts the visual appearance of the cat with the ball inside him, and also something of the kinesthetic sensation. Finally, in (11.27), the gesture space is not distinguished from the surrounding physical space, as the child turns around completely in her chair to point to the destination of the cat (the room next door, where the experimenter was).

The changes between early childhood and adulthood have to do with the declining role of enactment and, simultaneously, the increasing symbolic structuring of gestures. A special problem is the phenomenon of viewpoint: young children, no less than adults, have both observer and character viewpoints; but the children's observers are considerably different from the adults'.

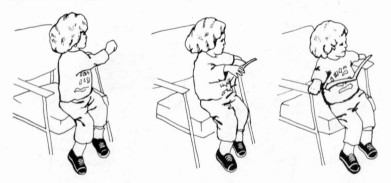

Figure 11.14. The 2½-year-old's version of the bowling ball scene with "and uh [he went away with that]." Compare this to the adult's version in fig. 11.4 which consists of a smooth sweep to the right. The child's hands open and close as she sweeps her arm. These hand movements possibly create what the child takes to be the experience of Sylvester's rotating movement. Such extra details often appear in the gestures of very young children.

Viewpoint

CHARACTER AND OBSERVER. Both C-VPT and O-VPT iconics occur from early ages although the C-VPT is far more frequent. The sub-two-year-olds reported in table 11.2 from Acredolo and Goodwin (to appear) produced gestures from both viewpoints, as already noted. Also, the O-VPT appeared with the two-and-a-half-year-old when she turned around to point at the room behind her. But these early O-VPT gestures are often of the inside observer type, where the child enters into the narrative space. The two-and-a-half-year-old's gesture incorporated the observer inside the scene who acted as if she could locate the cartoon events in the room behind her. Another illustration is the following by a four-year-old. The cat (called a wolf) is shown going up the pipe; the pipe is located directly over the child's own head, putting the child inside the scene:

(11.28) [a wolf went up the pipe]
Iconic: right hand points straight overhead.

The target of the gesture was straight up, and included the same space that the child himself was occupying (see fig. 11.15).

Even when young children have an O-VPT and the child himself is outside the gesture space, the gesture incorporates elements of an enactment. There may be extra movements that simulate the feel of the action from the character's point of view. There thus is an element of C-VPT incorporated into the hand movement. Again the two-and-a-half-year-old's example showed this when she opened and closed her hand repeat-

Figure 11.15. An inside observer iconic gesture with "[a wolf went up the pipe]." The child is 4 years old. He points directly overhead, placing himself in the scene as an observer. Such gestures are rare with adults but common with children and again reveal a space that approximates the space of actual actions.

edly while it swept across the gesture space. This outside observer gesture with enactment was immediately followed by the inside observer gesture where the character was shown rolling into the next room. The child's entrance into the gesture space was thus continuous.

Other examples similarly suggest that children adopt viewpoints in parallel contexts to adults, but while so doing incorporate aspects of enactment that adults do not have. Direct quotations, for example, may be accompanied by chimerical dual C-VPT gestures, as with adults (see fig. 4.18), in which one C-VPT is for the speaker and the other C-VPT is for the addressee. However, while adults confine the dual C-VPT to situations where the gesture is pointing and the relationship represented in the gesture is specifically that of a speaker directing an utterance to an addressee, children have dual C-VPTs where the relationships are not confined to an abstract diagram of interpersonal communication but involve physical actions of one character on the other; this physical action is what the gesture enacts. At the same time, speech also may contain an enactment (verbal pantomime). The following is an example from an eight-year-old (see fig. 11.16):

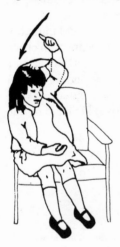

Figure 11.16. An 8-year-old's chimerical gesture taking the viewpoint of two characters simultaneously. This accompanied "and she goes '[aah!] I got you'," and is a gestural quotation that accompanies a direct verbal quotation. The child is enacting Granny both in speech and movement, but the extended index finger adds narrative distance to the gesture. Compare with fig. 4.18, which is an adult chimerical C-VPT.

(11.29) and she goes "[aah!] I got you!"
         . . . .

Iconic: left arm with index finger extended (= umbrella) moves down and finger strikes own head.

The gesture incorporates both characters: the arm movement the agent, her head the recipient. The linguistic references are only to the agent (this is clear from the feminine pronoun and the vocal pantomime). The child's speech is a direct quotation and thus agrees with the arm use in the gesture. Her head then represents a totally separate character.

VOICES. The distinction between O-VPT and C-VPT is blurred because the gestures of young children combine enactment with the O-VPT and use dual C-VPTs in an enactment mode. Nonetheless, two voices exist even before age two. Perspective and role playing seem to be fundamental. Moreover, by age four at least, children differentiate by means of gestures between the central and peripheral story events in the cartoon narration, using C-VPT with the former and O-VPT with the latter. They do not do this as sharply as older children or adults, but the capability to draw this distinction is clearly present (see fig. 11.17, taken from Church et al. 1989).

Late Development of Gestures: Beats, Metaphorics, and Abstract Pointing

The occurrence of two gestural viewpoints does not necessarily mean that little children differentiate two lines of cohesiveness, one the story line itself and the other a line of comments by the observer. Rather, children may not differentiate these event lines but move about without exploiting the distance of the observer and character voices. The child's ready inclusion of himself with the observer voice in the observed gesture space is another indication that the voices, while available, are not functionally distinct; there is just a variety of things the child does without much meaning (or at least, without much adult meaning) being attached to them. If the child's deployment of voices is not consistent with functional distinctions, that would fit in with other gesture evidence, for children also don't systematically differentiate narrative levels. It is not that the child is confined to the narrative level but that the child drifts between what, for an adult, would be the narrative, metanarrative, and paranarrative levels, without ever signaling the fact that there are these shifts of level; children in fact do not have definite levels. Not surprisingly, therefore, the gestures that convey discourse content are all late to emerge. The arrival of these gestures constitute the final stage of speech-gesture development, and this extends over a five- to seven-year span. The last gestures to be used by children are those that refer specifically to discourse: beats, metaphorics, and abstract pointing. The lateness of abstract pointing is particularly striking given that concrete pointing is the first of all gestures to emerge; abstract pointing is, however, one of the

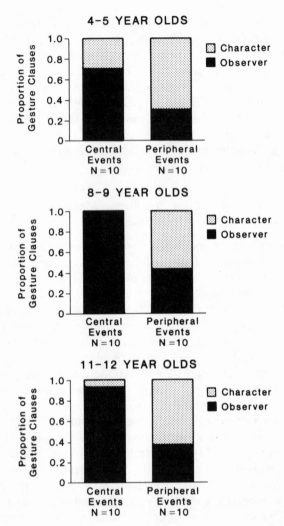

Figure 11.17. Gesture voice and story centrality at three ages (from Church et al. 1989).

last. The gradual development of gestures on meta-levels implies that children's ability to think on multiple levels is expanding at the same time.

All of these discourse gestures, though simple and utilizing movements of a kind children have been able to perform for years, require the ability to understand relationships between entities and different levels of structure. A beat, even though it is just a flick of the hand, is cognitively complex. To refer to a metanarrative relationship demands comparing the given word to its context. Abstract pointing likewise: to point abstractly demands the ability to compare the current frame of reference to a new one that the child is introducing. A metaphoric gesture similarly depends on the ability to view the story as an object, which is a way of standing outside the story, adding distance. Cohesive repetitions of gestures or space demand the ability to compare the current reference to the previous one. All of these uses of gesture imply that meta-level abilities emerge late (Flavell, 1976). In contrast, on the narrative level the child needs only to think about one thing, the object or act the gesture is depicting.

Linguistic references to pragmatic meanings also are emerging at this same time and this emergence is equally slow. The cohesive use of pronouns, for example, is lacking until school age according to Annette Karmiloff-Smith (1979a). Gestures and language develop parallel to each other with the late emergence of pragmatic thinking.

Emergence of Beats and Abstract Pointing

As noted earlier, the semiotic value of the beat derives from the fact that emphasis on a word in its normal context induces us to seek a different, extra-normal context for it. Young children do not have beats because they lack the additional levels of *structure* in terms of which such new contexts can be sought. To a child, the story is the complete world at the moment, and to step out of it is to leave the story altogether; there is no possibility of stepping out to better frame what is going on in the story world.

Two lines in the development of beats have to be followed. The first involves gestures with the correct biphasic form. These first appear at about age five, and mark, at this stage, discontinuities that are *metalinguistic*, rather than *metanarrative*. The beat, that is, signals a comment on the use of language itself, not a reference to the pragmatic structure. Beats in this biphasic form start at age five but are not abundant until age eleven by which time they function as metanarrative signals. An example from a five-year-old on the metalinguistic level is the following which accompanied the child's insistence on the proper definition of a word (see fig. 11.18). This is one of the earliest beats that we have observed:

Figure 11.18. A 5-year-old's meta-linguistic beat with "execute [/ it's something else]." This is one of the earliest true beats we have seen (i.e., it has two movement phases, peripheral space, minimal effort, and a meta-level function).

A 5-year-old:

(11.30) execute [. . . it's something else] . . . it's when you're killed

Beats (3X).

The other line of development takes into account what can be termed "protobeats" (Cassell 1989a, 1991). These are beat-like in the sense that they lack any semantic references, but have a variety of forms, not the canonical biphasic form of an adult beat. For example, the child might tap on the armrest of the chair, or touch the interlocutor, or wiggle his hands.

MARKING METANARRATIVE STATEMENTS. Cassell (1989a; 1991) investigated the development of protobeats, canonical beats, and abstract deixis, and found a striking upright U-shaped relationship: protobeats decline after age five while canonical beats increase from age eight (see fig. 11.19). Abstract deixis increases from age eight as well.

What kinds of linguistic contexts do the protobeats at five years accompany? Since there are few metanarrative statements, there must be something besides metanarrative content to trigger protobeats. Cassell looked at the production of temporal adverbs and conjunctions—words and phrases that specify temporal reference points, like "one Sunday morning," or indicate temporal relationships, such as "while Sylvester was coming up" or "and then Granny hit him." Such terms introduce discontinuities on one level into narratives but do not necessarily evoke new episodes. For example, "while Sylvester was coming up" interrupts the narrative flow to specify a relationship between two events, but does not refer to a new episode. Cassell knew from earlier research (Cassell,

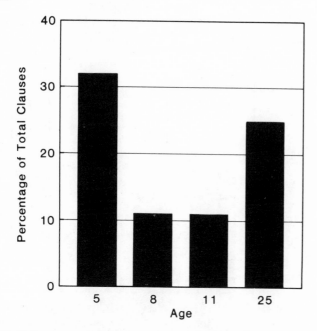

Figure 11.19. Frequency of beat and protobeat movements at 4 ages (from Cassell 1989a).

1984) that these kinds of temporal terms are extremely common in five-year-olds' speech. Figure 11.20 shows the upright U-shaped curve broken down into two curves, a declining curve of protobeats associated with the child's use of temporal terms and a rising curve of canonical beats associated with metanarrative statements. Abstract deixis rises at the same rate as the canonical beat curve and also seems to reflect meta-narrative references. There is a period, around eight years, where neither protobeats nor true beats take place, and this would be a period where the child makes little use on any level of devices for signaling discon-tinuities: "The temporary behavioral regression in the production of beats is indicative of progression at the underlying representational level, where children are re-evaluating the nature of the procedure being ac-quired, and constraining local production for reasons of more global concerns. That is, as children begin to represent the story as a whole more important than the sum of its parts, they must re-evaluate where beats are to occur" (Cassell 1989b, 10).

BEATS AND REPAIRS. Besides their use for signaling metanarrative state-ments, beats also mark the breakdown-repair cycle. In adult speech beats

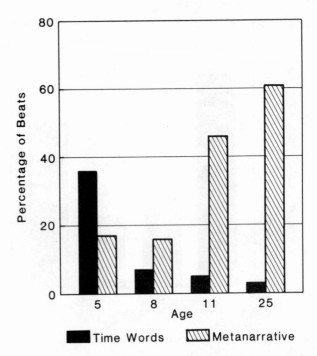

Figure 11.20. Percentage of beat and protobeat movements with time words and meta-narrative clauses at four ages. The gestures with time words were mainly protobeats, while those with metanarrative references were mostly true beats (from Cassell 1989a).

accompany the *repair*—the second element. An example given in chapter 6 was the repair of "bird" by "canary" (example (6.32), repeated here):

(An adult)

(11.31) <u>and the bird . . . the ca[NAR]y . . . throws a bowling ball</u>
                                    Beat.

The beat signaled that the repairing word "canary" was the discontinuity. Adults typically produce beats at these points where the repair is made, but with children it is exactly the opposite: they produce beats that mark the source of trouble, not the repair.

For example, here is an eight-year-old producing a beat along with a false start:

(An 8-year-old)

(11.32) <u>um the eh he [p∗] the pussy cat go- um looks at the bird</u>
                    Beat.

The discontinuity highlighted by the beat exists *within* the speech flow, the beat marks a breakdown flow of speech itself, not a discontinuity on the metanarrative level in the relationship of speech to context. Again, we see that children's lack of meta-level perspective affects their gestures.

Emergence of Metaphorics

Conduits appear in small numbers at early ages. The following gesture looks like a conduit; if in fact it is a conduit, it is the youngest such gesture that we have recorded (see fig. 11.21):

Figure 11.21. Possible conduit gesture from a 3½-year old with "[the mother one ahm took!]." The gesture appears to depict an event as an object, but the remark is not metanarrative. Alternatively, the gesture could be an "all gone" emblem.

(A 3½-year-old)

(11.33) [the mother one ahm took!]

Potential metaphoric: both hands spread apart, palms up, fingers spread, presenting story to listener, on whose lap she is sitting. She also turns to look at her listener's face while she makes this gesture.

The verbal expression however is not recognizably metanarrative, and we might be better off to classify the gesture as an emblem (meaning "all gone"). The next example is a more convincing illustration of a conduit from a child a little older. Speech also contains a hint of the metanarrative in a remark of the summing-up type:

(A 5-year-old)

(11.34) [n' he didn't work]

Metaphoric: both hands present object.

Another metaphoric usage at five years is the "eidola" gesture. This appeared earlier in an example (11.7) to illustrate the addition of extra movements. The following is another illustration from a different five-and-a-half-year-old:

(A 5¹/₂-year-old)

(11.35) the pussy cat first he was lookin' [through] these things

Metaphoric and iconic: right hand in ring moves up and away from eye to full arm extension.

The child possibly didn't know the word "binoculars," but the gesture accompanied "through," rather than the substitute "these things" for binoculars. It thus seems to have depicted the act of looking through, rather than the binoculars as such, with a beam in the shape of a binocular lens that was sent out from the eye.

More abstract gestures are absent from these four- and five-year-olds. A use of space to differentiate options emerges only much later. I have seen no examples of this type of metaphor from children younger than eleven. The following is from an eleven-year-old:

(An 11-year-old)

(11.36) and [Sylvester somehow gets up on the ledge]

Pointing to center space for the location of the ledge.

(11.37) an' then uh Tweety doesn't [know]

Pointing: thumb points behind right shoulder.

The gesture in (11.36) is an example of abstract deixis, pointing to the locus of an event in symbolic space. The one in (11.37), pointing in the opposite direction, signals the opposition between Sylvester's actuality on the ledge and Tweety's ignorance of this. This use of space for abstract contrasts is adultlike, although the orientation of the space, in the third dimension, is still as with younger children. The implication is that the development of the use of gesture space for abstract meanings continues into adolescence; however, we have no observations of older children.

Gestural Motherese

When adults talk to little children, they often modify their speech quite extensively from the kind of speech they address to other adults. Grammatical structures are simplified, vocabulary is limited, intonation is exaggerated, voice pitch goes up, and other changes occur that are collectively termed, "Motherese" (Newport 1977). Motherese might perform a useful job of making clear to the child the structure of language, and thus help the child's language learning, although the effectiveness of Motherese for this is in some doubt (Gleitman, Newport, and Gleitman 1984). Still, there is no doubt of the reality of the special register of adult talk to children. Trevarthen (to appear) has observed Motherese in the speech of adults to tiny newborns, and in a variety of different cultures.

There is also a Motherese of gestures. Just as Motherese speech is characterized by simplicity, exaggeration, and hoped-for clarity, so in the gesture mode there is emphasis on concrete deixis, display, and demonstration; the standard iconic, metaphoric, and beat gestures of adults practically disappear. Gestures in talk to babies are thus radically different from gestures by the same mothers addressing an adult, even an adult in the same room, at the same time, and talking about the same things in general (Bekken 1989).

Bekken set up an experiment that involved the videotaping of three people: a mother, her child of two, and an adult assistant, who was present as an on-screen collaborator and interlocutor. To this adult interlocutor mothers used the full range of typical gestures in conversations. In decreasing order of frequency, to the adult the mothers addressed metaphorics, deictics (abstract and concrete), iconics, and beats. To their children, however, by far the most frequent type of gesture was concrete pointing, followed by manipulative forms of deixis (holding objects up or holding them out, and demonstrations of objects). All the even slightly abstract gestures, including iconics and especially metaphorics and beats, virtually disappeared from the repertoire. Mothers who

Table 11.3 Percentage of Mother's Gestures in Different Categories (from Bekken 1989)

				Mother to Adult Gesture Type				
N	Hold	Demon-stration	Concrete Deictic	Abstract Deictic	Iconic	Meta-phoric	Beat	Emblem
378	<1	0	32	9	18	28	10	2

				Mother to Child Gesture Type				
N	Hold	Demon-stration	Concrete Deictic	Abstract Deictic	Iconic	Meta-phoric	Beat	Emblem
324	17	6	61	0	9	1	1	6

showed the largest Motherese changes in speech were the same whose gestures changed the most. Thus, equivalent shifts seemed to be taking place in speech and gesture. In both cases the attempt appeared to be to make the referential situation clear.

Mothers talking to their children also increased their use of emblems—the socially constituted speech substitutes ("Italianate" gestures, see chap. 2). Emblems by the mother hardly occur at all to the adult, but are used by her to the child (ten times more frequently than beats)—a paradoxical fact, since the emblem is precisely a gesture that has to be learned.

The accompanying table (table 11.3) shows the proportion of total gestures made by the mother to the child and to the adult, classified into various types (based on Bekken 1989, table 21). Six mother-child-adult trios are represented. We see from this table that mothers' gestures to children match fairly closely the gestures that we know in general children themselves produce at two: pointing, holding up, but almost no iconics, metaphorics, or beats. It is easy to see, finally, how deictic gestures would become selected by children in the interactions with their mothers, since the mothers offer abundant examples of deixis but few gestures of other kinds.

There are several routes over which the question of cerebral control of spontaneous gestures can be approached and all lead to the same conclusion, which I will present at the end of the chapter as a hypothesis regarding how the brain controls and interrelates gestures and speech. First, there is gesture handedness: are all gestures lateralized in the same way? Second, there is gesture in aphasia: what do we see when language is disturbed—words not available, content gone, structure ruined? Finally, what are the gestures and speech like of split-brain patients? (The material in this chapter is an expanded version of a paper written jointly with Elena T. Levy and Laura L. Pedelty: McNeill, Levy, and Pedelty, 1990.)

As is well known, the human brain is separated into two cerebral hemispheres with distinct functions. The left side controls the movements on the right side of the body, the right side those on the left. In terms of psychological function, the left side (for right-handed people) is usually the locus of the speech centers—the parts of the brain specifically engaged in speech articulation and perception; the right side houses the more global spatial and visual kinds of operations. These hemispheres are the last parts of the brain to develop in babies but some hemispheric asymmetries exist as early as four months before birth (Trevarthen 1987a).

Given the differences between the two hemispheres, disease and injury of the brain are likely to have quite different effects depending on the hemisphere that is injured and where in the hemisphere the specific lesion occurs. Aphasia (difficulty or inability in communicating by speech or writing) can be the result of lesions in the speech areas of the left hemisphere (of typical right-handers). It thus reveals aspects of language that depend on these brain regions. Symptoms include agrammatism (difficulty in constructing grammatical sentences), severe word-finding problems, neologisms (substituting nonwords), paraphasias (substituting inappropriate words), and losses of semantic content (without concomitant loss of grammatical output). In the case of all these disorders of speech, we can ask what the gestures are like. Furthermore, we can attempt to use gestures and speech to infer the growth points of utterances, which may show some abnormalities of their own. Besides specific linguistic disturbances, about two-thirds of aphasic patients also suffer apraxia: a blockage of symbolic actions in which they are unable to pretend to carry out actions such as breaking an egg or hammering a nail, even

329

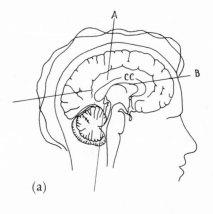

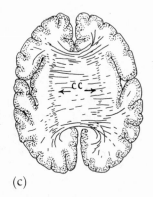

(a)   (c)

Figure 12.1. Three cutaway views
of the brain. Panel (a) is a side view;
(b) the section along line A viewed
from the front; and (c) the section
along line B viewed from the top.
The corpus callosum is CC (from
Trevarthen 1987b).

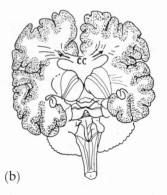

(b)

though they can do both of these things with real objects. Again, we can
ask what the gestures of such patients are like.

The two sides of the brain are normally in constant communication
through the corpus callosum, a thick band of fibers running between the
two half-brains. Without the corpus callosum, the hemispheres are otherwise quite separate, the only connections being through noncortical
lower brain centers (see fig. 12.1). Surgical interruption of the corpus
callosum—a procedure termed commissurotomy—has been carried out
for treatment of certain forms of epilepsy, and this procedure effectively
isolates each hemisphere from the other (producing a so-called split
brain). In these cases it is possible to stimulate and test each half-brain
separately. Since the gestures of normal speakers suggest that not only
words and sentences are involved in the process of speaking but also
closely linked images, the question of what sorts of gestures split-brain
speakers perform becomes extremely interesting. It would seem impos-

sible that their gestures could be integrated with speech in a way that is normal.

Gesture Handedness

While gestures may be performed by either hand, or both together, most speakers tend to use one hand rather than the other during extended stretches of speech. Gestures are manual actions, and thus might be lateralized to the dominant hand like other manual actions. But they also are part of the symbolic process, and thus might be lateralized depending on functional factors, such as the role of the gesture in the discourse. Thus observing gesture hand preferences can provide insights into the cerebral control of gesture and the neurological underpinnings of gestures in relation to speech and discourse.

Studies of gesture performance generally show gestures being made with the dominant hand but find no such lateralization for nongesture movements, like smoothing the hair or fiddling with objects (Sousa-Poza, Rohrberb, and Mercure 1979; Kimura 1973a, 1973b). The dominant hand for most complex motor movements is controlled by the language-dominant hemisphere in right-handed people, although left-handers show more complicated relationships (Rasmussen and Milner, 1976; Milner, Branch, and Rasmussen 1964). Kimura tested speech laterality in her subjects by means of dichotic listening experiments, and found that the right-handed gesture preference went along with left-hemisphere speech (in a dichotic experiment, the subject hears different speech sounds simultaneously in the two ears: if the sound in the right ear is reported more accurately, the inference is that the left hemisphere is the dominant half of the brain for the perception; see Shankweiler and Studdert-Kennedy 1967 for a description of the technique and its interpretation). The few right-handed speakers who preferred their left hands for gestures were also more likely to have a left-ear advantage (implying a right-hemisphere involvement in speech). Left-handers whose dichotic results implied a right-hemisphere involvement in speech tended to make gestures with their left hands, while left-handers with an inferred left-hemisphere speech process showed no lateralization tendency for gestures at all.

Thus the half of the brain that is dominant for language also appears to be the significant locus for the production of the gestures that accompany speech. Kimura (1976) and Kimura and Archibald (1974) proposed a hypothesis that elegantly accounts for the speech-gesture correlations. They said that the specific quality of the language-dominant hemisphere that is responsible for this lateralization is the programming of complex movement sequences. Complex movements—either oral or manual—would engage the left hemisphere of right-handed people (the right hemisphere of left-handed people), and this is the case even when the speaker may have learned to write with the other hand (thus being classified as dominant in the other hand).

Kimura did not classify gestures into types. This was done by another investigator, Stephens (1983), who found that right-handers during narrations of a full-length Hitchcock film used their right hands (and left-handers their left hands) to make *iconics,* but not to make *beats.* With beats there were no hand preferences: either the right or the left hand was used or both hands performed the beat simultaneously. Beats, of course, being motorically simple, could be simple enough for the nonspeech hemisphere to program.

A further observation, however, shows that other factors also must be considered. Stephens discovered that *metaphorics* are also performed with the dominant hand. The metaphorics in her study were generally conduits and spatial metaphorics and such gestures tend to be performed with simple movements and not be more complex motorically than beats (e.g., a simple hand rotation for a conduit, or a hand flicking out in an arc and returning for a spatial metaphor of the timeline). If simplicity of the movement alone were responsible for the nonlateralization of a gesture, the pattern with these metaphorics should have been like beats; but in fact the pattern was like iconics: the metaphorics went to the dominant hand. It thus appears that more than motoric complexity engages the speech-dominant hemisphere in the production of gestures, and that the specific symbolic character of the movement also must be taken into account.

Gestures in Aphasia

The importance of the symbolic character of movements is borne out by studies with brain-damaged patients. Pedelty (1987) is my source of information for this section. A review of the effects of unilateral brain damage on gesture performance has been presented by Feyereisen (1986). Pedelty's study, however, is particularly relevant to my discussion since she observed nine aphasic patients narrating the standard cartoon stimulus that has been the source of observations throughout this book and classified the gestures in terms of the iconic, metaphoric, beat, and deictic gesture categories that have figured in earlier sections. The chief conclusion that I will draw from her work is that the posterior or

Wernicke type of aphasic ("fluent" aphasics) are deficient because they add linguistic differentiation without corresponding imagery; the anterior or Broca type of aphasic ("nonfluent" aphasics) are deficient because they create imagery but fail to add linguistic differentiation. The two kinds of aphasic patient present opposite patterns of imbalance during the interaction of imagery and language. From the point of view of self-organization, the damage to their brain has interrupted the synthesis of image and language, in the Wernicke's case at an early phase of the self-organizational cycle, and in the Broca's case at a late phase.

An issue that has arisen in discussions elsewhere on the topic of aphasia is whether aphasia impairs gesture and speech in parallel. Feyereisen (1986), in his review, concludes that "in none of these studies was there a noticeable impairment of the gestural production in the aphasic groups and no clear differences between the kinds of aphasia were observed. Taken together, these results do not argue for a common cerebral basis underlying speech and gestures; the hypothesis of a nonverbal impairment parallel to the verbal deficit is not confirmed" (87). However, Feyereisen lumped together all types of gesture. When the types are distinguished, as in Pedelty's study, a parallel interference of speech and gestures does appear, and the different kinds of aphasics do not gesture in the same way.

POSTERIOR AND ANTERIOR PATIENTS. Classically, discussions of aphasia have concentrated on two types. Damage to the anterior portions of the language-dominant hemisphere results in a form of language disruption first described by Paul Broca (1861), which is often accordingly called Broca's aphasia (see fig. 12.2). A patient with this kind of aphasia

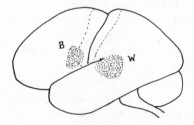

Figure 12.2. View of the left hemisphere, showing Broca's (anterior) and Wernicke's (posterior) areas (from Penrose 1989).

has relatively good comprehension of events and has what neurologists call "drive to communicate," but is able to speak only haltingly, dysfluently, and with great difficulty. Such speech is agrammatic and often termed "telegraphic"—to convey the picture of speech with minimal grammatical structuration. Utterances by Broca's aphasics largely lack grammatical functors (articles, prepositions, and other structural words) and rely heavily on content-bearing ("open-class") words. Howard Gardner, in his book *The Shattered Mind*, quotes this example of Broca's aphasic speech: "I'm a sig . . . no . . . man . . . uh well . . . again," where each word was uttered slowly and with painful effort. Later in the conversation he was asked what he has been doing in the hospital, and he replies: "Yes, sure. Me go, er, uh P.T. nine o'cot, speech . . . two times . . . read . . . wr . . . ripe, er, rike, er, write . . . practice . . . getting better" (Gardner 1974, 60–61).

The converse picture appears in patients with more posterior damage, a syndrome first described by Karl Wernicke (1874), and called Wernicke's aphasia (see fig. 12.2). Speech in these cases is fluent or even hyperfluent and makes use of a rich variety of syntactic patterns, but is prone to neologism and paraphasia—using nonwords or words of approximately the right sound but the wrong meaning—and is notoriously lacking in coherence and content, as in this example (quoted in Gardner 1974, 68): "Boy, I'm sweating, I'm awful nervous, you know, once in while I get caught up, I can't mention the tarripoi, a month ago, quite a little, I've done a lot well, I impose a lot, while, on the other hand, you know what I mean, I have to run around, look it over, trebbin and all that sort of stuff." The neologisms ("tarripoi" and "trebbin") and the paraphasia ("impose" for "improve") are only the more easily pointed out aphasic characteristics; the rambling and empty style are even more impressive in this example.

The two kinds of aphasic thus have complementary patterns of skills retained and lost. Where the anterior patient is hesitant, agrammatic, and struggles to produce almost every word, the posterior patient is fluent, grammatical, and speaks all too freely—like an amateur double-talk artist, as Gardner says. But while this posterior speaker is rattling on there is no coherence or meaning, and here the hesitant anterior aphasic, despite his lack of fluency, retains what the posterior has lost, for the anterior clearly is attempting to communicate meaning and we can share it.

Pedelty's anterior and posterior patients presented similar speech patterns to those illustrated in Gardner's examples. Despite severe disruptions of speech, both types of patient made gestures. However, their gestures were not the same; gestures did not survive aphasia intact. Described globally, the deficits of gesture and of speech are parallel. This is apparent when the type of gesture and the locus of the gesture on Kendon's continuum are taken into account (see chap. 2). Broca's aphasics tend to perform meaningful interpretable gestures, while Wernicke's aphasics have gestures that are (like their speech) vague, meaningless, and uninterpretable (Cicone et al. 1979; Goldblum 1978; Feyereisen, 1983). The gestures of the Broca's aphasics are brief and isolated, while those of Wernicke's aphasics occur in fluent streams (Cicone et al. 1979; Delis et al. 1979). Pedelty's nine aphasics were divided into four non-fluent Broca patients with damage to anterior areas, and five fluent Wernicke patients with posterior damage. She devised a completely formal method for coding the gestures that did not require any reference to speech; thus the distortions of linguistic content that are inevitable with aphasic speech did not influence her judgments of iconicity. Her method was to utilize the concept of a canonical gesture for each of the events of the cartoon. For example, in the scene where the bird drops the bowling ball into the pipe, a canonical gesture would include dropping something down. If a patient performed such a gesture, the gesture could be described as iconic, even if speech was unintelligible or otherwise inaccurate (see fig. 12.3 for an example of such a gesture). As Feyereisen (1986)

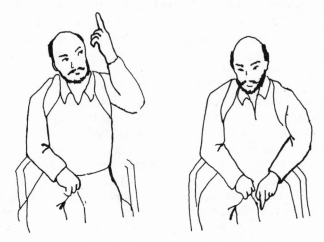

Figure 12.3. A semantically appropriate gesture with interruption of speech in one of Pedelty's (1987) Broca patients. The gesture appropriately depicts an episode of the cartoon story despite the total cessation of speech (the bowling ball rolls Sylvester out of the drainpipe): "ah ah [   ]."

concluded in his review, there was no special tendency for one group of patients to gesture more than the other or to produce gestures in longer strings. The one physical trait of their gestures that did differ was the use of the gesture space. The fluent Wernicke patients used a space similar to that of normal adult speakers: a flat plane parallel to the torso. The non-fluent Broca patients, in contrast, had extremely large gesture spaces of the type also used by young children, with gestures taking place high above their heads and often reaching far out into the periphery. The reason for this gigantically enlarged space is not clear, but it might have something to do with the types of the gestures that appear in the performance of the two groups.

The fluent Wernicke aphasics resembled normal speakers in another way: their gestures arose almost exclusively from the gesticulation end of Kendon's continuum: beats, occasional deictics, iconics, and metaphorics, but little from the more language-like regions. The nonfluent Broca aphasics, in contrast, produced movements with communicative significance from all points along Kendon's continuum except the sign language extreme. They performed unique and clearly interpretable iconics, much like those we see from normals, but they also moved into the more codified regions—emblems (e.g., a wave-of-the-hand hello, yes, no, the OK sign, etc.), words spelled out with their fingers in the air, and whole-body pantomimes of the kind also seen with children, often with vocal sound effects. Thus, the anterior, nonfluent aphasic patients exploit more fully the entire range of nonverbal communicative possibilities and perform larger physical movements that occupy the space of actual actions in the process.

Aphasic patients often have some paralysis of the dominant hand, and this limits the complexity of their gestures. For example, the number of gesture components and the complexity and trajectory of the stroke phase correlated with performance on standard tests of manual skill. Nonetheless, the propensity to perform iconics in general—i.e., the proportion of utterances accompanied by such gestures—did not correlate with either type of patient's practic skill. While motor skill is an important component of gesture, as Pedelty points out, it is neither necessary nor sufficient to explain the role of the language-dominant hemisphere in the production of gestures.

ICONIC TO BEAT RATIOS. Concentrating now just on the gesticulation end of the continuum, we find that the nonfluent Broca aphasics have a more heavily iconic, imagistic gesture output. Table 12.1, based on Pedelty (1987), compares the two kinds of aphasic patient in terms of their production of iconics and beats, expressed in the ratio of the frequency of the first to the frequency of the second. This ratio is much higher for the Broca patients than the Wernicke patients. The Wernickes, in two cases, had more beats than iconics, whereas every Broca had more iconics than beats (and two Brocas had no beats at all, but did have iconics). No Wernicke aphasic had as many iconics relative to beats as any Broca aphasic; so the two classes of patient were nonoverlapping in this regard.

Table 12.1 Production of Iconics and Beats
by Nonfluent and Fluent Aphasics (based
on Pedelty 1987)

Type of Patient	Patient	Frequency Ratios Iconic : Beat
Anterior	1	2.63
(Nonfluent)	2	no beats
	3	3.84
	4	no beats
Posterior	1	1.54
(Fluent)	2	0.22
	3	0.45
	4	1.67
	5	1.00

The ratios show that Brocas have a strong preference for imagistic iconic gestures. The Wernickes are capable of producing iconics, but their gestures are weighted in varying degrees to the motorically simple gestures that are more strongly related to discourse relationships (beats, metaphorics) than to referential content. Thus the agrammatic Brocas tend to avoid the specific gesture type (beats) that emphasizes relationships, while the semantically empty Wernickes tend to avoid the specific gesture type (iconics) that presents semantic content. In this global sense, gestures and speech dissolve together in the two kinds of aphasia. It is important to emphasize, however, that for the most part both kinds of aphasic performed both kinds of gesture. Moreover, the gestures of the two kinds—iconic and beat—patterned themselves in narrations in much the same way as they do with normals. The iconics of both the Brocas and the Wernickes appeared in narrative contexts, while the beats of both types of patient (if beats were occurring) appeared in metanarrative clauses conveying background information, locating events in time, or otherwise overtly structuring the narration. The gestures of these patients, despite gross abnormalities of language, are clearly tied to their linguistic systems in ongoing narrations, and play a role vis-à-vis language not unlike that played by gestures with normal speakers.

COMPENSATION WITH GESTURES. The gestures in aphasic speakers are thus closely linked to their speech with all its peculiarities; this is true globally, but it does not mean that gestures and speech are necessarily doing exactly the same things in every utterance by aphasic speakers. Gestures can compensate for speech, replace speech, or repair it when language fails. Both the nonfluent and fluent patients had lapses of language, but of different kinds. The nonfluent Brocas often were unable to produce a word or sentence to describe a particular entity or event from the cartoon. In these circumstances, iconics could take over, as in the following case (see fig. 12.3):

(12.1) (Experimenter: What was the cat doing?)

ah ah [   ]

Iconic: left hand with index finger pointing up, rises up over head and then straight down to lap—the cat plunging to earth.

Although the narrator could not say anything at all, he could perform a clear iconic gesture that depicted the scene in which a character was rolling out of a drainpipe with a bowling ball inside him.

With fluent Wernickes we find gestural repairs. The speech of these patients tends toward neologism and semantic emptiness, and this seems to reflect an equally unorganized and empty conceptual storehouse. Most of the neologisms and paraphasic speech by these patients were accompanied by beats or by no gesture at all: thus, compensation was not attempted in such cases. There were rare but stunning cases, however, where paraphasias were accompanied by iconic gestures. In these cases, *the gesture was always appropriate to the target word,* not to the erroneous word (which Pedelty could identify from the context, since the speakers were narrating the cartoon story). For example, a Wernicke patient substituted the word "person" for "umbrella" but performed the grasping and swinging movement that is standard for the umbrella in the cartoon (the umbrella was used as a weapon):

(12.2) and she had to use a [person] for a . . . a stick and a

Iconic: curled hand grasps "umbrella" and moves outward and to the right.

Another Wernicke-type patient described the cartoon scene in which a character had a bowling ball dropped on him while inside the drainpipe, and produced the word "pillow" followed by a neologism "tscher." All of this was accompanied by very clear iconic gestures that depicted the locus and shape of the pipe, and the character's falling through it (see fig. 12.4):

(12.3) see he went through the [pillow] and [all around]
                                    (1)   (2)

(1) Index finger rises and moves down, indicating locus of drainspout.
(2) Hand curls to grasp the "bowling ball."

(12.4) through [that tscher] . . .
                    (3)

(3) Hand swoops down, depicting descent of ball and character.

Figure 12.4. A semantically appropriate gesture with a neologism in one of Pedelty's (1987) Wernicke patients: "through [that tscher]." The gesture stroke depicts the bowling ball and Sylvester rolling out the pipe.

Insofar as we can judge, the patient preserved semantic synchrony of gestures and speech: the gesture for the pipe at (1) accompanied the reference to the pipe in the form of the word "pillow"; the gesture for the bowling ball at (2) accompanied the reference to the ball in "all around" (although this is so vague that we can't be sure of the reference); and the gesture for plunging down the pipe at (3) went with "that tscher," which may have been an attempt at a sound effect for this event. Thus, despite a paraphasia, a neologism, and a typical content-poor lexicalization ("all around"), semantic synchrony is preserved in this aphasic speech example.

Uses of gesture to replace or compensate for speech suggest that with aphasics, as with normals, speech and gesture are coexpressive but potentially nonredundant unfoldings of idea units into communicative behavior. When the spoken output goes awry, gestures can proceed fluently and the idea unit be expressed in an appropriate iconic gesture.

GESTURE TO CLAUSE CORRESPONDENCE. In chapter 3 we saw that for normal speakers most gestures are one to a clause. Where there are departures from this rule, the speaker most often produced multiple gestures within a single clause, implying that an attempt was made to unpack more than one idea unit with just one linguistic program. The output of speech in such cases is usually dysfluent, suggesting that the speaker was experiencing some difficulty in mapping the idea units onto a single clause. The gesture to clause ratios for Wernicke and Broca aphasics are given in table 12.2 from Pedelty (1987). As the table reveals, the ratios differ from each other and from those of normals. The differences are interesting and suggest some insights into the nature of the aphasic deficits

Table 12.2 Frequency of Gestures to Clauses (based on Pedelty 1987)

	Gesture to Clause Ratio					
	1 : 4	1 : 3	1 : 2	1 : 1	2 : 1	3 : 1
Nonfluent	—	1	4	71	14	2
Fluent	4	7	16	87	3	—
Normal	2	5	19	290	82	35

for speech. The first notable point is that, with both types of aphasics, as with normals, most gestures are one to a clause. However, when aphasic speakers depart from this pattern the two types move in opposite directions. The fluent Wernicke patients are more likely to cover several clauses with a single gesture, while the nonfluent Broca patients are more likely to perform several gestures during a single clause.

INFERRING THE GROWTH POINTS OF APHASIC UTTERANCES. The impression of speech running amok by the Wernickes may thus be related to an unfolding of a single idea unit into several grammatical clauses. This interpretation is supported by the grammatical structure of these utterances, which tend to be simple declarative clauses either embedded inside other clauses or concatenated inside stereotyped frames. In contrast, the nonfluent Brocas seem to suffer from a mismatch of too many idea units for their linguistic clauses. For them there are several idea units (i.e., individual iconic gestures) squeezed into a single dysfluent clause. The quite different iconic to beat ratios shown in table 12.1 point in a similar direction. The Wernickes, having many linguistic clauses for a single idea unit (gesture), have ample opportunity to code relationships, but these are relationships not between ideas but between linguistic output segments; thus they produce beats and few iconics. The Brocas, having a single clause for several idea units, have little experience of relationships but many separate and inadequately combined ideas; thus they produce iconics but few beats. This interpretation of the contrast between Wernicke and Broca aphasics is consistent with a recent idea of Friederici (1988) that what causes agrammatism—the characteristic nonfluency of Broca aphasia—is an inability to quickly retrieve closed-class items (the grammatical function words). This leaves them with onrushing images without sufficient syntactic means to interrelate them, and thus with several images or idea units attempting to crowd their way into one clause or semiclause.

In terms of growth points, we have the following contrasts between the two types of aphasic speaker. Wernickes have extensive *already un-packed* growth points that make little contact with imagery. For these patients language seems to come too quickly and cannot be broken down into independently manipulated segments. This leads to the impression of semantic emptiness. A growth point might consist of several clauses which the patient cannot break down into smaller segments to contact the imagery. Thus, for these aphasics, language is inaccessible because they cannot get inside complex linguistic structures and relate the parts to distinct images. Such a picture is compatible with the findings of others. Milberg and Blumstein (1981) and Blumstein, Milberg, and Shrier (1982) have concluded that Wernickes retain intact semantic knowledge but have impaired access to it.

Brocas, in contrast, have tiny *unpackable* growth points that make excessive contact with images. The growth points are unpackable because (in part) the patient cannot activate the necessary closed-class items quickly enough. To these patients, language is inaccessible because they cannot find the parts with which to build up a linguistic representation of holistic images. Thus, according to this analysis, the Wernicke and Broca aphasic types differ in two ways, both of which lead to abnormalities of image-language synthesis. The patients have inversely abnormal growth points in terms of size: they are too large in the Wernicke case, too small in the Broca case; and they also have inversely abnormal relationships with imagery: too little in relation to the availability of linguistic structure in the Wernicke case, too much, or too rapid, in relation to linguistic resources in the Broca case. As a consequence, the Wernicke speaker appears to produce fluent speech, but it is weakly related to imagery. The Broca speaker cannot produce fluent speech at all, but what speech he produces is heavily laden with imagistic content. The Broca speakers may have scattered or less dense or otherwise inaccessible linguistic representations. This inaccessibility could slow their access to the modules necessary to carry forward self-organization. The Wernicke speakers seem unable to relate their growth points to their imagistic thinking processes because the growth points are so large and contain internal linguistic structures that have become inaccessible. If they could be taught to break down these large growth points, they might be able to overcome some of their speech disturbances.

APRAXIA AND OTHER REGIONS OF KENDON'S CONTINUUM. As noted, fluent aphasics generally confined their gestures to the gesticulation end of the continuum. The nonfluent speakers, however, ranged freely over the continuum, producing pantomimes and emblems, as well as spontaneous-looking iconics. It is crucial to note that pretending to hammer a nail is pantomime, not gesticulation. It thus resides in the middle of Kendon's continuum, free of any necessary dependence on linguistic processes. It is precisely this dissociation from the damaged linguistic system that enables Broca aphasics to use pantomime and emblems to open up a communicative channel. Researchers on aphasia often fail to distinguish the different regions of the continuum (e.g., Feyereisen 1987), but distinguishing gesticulation from pantomime and emblems is crucial if the relationship of gestures to speech in these patients is to be properly understood. Enacting a pretended action in the absence of speech does not engage the synthesis of imagery and linguistic form that is the hallmark of speech and gesture production, and thus a symbolic movement can occur even when speech is totally blocked. The phenomenon of apraxia, as noted earlier, refers to the inability of some aphasics to perform imaginary actions like brushing their teeth or hammering a nail, even though they have no difficulty doing these things with real objects. Apraxic patients described by Skelly (1979) were able to learn and use signs based on American Indian Sign Language, and were able to produce speech specifically with these signs; but no observations seem to have been described of spontaneous speech-accompanying gestures in such patients. According to classical data (Liepmann 1905), two-thirds of aphasics are apraxic. More recent data suggest that most aphasics are not apraxic (none of Pedelty's patients were, for example, and this seems typical, see Feyereisen 1987), but when there is apraxia there most often also is aphasia (Duffy and Duffy, 1981). This one-way relationship suggests that aphasia and apraxia are separate disorders, but that when there is apraxia it tends to disturb speech (e.g., if a person cannot form meaningful images of actions, he lacks a major input to speech).

COMPARISON TO DEAF APHASICS. When deaf people suffer lesions of the speech areas in the left half of the brain, what are the consequences? This question has been studied in detail by Poizner, Klima, and Bellugi (1987), for both fluent and nonfluent ASL aphasics. Fundamentally, the same pattern of symptoms appears in the ASL aphasics as in hearing/speaking ones. In ASL many of the same formal properties of kinesic form and space are used as in spontaneous gestures, but they are organized into a system of contrasts and standards of well-formedness that have no counterpart in gestures (see chap. 2). In particular, ASL syntax is conveyed spatially, and this spatial syntax is differentially impaired by left hemisphere damage, while nonlinguistic uses of space by ASL users are differentially impaired by damage to the right hemisphere. Right hemisphere damage grossly distorts the ability to make use of the left side of space; patients, for example, avoided the left side of space completely in describing the layouts of rooms. Yet these same patients perform ASL signs in the left space. That is, there is no distortion with the ASL use of space, implying that space for language is organized by the intact left side of the brain in these patients. The gestures of deaf signers have not been described, although informal observation of ASL cartoon narrations suggests that true gesture does accompany ASL use; it is not the case that ASL occupies all the communicative potential of the visual-kinesic modality. If this impression is valid, and signers indeed use spontaneous gestures along with their sign production, we would expect, in cases of sign aphasia, that the gestures would be like the gestures of hearing aphasics, in general parallel to ASL disturbances but with compensations occasionally appearing as well.

Gestures of Commissurotomy Patients

"Split-brain" patients are individuals who have had their two cerebral hemispheres disconnected in a surgical treatment for epilepsy in which the corpus callosum and other smaller interhemispheric connections are severed, leaving only brain stem connections. Each hemisphere remains intact and functions in a normal way apart from its inability to interact with the other hemisphere plus any abnormality associated with the patient's epilepsy. It is thus possible to study the special functions and limitations of the two hemispheres in isolation in such patients. The effects of the operation are subtle but profound. There is a complete division of the patient's awareness into two halves (Trevarthen 1987b). Neither half is directly aware of the other—indirect awareness is possible, and this is achieved through one hemisphere's observing the effects of the other hemisphere on "its" body, as if observing a second person. For example, in one of the classic tests (Gazzaniga 1970), a female split-brain patient was unexpectedly shown a pinup, in such a way that it was confined to her right nonspeech hemisphere.[1] The patient laughed but when the experi-

1. This is possible since the right visual field of each eye goes to the left hemisphere and the left visual field to the right hemisphere. The dividing line is the midline. This anatomical separation permits precise optical testing of split-brain patients. As long as the patient does not move his eyes, which can be assured by presenting the stimulus for less than the eye movement reaction time, a figure flashed to the right of the fixation point will be received only in the left hemisphere and one flashed just to the left will be received only in the right hemisphere. Split-brain patients "hallucinate" complete figures when a visual stimulus crosses the midline, even though each hemisphere sees only what is in the opposite visual field. Another avenue for testing the two hemispheres separately is through the hands, since each hemisphere receives information from and primarily controls the opposite hand, but here the separation of the hemispheres is not absolute.

menter asked her why she had laughed she answered (the left hemisphere speaking) that she didn't know, that the "machine was funny, or something." The left hemisphere was trying to make sense of why there had been this laughter. When the pinup was flashed to the left hemisphere, there was again laughter but now the laughter was spontaneously accompanied by a report that among the apples and the other ordinary objects that were being shown there had been a nude woman.

Separate tests of the two hemispheres in these kinds of experiments show a sharp division of linguistic and visual-spatial capabilities. Drawings shown to the left hemisphere can be described verbally in the normal way, but the same drawings shown to the right hemisphere usually evoke no response at all. If the patient is urged to respond he will say (the left hemisphere speaking) that there was some kind of vague event or he will simply make up some story. On the other hand, the right hemisphere is far superior to the left in perceiving through palpation oddly shaped objects that do not have recognizable components. Thus the right hemisphere seems better at taking in global holistic perceptual patterns. The left hemisphere tries to build up complex objects out of components rather than take them in as wholes. For a general description of the split-brain patient and the results of these psychological tests and others, see Trevarthen (1987b).

Collecting Narratives from Split-Brains

With the help of Colwyn Trevarthen, who put me into contact with Dahlia Zaidel, I have been able to obtain narrations by two commissurotomy patients.[2] One (L.B.) was a 35-year-old man at the time of testing and the other (N.G.) a 57-year-old woman. Both patients are right-handed, and both had the corpus callosum, the anterior commissure, and the hippocampal commissure disconnected for treatment of intractable epilepsy (the disconnections have been confirmed by MRI scans). So far as I am aware, these are the first commissurotomy patients in whom narrative and gesture performance have been studied.

Each subject was shown the cartoon in three segments, to improve chances for recall, and each attempted to retell the story after each segment. Vision was free, so visual input was available to both cerebral hemispheres. This point will be important later when we interpret the

2. I am grateful to Dahlia Zaidel of UCLA for making available L.B. and N.G. and for generously setting up the video equipment and collecting these narrations, and to Kaaren Bekken for transcribing and analyzing the gestures. The patients live in southern California. I am also grateful to Dahlia Zaidel for advice on how to present the results of this study of the narratives of commissurotomy patients.

performance of L.B. and N.G. Both subjects have impairment of memory, but there was some recall of most episodes. For L.B. there were some 50 clauses and gestures. For N.G. there were more than 50 clauses and 20 gestures. Both the narrations and the gestures, however, were different from those of normal speakers. L.B. and N.G. also were different from each other in certain respects but similar in others.

What One Sees

The specific contributions of the left and right hemispheres must be integrated in the construction of a well-formed, accurate, and appropriately meaningful narration. What sort of narration might be produced by a commissurotomy patient? It is conceivable that each hemisphere would control its own domain of functions, but these functions not be integrated—for example, spatial gestures might be made exclusively with the left hand, or metaphorics might be made with the left hand, while the right hand performed beats to accompany the speech flow.

The analysis of L.B. and N.G. suggests that the left hemisphere controlled both speech and gesture, to the detriment of each channel of expression. The style of commissurotomy patients is to distance themselves from the events of the cartoon: instead of describing the events of the cartoon directly, they produce a metanarrative description with gestures to match. In keeping with speech-gesture coexpression, the subject's gestures functioned on the same metanarrative level as the spoken narration. Both gestures and speech in the split-brain style thus slight the story text and overemphasize the metanarrative text. While a normal speaker's narrative also makes extensive use of metanarrative perspectives, the metanarrative is always at the service of organizing and presenting the narrative content. It is conceivable that a metanarrative perspective without strong narrative content is the form in which the left hemisphere apprehends, stores, and reproduces visually presented narrations, such as a cartoon. There is not use of the gesture channel to compensate for a lack of visuospatial content in the speech channel. L.B. made beats and other small movements of such generic form as to be impossible to relate to narrative content. Sixty-two percent of L.B.'s gestures were beats and only 11% iconics (whereas with normals the number of iconics and beats is about equal). In general, L.B.'s gestures were what one would expect from an image-poor, language-rich left cerebral hemisphere. This implies that the gestures of the subject were organized in his left hemisphere, along with his speech, and did not draw on the (presumed) greater resources of visual memory and organization in the right hemisphere. N.G. made more iconic gestures than did L.B., but her iconics were of stereotyped form, often deictic as well as iconic, and, crucially, they also were not on the narrative level. That is, even though they were iconic they could have been left hemisphere gestures, a source that would explain their stereotyped form.

Moreover, with both L.B. and N.G., there is evidence of a trade-off between speech fluency and gesture. This is most clear in the case of L.B., but also can be discerned in N.G.. Most of L.B.'s speech was normally fluent. As noted above, this fluent speech was on the metanarrative level and occurred with minimal gestures. However, a much smaller part of his speech was markedly dysfluent and that speech was on the narrative level and occurred with true iconic gestures.

The breakdown of speech with iconic gestures has more than one possible explanation. First, the gestures in these cases may arise from the *other* hemisphere and the left hemisphere finds itself stumbling because it is unsupported by its own gestures. Alternatively, we may be hearing the *right* hemisphere attempting to have voice. Speech may be dysfluent in these cases because speech, together with gesture, arises from the right hemisphere whose abilities for linguistic production are limited.

The Two Patients

PATIENT L.B.   The difference in L.B.'s narration from normals is difficult to quantify, but obvious on inspection. The narration was conducted at a level of abstractness that, in the speech of a normal person, would be regarded as metanarrative. That is, rather than recount the events of the cartoon, which requires thinking of the sequence of cartoons events as primary, the speaker appeared to remain in the real world and tell a story about looking at the cartoon. For example, here are two contrasting versions of the scene from the cartoon where a character swallows a bowling ball:

A normal speaker (the most laconic available; no gestures occurred):

(12.5) Tweety drops a bowing ball. The bowling ball falls into Sylvester's mouth. Sylvester falls back down the drainpipe.

The commissurotomy patient:

(12.6) he had a bowling ball dropped on him a[mong] other things

                                        (1)

(1) Raises eyebrows, nods.

[while he was coming up] the drainpipe

(2)

(2) Left-hand fingers rise up then fall.

The normal speaker's description was more detailed. Crucially, the order was the same as the order of events in the cartoon. The split-brain narrator's version reversed this order—and this type of time-reversal implies a nonnarrative context. His gestures confirm the nonnarrative perspective: nonimagistic beats highlighting the discourse content (which was metanarrative, "among other things," and background information, "while he was coming up").

To give a further idea of this patient's narrative style, I quote here his description of a scene in which a character is running along trolley wires, pursued by a streetcar that the other two characters are driving; each time the streetcar catches up with the character on the wires, there is an explosion. While the patient had reasonably good recall of the descriptive details for this episode, he embedded these details within meta- and paranarrative comments, rather than place them at the focus of the discourse.

(12.7) and . . . again landed on the [wires / for [streetcars]
         (1)   (2)

(1) Left hand opens with palm outward, and holds.
(2) Superimposed beat.

(12.8) and it turned out the car that was [chasing him]
                                            (3)

(3) Superimposed beat, hand position still holds.

(12.9) was being driven by [Tweety][/ and]
                            (4)   (5)

(4) Left hand little finger drops down, and head nods, while hand position still holds.
(5) Palm rotates inward to face self, while position still holds.

(12.10) [good [old granny]]]
          (6)   (7)

(6) Head dips to the left side.
(7) Superimposed beat and end of the held position of the hand.

The structure of this text is similar to the inertia example described in chapter 7, which also was constructed on the metanarrative level with embedded narrative accounts. It is possible that dominance of the metanarrative is common when memory for the story line is flawed. The speaker is forever breaking the narrative flow to insert missing information out of sequence. In the example in chapter 7, a normal speaker inserted a succession of quick summaries, each with its own description of an event, into a prevailing metanarrative comment on the structure of the story. The split-brain is similar in that he inserts descriptive details into metanarrative comments. He said, for example, "it turned out the car that was chasing him," where the descriptive detail is the fact that the character is being pursued by the streetcar, but this is embedded (literally) within an explicit metanarrative comment, "it turned out that." Or, again, the full complex sentence, "and it turned out that the car that was chasing him that kept shocking him was being driven by Tweety and good old Granny," placed the focus on the outcome of the scene—the comical realization that the tables had been turned on the first character. It subordinated the descriptive to this metanarrative level comment. Finally, at least with respect to the order in which events were revealed in the cartoon itself, there is a time reversal in that the patient describes the streetcar and who was driving it before mentioning the character being shocked (in the cartoon, we are shown the character running and being shocked first). Thus, in several respects, the text of the narration exhibits a weakened narrative focus compared to a strong metanarrative emphasis.

The gestures are similar in the sense that they are exclusively non-iconic. The palm posture at (1)–(4) is conceivably a kind of metaphoric gesture for presenting the outcome (palm out phase), and then, at (5), is a contrasting movement for the cause of the outcome (palm in). Various beats are superimposed on these gestures. Thus, all the gestures highlight nonnarrative relationships, and there is no iconicity in the gesture channel at all.

On the other hand, when iconics are clear and well developed, the accompanying speech is often disrupted and incomplete—as if there were too little linguistic information in the gesture channel. This too, of course, is quite different from the gestures of normal speakers. Here is an example where a C-VPT enactment of Tweety's startled reaction to Sylvester accompanied a quoted exclamation but speech otherwise is in a state of collapse:

(12.11) some . . . what . . . shady scene of just ["aah!"] ["help!"]

                                    (1)   (2)

(1) *Both hands, palms down, 5-shape, move together to left.*
(2) *Shakes head.*

That is, either the speech is complete and the gesture minimal, or gesture is complete and speech minimal. The patient does not seem able to combine speech and gesture when both are well developed.

Although each hemisphere dominates the hand on the opposite side of the body, the subject performed gestures with either the right or the left hand and several times performed gestures bimanually. All but one of the bimanual gestures were symmetrical—the hands performing the same movements in mirror images. It would seem likely that symmetrical bimanual gestures could arise from a single hemisphere (viz., the left). Thus, one interpretation of L.B.'s narrative performance is that most of the time he was generating both speech and gestures in the left hemisphere. Occasionally his right hemisphere attempted to perform a gesture, and when this occurred speech was degenerate but iconic gestures were well developed.

L.B.'s one nonsymmetrical bimanual gesture was quite unusual, since each hand did something different (see fig. 12.5). With normal speakers, if a gesture is bimanual with the hands performing different motions, the hands interact cooperatively to present a single image that incorporates the semantic quality of an accomplishment or End State (Vendler 1967; see chap. 4). An example cited earlier is the right hand depicting a character's open mouth while the left hand depicts the bowling ball going into it (e.g., line 33 of the narrative in chapter 3). In the split-brain's one non-symmetrical bimanual gesture, one hand showed a character rushing to answer a phone (the left hand flicking off to the left), while the other hand depicted picking the phone up (grabbing something to the right). These are two independent gestures for the same scene. They involve different uses of space and do not cooperate to present a single complex meaning. Perhaps, therefore, they show the separate contributions of each hemisphere or the cross-cuing of one by the other. This patient was described by Levy, Trevarthen, and Sperry (1972) as manifesting an ex-

Figure 12.5. An asymmetrical bimanual gestures by a split-brain patient in which the hands independently depict different elements of the scene. The utterance was "[/rushed to the phone]," and the right hand shows the character grabbing the phone (an old-fashioned upright) while the left shows him rushing. The gestures are uncoordinated in space, since they place elements of the action on opposite sides, but synchronous in time. What is most striking, however, is that such independent right and left gestures appear but rarely with split-brains.

ceptional amount of verbal control in tests of the minor (right) hemisphere. They suggest various explanations for this, including control of
speech by the right hemisphere, use of mid-brain visual mechanisms (accessible to the left hemisphere), and cross-cuing of the left hemisphere by
the right hemisphere. The latter mechanism could have been involved in
generating these two gestures (see line 20 of L.B.'s narrative, below).

OBSERVATIONS ON L.B.'S MEMORY. L.B.'s narrative style was characterized by one colleague to be as if he were reading events off from a list.
In fact, L.B. often did stop talking and silently mouth words while seeming to tick points off with his fingers, and he did the same while he
watched the cartoon (the camera was left on). This suggests the phenomenon of extremely poor memory that has been documented for
split-brain patients, including patient L.B. (Zaidel and Sperry 1974).
Forgetting in itself is no mark of an abnormal narrative performance.
Narrations by normal speakers are certainly riddled with it. They forget
details and often whole episodes. However, separate episodes are not
normally run together. The episode is the basic memory unit in that it
preserves its integrity even when the speaker has lost many details. At one
point L.B., however, in contrast to this normal pattern, short-circuited
from one episode to a different episode. The episodes were not adjacent
in the cartoon itself, so it is not that he forgot that there was a boundary
between episodes. Nor did he confuse episodes that had similar actions in
them, such as two episodes where Sylvester dresses up in a costume. The
confusion, rather, appeared to be visuospatial. L.B. made a leap from one
episode to the other at a point where the two episodes could be joined
visually. In the first episode Sylvester catapults himself up to Tweety's
window and comes back down. In the second episode Sylvester is running overhead on trolley wires. This is where L.B. short-circuited; he described Sylvester coming back down but then, suddenly, had him landing
on the wires. Thus his memory leapt to a point where the second episode
was visuospatially homologous with the first and could logically serve as
a continuation of it.

Here is L.B.'s description; the short-circuit takes place between
(12.14) and (12.15):

(12.13) he went [up]
Head rises up.
(12.13) came [down]
Head drops.

(12.14) the prism came dow- or the [weight came back] over him and then on him

Left-hand fingers open and close.

(12.15) and / (the?) again landed on the [wires for [streetcars]
. . . .
(1)   (2)

(1) Left-hand fingers open and held out.
(2) Beat.

(12.16) and it turned out the car that was [chasing] him
. . . .
(3)

(3) Beat.

(12.17) that kept [shock][ing him]
. . . . (end of 1)
(4)   (5)

(4) Beat.
(5) Left hand held down.

(12.18) was being driven by [Tweety] [/ and]
(6)   (7)

(6) Left-hand fingers moves downward.
(7) Head nods.

(12.19) [good] [old Granny]
(8)   (9)

(8) Head dips left.
(9) Beat.

Once the switch to the trolley car episode had taken place another revealing development occurred. Apparently L.B. reconstituted the missing parts of the trolley car episode. This is apparent in his use of cohesive linguistic referring forms (relative clauses) in (12.16) and (12.17): "the car that was chasing him that kept shocking him," where he presupposes prior mentions of the trolley and the fact that it was pursuing Sylvester and delivering shocks. Neither had actually been mentioned by L.B., but he seems to have forgotten his own speech and referred to the nonexistent prior mentions of these things.

It is possible that this series of confusions also is a manifestation of the left hemisphere trying to recount the cartoon alone. If there had been a clear visual memory to guide L.B., it seems unlikely that he would have short-circuited in the first place (there is nothing in the catapult scene to suggest visually that Sylvester landed on the trolley wires). Normal speakers do not run episodes together, in part, because they can remember distinctive visual details that identify each episode. L.B. presumably lacks such visual memories in his left hemisphere. The switch from one episode to the other is the kind of confusion the image-starved left hemisphere might be expected to make. Also, reconstituting the missing parts of the trolley scene without awareness of its visual inappropriateness would be more likely in the isolated left hemisphere if it were relying on a verbal, list-like record of the cartoon with minimal imagery.

PATIENT N.G. Patient N.G. demonstrates even more clearly the importance of the narrative level of utterances for explaining the split-brain's gestures. She produces more iconic gestures than patient L.B. and more directly describes the episodes of the cartoon. Some of her iconics, moreover, co-occur in some cases with fluent speech. However, these fluent gestures, even though they are iconic, are used with metanarrative speech. She also used numerous spatial gestures that indicated the pragmatic structuring of the narrative. These, too, were accompanied by fluent speech. Thus N.G.'s performance approximates that of a normal speaker. Nonetheless, she resembles L.B. in some crucial respects. While she has fluent speech and gesture co-occurrences on the metanarrative and paranarrative levels, the general picture of a trade-off between speech fluency and gesture remains on the narrative level; that is, more gestures, more dysfluency.

In the following excerpt, the patient sets up a series of abstract spatial oppositions while she gropes for the correct word. There are two gestures that appear to have iconic significance, (4) and (5), and the rest function metanarratively, i.e., (1)–(3). Speech is nonfluent—full of false starts and repairs—as long as gestures continue. The example also demonstrates, however, that once gestures cease, more fluent speech occurs (she folded her arms). All of the descriptions are on the narrative level.

(Experimenter: Tell me what happened here. What d'you remember?)

(12.20) <u>ok the cat was running after that uh</u> /
(12.21) [I mean] <u>the MONkey</u>
    (1)

(1) Right hand moves to right (metaphoric of contrast).

(12.22) the [cat] [was] runnin' [after that] bIRd /
       (2) (3)   (4)

(2) Right hand moves to left (probavbly a noniconic contrast with (1)).
(3) Right hand shifts back to right (possibly a retraction).
(4) Right hand arcs and rotates to left (iconic for running).

(12.23) the [bird] the CAT in that
       (5)

(5) Right hand rises straight up overhead (pointing to Tweety).

(12.24) then he is dressed up in a monkey's outfit / and uh / he was
     (Arms folded)

(12.25) running away and then that old lady uh / in the room wanted
     (Arms folded)

(12.26) some uh / (unintelligible)
     (Arms folded)

The next excerpt demonstrates that N.G. is capable of generating reasonably fluent speech with iconic gestures. The utterances in (12.27) to (12.30) are not grossly malformed, and there are iconics and deictics throughout. However, (12.28) and (12.29) are scene-setting statements; thus there is scant evidence of coexpressivity on the narrative level.

(12.27) 'n' he came down and he hit a board /

(12.28) [fixed a board] across there
     . . . .
     (1)

(1) Right hand moves from left to right and holds with palm facing down.

(12.29) so then he can [jump] (unintelligible)
     . . . .
     (2)

(2) Right hand plunges straight down.

(12.30) 'n' [he got up there]
     (3)

(3) Right hand rises straight up.

These are not isolated examples of reasonably fluent speech with iconic imagery. Here is another case, where N.G. is trying to remember what to call a hand organ. Again, however, the level is nonnarrative (here, it is metalinguistic, she is discoursing about language itself):

(12.31) [/ what do ya call 'm / that little machine?] uh
Right hand appears to turn organ crank.

(12.32) this box singing / [that little thing that /] oh that
Right hand appears to turn organ crank.

(12.33) that thing / [that goes 'round like that]
Right hand appears to turn organ crank.

The crank-turning movement seems to have been organized jointly with the coexpressive speech references to the organ ("that thing," etc.), just as the horizontal and up-and-down movements of the earlier examples were organized jointly with their coexpressive references.

PATIENTS L.B. AND N.G. COMPARED. Despite the considerable differences between L.B. and N.G., they present a similar picture on one crucial point: *What the left hemisphere seems unable to accomplish is fluent, narrative-level speech and iconic gestures at the same time.* In normals, the imagery for the iconics can come from the right hemisphere, but this is impossible in both L.B. and N.G. On the narrative level, this duality of gesture and speech appears to overload or somehow distract the subject in his or her speech production effort. Only the gesture survives intact. However, when the left hemisphere can structure speech and gesture on nonnarrative levels, there is no breakdown of speech. This implies that the different narrative levels may have distinct brain representations. It is perhaps this potential for structuring space by the left hemisphere in terms of distinctions between levels that is also tapped by the deaf, as noted before, so that although right hemisphere damage interferes with the representation of general space, *linguistic* space is spared since it is represented in the left hemisphere (Poizner, Klima, and Belluai 1987).

While Patient N.G.'s examples can be regarded as demonstrating left hemisphere control over the combination of speech and imagery when the level is nonnarrative, there is another explanation. This is cross-cuing between the two hemispheres. In such a process N.G. would blend the separate outputs of the two hemispheres into one more or less unified overt performance. The iconic gestures with these discourse references would be the contribution of the right hemisphere. If we look carefully at L.B.'s gestures with fluent speech, we in fact find some oddities that could arise from cross-cuing. The horizontal movement in (12.28), for instance, did not take place with the most coexpressive linguistic element ("across"), but with "fixed a board." This could be an anticipation, but the next iconic gesture, in (12.29) for "jump," actually was *down*, and only the upward gesture in (12.30) fits its speech segment ("he got up there"). In other words, there are mismatches on the microlevel that could have arisen from the two hemispheres cuing each other, the left structuring speech on the meta-level and the right providing the images that it believed would go with the speech but not always getting it exactly right. Such cuing could work in the other direction too. The references in (12.31) to (12.33) to the hand-organ also are on the meta-level and the cranking gestures could be explained as the left hemisphere's verbally referring to the right hemisphere's gestures (the verbal forms include demonstrative pronouns: "that" in fact indexes the gestures in these utterances). The chief obstacle to this right-hemisphere explanation, however, is the handedness of N.G.'s gestures: all were performed with her right hand, implying left hemisphere control.

A POTENTIAL EXPERIMENTAL TEST OF COMMISSUROTOMY PATIENTS. For both L.B. and N.G. there is an experimental test that one would like to carry out. It would be most interesting to expose the cartoon separately to the demi-visual fields (which is possible using a so-called Z-lens; Zaidel 1975). There are clear predictions for such an experiment: if the right visual field (left hemisphere) is shown the cartoon, the resulting narrative should be devoid of appropriate iconic gestures with both subjects, including N.G.'s. Patient N.G., if she is cross-cuing, might attempt to add iconics, but it would be hard for her to make them appropriately since her right hemisphere would not have seen the cartoon. If the left visual field (right hemisphere) is shown the cartoon, speech should be very hesitant and poorly formed, but iconic gestures should be abundant. With both patients metanarrative structuring should suffer badly, but N.G., again if she is cross-cuing, might try to refer verbally to her gestures. The question of greatest interest concerns the pragmatic references in both the speech and gesture channels. The arguments I have been presenting suggest that such references are organized in the left hemisphere, and thus would be more characteristic of right visual field (left hemisphere) exposures.

Summary of Cerebral Control of Gesture and a Hypothesis

I can sum up the observations of this chapter in four points of importance for understanding the cerebral control of speech and gesture (see McNeill, Levy, and Pedelty, 1990):

1. Fluent aphasics appear to unpack single idea units into several clauses; this shows that semiautonomous speech is possible with scant imagistic content.

2. Nonfluent aphasics try to squeeze several idea units into single clauses; this shows that imagery is not sufficient for fluent speech production.

3. The handedness results suggest that it is precisely the imagistic content of gestures that requires the linguistic hemisphere's action. Beats, since they do not incorporate images, are less tied to the specific processes of integration in the speech hemisphere whereas certain metaphorics that are simple like beats but do incorporate imagery, are lateralized in the same way as iconics.

4. The peculiar speech and gesture patterns of the commissurotomy patients suggest that the isolated left hemisphere is unable to present narrative events on their own level. It cannot ground these events in imagery; it always keeps them at a distance, seeing them from a metanarrative perspective. The left hemisphere, working alone, thus constructs a meta-narrative discourse with gestures to match, presumably basing it on a list-like verbal memory of the cartoon. It does not, cannot, combine its meta-narrative construction with a visuospatial representation of the discourse, as normal speakers do.

Thus we can make the following proposal, which Pedelty, Levy, and I put forth very tentatively. In addition to controlling visuospatial cognition and affect, the so-called nonlinguistic hemisphere may play a crucial role in the integration of verbal processes. Normal narrative production appears to involve the cooperative interaction of both hemispheres, each making its own specific contributions. The locus of the convergence may be the left hemisphere for purposes of output control, but the right hemisphere plays a crucial part in the overall linguistic process. The close temporal, semantic, and functional relationships of speech to gesture may then arise because the two hemispheres converge and interact to construct a unified verbal-gestural operation. The result is an integral whole constructed with both imagistic and linear-segmented aspects. Although the aphasia patients had intact right hemispheres, imagistic data could not interact normally with verbal processes in their damaged left hemispheres. Damage in the linguistic part of the brain disturbs the convergence but leaves open the gesture channel itself, hence the globally parallel speech and gesture disruptions that we observed, but also the rare instances of gestural compensations.

Self-Organization and the Brain

The foregowing observations point to the conclusion that, in addition to controlling specific linguistic operations and skilled movement, the lin-guistic hemisphere integrates imagistic and verbal processes.It is here that the unpacking and sound image phases of the self-organizational cycle would take place. A vast number of active modules are presumably used for this process, but the requirements would not seem larger than with many other cerebral functions, such as vision. In addition, the ne-cessity of a rhythmical pulse is clarified, since different sources must be combined by the left hemisphere into a single chain of output and the pulse provides the vehicle for this. However, gesture anticipation move-ments can occur independently and at uncorrelated times out of the right hemisphere.

This is because the right hemisphere is the locus of another con-vergence which goes on separately from the convergence in the left, that of the image and the linguistic meaning category components of the growth point. The right hemisphere may be the locus of speech's primi-tive stage. By implication, therefore, the right hemisphere is the locus of the fragmentation phrase of the self-organizational cycle, the locus of the speaker's refocusing of attention, and of his or her new focus of interest. The "limited" linguistic abilities of the right hemisphere can thus be ex-plained as a *necessary* part of normal speech production, which depends on fragments, both linguistic and imagistic.

Text of the Cartoon Story Told by L.B.

Since narratives by split-brain patients have not been described before, I reproduce here the complete narrative by patient L.B. Gestures and other movements that possibly are gestural are shown in brackets. Post-stroke holds are shown with dotted underscoring (. . .), and pauses are indicated with slash marks (/). Boldface is for comments.

FIRST SECTION:

Tape starts: both hands on right leg, right holding left down

1. the cat goes over to quote the the [Bro]ken

Slight head dip.

2. Arms Apartment, which is where the bird is

3. and [attempts] [/] to . . . get the bird
    (1)   (2)

(1) Raises eyebrows.
(2) Repeats.

   4. the bird [pulls]
Slight left index finger movement to side.

   5. some . . . what . . . shady scene of just ["Aah!"] ["Help!"]
                                  (1)   (2)

(1) Both hands, palms down, 5-shape, move together to left.
(2) Shakes head.

The gesture at (1) is the first substantial movement. The preceding clauses, all of which are narrative in function, were accompanied by small uninterpretable movements. The gesture at (1), in contrast, seems an appropriate part of the quoted exclamation, and is a kind of C-VPT gesture. It is noteworthy that this well-developed gesture was accompanied by an almost total breakdown of speech.

   6. [and] uh /
Shakes head.

   7. Bird's owner raly (lady?) a [granny, if you] will
Right hand to center, palm down, 5-shape, also shakes head and smiles.

This movement is similar to the preceding, including the head shake, and would be appropriate if we assume the gesture is metaphoric for "if you will." It is unclear if that assumption could account for the head shake and smile.

   8. starts beating [/][Syl]vester with a . . . an um[brel]la
              (1) (2)   (3)

(1) Right-hand fingers rise up slightly.
(2) Left-hand fingers rise up.
(3) Nods head.

These could be iconic or metaphoric. Notice that the right and left hands alternate.

   9. and this is after he's already had a bowling ball dropped on him /
a[mong] other things
Raises eyebrows, nods.

10. [while he was coming up] the drainpipe
Left-hand fingers rise up slightly and fall.

This example was cited earlier. In contrast to the elaborate descriptions of the bowling ball episode given by other speakers, this speaker presents it as a metanarrative afterthought with minimal elaboration of gesture.

11. and / where the devil was he? He was at the Broken Arms for /
12. for / uh [Tweety /] [and then what did he do? I had it in my

....
    (1)   (2)

(1) Right-hand index points to left and holds.
(2) Moves finger to different spot and holds. Shakes head and moves finger around throughout.

These clear movements refer to the nonnarrative structure of the discourse. In contrast to the impoverishment of the speaker's narrative level iconics, his metanarrative (in (1)) and paranarrative (in (2)), deictics are presented clearly and appropriately.

13. head and I forgot / that's the sum total of it /
.... *(end of 1 and 2)*

SECOND SECTION

At tape start: both hands intertwined on lap, twiddling thumbs.

14. this one is about Sylvester trying to get Tweety, this time in
15. the apartment building and dressed as / a [bellboy /]
Eyebrows raised.
16. room / 358
17. (mouths words, not intelligible)
Thumbs separate, hands still entwined.
18. he's got / when the [lady] called down
Lifts both hands up, left index points to right.

This deictic could be on the metanarrative level, assuming the speaker was attempting to set up the new episode on the right.

19. [one thing I remember clearly was the desk clerk was very [irritated]]
....
    (1)   (2)

(1) Left hand points to interlocutor.
(2) Head nods.

Paranarrative point is performed normally.

20. I mean he [/ rushed to the phone]
     . . . .
                          (3)

(3) Right hand closes to fist and left hand moves to left away from body. Right hand holds clench.

These gestures also were cited earlier; they are the one case in which the left and right hands simultaneously perform two separate actions.

21. like he was ready to [hit] somebody
     . . . .
                          (4)

(4) Left hand beats. Right-hand fist still clenched.

22. and the [min]ur he minute he answered
     . . . .
                          (5)

(5) Left hand beats. Right hand still clenched.

23. "hello" [with a]] [nice /][pleasant] voice
         . . . . (end of 1)
                       . . . .
             (6)   (7)   (8)

(1) Right hand unclenches.
(6) Left hand begins to rise and holds.
(7) Right hand moves to center space to prepare for (8).
(8) Both hands form large conduit.

24. which was different

The beats at (4) and (5) accompany metanarrative references. The conduit on the metanarrative level at (7) and (8) is well developed.

25. (mouthing words, unintelligible)

Right hand rotates upward.

26. / [when /]

Left-hand fingers rise, one at a time.

These could be iconic for going upstairs.

27. Syl[ves]ter got to the [room]
         (1)   (2)

(1) Left hand points down.
(2) Left hand beats.

  28. <u>he [heard [quote] [Granny say]</u>
         . . . .
       (1)   (2)   (3)

(1) Left thumb contacts palm of other hand and holds.
(2) and (3) Left hand beats, and holds.

  29. "the [bags] are right][inside]"
        . . . .*(end of 1)*
       (4)   (5)

(4) and (5) Left hand beats.

  30. and she would meet him <u>[down in the lobby]</u>
                               (6)

Left hand in point arcs down and right.

The beats at (2) to (4) seem to signal references to discourse structure. The deictic at (6) is appropriate at the narrative level.

  31. <u>[so he picked up the bags /</u>
        . . . .
       (1)

(1) Right thumb rises slightly and holds.

  32. [discards] the suitcase that came with [birdcage]
        . . . .
       (2)   (3)

(2) Left hand arcs to left with palm facing center and holds.
(3) Left hand rotates palm facing up and holds.

This appears to be iconic for trajectory but not for handshape. If the gesture depicts discarding, it was not synchronous with the coexpressive speech.

  33. go <u>[down to the lobby /]</u>
        . . . .
       (4)

(4) Left hand rotates downward slightly and holds.

  34. [/ lifted up the top of the birdcage] surprise
        . . . .
       (5)

(5) Left hand drops and is held with palm up below knee.

35. Granny was [there]]
.... *(end of 5)*
(6)

(6) Right hand rises slightly.

The movements at (4), (5), and (6) are more like beats than iconics.

36. [/ that's / [about where it ended]]
....
(1)   (2)

(1) Right-hand 2 fingers rise and hold.
(2) Right hand rises slightly and rotates slightly out.

These movements are small and uninterpretable.

THIRD SECTION:

Subject has both hands folded on lap, leaning on left arm on chair armrest.
Experimenter: tell us everything you can remember from the last strip.

37. it starts out with him stacking boxes / the [cat //]
....
(1)

Experimenter: The cat was doing it?

38.   [   ]
....
(2)

(1) Both hands separate, fingers spread, palms facing each other.
(2) Both hands shift to horizontal and change shape to C.

The gesture at (1) is a conduit metaphoric; the shape and space changes at (2) might be due to relaxation while listening to the experimenter and be without significance. Thus, the one clear gesture had a metanarrative reference.

39. stacking boxes to get to / the window I believe

40. and he's hurriedly (?) trying to get up

41. (mouths: what happens to him? I don't remember)

Shakes head.

42. (mouths: / I forgot)

Eyebrows raised.

Experimenter: What did you say?

43. I said I forgot

Nods head.

44. Guess the next thing I remember is him trying to send himself

45. over as a prism using a 500 pound weight, which didn't work

46. he went [up]

Head rises up.

This is possibly an iconic movement of the head.

47. came [down]

Head drops.

Again, this is possibly an iconic movement of the head.

48. the prism came dow- or the [weight came back] over him and then on him

Left-hand fingers open and close.

49. and / (the?) again landed on the [wires for [streetcars]
                    . . . .
                       (1)   (2)

(1) Left-hand fingers open and held out.
(2) Beat.

The speaker has run together two episodes of the cartoon: the weight and the trolley car. Such confusions are virtually unknown in normal narratives.

50. and it turned out the car that was [chasing] him
    . . . .
                          (3)

(3) Beat.

51. that kept [shock]][ing him]
    . . . .
         (4)   (5)

(4) Beat.
(5) Left hand held down.

52. was being driven by [Tweety] [/ and]
    . . . .*(end of 1)*
               (6)   (7)

(6) Left hand fingers move downward.
(7) Head nods.

   53.   [good]   [old Granny]
        (8)   (9)

(8) Head dips to left.
(9) Beat.

All the gestures in (1) to (9) make metanarrative discourse references; no iconics appear.

Appendix: Procedures for Eliciting, Recording, Coding, and Experimenting with Gestures

In presenting the main arguments of this book I deliberately have not given specific details of how to elicit, record, code, and experiment with gestures during narratives. These details would be crucial to someone who wished to carry out this type of investigation, however, and it is now time to provide them. This Appendix is organized in the following way: first I explain the physical arrangement for collecting videotaped data; then I explain how to transcribe gestures; and finally I explain the coding of gestures and give some examples. In addition, I present a line-by-line description of the cartoon stimulus and a line-by-line text of the stimulus used for the "mismatch" experiment described in chapter 5.

Collecting the Data

THE STIMULUS. Subjects view an animated color cartoon or a full-length black-and-white film (a 1929 Hitchcock, *Blackmail*). They immediately afterwards narrate the story of the cartoon or film to a listener. In some cases (children, aphasics, the split-brains), where memory and/or attentiveness may be limited, we present the stimulus (always the cartoon in these cases) in three parts, and have the subject narrate the story of each part before viewing the next part. The cartoon is about seven minutes long and takes about the same amount of time to narrate. The film is an hour and a half long and takes between a half and a full hour to narrate.

We chose the cartoon for its simplicity of structure, its concreteness, its near absence of spoken dialogue, and also its potential to evoke a variety of iconic gestures (McNeill and Levy 1982). A cartoon stimulus is usable with a wide variety of speakers: educated adults, children, pathological speakers, and non-English speakers. The film *Blackmail* has been used exclusively with educated adults. It evokes a higher proportion of metaphoric gestures than the cartoon. It was originally chosen for a study of gesture handedness (Stephens, 1983). In addition to these film and cartoon narratives, one can also present subjects with printed material (e.g., comic books) and have them recount the stories to listeners (Marslen-Wilson, Levy, and Tyler (1982). The mathematics discussion was arranged by one of the participants (Robert Morris), and in a sense was nonspontaneous, although the discussion was genuine and the participants appeared to forget that they were being videotaped (every now and then the cameraman would move, and this caused the participants to look up in evident amazement, as if they had forgotten that a third person was there). The conversation between the law student and the social work student was recorded by Starkey Duncan as part of his ongoing research on face-to-face interaction.

THE STIMULUS. The cartoon stimulus is an animated color cartoon in the Sylvester and Tweety Bird series (*Canary Row,* Warner Brothers). It consists of some 9 to 12 episodes—12 if an episode is defined by the use of a distinct major prop; 9 if it is a section separated by fadeouts. The episodes all have basically the same "deep structure" (Sylvester attempts to capture Tweety but is thwarted by Tweety or Granny), but are differentiated on the surface by inventive and amusing variations. The cartoon recommended itself because of its simple and repetitive event structure, its surface variety, and its minimal use of spoken dialogue. Obviously, no narration contains every detail of the cartoon, and some details are never mentioned by any narrator. The following is full analysis of the cartoon at the micro level (S = Sylvester, TB = Tweety Bird, G = Granny):[1]

1. camera moves across buildings
2. camera stops on sign, "Birdwatcher's Society," over a window
3. S's head peeks up over window sill
4. S's eyes move right and left
5. camera zooms in on S's head (eyes still to left)
6. eyes move right
7. S moves down
8. S reappears with binoculars
9. S looks right with binoculars
10. S moves binoculars to center
11. S stops and you see his eyes magnified through binocular lenses
12. you see "through S's eyes"—the door of an apartment building with sign over it—"Broken Arms Apartments"—building #814
13. still seeing "through S's eyes," the binoculars move up to a window above the door
14. binoculars continue moving up to the second window above the door, where there's a bird cage in the window
15. still seeing through S's eyes you get a closer shot of the bird cage and see TB with binoculars and very large eyes looking dead center
16. TB lowers his binoculars
17. TB says, "I taught I taw a putty cat"
18. TB puts the binoculars back to his eyes
19. camera shifts to S looking through binoculars
20. camera shifts to TB looking through binoculars
21. TB puts down binoculars
22. TB says "I did! I did saw a putty cat!"
23. you see S from a side angle looking out the window with binoculars; you see the Birdwatcher's Society sign over the window
24. S moves the binoculars away from his eyes and smiles
25. S dashes away from the window

FADEOUT

1. This analysis was carried out by Elena Levy.

26. scene shifts to a street corner
27. S runs across the street
28. scene shifts to, presumably, across the street; scene is a building with an awing
29. S runs into the building
30. camera zooms in on the door of the building; sign next to door says "Broken Arms Apartments/No Dogs or Cats Allowed"
31. S comes flying out the door
32. same scene as 30; man's voice says "and . . ."
33. scene shifts to S lying in a pile of garbage; man's voice says "stay out!"
34. S lifts a tin can off his head
35. S lisps "thpoiled thport"
36. S moves his head forward

FADEOUT

37. TB swinging on swing in his bird cage, singing "When Irish Eyes are Smiling"
38. scene shifts to S climbing up a drainpipe; TB is still singing
39. scene shifts back to TB swinging
40. as camera moves back from bird cage, you see S's hand off to the right moving back and forth, conducting; TB still singing
41. camera stops movement back when you see all of S; still conducting; TB still singing
42. TB turns his head to right and looks at S; TB stops singing
43. S waves
44. TB moves around in bird cage; S looks surprised; TB says "help, help, the bad ole putty cat is after me!"
45. TB flies out of cage; S goes after him
46. scene is of bird cage in window; sounds of fighting
47. S comes flying out of window
48. G comes to window and looks out of it, holding umbrella; sounds of crash
49. G says "ye-e-es, that'll teach you" and points a finger down, apparently at S
50. G still talking, shakes umbrella, presumably at S; G says "next time I'll give you what fer"
51. TB flies to top of bird cage and stands there
52. camera zooms in on TB, who's pointing a finger down, and saying "bad old putty cat"
53. TB lifts chin way up

FADEOUT

54. scene is side of building, bottom of drainpipe; S pacing back and forth
55. S stops and looks up, then down at bottom of drainpipe,then up
56. S crawls in the drainpipe
57. scene shifts to top of drainpipe; TB standing on window sill looking down
58. TB looks surprised
59. scene shifts to central portion of drainpipe; camera moving up drainpipe
60. camera reaches top of drainpipe again; still see TB

61. TB looks excited, jumps up and runs to left
62. same scene, but TB absent
63. TB reappears carrying bowling ball
64. TB dumps bowling ball into top of drainpipe
65. scene shifts to side of building, central portion of drainpipe
66. bulge moves down drainpipe
67. camera angle shifts so that looking down on drainpipe from above
68. bulge moves down drainpipe
69. scene shifts to side angle of drainpipe
70. bulge moves down
71. bulge explodes
72. scene shifts to street
73. S falls into street with bowling ball–shaped bottom
74. S rolls down street on bottom, feet rotating above the ground
75. S rolls down different part of street, looks upset
76. scene of empty street
77. scene shifts to end of street; bowling alley
78. S rolls into entrance of bowling alley
79. same scene as 76 (without S); sounds of bowling pins crashing
FADEOUT
80. same as 54
81. S stops; thrusts head rapidly to his left
82. scene switches to other street corner; organ grinder playing, organ and
    monkey moving back and forth
83. S sneaks around corner; monkey takes off cap to him
84. same corner without S or organ grinder or monkey
85. scene switches to around corner
86. S peaks his head out
87. S says "psst, psst . . ."
88. S holds out a banana and says "here's a nice banana for ya"
89. the monkey tiptoes up to S
90. S disappears behind the corner; the monkey follows him
91. the monkey disappears behind the corner; sound of bang
92. S pops out from the corner dressed in the monkey's uniform
93. S hops around, making monkey sounds, then hops off camera
94. same as 85
95. scene shifts to TB in cage, looking down
96. TB says "uh oh, that putty cat after me again"
97. TB looks down
98. scene shifts to drainpipe on side of building and S climbing up it
99. scene shifts to TB in cage on window sill
100. S's hand appears
101. S jumps onto window sill
102. TB hides in cage
103. TB jumps out of cage

104. S follows him
105. scene shifts to living room with G standing there
106. TB runs in, across the floor as G watches
107. S runs in and plays monkey for G
108. G smiles as S jumps up and down, making monkey noises
109. camera zooms in on G holding up her hand and saying "well, look at this, a darling little monkey"
110. G claps her hands
111. scene shifts to S on living room floor, a table in view
112. S moves to left to table covered by tablecloth
113. S peeks under tablecloth
114. scene switches to different part of living room, an armchair in view
115. S looks around
116. S peeks under armchair
117. S lowers skirt of armchair
118. scene switches to different part of living room, a blue thing in view
119. S appears on scene
120. S runs over to blue thing
121. S looks around
122. S lifts blue thing and see G's legs
123. S looks away
124. S turns head several times
125. S moves over to rug
126. S lifts rug and looks under it
127. S lets go of rug
128. scene shifts to G's smiling face
129. G opens a purse and says "here monkey . . ."
130. scene shifts to S looking up at G (in confusion) as G says "here's a nice new penny for you"
131. a coin appears in G's hand and S moves cup toward it
132. S walks up to G and holds out cup; holds head high and smiles
133. G drops the coin in
134. scene shifts to close-up of S
135. S moves head down and looks into cup
136. S lifts his hat
137. an umbrella handle comes down and bops S on the head; sound of a crash
138. S disappears (down) from camera
139. S reappears on screen
140. scene shifts to living room; S and G on screen; G holding the umbrella up and S looking dizzy
141. G puts hands on her hips and says, "aha! thought you'd outfoxed ol' Granny, heh? well I was hep to yer all the time"; S walks around in circles and finally raises his hat, an enormous welt appearing under it.
FADEOUT
142. scene shifts to hotel desk; sign says "desk clerk"; sound of phone ringing

143. desk clerk runs on camera and picks up phone (old-fashioned pedestal type), looking angry
144. desk clerk talks on phone, looking courteous; says in a smarmy voice "ye-e-es"
145. desk clerk still talking on phone, smiles bigger; G's voice says "hello, desk clerk . . ."
146. desk clerk moves eyebrows up and down, still smiling; G says "would you please send up a boy to get . . ."
147. desk clerk nods head, still smiling; G's voice says "my bags and bird"
148. desk clerk blinks eyes, still smiling with head still; G's voice says "I'm checking out"
149. scene shifts to mailboxes behind desk clerk; S peeking out
150. S raises an ear; desk clerk's voice says "room 158? yes, ma'am, right away"
151. S grins wickedly and looks right and left

FADEOUT

152. scene shifts to door #158 with open transom; hear knocking on door
153. camera moves down to S, dressed as bellhop, standing at bottom of door
154. S knocks on door; hear knocking sound
155. scene shifts to 152, and shows G looking out of the transom; says "yes, who is it?"
156. scene shifts back to 153; S lisps "your bagth, madam"
157. scene shifts to 155; G says "oh yes . . . uh . . . just a minute"
158. G disappears quickly from transom
159. scene shifts to 152
160. S grins evilly as G says "OK . . . they're right behind the door. I'll see you in the lobby"
161. S looks around, rubs his hands together, reaches for the doorknob
162. scene shifts to other side of closed door
163. door opens and S walks in
164. S looks around
165. S looks at covered bird cage and smiles
166. S walks up to bird cage and suitcase
167. S picks up bird cage and suitcase
168. S walks toward door with bird cage in one hand and suitcase in other
169. S disappears through door
170. door shuts
171. scene shifts to hallway; S tiptoeing and carrying bird cage and suitcase
172. as S walks along, more of hallway appears; walks toward "Stairs to Rear" sign
173. S stops and looks around
174. S lets go of bird cage and suitcase
175. S lifts suitcase over his head
176. S throws suitcase left off screen and you hear a crashing noise
177. S smiles
178. S picks up bird cage in both arms

179. as S moves closer to stairs, camera follows him and scene shifts
180. camera stops at staircase (scene stabilizes); S tiptoes down, clutching bird cage and grinning
181. scene shifts to back alley
182. S appears, tiptoeing and clutching bird cage
183. S runs down alley and turns around corner to left
184. scene shifts to other part of alley; S rubbing his hands and grinning evilly while looking at covered bird cage on platform
185. S looks around, still rubbing hands
186. S reaches for cover of bird cage
187. as S pulls off cover, G appears in bird cage, holding umbrella
188. S screams and his hat flies up as G reaches out with her umbrella and says "aha!"
189. G bops S on the head with umbrella; hear sound of umbrella hitting the head; S falls
190. S gets up and G bops him again; hear sound of umbrella hitting S
191. S gets up and runs off screen to left
192. G follows S, still in bird cage
193. scene is corner of alley without S or G
194. scene shifts to street
195. S appears on screen to right, running
196. G appears after S, still in cage with her feet sticking out, running and hitting him with umbrella; hear sound of umbrella hitting S
FADEOUT
197. scene is street corner, bottom of drainpipe
198. S runs onto screen, carrying large crate
199. S stops, looks up, puts down crate; hear sound of crate hitting ground
200. S runs off screen deviously
201. scene is 197, with crate on ground
202. S runs onto scene, deviously, carrying long board
203. S stops, looks up
204. S lays board on crate; hear sound of board contacting crate
205. S runs off screen deviously
206. scene is 197, with crate and board
207. S walks on screen, carrying 500 pound weight
208. scene shifts to TB in cage on window sill; TB looking down
209. scene shifts to crate and board, S on one end carrying 500 pound
210. S throws weight up
211. weight disappears off top of screen, S looking up and smiling
212. weight lands on other side of board; hear crashing sound
213. S disappears off screen
214. scene is crate and board, with 500 pound weight on one end
215. scene shifts to side of building
216. S appears on scene and flies past vertically, then leaves scene
217. same as 215

218. scene shifts to TB in cage on window sill, looking down
219. S appears at bottom of screen
220. S reaches out hand and grabs TB, smiling
221. S with TB in his hand moves down toward bottom of screen and disappears off screen
222. scene shifts to crate, board, and weight
223. S with TB in his hand lands on opposite end of board from weight; hear crashing sound
224. end of board with weight flies up
225. S jumps up and runs to right
226. camera follows S running down street with TB in hand
227. weight appears at top of screen
228. weight falls on S's head; hear banging sound
229. TB flies off to left and weight to right
230. TB and weight off screen; S in a heap on ground
231. S looks up, head flattened; hear a crashing sound (presumably of weight hitting the ground)
232. S looks around with flat head

FADEOUT

233. scene shifts to inside room; S at drawing board drawing a blueprint; telescope pointing out window to left
234. S looks to left
235. S moves to telescope at window; camera follows him
236. S looks through telescope
237. S moves back to drawing board, smiling; camera follows him
238. S jumps on stool at drawing board and continues to draw
239. scene shifts to TB in cage on window sill
240. camera zooms in on TB in cage
241. TB says "well, what you 'ppose that putty cat's up to now?"
242. TB looks to right
243. scene shifts to outside of window; S on ledge holds on to end of rope
244. S jumps off window ledge and flies across screen
245. same as 243, minus S and rope
246. scene shifts to side of other building, with TB sitting in window
247. S flies across screen
248. camera angle shifts and shows S smashing against wall next to TB's window
249. S drops down vertically
250. same as 246, but TB looking down
251. scene shifts to close-up of TB in cage, looking down; hear banging sound, presumably as S hits the ground
252. TB says "that putty's gonna hurt himself if he's not more careful!"
253. TB looks down

FADEOUT

254. scene shifts to S pacing up and down in front of bottom of drainpipe
255. S stops and looks up and to right

256. S looks up to left, presumably in direction of TB's window
257. S runs to right, off screen
258. scene shifts to street, with trolley wires overhead
259. S appears at left, running down street (across screen)
260. S stops at right of screen and looks up
261. S looks to right
262. S runs off screen to right
263. same as 258
264. scene shifts to crisscrossing trolley wires
265. S appears at right, tightrope walking on wires with arms outstretched at sides; S stops periodically to regain balance
266. scene shifts to different angle on wires
267. trolley car appears and runs across screen; hear bell ringing
268. trolley car disappears; same as 266
269. shifts to different camera angle on wires; S walking on wires
270. S looks to right; looks worried
271. S jumps up
272. S starts running
273. connector from wire to trolley passes along screen from right to left; hear bell ringing; disappears off screen
274. same as 269, but without S
275. camera follows S running and trolley car connector following him; hear bell ringing
276. connector touches S; he turns white and jumps up "exploding"; exploding noise
277. S lands on wire, and runs with trolley connector following him
278. repeat of 276; exploding noise
279. repeat of 277
280. shift to different camera angle on wires
281. S appears on screen, runs across screen along wire, and disappears off screen
282. trolley appears on screen and runs across it
283. shift to different camera angle on wires; hear bell ringing
284. S appears on screen, runs across screen and disappears off screen; hear bell ringing
285. same as 283
286. scene shifts to TB with conductor's cap driving the trolley
287. TB says "I taught I taw a putty cat," as trolley moves along
288. camera moves back, and both TB and G are on screen, over sign saying "pay as you enter"
289. G says "you did, you did, you did see a putty cat!"
290. G and TB look at each other
291. TB looks ahead as G pulls bell several times; hear sound of bell ringing
292. TB looks at G again
293. scene shifts to wires, with S running and trolley following

294. S is shocked; you hear exploding sound
295. S keeps running
296. S is shocked; exploding noise
297. S and trolley disappear off screen
FADEOUT

THE PROCEDURE. In the cartoon and film narratives, the subject (the viewer/narrator) was brought into the lab, was shown the video screen where the stimulus would be presented, and was told more or less the following:

We are going to show you a cartoon (or Hitchcock film). It will last about seven minutes (or an hour and a half). After you have seen the cartoon (or film), you will tell (the listener's name) the story of the cartoon (or film). After that, (the listener) will tell the story to someone else. He will not get to see the cartoon (or film), so it is very important for you to tell him the story clearly and completely, so that he will be able to tell the story to someone else.

The emphasis on accuracy and completeness was to motivate the narrator to tell the story in a clear and comprehensible manner. At some time during the experimental session, before the actual narration began, we would mention that the focus of interest in our study was on the process of storytelling itself. Note that the instructions did not mention gestures or video recording. No subjects ever commented on their own gestures and it appears that we were successful at not drawing attention to this aspect of the narration. The subject then watched the stimulus (either straight through or in three parts). The exhortation to completeness and clarity was repeated when the listener was brought into the room with the narrator.

The listener was a genuine listener, however in most cases we did not actually have the listener tell the story to a third person. With children, the distinction between narrator and listener is less sharp, and often both children would tell the story during the same taping session to each other. The listener was allowed to interact with the narrator and to ask questions when the narration was unclear; he or she was not prohibited from the usual feedback signals that occur spontaneously in such situations. While the narrative context is fundamentally asymmetrical and tends to be monologic—the narrator is in charge and does most of the talking—it is by no means nonsocial.

At the end of the full-length film narration, the speaker and listener were asked to discuss a prepared set of questions, and this too was videotaped. The questions, written by Debra Stephens, were quite successful at eliciting a more conversational type of interaction. The narrator and listener were placed face-to-face in comfortable chairs at an angle of about 130°. The camera was off to one side, at an angle of about 60° with respect to the narrator's forward direction. In this way, one camera could resolve most movements in all three dimensions and was out of the speaker's direct view (however, no attempt was made to hide the camera).

Transcribing the Data

The following description obeys a recipe format that, one hopes, the reader will find accessible. In practice, of course, individual transcribers work out their own methods and shortcuts. The recipe format does not convey the great extent to which our procedure relies on discussion. We hold weekly lab meetings where transcriptions are gone over line by line. This procedure cannot be used when a formal reliability study is underway since it is of the essence then to see to what extent different transcribers agree, but for the greatest accuracy of transcription we are convinced by our experience that the method of transcribing the narrative by one worker, followed by group discussion and debate, and ending in the resolution of all disputes on the spot, is the best one to follow.

SPEECH. Speech is transcribed fully from the videotape in ordinary orthography (in standard romanizations in the case of Chinese, Japanese, Swahili, and Georgian). The speech transcription is supplemented with notations for hesitations, both filled and unfilled, and all speech errors, false starts, word changes, repairs, etc., are carefully noted:

[ ]	gesture phrase (stroke in boldface)
‡	breath pause (must be audible)
/	silent pause (multiple slashes for longer pauses)
*	self-interruption
—	other interruption
< >	filled pause; the brackets go around the relevant phonological transcription
(. . .)	post-stroke hold

The "/" notation allows one to record the approximate length of the silent pause. It is also possible to measure hesitations if a visual record of the speech is available as either an oscillograph trace or a speech spectrograph trace.

GESTURES. The transcription takes place in several steps:

1. Identify the movements that are gestures, i.e., all hand, arm, leg, and head movements, regardless of size, complexity, or location, except self- and object-"adaptors" (manipulations). The reliability of these identifications, determined by comparing the results of independent coders, ranges between 77% and 96% (this compares favorably to reliabilities reported by Freedman 1972, which were from 69% to 88%).

2. Identify the preparation, stroke, and retraction phases of the gestures. If there is no separate preparation or retraction phase, identify the phases that do occur. Determining the onset and offset of movement is quite easy. To determine the gesture phase we employ teams of coders working jointly.

The stroke phase is defined in both semantic and kinesic terms. Semantically, it is the content-bearing part of the gesture. Kinesically, it is the phase carried out with the quality of "effort," a concept developed for dance notation (Laban 1966). Of dance, Cecily Dell (1970) wrote:

When someone moves, you perceive it as more than a change of place or change in the mover's body shape. Movement does not flow along in a monotone—you see swellings and subsidings, quick flashes, impacts, changes in focus, suspension, pressures, flutterings, vigorous swings, explosions of power, quiet undulations. All this variety is determined by the way in which the mover concentrates his exertion or effort. This exertion or effort may, at any particular moment, be concentrated in the changes in the quality of the tension, or the flow of movement; it may be concentrated in changing the quality of the weight, or the quality of time in the movement; or it may be concentrated in the mover's focus in space. Flow, weight, time and space are called Effort factors. (P. 11)

Gesture movements are rarely so extensive, but the same considerations apply. The preparation and retraction phases are such that the effort is concentrated on reaching the end-point of the phase (with the retraction phase there may be no discernible effort at all). In the stroke the effort is concentrated on the form of the movement itself—its trajectory, shape, posture. In the example given in chapter 1 (1.11), where a gesture accompanied "[so he ignites him] [self and flies] [off out the window]," in which the hand moved up and out and opened as it went, the stroke phase concentrated its effort factors on the movement upward and the expansion, whereas the preparation phase concentrated on reaching the start of the stroke and the retraction phase concentrated on reaching the rest position.

The rest position is prototypically the speaker's lap or armrest of the chair, but also can be the hand resting next to his or her head, behind the head, on the knees, etc. It is difficult to give an exceptionless definitions of a rest position (but see the "beat filter" below). Generally it is where the hands are relaxed and are not supported solely by the arms in midair. If identification of the separate phases of the gestures is not a crucial issue (e.g., because the timing of the phases is not of interest), the gesture can be located just with respect to the beginning and cessation of movement.

3. Locate the boundaries of the gesture phases in the relevant part of the phonological transcription. Square brackets [ ] are conventionally used to locate the onset and cessation of movement; (since the transcriptions include all three gestures phases, a left bracket is used for the onset of preparation, boldface is used for the stroke, and a right bracket is used for the close of retraction). Thus, for example, a finished notation will look like this:

in the Birdwatcher's Society [which is **way** up] in a building

In other words, there was no gesture activity until the "which," and then the preparation movement started. The stroke was during "way," and the retraction during "up"; then again there was no gesture activity.

A delicate issue is considering what to do with pauses in the gesture. If the handshape does not change, the pause is considered to be part of the preceding gesture. If the handshape does change, it is not considered part of that gesture, and may mark the onset of preparation for the next gesture.

Crucial to carrying out a transcription is to add to each video frame a sequential frame number (which counts in 30ths of a second), and to remove the muting function of the VCR so that it produces continuous sound (you need sound during slow-motion and immediately upon starting the tape after a pause). The accuracy of placement of the gesture can then be made to within one syllable by using the slow-motion and freeze-frame features of the VCR: (1) move the tape in slow-motion until you just reach the onset of the movement you are interested in; (2) pause the tape and note down the frame number; then (3) release the tape: you will hear the syllable that was in progress at this frame number.

As an aid to the process of aligning gestures and speech, you can add to the video frame an oscilloscope trace of the speech along with the frame number. With this data, based entirely on visual information, you can determine the point in speech where movements of the speaker occurred to an accuracy of one-half video frame.

4. Locate gesture movements in space. Figure A.1 shows a system of concentric squares into which the gesture space is subdivided. (This figure was originally discussed as figure 3.1.) The space is usually a flattened disk in front of the speaker. It includes the speaker when the viewpoint is the character's.

Coding the Data[2]

Assess where the gesture occurs with respect to the speech and bracket the speech accompanied by the gesture. Mark the onset of the preparation and end of the retraction phases separately with square brackets [ ], and mark the stroke in bold types. If any phrase is held, mark this with dots.

The following instructions should be followed in the sequence given:

I. Analysis and classification of gestures
   A. Code the gesture type
      1. Representational (i.e., represents attributes, actions, or relationships of objects or characters); two kinds:
         a) iconic
         b) metaphoric
      2. Deictic (i.e., finger points or other indications of either concrete or imaginary objects or people)
      3. Beats (i.e., formless hands that convey no information but move in rhythmic relationship to speech). This category can be confirmed by means of the beat filter below.
      4. Confidence scale. This is a number reflecting your confidence in

2. This coding scheme is the work of R. Breckenridge Church, and was developed in 1989. It is an evolved version of the code devised originally by McNeill and Levy (1982).

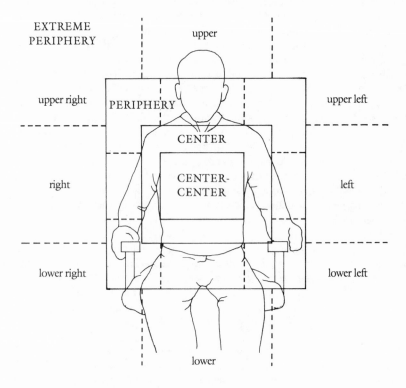

Figure A.1. Division of the gesture space for transcription purposes. From Pedelty (1987).

your typing of each gesture: 1 = marginally confident, 3 = confident, 5 = totally certain.

II. Code the form and meaning of the gesture
  A. If representational: code using the system described below.
  B. If deictic: use system below.
  C. If beat: do not code unless the form varies from the typical (i.e., if the shape of the hand is other than a B-shape and the movement is other than short up and down strokes).

III. System for coding representational and deictic gestures
  A. Gesture will be coded in two parts
    1. Hand
      a) form
      b) meaning (what the hand is representing)
    2. Motion

        a) form
        b) meaning
  B. Coding the form of the gesture
    1. Hand: describe on 4 dimensions
        a) handedness (which hand, or both hands; if both, are they symmetrical or doing different things; if different, are they coordinated?)
        b) shape of the hand (use ASL handforms to approximate; see Friedman 1977 and table 3.5, for illustrations)
        c) palm and finger orientation
        d) place in gesture space where gesture is articulated[3]
    2. Motion: describe on 3 dimensions
        a) shape of the motion (trajectory, etc.)
        b) place in space where motion is articulated
        c) direction of motion
  C. Coding the meaning of the gesture
    1. Hand: describe on 2 dimensions:[4]
        a) what does the hand represent?
        b) what viewpoint is the hand representing?
    2. Motion: describe on 2 dimensions:
        a) what does the motion represent?
        b) what viewpoint is the motion representing?
    3. Body: you will want to decide what the body is representing if it is representing a different entity from the hand or the motion.
IV. Code for gestural form and meaning
  A. Form
    1. Hand form
        RH, LH
        2 SH means both hands have the same shape
        2 DH means the hands have different shapes
        Represent shape by ASL finger-spelling shapes: find the shape that most closely approximates the gesture and if needed add a modifier to describe how the gesture differs from the ASL form.

    3. If the gesture is *deictic*, just code handedness, shape, and the place where the finger is directed.
    4. If the gesture is *deictic*, the meaning will be what is being indicated and there will be no viewpoint. Some deictic gestures set up a space for locating different referents, and these may persist through the story for a while; if so, the meaning would also include this spatialization of the reference space. If the gesture is *metaphoric*, you will code two different levels: (1) the Base, i.e., the concrete representation of the gesture; (2) the Referent, i.e., the abstract meaning being represented in the Base (cf. Mandel 1977). If the gesture is a *beat,* the meaning is simply that what it accompanies in the speech is emphasized, but some beats also highlight that an opposition is being set up between the thing referred to in the speech it accompanies and a simultaneous iconic or metaphoric gesture or something else earlier or later in the story, and this opposition should be noted.

2. Palm/Finger orientation

P/FTU: palm/finger toward up

      TD: toward down

      TC: toward center

      AB: away from body (outward)

      TB: toward body (inward)

      AC: away from center (left or right)

3. Motion

    TB: toward the body

    AB: away from body

    PF: parallel to front of body

    PS: parallel to side of body

4. Direction

    Uni-1:   unidirectional, one movement

    Uni-2:   two movements, effort exerted in one direction, the other movement returning the hand to starting place.

    BiDir: bidirectional, two movements with effort exerted in both directions

    2SM: both hands move in same way (mirror images)

    2DM: each hand moves in its own way (describing one action)

B. Meaning

1. Hand represents

    a) which character?

    b) which object?

    c) any marked (highlighted) features? List them.

2. Motion represents

    a) what action?

    b) any marked features? List them.

3. Viewpoint: specify whether

    a) character (identify which one)

    b) observer (inside or outside)

    c) dual (specify which viewpoint goes with shape and motion)

V. Beat filter[5]

This is a completely formal method of distinguishing beats from iconics and metaphorics, or any gesture in which there is an active adoption of shape and other than two movement phases. It makes no reference to content or function, but looks only at the kinesic qualities of gestures.

The beat filter applies to any movement of the hands that takes place between two rest positions (a gesture unit in Kendon's 1972 sense). Any gesture that moves the hands from a position outside the central gesture space into the central

---

5. This filter is the work of Bill Eilfort.

space is iconic (or metaphoric). Beats also occur inside the central space, but only if they begin and end there. Therefore, beats are restricted to movements in the periphery of the gesture space or movements that are superimposed on central iconics or metaphorics.

Any gesture that does not include movement of the wrist is iconic. This condition ensures that beats incorporate the minimum of effort. Any gesture containing two or more phases is iconic. Any gesture containing a component with two or more features (shape change, movement change, space change) also is iconic. When combined with the next condition, these conditions limit beats to maximally simple two-phase gestures. Any gesture not returning to its origin within two phases is iconic. This condition forces beats to be gestures consisting of exactly two phases, which are thus simply hand pulsings at the wrist.

A major problem is the correct classification of successive beats or beats superimposed on iconics and metaphorics. This is a problem that involves a decision as to how to segment movements into gestures and thus, given the above definition of a gesture, the definition of a rest position. Whenever the hands are static and relaxed, this configuration is the *canonical rest position*. To capture superimposed and successive beats, we say that whenever one phase of a gesture ends where another phase begins, these phases and any intervening phases comprise a single gesture. We then call the position between the two gestures a *local rest position* if it is not a canonical rest position. Further, whenever one hand is in motion while the other hand is at rest, subsequent motion of the static hand indicates a new gesture. Thus, superimposed beats are two-phase gestures that occur between local rest positions during an iconic or metaphoric gesture, which itself occurs between two canonical rest positions.

According to these definitions, then, we have these rules: any gesture superimposed on another gesture is a beat, while any gesture with another gesture superimposed on it is iconic or metaphoric. Finally, any iconic or metaphoric gesture must either begin or end in a canonical rest position. Bimanual gestures must start at the same time but need not start from the same place, and can end at different times. The chief shortcoming of these definitions is that they do not distinguish between successive iconics and successive beats, unless the iconics have rest position between them (but this requirement is in fact met by many iconics).

These considerations lead to a scoring system, which is the beat filter. Beats pass through the filter. You find the score by adding a 1 for each yes answer:

1. Does the gesture have other than two phases of movement? (Yes for either more or less than two.)
2. How many times does wrist or finger movement or tensed stasis appear in any movement phase not ending in a rest position? (Add this number to the score.)
3. If the first movement is in noncentral space, is any other movement performed in central space?

4. If there are exactly two movement phases,[6] is the initial phase in the same place as the second phase?

A score of zero means a beat on formal grounds; higher scores reflect increasing iconicity, on formal grounds.

VI. Format

Use the following format for transcribing the gestures accompanying speech:

Frame number
Speech (bracketed, in boldface type, and underscored with dots to show movement phases and post-stroke holds)
Gesture type
Which hand, shape, palm/finger orientation, hand place, motion shape, motion place
H (hand meaning); M (motion meaning); B (body meaning); S (space meaning, if any)
Gloss of entire gesture
Viewpoint (and which character in C-VPT)
Beat filter score
Confidence score.

VII. Examples

A. *An iconic gesture in which the two hands make rings in front of the eyes* (see fig. A.2):

Figure A.2. An iconic gesture on the narrative level with "so he's [looking at] Tweety Bird."

Frame number:	0199
Speech:	[so he's **looking** at Tweety Bird]

Gesture type:	iconic
Which hand:	2SH
Shape:	O-hand
Palm/finger orientation:	PTC and FAB
Hand place:	at eyes

6. A movement phase is one of the following: preparation, stroke, or retraction.

Motion shape and place: no motion
Hand meaning   H = S's hands holding binoculars
Motion meaning   M = no motion
Body meaning   B = Sylvester
Space meaning   S = space between Sylvester and Tweety Bird
Gloss: S is looking through binoculars at TB
Viewpoint: C-VPT (Sylvester)
Beat filter: 4 (Q1 = yes, Q2 = 2, Q3 = yes, Q4 = nonapplicable)

Confidence: 5 (metaphysical certitude)

    B. *A metaphoric gesture in which one hand appears to support an object and hand it to the listener* (see fig. A.3):

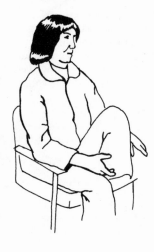

Figure A.3. A metaphoric gesture on the metanarrative level with "[some of the ways that he goes about trying to catch Tweety Bird.]"

Frame number: 2741
Speech: [some of the ways that he goes about trying to]
       ....

Gesture type: metaphoric
Which hand: RH
Shape: B-spread
Palm/finger orientation: PTU
Hand place: lower center periphery
Motion shape and place: no motion
Hand meaning   H = container/"some of the ways"
Motion meaning   M = no motion
Body meaning   B = none
Space meaning   S = none
Gloss: presenting "some of the ways" to the listener
Viewpoint: O-VPT

Beat filter: 3 (Q1 = yes, Q2 = 2, Q3 = no, Q4 = nonapplicable)
Confidence: 4 (moderately confident)
   C. *A pointing gesture made with one hand in a paranarrative context* (the Georgian speaker; see fig. A.4):

Figure A.4. A deictic gesture on the paranarrative level (in the Georgian language) with "oh, this is [funny]." Note that the gesture includes the listener in the space (but avoids pointing directly at him).

Frame number: 6036
Speech: [o, **sa**saci]lo es aris rom #
                            .....
                            [oh, fun]ny this is that
                            'oh, this is funny'
Gesture type: deictic
Which hand: RH
Shape: G with 2 fingers extended
Palm/finger orientation: PTD/FAB
Hand place: upper right periphery
Motion shape and place: Uni-2 AB
Hand meaning   H = index
Motion meaning   M = toward shared space with interlocutor (but off to side to avoid pointing directly at him)
Body meaning   B = none
Space meaning   S = interaction space
Gloss: invoking paranarrative level
Viewpoint: not applicable
Beat filter: 3 (Q1 - yes, Q2 = 2, Q3 = no, Q4 = nonapplicable)
Confidence: 5 (metaphysical certitude)
   D. *A beat with a metanarrative evaluation* (see fig. A.5):

Frame number: 5803
Speech: when[**ever she**] looks at him he tries to

Figure A.5. A beat with specific metanarrative content in "when[ever she] looks at him he tries to make monkey noises."

Gesture type:	beat
Which hand:	LH
Shape:	loose 5
Palm/finger orientation:	PTD/FTC
Hand place:	lower periphery
Motion shape and place:	Unit-2 TD
Hand meaning	H = none
Motion meaning	M = none
Body meaning	B = none
Space meaning	S = none
Gloss:	emphasis on "whenever"
Viewpoint:	none
Beat filter:	1 (Q1 = no, Q2 = 1, Q3 = no, Q4 = no)
Confidence:	5 (metaphysical certitude)

Gesture Complexity

Iconic and metaphoric gestures can vary in their internal complexity and it is important to have an established procedure for describing the differences. The following rules were devised by Kita (1990). To calibrate the degree of elaboration of a gesture, add one point for each of the following (the examples are found in chapter 4):

use of two arms (4.21)
movement of the fingers (4.19)
change of hand shape during the stroke (4.20 and 4.21)
other than a fist or open shape (4.20 and 4.21)
other than rest position (4.19, 4.20, and 4.21)
The sum of these points is the complexity score.

Totally Nonverbal Gesture Coding

As the preceding descriptions make clear, judgments of iconicity depend on knowing the semantic content of speech, for an iconic is defined as a gesture whose content is relevant to that of the concurrent speech. In certain problem areas, however, it is not possible to rely on our ability to interpret the speech accurately. Aphasic speech in particular may be disrupted so that interpreting it is highly impressionistic. In these cases it may be necessary to code the gestures for iconicity without reference to speech. Pedelty (1987) in her study of the gestures of aphasics employed a totally nonverbal method for coding the gestures in the cartoon narrative (the method could be used with discourse of other kinds). I quote here at length from her description of this method. Pedelty's thesis is the one study I am aware of where gestures have been identified as iconic, metaphoric, and beat exclusively by means of formal criteria:

For the purposes of the current study, it was desirable, for several reasons, to categorize gestures independently of any aspect of the concurrent speech. Because aphasic speech may be garbled or highly elliptical, it can be difficult to interpret, and is sometimes unreliable as an index of meaning; moreover, if the content or representational value of gesture is to be compared or contrasted to that of speech, independent coding helps to avoid circularity.

Certain conventional gestures are widely recognized within a community, and can be identified and interpreted on the basis of their form. Included in this category are emblems . . . , self-referential gestures to the speaker's own head, mouth, or throat, and pointing gestures. . . .

The remainder of the gestures were classified as representational or nonrepresentational according to objective formal criteria. Among normal speakers, iconic and beat gestures have been observed to differ along purely formal (movement-based) dimensions such as size, complexity, hand configuration, and spatial location [these being the dimensions represented in the beat filter]. These formal distinctions were incorporated into a formal coding scheme. According to this scheme, gestures comprising a clear preparatory, stroke, and refractory phase, with marked hand configuration (i.e., hand configuration other than a relaxed hand exhibiting only normal tonus) [cf. the scale of gesture complexity above], were classified as "iconic." Included in this category were "deictic iconic" gestures, points to loci within the gesture space. . . .

Another major class of unique representational gestures observed in normal speakers is metaphoric gestures, gestures that depict a concrete metaphor for a more abstract idea. True, spontaneous metaphoric gestures are often highly personal, and difficult to interpret independent of the narrative context; however, work with normal speakers has revealed at least two gestural forms that are reliably associated with metaphoric ideas. One form, the "conduit gesture," in which the flat or cupped hand is rotated or extended, palm up, is associated with the idea of producing speech or conveying information. In another, the "equivocation" gesture, the fully spread hand is oriented with the palm down, and rocks back and forth at the wrist to indicate vacillation between two options, or general uncertainty. Gestures taking these forms were accordingly classified as "metaphoric."

The remaining gestures comprised a class of simple movements (one or two components), with an unmarked (relaxed or flat form) hand posture, usually performed from the wrist. These were termed "beats." They were observed to occur in isolation at rest position, concatenated in strings of nearly identical movements, and superimposed on more complex gestures. (Pedelty 1987, 32–34).

Shortcuts

For many purposes a less detailed transcription of gesture will suffice. This can lead to very significant savings of time and effort. One simple but very significant economy is to omit exact speech-gesture synchronization, and register just the words with which the gesture coincided. To achieve accuracy to the nearest syllable is highly time consuming. Often accuracy to the nearest word, however, can be achieved in real time, while watching someone speak. Other shortcuts, roughly in the order in which they would sensibly be taken, are (a) to omit the beat filter; (b) not to subdivide the gesture into phases, but only mark the stroke; (c) not to analyze the gesture into the kinesic components of trajectory, shape, and space, but to give only the verbal description of the movement (much the way gestures have been described in this book); this entails also not analyzing the meaning of the kinesic components, but giving only a gloss for the gesture as a whole; and (d) not to record the viewpoint (however this is almost effortless).

A minimally useful transcription would consist of a classification of the gesture type (iconic, etc.), a recording of the word(s) with which the gesture stroke co-occurred, a verbal gloss of the presumed meaning or function, and the viewpoint if any. Of course, the value of the information derived from the gesture channel diminishes in proportion to the number of shortcuts taken in the transcription while the ease and speed of transcription increase.

Mismatch Experiment

Situation

Subjects were told that they would see a videotape of someone telling a cartoon story. They themselves would not see the cartoon, but would retell the story to a friend from this videotaped narration. To explain why we were asking them to do this, we said that we were interested in the process of storytelling. No mention of gestures was made. The tape was presented in three segments (break points are indicated below by a broken line) and each segment was narrated before the next segment was seen; this was to increase the likelihood of recall (which we found poor when the video narration was viewed in a single sitting). After they had viewed and retold all three sections of the tape, we asked the subjects whether they had noticed anything unusual in the videotaped narrator's performance. At this point we directed the subjects' attention to gestures, and specifically asked if they had noticed his gestures and whether they saw anything unusual (all subjects said they did not notice anything unusual, and some spontaneously admired the videotaped narrators "lively" and "spontaneous" style).

Script

Several stimulus tapes were constructed; the following is one of them.[7] The spoken text is to the right. The type of mismatch is given on the left. Mismatches are indicated (in italics) and explained (in boldface) within the text. The narrator performed other, normal gestures at other places in the text where specific mismatches were not called for.

A = spatial anaphor mismatch (that is, the characters suddenly exchange places in the gesture space).

V = verb mismatch (that is, the gesture displays a manner of action that the spoken verb does not encode)

O = origo mismatch (that is, the point of origin of an action by the same character suddenly shifts in gesture space)

Type of Mismatch	*Text*
	OK it was a cartoon called Canary Row and it was one of the old Sylvester and Tweety cartoons.
A	First you see Sylvester (*LH*) and he's in the window of the Bird Watcher's Society, and he's looking through binoculars at Tweety Bird (*RH*) who's in the Broken Arms Apartment building, and Tweety Bird (*RH*) is looking back at Sylvester through binoculars too. Sylvester decides to go get Tweety and so (*RH*) he dashes out of his building and runs across the street. [**Here the right hand has been set up to be Tweety and the left hand to be Sylvester, but all of a sudden the right hand becomes Sylvester.**]
V	Sylvester runs into the apartment building (*RH moves into LH*), [**The manner corresponds to "slams into" or "enters into," not just "runs."**]
V	but he comes right back out again (*RH describes walking motion*) [**The manner corresponds to "walks" or "runs," not just "comes."**] and lisps "spoil sport."
V	Next Sylvester decides to climb up to Tweety's window, so he goes up the drainpipe (*BHs describe climbing motions*). [**The manner corresponds to "climbs" or "crawls," not just "goes."**]

7. This is the work of Justine Cassell. It is based on the scene-by-scene analysis of the original cartoon presentation, which was prepared by Elena Levy, and it incorporates fragments of actual narrations by subjects who have viewed the cartoon in the usual manner.

A Tweety (*LH*) is singing and swinging in his window, and Sylvester (*RH*) is right near him watching him and then suddenly he (*LH*) lunges for him and runs into the apartment after him. [**The left-hand space has been associated with Tweety and the right-hand space with Sylvester, but then suddenly the left space become Sylvester.**]

O But Granny is there, Tweety's friend, and she whacks him one (*punches to front*) and throws him back out the window (*hand moves towards self*). [**The point of origin of Granny's first action was the speaker's locus, the origin of her second action was in the space in front.**]

Tweety is all happy and sits on top of his cage saying "bad ole putty cat."

Well Sylvester doesn't stop there. He goes back up, barreling up through the drainpipe.

O But Tweety sees him (*points away from self*) and runs and gets a bowling ball, and drops it into the top of the drainpipe. So obviously Sylvester and the bowling ball meet halfway and Sylvester swallows it (*swallowing towards self*) and falls back down the pipe. [**Sylvester's first locus is away from the speaker, then he swallows the ball at the speaker's locus.**]

V He comes out the bottom of the pipe and goes down the street (*bouncing motion*) with the bowling ball in his stomach until he goes right in the door of a bowling alley. And from the bowling alley you hear someone yell "strike!" [**The manner corresponds to "bounce," but the verb was "goes."**]

O So then Sylvester sees an organ grinder and a monkey on the street. He hides around the corner from them and he gets the monkey to come and then he mugs the monkey and steals his costume (*grabbing movement toward self*). Then Sylvester dresses up in the monkey's costume (*hands dress another in center space*) [**Sylvester's locus appears to shift from self to the center space.**] and climbs back up the pipe.

A He gets into the apartment and is chasing the bird around when Granny sees him and says "Oh, what a nice little monkey." And then she offers him a penny (*RH offers toward self*). And Sylvester has to stop and he bows and takes (*RH*) his hat off (*hat removed from other's O head in central space*). And then Granny sees that it's him and she whams him again with her umbrella and chases him out of the apartment. [**The A mismatch is that the right hand was first identified with Granny, then becomes Sylvester. The O mismatch was that Sylvester was first at the speaker's locus, then was in the center space.**]

O   Next you see the desk clerk at the front desk acting all smooth. And he answers the phone and it's Granny saying that she wants someone to come and take her bags (*two hands lift bags from front of speaker*) 'cos she's checking out. [**The speaker suddenly becomes the person lifting the bags.**]

O   Sylvester overhears this and so he dresses up like a bellhop and he goes upstairs and knocks (*hand knocks*) on the door. And Granny looks out from the transom (*points down and away*) and shouts "Oh, the bags are right behind the door—I'll meet you down in the lobby." [**The speaker was first Sylvester, then became Granny.**]

A   So he goes in (*RH*) and takes the suitcase (*LH*) and the birdcage which is all covered up and he leaves. [**The right hand is Sylvester moving in, then the left hand is Sylvester lifting up the suitcase.**]

V   And immediately he gets rid of the suitcase (*one hand shoves something under the other hand*) and runs down the stairs with the birdcage. [**The manner corresponds to "hides" or "buries," but the verb is just "gets rid of."**]

A   He carries the birdcage into an alley and he's sort of licking his lips and then he removes (*RH*) the cover from the birdcage. But when he uncovers it Granny springs out (*LH springs out*) and she hits him and chases after him (*RH hits and chases*). [**The right hand had been identified with Sylvester, the left with Granny, but then the right hand became Granny.**]

A   So then Sylvester goes and puts this box underneath the drainpipe with a board on top to make a seesaw. And then he stands on one end of the seesaw (*LH*) and throws a huge weight onto the other end

O   (*RH*), and so he goes shooting up into the air (*RH*) and grabs Tweety on his way back down. But this doesn't work either, 'cos as he's running away with Tweety the weight falls back down and squishes him (*two hands fall on own head*). [**The A mismatch is that the left hand was identified with Sylvester, the right hand with the weight, but** then the right hand becomes Sylvester. The O mismatch was that the weight's movement was in the space in front of the speaker, but then shifted to the speaker's own space.]

V Next you see Sylvester in his apartment making plans (*RH taps fore-head*). He gets some kind of rope and tries swinging down from his window (*RH*) into Tweety's window. But he miscalculated and

A crashed right into the wall and slid down (*both hands meet and LH slides down*). [The V mismatch was that the manner corresponds to "thinking up," but the verb was just "making." The A mismatch was that at first Sylvester was identified with the right hand, but then was the left hand.]

And then, let me think, how does it end? Oh! you see him crossing the

V trolley wires (*arms outstretched to balance*) to try to get to Tweety's window that way when all of a sudden the trolley car comes along (*RH*), and he's trying to run ahead of it (*LH*) and it catches up to him

A (*RH*) and he gets shocked and then he escapes (*RH*) and it continues like that, and then you see that the driver of the trolley car is the Tweety Bird and Granny is there too. [The V mismatch was that the manner corresponded to "tightroping" or "tightrope walking," but the verb was just "crossing." The A mismatch was that the right hand had been identified with the trolley, the left hand with Sylvester, but then the right hand became Sylvester escaping.]

References

Acredolo, L., and Goodwyn, S. To appear. Sign language in babies: The significance of symbolic gesturing for understanding language development. In R. Vasta (ed.), *Annals of child development*, vol. 7. Greenwich, CN: JAI Press.

Altmann, G., and Steedman, M. 1988. Interaction with context during human sentence processing. *Cognition*, 30: 191–238.

Arnheim, R. 1969. *Visual thinking*. Berkeley and Los Angeles: University of California Press.

Bahktin, M. M. 1981. *The dialogic imagination* (M. Holquist, ed.; C. Emerson and M. Holquist, trans.). Austin: University of Texas Press.

Barroso, F.; Freedman, N.; Grand, S.; and van Meel, J. 1978. Evocation of two types of hand movements in information processing. *Journal of Experimental Psychology: Human Perception and Performance* 4: 321–329.

Barsalou, L. 1987. The instability of graded structure: Implications for the nature of concepts. In U. Neisser (ed.), *Concepts and conceptual development: Ecological and intellectual factors in categorization*, 101–140. Cambridge: Cambridge University Press.

Bates, E.; Bretherton, I.; Shore, C.; and McNew, S. 1983. Names, gestures, and objects: Symbolization in infancy and aphasia. In K. E. Nelson (ed.), *Children's language*, vol. 4, 59–123. Hillsdale, NJ: Erlbaum.

Bates, E., and MacWhinney, B. 1982. Functionalist approaches to grammar. In E. Wanner and L. Gleitman (eds.), *Language acquisition: The state of the art*, 173–218. Cambridge: Cambridge University Press.

Bekken, K. 1989. Is there "motherese" in gesture? Ph.D. diss., Department of Psychology, University of Chicago.

Berger, J. 1972. *Selected essays and articles: The look of things*. Harmondsworth, England: Penguin Books.

Bever, T. G., and Chiarello, R. J. 1974. Cerebral dominance in musicians and nonmusicians. *Science* 185: 537–539.

Black, M. 1962. *Models and metaphors*. Ithaca, NY: Cornell University Press.

Bloom, L. 1973. *One word at a time: The use of single word utterances before syntax*. The Hague: Mouton.

Bloom, R. 1979. Language creation in the manual modality: A preliminary investigation. Bachelors thesis, Department of Behavioral Sciences, University of Chicago.

Blumstein, S. E.; Milberg, W.; and Shrier, R. 1982. Semantic processing aphasia: Evidence form an auditory lexical decision task. *Brain and Language* 17: 301–315.

Bock, J. K. 1982. Towards a cognitive psychology of syntax: Information processing contributions to sentence formulation. *Psychological Review* 89: 1–47.

————. 1986. Syntactic persistence in language production. *Cognitive Psychology* 18: 355–387.

Bock, J. K., and Warren, R. K. 1985. Conceptual accessibility and syntactic structure in sentence formulation. *Cognition* 21: 47–67.

Bosch, P. 1988. Representing and accessing focussed referents. *Language and Cognitive Processes* 3: 207–231.

Broca, P. 1861. Remarques sur la siège de la faculté du langage articule, suivies d'un observation d'aphemie. *Bulletin de la Société anatomique* 6: 330–357.

Brooks, C., and Warren, R. P. 1959. *Understanding fiction,* 2d ed. New York: Appleton-Century-Crofts.

Brown, R., and Lenneberg, E. H. 1954. A study in language and cognition. *Journal of Abnormal and Social Psychology* 49: 454–462.

Bruner, J. 1966. On cognitive growth, I and II. In J. Bruner, R. Olver, and P. M. Greenfield (eds.), *Studies in cognitive growth,* 1–29, 30–67. New York: Wiley & Sons.

————. 1986. *Actual minds, possible worlds.* Cambridge, MA: Harvard University Press.

————. 1990. *Acts of meaning.* Cambridge, MA: Harvard University Press.

Bühler, K. 1934. *Sprachtheorie: Die Darstellungsfunktion der Sprache.* Jena: Fischer. (Reprinted by Gustav Fischer Verlag, Stuttgart, 1965.)

Bulwer, J. [1644]1974. *Chirologia: Or the natural language of the hand and Chironomia: Or the art of manual rhetoric.* Carbondale, IL: Southern Illinois University Press.

Butcher, C. 1989. A point for this, a word for that: Two methods for referring to objects non-literally. Bachelors thesis, Department of Psychology, University of Chicago.

Butcher, C., Mylander, C., & Goldin-Meadow, S. To appear. Displaced communication in a self-styled gesture system: Pointing at the non-present. *Cognitive Development.*

Butterworth, B., and Beattie, G. 1978. Gesture and silence as indicators of planning in speech. In R. N. Campbell and P. T. Smith (eds.), *Recent advances in the psychology of language: Formal and experimental approaches,* 347–360. New York: Plenum Press.

Butterworth, B., and Hadar, U. 1989. Gesture, speech, and computational stages: A reply to McNeill. *Psychological Review* 96:168–174.

Carey, S. 1985. Conceptual change in childhood. Cambridge, MA: MIT Press.

Cassell, J. 1984. Then and then . . . and then temporality in children's narrative. M. Litt. thesis, Department of Linguistics, University of Edinburgh.

————. 1989a. The development of metanarrative speech and gesture in children's storytelling. Paper presented at the Biennial Meeting of the Society for Research on Child Development, Kansas City, MO.

————. 1989b. Gesture and the development of metanarrative ability. Paper presented at the 1989 Annual Meeting of the Linguistic Society of America, Washington, D.C.

————. 1991. The development of time and event in narrative: Evidence from speech and gesture. Ph.D. diss., Departments of Linguistics and Psychology, University of Chicago.

Cassell, J. & McNeill, D. 1990. Gesture and ground. In K. Hall, J.-P. Koenig, M. Meacham, S. Reinman, and L. A. Sutton (eds.), *Proceedings of the 16th Annual Meeting of the Berkeley Linguistics Society*, 57–68. Berkeley: BLS.

———. To appear. Gesture and the poetics of prose. *Poetics Today* (special issue on narratology).

Chafe, W. L. 1974. Language and consciousness. *Language* 50: 111–133.

———. 1976. Givenness, contrastiveness, definiteness, subjects, topics, and point of view. In C. N. Li (ed.), *Subject and topic*, 25–55. New York: Academic Press.

Church, R. B.; Baker, D.; Bunnag, D.; and Whitmore, C. 1989. The development of the role of speech and gesture in story narration. Paper presented at the Biennial Meeting of the Society for Research in Child Development, Kansas City, MO.

Church, R. B., and Goldin-Meadow, S. 1986. The mismatch between gesture and speech as an index of transitional knowledge. *Cognition* 23: 43–71.

Cicone, N.; Wapner, W.; Foldi, N. S.; Zurif, E.; and Gardner, H. 1979. The relation between gesture and language in aphasic communication. *Brain and Language* 8: 324–349.

Clark, E. V. 1988. On the logic of contrast. *Journal of Child Language* 15: 317–335.

Clark, H. H., and Clark, E. V. 1977. *Psychology and language: An introduction to psycholinguistics*. New York: Harcourt Brace.

Cohen, E.; Namir, L.; and Schlesinger, I. M. 1977. *A new dictionary of sign language*. The Hague: Mouton.

Condillac, E. B. de [1756]1971. *An essay on the origin of human knowledge: Being a supplement to Mr. Locke's Essay on the human understanding* (T. Nugent, trans.). Gainesville, FL: Scholars' Facsimile and Reprint.

Cosnier, J. 1982. Communications et langages gestuels. In J. Cosnier, A. Berrendonner, J. Coulon, and C. Orecchioni (eds.), *Les voies du langage: Communications verbales, gestuelles, et animales*, 255–304. Paris: Dunod.

Crain, S., and Steedman, M. 1985. On not being led up the garden path: The use of context by the psychological syntax processor. In D. R. Dowty, L. Kartunnen, and A. M. Zwicky (eds.), *Natural language parsing: Psychological, computational and theoretical perspectives*, 320–358. Cambridge: Cambridge University Press.

Curme, G. 1931. *Syntax*. New York: D. C. Heath.

De Casper, A. J., and Fifer, W. P. 1980. Of human bonding: Newborns prefer their mothers' voices. *Science* 208: 1174–1176.

Delancey, S. 1981. An interpretation of split ergativity and related patterns. *Language* 57: 626–657.

———. 1987. Transitivity in grammar and cognition. In Russell S. Tomlin (ed.) *Coherence and grounding in discourse*, 53–68. Amsterdam: John Benjamins.

Delis, D.; Foldi, N. S.; Hamby, S.; Gardner, H.; and Zurif, E. 1979. A note on temporal relations between language and gestures. *Brain and Language* 8: 350–354.

Dell, C. 1970. A primer for movement description: Using effort-shape and supplementary concepts. New York: Dance Notation Bureau.

Dell, G. S. 1986. A spreading activation theory of retrieval in sentence production. *Psychological Review* 93:283–321.

Di Jorio, A. 1832. *La mimica degli antichi investigata nel gestire Napolitano*. Napoli: Staperia del Fibreno.

Dimmendaal, G. J. 1983. *The Turkana language*. Dordrecht, Holland: Foris.

Dray, N. L., and McNeill, D. 1990. Gestures during discourse: The contextual structuring of thought. In S. L. Tsohatzidis (ed.), *Meanings and prototypes: Studies in linguistic categorization*, 466–488. London and New York: Routledge.

Du Bois, J. W. 1987. The discourse basis of ergativity. *Language* 63: 805–855.

Duffy, R. J., and Duffy, J. R. 1981. Three studies of deficits in pantomimic expression and pantomimic recognition in aphasia. *Journal of Speech and Hearing Research* 46: 70–84.

Duncan, S., Jr., and Fiske, D. W. 1977. *Face-to-face interaction: Research, methods, and theory*. Hillsdale, NJ: Earlbaum.

Efron, D. 1941. *Gesture and environment*. Morningside Heights, NY: King's Crown Press.

Ekman, P., and Friesen, W. V. 1969. The repertoire of nonverbal behavioral categories: Origins, usage, and coding. *Semiotica* 1: 49–98.

Fauconnier, G. 1985.*Mental spaces: Aspects of meaning construction in natural language*. Cambridge, MA: MIT Press.

Feldman, H.; Goldin-Meadow, S.; and Gleitman, L. 1978. Beyond Herodotus: The creation of a language by linguistically deprived deaf children. In A. Lock (ed.), *Action, symbol, and gesture: The emergence of language*, 351–414. New York: Academic Press.

Ferreira, F., and Clifton, C., Jr. 1986. The independence of syntactic processing. *Journal of Memory and Language* 25: 348–368.

Feyereisen, P. 1983. Manual activity during speaking in aphasic subjects. *International Journal of Psychology* 18: 545–556.

———. 1986. Lateral differences in gesture production. In J.-L. Nespoulous, P. Perron, and A. R. Lecours (eds.), *The biological foundations of gestures: Motor and semiotic aspects*, 77–94.

———. 1987. Gestures and speech, interactions and separations: A reply to McNeill. 1985. *Psychological Review*, 94: 493–498.

Feyereisen, P.: Van de Wiele, M.; and Dubois, F. 1988. The meaning of gestures: What can be understood without speech? *Cahiers de Psychologie Cognitive* (listed in some libraries as *European Bulletin of Cognitive Psychology*) 8: 3–25.

Fillenbaum, S. 1966. Memory for gist: Some relevant variables. *Language and Speech* 9: 217–227.

Fillmore, C. J. 1968. The case for case. In E. Bach and R. T. Harms (eds.), *Universals in linguistic theory*, 1–90. New York: Holt.

———. 1977. Topics in lexical semantics. In R. W. Cole (ed.), *Current issues in linguistic theory*, 76–138. Bloomington, IN: Indiana University Press.

———. 1982. Frame semantics. In Linguistic Society of Korea (eds.), *Linguistics in the morning calm*, 111–137. Seoul: Hanshin Publishing Co.

———. 1985. Frames and the semantics of understanding. *Quaderni de Semantica* 6: 222–253.

Fillmore, C. J., and Atkins, B. T. 1991. Toward a frame-based lexicon: The semantics of RISK and its neighbors. MS, Department of Linguistics, University of California, Berkeley.

Firbas, J. 1964. On defining the theme in functional sentence analysis. *Travaux linguistiques de Prague* 1: 267–280.

———. 1971. On the concept of communicative dynamism in the theory of functional sentence perspective. *Philologica Pragensia* 8: 135–144.

Flavell, J. 1976. Metacognitive aspects of problem solving. In L. B. Resnick (ed.), *The nature of intelligence*, 231–235. Hillsdale, NJ: Erlbaum.

Fodor, J. A. 1980. Methodological solipsism considered as a research strategy in cognitive psychology. *The Behavioral and Brain Sciences* 3: 63–73.

———. 1983. *The modularity of mind*. Cambridge, MA: MIT Press.

Fodor, J. A., Bever, T. G., and Garrett, M. F. 1974. *The psychology of language: An introduction to psycholinguistics and generative grammar*. New York: McGraw-Hill.

Frazier, L., and Fodor, J. D. 1978. The sausage machine: A new two-stage parsing model. *Cognition* 6: 291–326.

Freedman, N. 1972. The analysis of movement behavior during the clinical interview. In A. Siegman and B. Pope (eds.), *Studies in dyadic communication*, 153–175.

Freedman, N., and Hoffman, S. P. 1967. Kinetic behavior in altered clinical states: Approach to objective analysis of motor behavior during clinical interviews. *Perceptual and Motor Skills* 24: 527–539.

Friederici, A. D. 1988. Agrammatic comprehension: Picture of a computational failure. *Aphasiology* 2: 279–284.

Friedman, L. A. 1977. Formational properties of American Sign Language. In L. A. Friedman (ed.), *On the other hand: New perspectives on American Sign Language*, 13–56. New York: Academic Press.

———. ed. 1977. *On the other hand: New perspectives on American Sign Language*. New York: Academic Press.

Frishberg, N. 1975. Arbitrariness and iconicity: Historical change in American Sign Language. *Language* 51: 696–719.

Fromkin, V. A. 1971. The non-anomalous nature of anomalous utterances. *Language* 47: 27–52.

Gardner, H. 1974. *The shattered mind*. New York: Vintage Books.

Gardner, H.; Brownell, H.; Wapner, W.; and Michelow, D. 1983. Missing the point: The role of the right hemisphere in the processing of complex linguistic materials. In E. Perecman (ed.), *Cognitive processing in the right hemisphere*, 169–191. New York: Academic Press.

Garrett, M. F. 1980. Levels of processing in sentence production. In B. Butterworth (ed.), *Language production*. Vol. 1: *Speech and talk*, 177–220. London: Academic Press.

Gathercole, V. C. 1989. Contrast: A semantic constraint? *Journal of Child Language* 16: 685–702.

Gazzaniga, M. S. 1970. *The bisected brain*. New York: Appleton-Century-Crofts.

Genette, G. 1980. *Narrative discourse: An essay in method* (J. E. Lewin, trans.). Ithaca, NY: Cornell.

Givón, T. 1985. Iconicity, isomorphism and non-arbitrary coding in syntax. In J. Haiman (ed.), *Iconicity in syntax*, 187–219. Amsterdam: John Benjamins.

——— 1990. Isomorphism in the grammatical code: Cognitive and biological considerations. MS, Department of Linguistics and Cognitive Science Institute, University of Oregon.

Gleitman, L.; Newport, E.; and Gleitman, H. 1984. The current status of the motherese hypothesis. *Journal of Child Language* 11: 43–79.

Glucksberg, S., and Keysar, B. 1990. Understanding metaphorical comparisons: Beyond similarity. *Psychological Review,* 97: 3–18.

Goldblum, M. C. 1978. Les troubles et gestes d'accompagnement de langage au cours de lesions corticales unilaterales. In H. Hecaen and M. Jeannerod (eds.), *Du contrôle moteur à l'organisation du geste*, 384–395. Paris: Masson.

Goldin-Meadow, S. 1982. The resilience of recursion: A study of a communication system developed without a conventional language model. In E. Wanner and L. Gleitman (eds.), *Language acquisition: The state of the art*, 51–77. Cambridge: Cambridge University Press.

Goldin-Meadow, S., and Feldman, H. 1977. The development of language-like communication without a language model. *Science* 197: 401–403.

Goldin-Meadow, S., and Mylander, C. 1983. Gestural communication in deaf children: Non-effect of parental input on language development. *Science* 221: 372–374.

———. 1984. Gestural communication in deaf children: The effects and non-effects of parental input on early language development. *Monographs of the Society for Research in Child Development* 49(3), no. 207.

———. to appear a. Beyond the input given: The child's role in the acquisition of language. *Language.*

———. To appear b. The role of a language model in the development of a morphological system. *Journal of Child Language.*

Goldin-Meadow, S., Nusbaum, H., and Garber, P. 1991. Transitions in learning: Evidence for simultaneously activated strategies. Paper presented at a symposium on transitional knowledge at the Biennial Meeting of the Society for Research in Child Development, Seattle, WA.

Goodwin, C., and Goodwin, M. H. To appear. Context, activity and participation. In P. Auer and A. di Luzo (eds.), *The contextualization of language*. Amsterdam: John Benjamins.

Graham, J. A., and Heywood, S. 1976. The effects of elimination of hand gestures and of verbal codability on speech performance. *European Journal of Social Psychology* 5: 189–195.

Greenfield, P. M., and Smith, J. H. 1976. *The structure of communication in early language development*. New York: Academic Press.

Grosz, B. 1981. Focusing and description in natural language dialogues. In A. K. Joshi, B. L. Webber, and I. A. Sag (eds.), *Elements of discourse understanding*, 84–105. Cambridge: Cambridge University Press.

Hadamard, J. 1945. *The psychology of invention in the mathematical field*. Princeton: Princeton University Press.

Halliday, M. A. K. 1967. Notes on transitivity and theme in English: I. *Journal of Linguistics* 3: 37–81.

Halliday, M. A. K., and Hasan, R. 1976. *Cohesion in English*. London: Longmans.

Hanks, W. F. 1991. *Referential practice: Language and lived space in a Maya community*. Chicago: University of Chicago Press.

Harris, R., and Taylor, T. J. 1989. *Landmarks in linguistic thought: The Western tradition from Socrates to Saussure*. London: Routledge.

Hecaen, H. 1967. Approche semiotique des troubles du geste. *Languages* 5: 67–83.

———. 1978. Les apraxies ideomotrices. Essai de dissociation. In H. Hecaen and M. Jeannerod (eds.), *Du contrôle moteur à l'organisation du geste*, 333–358. Paris: Masson.

Hockett, C. F. 1958. *A course in modern linguistics*. New York: Macmillan.

Hopper, P. 1979. Aspect and foregrounding in discourse. In T. Givón (ed.), *Syntax and semantics: Discourse and syntax*, vol. 12, 213–241. New York: Academic Press.

Hopper, P., and Thompson, S. A. 1980. Transitivity in grammar and discourse. *Language* 56: 251–299.

James, W. [1890]1961. *Psychology: The briefer course* (G. Allport, ed.), New York: Harper & Row.

Jarvella, R. 1971. Syntactic processing of connected speech. *Journal of Verbal Learning and Verbal Behavior* 10: 409–416.

Jarvella, R., and Klein, W. 1982. *Speech, place, and action*. Chichester, England: Wiley & Sons.

Johnson, M. 1987. *The body in the mind: The bodily basis of meaning, imagination, and reason*. Chicago: University of Chicago Press.

Johnson-Laird, P. N. 1983. *Mental models: Towards a cognitive science of language, inference, and consciousness*. Cambridge, MA: Harvard University Press.

Kant, Immanuel. [1787]1973. *Immanuel Kant's Critique of pure reason* (N. Kemp Smith, trans.). London: Macmillan Press.

Karmiloff-Smith, A. 1979a. *A functional approach to child language: A study of determiners and reference*. Cambridge: Cambridge University Press.

———. 1979b. Micro- and macrodevelopmental changes in language acquisition and other representational systems. *Cognitive Science* 3: 91–118.

Kempen, G., and Hoenkamp, E. 1987. An incremental procedural grammar for sentence formulation. *Cognitive Science* 11: 201–258.

Kendon, A. 1972. Some relationships between body motion and speech. In A. Siegman and B. Pope (eds.), *Studies in dyadic communication*, 177–210. New York: Pergamon Press.

———. 1980. Gesticulation and speech: Two aspects of the process of utterance. In M. R. Key (ed.), *The relation between verbal and nonverbal communication*, 207–227. The Hague: Mouton.

———. 1981. Geography of gesture. *Semiotica* 37: 129–163.

———. 1982. The study of gesture: Some remarks on its history. *Recherches Semiotique/Semiotic Inquiry* 2(1982): 45–62.

———. 1988a. How gestures can become like words. In F. Poyatos (ed.), *Cross-cultural perspectives in nonverbal communication*, 131–141. Toronto: Hogrefe.

———. 1988b. *Sign languages of Aboriginal Australia: Cultural, semiotic and communicative perspectives*. Cambridge: Cambridge University Press.

Kimura, D. 1973a. Manual activity during speaking—I. Right-handers. *Neuropsychologia* 11: 34–50.

———. 1973b. Manual activity during speaking—II. Left-handers. *Neuropsychologia* 11: 51–55.

———. 1976. The neural basis of language qua gesture. In H. Whitaker and H. A. Whitaker (eds.) *Studies in neurolinguistics*, vol. 2, 145–156. New York: Academic Press.

Kimura, D., and Archibald, Y. 1974. Motor functions of the left hemisphere. *Brain* 97: 337–350.

Kingdon, R. 1958. *The groundwork of English intonation*. London: Longmans Green.

Kita, S. 1990. The temporal relationship between gesture and speech: A study of Japanese-English bilinguals. MS, Department of Psychology, University of Chicago.

Klima, E., and Bellugi, U. 1979. *Signs of language*. Cambridge, MA: Harvard University Press.

Kolstad, V., and Baillargeon, R. 1990. Perceptual and functional categorization in 10-1/2-month-old infants. MS, Department of Psychology, University of Illinois, Champaign.

Kozhevnikov, V. A., and Chistovich, L. A. 1965. *Speech, articulation, and perception* (JRPS #30,543). Washington, DC: National Technical Information Service.

Laban, R. 1966. *Choreutics*. London: Macdonald and Evans.

Labov, W., and Waletsky, J. 1967. Narrative analysis: Oral versions of personal experience. In J. Helm (ed.), *Essays on the verbal and visual arts* (Proceedings of the 1966 Annual Spring Meeting of the American Ethnological Society), 12–44. Seattle: University of Washington Press.

Lakoff, G. 1987. *Women, fire, and dangerous things: What categories reveal about the mind*. Chicago: University of Chicago Press.

Lakoff, G., and Johnson, M. 1980. *Metaphors we live by*. Chicago: University of Chicago Press.

Lane, H., and Grosjean, F., eds. 1980. *Recent perspectives on American Sign Language*. Hillsdale, NJ: Erlbaum.

Lapointe, S. G. 1983. Some issues in the linguistic description of agrammatism. *Cognition* 14: 1–39.

———. 1985. A theory of verb form use in the speech of agrammatic aphasics. *Brain and Language* 24: 100–155.

Lenneberg, E. H. 1967. *Biological foundations of language*. New York: Wiley & Sons.

Levelt, W. J. M. 1983. Monitoring and self-repair in speech. *Cognition* 14: 41–104.

———. 1989. *Speaking: From intention to articulation*. Cambridge, MA: MIT Press/Bradford Books.

Levelt, W. J. M, and Kelter, S. 1982. Surface form and memory in question answering. *Cognitive Psychology* 14: 78–106.

Levelt, W. J. M.; Richardson, G.; and La Heij, W. 1985. Pointing and voicing in deictic expressions. *Journal of Memory and Language* 24: 133–164.

Levy, E. T. 1982. Toward an objective definition of "discourse topic." In K. Tuite, R. Schneider, and R. Chametsky (eds.), *Papers from the 18th Regional Meeting of the Chicago Linguistic Society*, 295–304. Chicago: Chicago Linguistic Society.

———. 1984. Communicating thematic structure in narrative discourse: The use of referring terms and gestures. Ph.D. diss., Department of Behavioral Sciences, University of Chicago.

Levy, E. T., and McNeill, D. To appear. Speech, gesture and discourse. *Discourse Processes*.

Levy, J.; Trevarthen, C.; and Sperry, R. W. 1972. Perception of bilateral chimeric figures following hemispheric disconnection. *Brain*, 95: 61–78.

Lewis, D. K. 1968. *Convention*. Cambridge, MA: Harvard University Press.

Liddell, S. K. 1980. *American Sign Language syntax*. The Hague: Mouton.

Liepmann, H. K. 1905. *Über Störungen des Handelns bei Gehirnkranken*. Berlin: Karger.

Lindsay, P. H., and Norman, D. A. 1977. *Human information processing*, 2d ed. New York: Academic Press.

Lock, A. 1978. *Action, gesture and symbol: The emergence of language*. London: Academic Press.

———. 1980. *The guided reinvention of language*. London: Academic Press.

Lucy, J. A. 1987. Grammatical categories and cognitive processes: An historical, theoretical, and empirical re-evaluation of the linguistic relativity hypothesis (2 vols.). Ph.D. diss., Department of Behavioral Sciences (Committee on Human Development), University of Chicago.

MacDougall, D., and MacDougall, J. 1977. *Lorang's way* [film]. Berkeley: University of California Extension Media Center.

MacWhinney, B. 1977. Starting points. *Language* 53: 152–168.

Mandel, M. 1977. Iconic devices in American Sign Language. In L. A. Friedman (ed.), *On the other hand: New perspectives on American Sign Language*, 57–107. New York: Academic Press.

Marcus, M. 1980. *A theory of syntactic recognition for natural language.* Cambridge, MA: MIT Press.

Marschark, M.; West, S. A.; Nall, S. L.; and Everhart, V. 1986. Development of creative devices in signed and oral production. *Journal of Experimental Child Psychology* 41: 534–550.

Marslen-Wilson, W. D. 1975. Sentence perception as an interactive parallel process. *Science* 189: 226–228.

———. 1984. Function and process in spoken word-recognition. In H. Bouma and D. B. Bouwhuis (eds.), *Attention and performance X: Control of language processes*, 125–150. Hillsdale, NJ: Erlbaum.

Marslen-Wilson, W. D.: Levy, E.; and Tyler, L. K. 1982. Producing interpretable discourse: The establishment and maintenance of reference. In R. Jarvella and W. Klein (eds.), *Speech, place, and action*, 339–378. Chichester, England: Wiley and Sons.

McClave, E. 1991. Ph.D. diss., Department of Linguistics, Georgetown University.

McNeill, D. 1979. *The conceptual basis of language.* Hillsdale, NJ: Erlbaum.

———. 1985a. Holophrastic noun phrases *within* grammatical clauses. In M. D. Barrett (ed.), *Children's single-word speech*, 269–285. Chichester, England: Wiley & Sons.

———. 1985b. So you think gestures are nonverbal? *Psychological Review* 92: 350–371.

———. 1987. *Psycholinguistics: A new approach.* New York: Harper & Row.

McNeill, D.; Cassell, J.; & Levy, E. T. To appear. Abstract deixis. *Semiotica.*

McNeill, D., and Levy, E. T. 1982. Conceptual representations in language activity and gesture. In R. Jarvella and W. Klein (eds.), *Speech, place, and action*, 271–295. Chichester, England: Wiley & Sons.

McNeill, D.; Levy, E. T.; and Pedelty, L. L. 1990. Gestures and speech in G. R. Hammond (ed.), *Advances in psychology: Cerebral control of speech and limb movements*, 203–256. Amsterdam: Elsevier/North Holland Publishers.

Mead, G. H. 1974. *Mind, self, and society.* Chicago: University of Chicago Press.

Meltzoff, A. N., and Moore, M. H. 1977. Imitation of facial and manual gestures by human neonates. *Science* 198: 75–78.

Milberg, W., and Blumstein, S. E. 1981. Lexical decision and aphasia: Evidence for semantic processing. *Brain and Language* 14: 371–385.

Miller, G. A., and Chomsky, N. A. 1963. Finitary models of language users. In R. D. Luce, R. R. Bush, and E. Galanter (eds.), *Handbook of mathematical psychology.* Vol. 2, 419–492. New York: Wiley.

Miller, G. A., and Johnson-Laird, P. N. 1976. *Language and perception.* Cambridge, MA: Harvard University Press.

Milner, B.; Branch, C.; and Rasmussen, T. 1964. Observations on cerebral dominance. In C. A. de Rueck and M. O'Connor (eds.), *Ciba Foundation symposium on disorders of language*. London: Churchill.

Montaigne, M. de. 1958. *The complete essays of Montaigne* (D. Frame, trans.). Stanford: Stanford University Press.

Morford, M., and Goldin-Meadow, S. To appear. Comprehension and production of gesture in combination with speech in one-word speakers. *Journal of Child Language*.

Morris, D.; Collett, P.; Marsh, P.; and O'Shaughnessy, M. 1979. *Gestures: Their origins and distribution*. New York: Stein & Day.

Morton, J. 1969. Interaction of information in word recognition. *Psychological Review* 76: 165–178.

Mylander, C., and Goldin-Meadow, S. To appear. Home sign systems in deaf children: The development of morphology without a conventional language model. In P. Siple and S. Fischer (eds.), *Theoretical issues in sign language research*. Chicago: University of Chicago Press.

Nandikesvara. 1917. *The mirror of gesture* (A. Coomaraswamy and G. K. Duggirala, trans.). Cambridge, MA: Harvard University Press.

Napier, J. 1980. *Hands*. New York: Pantheon Books.

Newport, E. 1977. Motherese: The speech of mothers to young children. In N. J. Castellan, D. B. Pisoni, and G. Potts (eds.), *Cognitive theory*, vol. 2, 177–217. Hillsdale, NJ: Erlbaum.

Newport, E., and Meier, R. P. 1985. The acquisition of American Sign Language. In D. I. Slobin (ed.), *The crosslinguistic study of language acquisition*, vol. 1: *The data*, 881–938. Hillsdale, NJ: Erlbaum.

Palmer, S. E., and Kimchi, R. 1986. The information processing approach to cognition. In T. J. Knapp and L. C. Robertson (eds.), *Approaches to cognition: Contrasts and controversies* 37–77. Hillsdale, NJ: Erlbaum.

Pedelty, L. L. 1987. Gesture in aphasia. Ph.D. diss., Department of Behavioral Sciences, University of Chicago.

Pedelty, L. L., and McNeill, D. 1986. Gesture form changes with level of discourse focus. In A. Farley, P. Farley, and K.-E. McCullough (eds.), *Papers from the 22d Annual Meeting of the Chicago Linguistic Society*, 336–343. Chicago: Chicago Linguistic Society.

Peirce, C. S. 1931–58. *The collected works of Charles Sanders Peirce* (C. Hartshorn and P. Weiss, eds.). Cambridge, MA: Harvard University Press.

Penrose, R. 1989. *The emperor's new mind*. New York: Oxford University Press.

Peterson, N., and Kirshner, H. 1981. Gestural impairment and gestural ability in aphasia: A review. *Brain and Language* 14: 333–348.

Petitto, L. A., and Marentette, P. F. 1991. Babbling in the manual mode: Evidence for the ontogeny of language. *Science* 251: 1493–1496.

Piaget, J. 1929. *The child's construction of the world*. London: Routledge and Kegan Paul.

————. [1941] 1965. *The child's conception of number.* New York: Norton and Company.

————. 1954. *The construction of reality in the child* (M. Cook, trans.). New York: Basic Books.

Poizner, H.; Klima, E. S.; and Bellugi, U. 1987. *What the hands reveal about the brain.* Cambridge, MA: MIT Press.

Prince, E. F. 1981. Topicalization, focus-movement, and Yiddish-movement: A pragmatic differentiation. Paper presented at the Seventh Annual Meeting, Berkeley Linguistics Society, Berkeley, CA.

Rasmussen, T., and Milner, B. 1975. Clinical and surgical studies of the speech area in man. In K. J. Zulch, O. Creutzfeldt, and G. C. Galbraith (eds.), *Othrid Forester symposium on cerebral localization.* Heidelberg: Springer-Verlag.

Rauch, I., and Carr, G. F. 1980. *The signifying animal: The grammar of language and experience.* Bloomington, IN: Indiana University Press.

Reddy, M. 1979. The conduit metaphor—a case of frame conflict in our language about language. In A. Ortony (ed.), *Metaphor and thought,* 284–324. Cambridge: Cambridge University Press.

Reinhart, T. 1984. Principles of gestalt perception in the temporal organization of narrative texts. *Linguistics* 22: 779–809.

Richards, I. A. 1936. *The philosophy of rhetoric.* New York: Oxford University Press.

Rimé, B. 1982. The elimination of visible behavior from social interactions: Effects on verbal, nonverbal and interpersonal variables. *European Journal of Social Psychology* 12: 113–29.

Riseborough, M. G. 1982. Meaning in movement: An investigation into the interrelationship of physiographic gestures and speech in seven-year-olds. *British Journal of Psychology* 73: 497–503.

Roth, E. M., and Shoben, E. J. 1983. The effect of context on the structure of categories. *Cognitive Psychology* 15: 346–378.

Rumelhart, D. E., and McClelland, J. L. 1986. *Parallel distributed processing: Explorations in the microstructure of cognition.* Vol. 1: *Foundations.* Cambridge, MA: MIT Press.

Saussure, F. de. [1916]1959. *Course in general linguistics* (W. Baskin trans.). Reprint. New York: Philosophical Library.

Schiffrin, D. 1987. *Discourse markers.* Cambridge: Cambridge University Press.

Searle, J. R. 1983. *Intentionality: An essay in the philosophy of mind.* Cambridge: Cambridge University Press.

————. 1984. *Minds, brains and science.* Cambridge, MA: Harvard University Press.

Selfridge, O., and Neisser, U. 1960. Pattern recognition by machine. *Scientific American* 203 (August): 60–68.

Shankweiler, D., and Studdert-Kennedy, M. 1967. Identification of consonants and vowels presented to the left and right ears. *Quarterly Journal of Experimental Psychology* 19: 59–63.

Silverstein, M. 1984. On the pragmatic "poetry" of prose: Parallelism, repetition, and cohesive structure in the time course of dyadic conversation. In D. Schiffrin (ed.), *Meaning, form and use in context*, 181–199. Washington, DC: Georgetown University Press.

Siple, P., ed. 1978. *Understanding language through sign language research*. New York: Academic Press.

Skelly, M. 1979. *Amer-Ind gestural code based on universal American Indian hand talk*. New York: Elsevier.

Solso, R. L. 1975. *Information processing and cognition: The Loyola symposium*. Hillsdale, NJ: Erlbaum Associates.

Sousa-Poza, J. F.; Rohrberb, R.; and Mercure, A. 1979. Effect of type of information (abstract-concrete) and field dependence on asymmetry of hand movements during speech. *Perceptual and Motor Skills* 48: 1323–1330.

Sparhawk, C. M. P. 1976. Linguistics and gesture: An application of linguistic theory to the study of Persian emblems. Ph.D. diss., Department of Linguistics, University of Michigan.

Sperber, D., and Wilson, D. 1987. *Relevance*. Cambridge, MA: Harvard University Press.

Stein, N. L., and Glenn, C. G. 1979. An analysis of story comprehension in elementary school children. In R. O. Freedle (ed.), *New directions in discourse processing*. Vol. 2: *Advances in discourse processing*, 53–120. Hillsdale, NJ: Erlbaum.

Stemberger, J. P. 1985. An interactive activation model of language production. In A. W. Ellis (ed.), *Progress in the psychology of language*, vol. 1., 143–186. Hillsdale, NJ: Erlbaum.

Stephens, D. 1983. Hemispheric language dominance and gesture hand preference. Ph.D. diss., Department of Behavioral Sciences, University of Chicago.

Stephens, D., and Tuite, K. 1983. The hermeneutics of gesture. Paper presented at the Symposium on Gesture, Meeting of the American Anthropological Association, Chicago, IL.

Sternberg, S.; Monsell, S.; Knoll, R. L.; and Wright, C. E. 1978. The latency and duration of rapid movement sequences: Comparisons of speech and typewriting. In G. Stelmach (ed.), *Information processing in motor control and learning*, 117–152. New York: Academic Press.

Stokoe, W. C. 1960. Sign language structure: An outline of the visual communication system of the American deaf. *Studies in linguistics*, Occasional papers No. 8. Buffalo, NY: University of Buffalo Press.

———. 1972. *Semiotics of human sign languages*. The Hague: Mouton.

Stromeyer, C. F., and Psotka, J. 1970. The detailed texture of eidetic images. *Nature* 225: 346–349.

Supalla, T. To appear. *Structure and acquisition of verbs of motion in American Sign Language*. Cambridge, MA: MIT Press/Bradford Books.

Supalla, T., and Newport, E. 1978. How many seats in a chair? The derivation of nouns and verbs in American Sign Language. In Siple (1978), 91–132.

Talmy, L. 1985. Lexicalization patterns: Semantic structure in lexical forms. In T. Shopen (ed.), *Language topology and syntactic description*, vol. 3: *Grammatical categories and the lexicon*, 57–149. Cambridge: Cambridge University Press.

Trevarthen, C. 1977. Descriptive analysis of infant communicative behavior. In H. R. Schaffer (ed.), *Studies in mother-infant interaction*, 227–270. London: Academic Press.

———. 1986. Form, significance and psychological potential of hand gestures in infants. In J. L. Nespoulous, P. Perron, and A. R. Lecours (eds.), *The biological foundation of gestures: Motor and semiotic aspects*, 149–202. Hillsdale, N.J.: Erlbaum.

———. 1987a. Brain development. In R. L. Gregory (ed.), *The Oxford companion to the mind*, 101–110. Oxford: Oxford University Press.

———. 1987b. Split-brain and the mind. In R. L. Gregory (ed.), *The Oxford companion to the mind*, 740–747. Oxford: Oxford University Press.

———. To appear. Signs before speech. In T. A. Sebeok and J. Umiker-Sebeok (eds.), *The semiotic web 1989*. Berlin: Mouton de Gruyter.

Tuite, K. n.d. Argument marking in the gestural "verb." MS, Department of Psychology, University of Chicago.

———. To appear. Towards a production-based model of gesture. *Semiotica*.

Tul'viste, P. 1989. Discussion of the works of L. S. Vygotsky in the USA. *Soviet Psychology* 27: 37–52.

Umiker-Sebeok, D. J., and Sebeok, T. A., eds. 1978. *Aboriginal sign languages* (2 vols.). New York: Plenum Press.

van Dyke, T. 1980. *Macrostructures: An interdisciplinary study of global structures in discourse, interaction, and cognition*. Hillsdale, NJ: Erlbaum.

Vendler, Z. 1967. *Linguistics in philosophy*. Ithaca, NY: Cornell University Press.

von der Malsburg, C., and Singer, W. 1988. Principles of cortical network organization. In P. Rakic and W. Singer (eds.), *The neurobiology of neocortex*, 69–99. Chichester, England: John Wiley.

Vygotsky, L. S. 1934. *Myshlenie i rech'* [Thinking and speech]. Moscow-Leningrad: Sozekgiz.

———. 1962. *Thought and language*, (E. Hanfmann and G. Vakar, trans.). Cambridge, MA: MIT Press.

———. 1986. *Thought and language* (A. Kozulin, ed.). Cambridge, MA: MIT Press.

Wanner, E. 1980. The ATN and the sausage machine: Which one is baloney? *Cognition* 8: 209–225.

Werner, H. 1961. *Comparative psychology of mental development*. New York: Science Editions.

Werner, H., and Kaplan, B. 1963. *Symbol formation*. New York: Wiley & Sons.

Wernicke, K. 1874. *Der Aphasische Symptomenkomplex*. Breslau: Cohn & Weigert.

West, L. 1960. The sign language (2 vols.). Ph.D. diss. Department of Anthropology, Indiana University. [Available from University Microfilms, Ann Arbor, MI.]

Whorf, B. L. 1956. Language, thought, and reality: selected writings of Benjamin Lee Whorf. (J. B. Carroll, ed.). Cambridge, MA: MIT Press.

Wittgenstein, L. 1961. *Tractatus logico-philosophicus* (D. F. Pears and B. F. McGuinness, trans.). London: Routledge & Kegan Paul.

Wundt, W. [1921]1973. *The language of gesture* (J. S. Thayer, C. M. Greenleaf, and M. D. Silberman, trans; with an introduction by A. L. Blumenthal and essays by G. H. Mead and K. Bühler). The Hague: Mouton.

Wylie, L. 1985. Language learning and communication. *The French Review* 57: 777–785.

Yngve, V. 1960. A model and an hypothesis for language structure. *Proceedings of the American Philosophical Society* 104: 444–466.

Zaidel, D., and Sperry, R. W. 1974. Memory impairment after commissurotomy in man. *Brain* 97: 263–272.

Zaidel, E. 1975. A technique for presenting lateralized visual input with prolonged exposures. *Vision Research* 15: 283–289.

Zinchenko, V. P. 1985. Vygotsky's ideas about units for the analysis of mind. In J. V. Wertsch (ed.), *Culture, communication, and cognition: Vygotskyian perspectives*, 94–118. Cambridge: Cambridge University Press.

Index